P9-EJH-341

The Cold War Reference Guide

To my parents, Evie and Bob, who chose to bring children into a crazy, dangerous world and empowered us with optimism, autonomy, and love;

To my sister, Laura, a life-long guide who has forged an ambitious, independent, and successful life despite lurking fears of nuclear bombs, government betrayals and foreign wars;

And to my wife, Ana-Maria, the love of my life whom I might never have met had the Cold War not brought us together.

The Cold War
Reference Guide

A General History and Annotated
Chronology, with Selected Biographies

by
RICHARD ALAN SCHWARTZ

McFarland & Company, Inc., Publishers
Jefferson, North Carolina, and London

YEARY LIBRARY
LAREDO COMM. COLLEGE
LAREDO, TEXAS

AUG 1 1 1998

YEARY LIBRARY
LAREDO COMM. COLLEGE
LAREDO, TEXAS

British Library Cataloguing-in-Publication data are available

Library of Congress Cataloguing-in-Publication Data

Schwartz, Richard Alan, 1951–
    The Cold War reference guide : a general history and annotated
chronology with selected biographies / by Richard Alan Schwartz.
      p.   cm.
    Includes bibliographical references and index.
    ISBN 0-7864-0173-7 (library binding : 50# alkaline paper) ∞
    1. World politics —1945– 2. Cold War. 3. Chronology, Historical.
4. Politicians — Biography. I. Title.
D843.S3365 1997
902'.02 — dc20
                                              96-38573
                                                CIP

©1997 Richard Alan Schwartz. All rights reserved

*No part of this book, specifically including the table of contents and index, may
be reproduced or transmitted in any form or by any means, electronic or
mechanical, including photocopying or recording, or by any information storage
and retrieval system, without permission in writing from the publisher.*

Manufactured in the United States of America

McFarland & Company, Inc., Publishers
  Box 611, Jefferson, North Carolina 28640

AUG 1 1 1998

Contents

Section IV: Prominent Cold War Figures

Preface

Modern science teaches us that an observer's point of reference determines to a large extent what he or she will experience. For instance, a pedestrian standing on a street corner will hear the horn of a car wail as it approaches and then pulls away, while the driver will hear a steady sound. Measuring devices would confirm that the frequency of the sound waves varied for the pedestrian and remained constant for the driver, even though they were listening to the same waves. Thus, even basic sensory facts — whether or not the horn wailed — change according to the observer's point of view. Likewise, human history looks different depending on where we stand, and historical facts can change with our point of reference. For instance, from the U.S. viewpoint the Vietnam War involved an attack by one sovereign nation, North Vietnam, against another, South Vietnam. But from the North Vietnamese vantage point it was a civil war in which the north was attempting to unify the nation. Even though they contradict one another and lead to vastly different interpretations of the war, each description can justifiably claim validity. Similarly, to the West rearming West Germany was a necessary defensive measure to protect against a Soviet-led invasion, but to the Soviets it was an offensive action that threatened them with a hostile German force for the third time in the twentieth century. Likewise, to President Reagan the Strategic Defense Initiative (SDI) proposed a defensive weapon designed to protect against a possible Soviet first strike. But the Soviets regarded it as an offensive system that could potentially allow a successful U.S. first strike. In each case the superpowers experienced the same situations and events in radically different ways.

The realization that viewpoint plays a central role in how we experience events underlines much of modern thought. It accounts in part for the multiple surfaces in Picasso's Cubism, the multiple narrators in Faulkner's novels, and the Lorentz transformations in Einstein's special theory of relativity. It would seem, therefore, that authors attempting to write a history should at least acknowledge their point of view. A professor of American literature and popular culture, I grew up with the Cold War (mostly in Miami) and experienced it from an American vantage point. I am from the generation that was raised to revere God and country and President Eisenhower, and hide under our school

1

desks during air raid drills for a possible nuclear attack. We are also the generation that fought and/or protested the Vietnam War and did not elect one of our own president until after the Cold War ended. This perspective is as good as any, but it is certainly not the only legitimate one: an account by a Russian, Hungarian, West German, Cuban, Angolan, or Nicaraguan would necessarily appear different. So would an account by someone who grew up 20 years later in a very different America and a very different phase of the Cold War. Rather than try to write a cubist history by superimposing multiple viewpoints of the same events, I am more modestly offering my American view of the Cold War.

For this reason I focus primarily on the superpowers — the United States and the Soviet Union — and to a lesser degree the People's Republic of China, Great Britain, France, and West Germany. Certain events loom larger than others from an American vantage point. For example, to a Czech citizen the Prague Spring of 1968 would represent a pivotal Cold War moment, whereas to most Americans it would not. Because I am presenting an American perspective, I have included more numerous and more detailed biographical profiles of American figures and shorter biographical sketches of the leaders of the other major powers.

In the earliest days of the Cold War even American opinion about Soviet intentions was mixed, but by 1949 a consensus emerged in which the Soviets appeared as an aggressive enemy intent upon achieving global dominance and destabilizing democratic governments. Whether this view accurately represented Soviet objectives is now a matter of scholarly debate, but that it was commonly shared among the American public and American policymakers is not. Apart from the shared belief that worldwide Communism posed a genuine threat to American interests and security, however, fundamental assumptions about key Cold War issues varied greatly. For instance, no complete consensus existed about the arms race, the Red Scare, foreign policy toward China, the Vietnam War, the desirability of a U.S.-Soviet détente, and the relative wisdom of pursuing strategies predicated on mutually assured destruction versus those based on the ability to survive and win a full-scale nuclear war. Moreover, crucial facts and interpretations of facts were disputed throughout the Cold War. For instance, short of going to war could the United States have negotiated a significantly better settlement at Yalta or prevented the Communist takeover of China? Were Alger Hiss and the Rosenbergs really guilty of spying? Was the threat from domestic Communist subversion and government infiltration as serious as the political right represented? During détente, were the Soviets seriously preparing to prevail in a major nuclear war? Assessments of U.S. actions rely heavily on these and other points that remain contested.

Though I experienced the Cold War more or less as a liberal, I listened to conservative arguments. Where appropriate I have tried to include both liberal and conservative perspectives on important disputed issues and to represent the rationale behind each position. Precisely because I recognize the essentially cubist nature of history I am not trying to promote any particular interpretation of the Cold War. Moreover, the act of writing this history has occasioned me to revisit aspects of the Cold War I lived through many years ago and now view them differently, with the advantages of retrospect, greater access to facts, and a more complete historical framework. Reviewing the Cold War after it has concluded is different from thinking about it while events are still unfolding.

Having at least roughly established my own point of view, I welcome you to review this account of the dominant political event of the second half of the twentieth century. The first section provides a relatively brief overview of the Cold War and identifies the major issues and events. The next section contains individual chapters that elaborate on some of the more significant developments such as the Korean War, the Red Scare, and the Cuban Missile Crisis. The third section gives an annotated chronology of Cold War events followed by a chronology of the international leadership. Next are the biographies of American figures and then biographical sketches of international leaders.

Because this volume is intended as a reference guide I have made each section free-standing. Thus someone interested in learning about John Foster Dulles, for example, can simply read his biographical entry without having also to read chapter 4 on massive retaliation. The cost of providing autonomy for each section is a certain amount of repetition among them. For instance, because Eisenhower and Dulles formulated the same policies their biographical entries overlap each other and chapter 4. But no entry merely repeats another entry.

In addition to providing factual information the annotated chronology offers an alternative way of perceiving the Cold War, since it presents information chronologically instead of as associated events. For instance, the relationship between the 1983 Grenada invasion and the deaths of peace-keeping Marines in Lebanon two days prior stands out when we regard the Cold War chronologically. Likewise, the biographies of presidents encapsulate the major events of their administrations, and the accumulated biographies of figures from any era provide a fuller account of the period. I have included biographies of every Cold War U.S. president, most of the secretaries of state and national security advisers and other influential individuals, mostly from the government or military. I have also included biographical sketches of all the Cold War–era leaders of Great Britain, France, West Germany, Formosa/Taiwan (the Republic of China), the Soviet Union, and the People's Republic of China. Thus someone wanting to learn about the Cold War's formative years would do well not only to read chapters 2 and 3 on the pre–Cold War and containment but also the biographies of Harry Truman, Dean Acheson, George Kennan, Douglas MacArthur, Bernard Baruch, James Byrnes, Alger Hiss, George Marshall, Julius and Ethel Rosenberg, Patrick McCarran, and Joseph McCarthy, as well as those of Winston Churchill, Clement Attlee, Joseph Stalin, Konrad Adenauer, Charles De Gaulle, Mao Zedong, and Chiang Kai-shek. The "Chronology of Superpower Leadership" lists when each American and foreign leader was in power;

"U.S. Presidential Administrations and Soviet Leadership" charts the presidential administrations and pairs them with the contemporary Soviet leadership; "Leaders of the Western Allies" and "Leaders of the Soviet Union and the People's Republic of China" likewise chart the terms of foreign leaders. At the risk of some repetition, readers can thus coordinate among the different sections of the book.

The Cold War hovered over human existence for some 43 years and influenced virtually every aspect of American life. I offer *The Cold War Reference Guide* as a basic introduction to that struggle.

Abbreviations

AAA	Agricultural Adjustment Administration
ABM	Antiballistic Missile
AEC	Atomic Energy Commission
ANF	Atlantic Nuclear Force
CDU	Christian Democratic Union (West Germany)
CENT	Central Treaty Organization
CFE	Conventional Forces in Europe
CIA	Central Intelligence Agency
CIG	Central Intelligence Group
CIO	Congress of Industrial Organizations
CND	Campaign for Nuclear Disarmament
COINTELPRO	Counter Intelligence Program
Cominform	Communist Information Bureau
Comintern	Communist International
DMZ	Demilitarized Zone
EEC	European Economic Community
EDC	European Defense Community
ERP	European Recovery Program
FBI	Federal Bureau of Investigation
FDP	Federal Democratic Party (West Germany)
GATT	General Agreement on Tariffs and Trade
HUAC	House Un-American Activities Committee
ICBM	Intercontinental Ballistic Missile
INF	Intermediate-Range Nuclear Force
KGB	Committee of State Security
MAD	Mutually Assured Destruction
MIA	Missing in Action
MIRV	Multiple Independently-Targeted Re-entry Vehicle
MPLA	Popular Movement for the Liberation of Angola
NAACP	National Association for the Advancement of Colored People
NASA	National Aeronautics and Space Administration

5

NATO	North Atlantic Treaty Organization
NIA	National Intelligence Authority
NLF	National Liberation Front
NSC	National Security Council
NSF	National Science Foundation
OAS	Organization of American States
OPC	Office of Policy Coordination (CIA)
OSS	Office of Strategic Services
PPBS	Planning Programming Budgeting System
SAC	Strategic Air Command
SALT	Strategic Arms Limitation Talks
SDI	Strategic Defense Initiative
SEATO	Southeast Asia Treaty Organization
SPD	Social Democratic Party (West Germany)
START	Strategic Arms Reduction Talks
UN	United Nations

SECTION I

A General History of the Cold War

Chapter 1

Overview

The Cold War lasted approximately from 1947 to 1990. It was a state of ongoing hostility between superpowers in which the United States led a loosely joined Western alliance, including allies in Western Europe (notably Great Britain, France, and West Germany), North America (Canada), the Middle East (notably Turkey and Israel), and Asia and the Pacific Rim (notably Japan, Taiwan, South Korea, South Vietnam, Australia, and the Philippines). The North Atlantic Treaty Organization (NATO), a military alliance, was formed in 1949 to contain Communist expansion in Europe. Led by the United States, NATO's original members included Belgium, Canada, Denmark, France, Great Britain, Iceland, Italy, Luxembourg, the Netherlands, Norway, and Portugal. Greece and Turkey joined in 1952, West Germany in 1955, and Spain in 1982. In 1966 France withdrew its forces from the integrated NATO command and ordered all U.S. and NATO troops to leave French territory; however, it proclaimed its willingness to adhere to the treaty in the event of an unprovoked attack against alliance members. Likewise, a public referendum in 1986 left Spain in NATO but removed it from the military command structure and continued to ban nuclear weapons on Spanish soil. An analogous Southeast Asia Treaty Organization (SEATO) was formed in 1954 after Vietnamese Communist nationalists under Ho Chi Minh forced the French evacuation of Indochina at the battle of Dien Bien Phu. SEATO included Australia, France, Great Britain, New Zealand, Pakistan, the Philippines, Thailand, and the United States.

The Soviet Union (USSR) headed the so-called Eastern alliance composed of its Eastern European allies and puppet states (notably Poland, Czechoslovakia, Hungary, East Germany, Romania, and Bulgaria), its Caribbean ally (Cuba), its Middle Eastern allies (the Arab states in conflict with Israel; notably Syria, and Egypt before the 1978 Camp David Accords), and its Asian allies (notably North Korea, North Vietnam, and the People's Republic of China before the late 1950s). In 1955 the Warsaw Pact formed in response to the remilitarization of West Germany and its admission into NATO. Led by the Soviet Union, the original Warsaw Pact members included Albania, Bulgaria, Czechoslovakia, East Germany, Poland, Hungary, and Romania. Albania ceased to be invited to meetings in 1962 and it formally withdrew in 1968. As of 1996 NATO remains intact, but the Warsaw Pact dissolved in 1991 after the Cold War ended.

In addition to these alliances, both superpowers also supported insurgent movements and/or reigning political regimes in civil wars and insurrections within Africa (notably Zaire and Angola), Southeast Asia (notably Vietnam, Laos, and Cambodia), Afghanistan, the Philippines, Nicaragua, El Salvador, Guatemala, the Dominican Republic, and other so-called "underdeveloped," nonindustrialized, agrarian countries. In the Korean and Vietnamese wars and the Soviet war in Afghanistan the superpowers engaged their own armies in prolonged warfare against indigenous forces. In other instances the superpowers supported warring factions in national disputes by supplying client governments or revolutionary movements with weapons, military advisers, military intelligence, and money in return for varying degrees of political allegiance.

The hostilities between the superpowers and their proxies took place within diplomatic, economic, and sometimes military realms, though the greatest fear — a major military confrontation between two nuclear superpowers — was never realized: hence the term Cold War.

Often represented by the United States and Soviet Union as a conflict between two incompatible economic ideologies — free-market capitalism and controlled-production/controlled-market Communism — the Cold War also pitted democracies whose citizens enjoyed a relatively high number of civil liberties against nondemocratic, totalitarian regimes that granted their citizens considerably fewer freedoms and less control over the conditions and choices in their lives. Though not all U.S. allies were truly freedom-granting democracies characterized by regular and honest elections and civil rights (South Vietnam, El Salvador, South Korea, and the Philippines under Ferdinand Marcos were highly suspect), in Europe profound contrasts existed between the freedoms of speech, assembly, movement, political organization, religion, and press enjoyed within the Western democracies and those within the Eastern totalitarian regimes. Consequently, the West frequently cast the Cold War in moral terms as a struggle for freedom. American policy gyrated during the Cold War from implacable opposition to an evil empire to attempts at peaceful coexistence with the Communist nuclear superpowers, and back again.

In addition to the ideological conflicts, the Cold War manifested several power struggles among international economic and military powers. Such conflicts typify human history, going back at least to Athens and Sparta, Rome and Carthage, England and Spain during the period of New World exploration, and England and Germany during periods of colonization and empire.

One of the many perspectives we can bring to the Cold War shows men in the ruling parties of their respective countries trying to consolidate and extend their personal power, both at home and abroad. (For whatever significance one wishes to attribute to this, the Cold War was initiated and fought at the highest levels almost exclusively by men.) Though often carried out more brutally within the Communist regimes than in the Western democracies, power struggles were fought in all countries against domestic opposition both within the same political party and between contesting parties. In the Soviet Union, for instance, Stalin purged many real and imagined enemies in the 1950s as well as in the more infamous purges of the 1930s in which millions were killed, and a coup removed Khrushchev in 1964. The Soviet Union intervened militarily in East Germany (1953), Hungary (1956), and Czechoslovakia (1968) to support Communist regimes threatened by internal opposition, and it backed the ruling Polish regime's internal suppression of the Solidarity Trade Union, which had demanded reforms in 1980. In China Mao Zedong killed thousands when he purged his enemies during the Cultural Revolution (1965–69).

The United States and Western European democracies transferred power more smoothly in presidential, congressional and parliamentary elections, but the U.S. Red Scare in the 1950s certainly purged many opposition members from positions of influence (see chapter 9). Moreover, files obtained under the Freedom of Information Act show that individual presidents, the FBI, CIA, National Security Council, Chicago Police Department, and other government agencies actively worked against political enemies. The Watergate investigations revealed that President Nixon kept an "enemies list" and used freelance espionage agents called "plumbers" to stop leaks, infiltrate the Democratic Party Headquarters, and undermine opponents to the Vietnam War. His Democratic predecessor, Lyndon Johnson, has been accused of similar abuses.

In addition to these internal clashes, the ruling groups in each alliance also struggled internationally for greater power, control, and wealth, and we can interpret the power politics of the Cold War in this light also. Thus, any complete representation of the Cold War must reveal the simultaneous workings of several forces, circumstances, and motivations: sincere commitment to ideologies and philosophies of government; the challenges of governing and implementing sound public policies within democratic and Communist Party–controlled environments; the political poses, hypocrisies, trade-offs, and betrayals necessary for maintaining and exercising power; the real dangers from external military threats and the opportunities for manipulating domestic politics that those threats afforded; and the personal ambitions and individual strengths, weaknesses, needs, and desires of the most important personalities. Some men and women made good decisions for selfish reasons; others made disastrous decisions for noble reasons.

The Periods of the Cold War

We can establish six roughly distinct periods characterized by U.S. policy toward the USSR: 1) the pre–Cold War (1945–47), 2) containment (1947–54),

3) massive retaliation, second strike and flexible response (1954–69), 4) mutually assured destruction and détente (1969–79), 5) winnable nuclear war, the evil empire, and the collapse of Communism in Eastern Europe and the Soviet Union (1980–90), and 6) the aftermath of the Cold War (1990–92).

Chapter 2

The Pre–Cold War
(1945–47)

In February 1945, when it had become apparent that the Allies would prevail over the Axis powers in World War II, Allied leaders met in Yalta to demand Germany's unconditional surrender and map out the general political arrangements for the postwar world. Attending were Franklin Roosevelt (United States), Winston Churchill (Great Britain), and Joseph Stalin (Soviet Union).

Though they called for representative governments and free elections in Eastern Europe, the agreements that emerged from the Yalta Conference implicitly acknowledged spheres of influence that essentially granted the USSR dominion over Eastern Europe and the Western allies dominion over Western Europe. These spheres of influence generally reflected military and political reality. The Soviet Red Army had already advanced through Eastern Europe into Germany and thus controlled most of the areas consigned to the Soviet sphere. In Yugoslavia the Western allies had no one to challenge the immensely popular partisan Communist leader, Marshal Tito. And the Czechs were unlikely to ally with the West after Great Britain and France had betrayed them in the 1938 Munich agreement that allowed Hitler to seize Czech territory (the Sudetenland). Likewise in Manchuria and the Far East, many of Churchill and Roosevelt's concessions permitting Soviet control reflected the existing presence of Soviet troops in those territories or their proximity.

Some American conservatives and others on the political right wing ferociously attacked the Yalta agreements as an American sellout to the Communists because the accords implicitly legitimized the Communist rule in Eastern Europe and Asia, a rule that these critics justifiably characterized as repressive. They also argued that a sly Stalin had duped an ailing Roosevelt into making bad bargains: that the West had conceded far more than necessary. (Roosevelt died two months after Yalta.) Right-wing rhetoric thus vilified Roosevelt and the Yalta agreements throughout the Cold War, especially during the 1950s and 1960s.

Historians disagree sharply over Yalta, ranging from those who believe it provided a realistic division of power given the anticipated military and political

13

conditions at the end of World War II, to those who believe that after defeating Germany the Western allies should have continued into the USSR to overthrow the repressive, anticapitalist Soviet government. Anyone assessing the probable success that a hypothetical American invasion of Russia might have had in 1945 should remember that the atomic bomb was not completed until after the Yalta Conference and that by the conclusion of World War II the Red Army was a formidable force that had conquered much of the highly vaunted German war machine. It is also questionable whether a war-weary American public would have supported a new war against a recent ally.

Roosevelt died suddenly on April 12, 1945, and Harry Truman ascended to the presidency. Truman assumed office at a dynamic moment in world history. Within two weeks of his inauguration he signed the UN charter; within a month Germany surrendered and World War II concluded in Europe; and within two months the terms of the Cold War were already beginning to emerge, as the Allies partitioned Germany into four sectors to be controlled individually by the United States, Great Britain, France, and the Soviet Union.

Initially, Truman, also a Democrat, sought to continue Roosevelt's policies of cooperating with the Soviets. Prior to the German surrender he turned down Winston Churchill's suggestion that the U.S. Army move deeper into Eastern Europe in order to give the United States a stronger bargaining position, and he reaffirmed Roosevelt's decision to acquire Soviet entry into the Japanese war in return for political and territorial concessions in Asia. In July Edward Stettinius stepped down as secretary of state and Truman appointed James Byrnes to replace him. Though the two men did not work easily together, they initially shared the same foreign policy objectives: to sustain the wartime alliance and inhibit Soviet attempts to take full control of Eastern Europe. Neither man viewed the Soviets as ideologues bent on world conquest. Instead, they regarded Stalin as a fellow politician willing to negotiate a political arrangement.

Truman and Byrnes promoted the founding of democratic governments in Germany and Eastern Europe and the eventual evacuation of Soviet troops from occupied European territories. The Soviets, on the other hand, insisted that their security required friendly governments in their Eastern European sphere of influence. Prior to the Potsdam Conference of July and August 1945, Truman insisted that the Soviets reaffirm the provisions of the Yalta Declaration calling for representative governments and free elections in Eastern Europe, and he reduced U.S. aid to the USSR to pressure Stalin on the issue. Harry Hopkins, one of Roosevelt's most trusted advisers, obtained an agreement for a compromise government in Poland and the Soviet entry into the war against Japan.

At Potsdam the so-called Big Three — the United States, Great Britain, and the Soviet Union — set policies for controlling Germany during the occupation. Based on their devastating experiences in World Wars I and II as well as their hopes for postwar domination of Europe, the Soviets wanted to keep Germany weak, disarmed, and possibly fragmented. On the other hand, Truman believed that a democratic, independent, economically strong, and unified Germany was crucial to the revitalization and security of Europe. This fundamental U.S.-Soviet disagreement over postwar Germany remained one of the central points of contention throughout the Cold War and accounted for why Germany was a flash point between 1948 and 1961. The Potsdam agreement called for the eventual unification of Germany as a sovereign democratic state independent from any of the superpowers, and the Soviets reluctantly acceded to its economic redevelopment. In return for Stalin's concessions Truman agreed to transfer part of eastern Germany to Poland, where it fell under Soviet control pending a final peace treaty (which was not signed until 1990). However, one year later at the 1946 Paris Peace Conference Byrnes became convinced that the Soviets would not honor their Potsdam commitment to create an independent, democratic Germany. Consequently the Truman administration moved toward establishing a separate, democratic West German government rather than allow a single, Soviet-dominated German state.

In November 1945 Byrnes went to Moscow where he agreed to recognize the Soviet-controlled regimes in Bulgaria and Romania in return for broader representation and democratic procedures within those governments. Truman, who had not been consulted during the negotiations, disassociated himself from the agreement and Republican Senator Arthur Vandenberg, a vocal critic of the administration's foreign policy, termed it "one more typical American give away."

Pushed to take a harder stance against the Soviets and increasingly convinced of their unwillingness to negotiate in good faith, Truman and Byrnes adopted a policy of patience with firmness in which the United States would negotiate with the USSR but would expect any further concessions to come from the Soviets. When Soviet troops occupied part of Iran in early 1946 in a dispute over oil rights, the administration exerted diplomatic pressure until Iran and the Soviet Union reached a formal agreement and the Soviets withdrew their soldiers. In February 1946 George Kennan wrote his detailed Long Telegram analyzing U.S. policy toward the USSR. Departing from Byrnes's earlier view that the Soviets were pragmatic politicians who sought to achieve their goals primarily through diplomacy, the Long Telegram maintained that Soviet foreign policy was predicated on the Communist ideological belief that conflict between Communism and capitalism was historically inevitable. Consequently, Kennan argued that Stalin would consolidate his power at home and insulate the Soviet Union by surrounding it with allied client states. Being too weak to attack the West militarily, the Soviets would attempt to isolate the United States by politically subverting other capitalist countries. Truman made the Long Telegram the intellectual basis for subsequent Soviet policy (see chapter 3).

Chapter 3

Containment
(1947–54)

Between 1947 and 1949 the East-West coalitions fell into place. The rapid Communist gains between 1947 and 1949 in Eastern Europe and China were often accomplished by military force and/or military threats. Moreover, the various Communist regimes frequently nationalized industry and collectivized agriculture through brutally repressive measures.

The events of these years did much to create the image in Western minds of the Soviet alliance as an evil empire bent on world conquest. Seizing and holding power by various deplorable means including assassination, insurgency, secret police, forced labor, and imprisonment of political opponents, the Communists also forged for themselves an image of iron-fisted tyranny. This image — all too similar in its brutality and oppression to Hitler's — was probably the strongest factor in mobilizing the American citizenry against Communism.

As the French and Italian Communists were removed from or squeezed out of their respective governments, Stalin purged non–Communists from his sphere of influence. In September 1947 the Soviet Communist Party and Communist parties in Bulgaria, Czechoslovakia, France, Hungary, Italy, Poland, Romania, and Yugoslavia loosely aligned through the Communist Information Bureau (Cominform), which replaced the Communist International (Comintern). In 1948 Communists took complete control of the government in Czechoslovakia. In 1947–48 they gained considerable control in Finland, capturing several high offices, briefly including that of the prime minister. Finland signed a treaty of cooperation with the USSR in 1948. In 1947 Communists forced a coalition Romanian government under a non–Communist leader to abdicate and replaced it with a Communist people's republic. Romanian industry and resources were nationalized and collectivized agriculture was instituted. Bulgaria also became a one-party Communist state aligned with the USSR, nationalizing industry and collectivizing farms. In early 1948 Hungarian Communists, through their control of the ministry of the interior, arrested leading politicians, forced the resignation of the premier, and gained full control of the state. In 1949 it was proclaimed a people's republic that also nationalized industry and resources and collectivized farms. During this time Albania solidified its Communist rule and its ties with the USSR, and in 1947 Communists took control of the Polish government and sovietized that country. In one East European country, however, events followed a different course. In 1948 Tito asserted Yugoslavia's independence from the USSR and initiated his own foreign policy. Yugoslavia was then banished from Cominform, which was dissolved in 1956 as a gesture of reconciliation when Yugoslavia reestablished friendly relations. In the interim Yugoslavia established ties with the West, receiving U.S. economic aid and signing a 1954 pact with NATO members Greece and Turkey.

One of the more dramatic moments in the Cold War was the Berlin Airlift of 1948–49. After World War II Allied troops occupied Germany, with the Soviets controlling the eastern part and the U.S., Great Britain, and France occupying the west. Though Berlin was situated well within the Soviet sector, the city was similarly divided and administered by the four allies. In an effort to force the Western allies to abandon plans to create a separate West German government and to accept a single, Soviet-controlled currency for all of Berlin, Stalin blockaded the land and river access routes to West Berlin in June 1948. Neither wanting to back down to the Soviets nor force a military confrontation, Truman initiated a massive airlift of vital supplies to the 2 million West Berliners. By spring 1949 the round-the-clock flights were averaging 8,000 tons of fuel and food supplies daily, with coal accounting for most of the tonnage. Unsuccessful in achieving their aims, the Soviets lifted the blockade in May 1949, thereby vindicating Truman and Secretary of State George Marshall who had opposed recommendations by General Lucius Clay and others that the United States send armed convoys to break the blockade.

Also during the Truman presidency (1945–53) Communists under Mao Zedong defeated U.S.-backed Chinese Nationalists led by Chiang Kai-shek. Chairman Mao formed a Communist People's Republic of China on October 1, 1949, while Chiang fled to the island of Taiwan (Formosa) and formed a government in exile 100 miles offshore in the Pacific Ocean. The United States continued to recognize Chiang's Republic of China as the sole, legitimate Chinese government until the 1970s. On June 25, 1950, Communist North Korea launched a surprise invasion of South Korea, inaugurating the Korean War. UN troops, primarily consisting of U.S. soldiers but also including forces from U.S. allies, intervened on behalf of South Korea, while the Chinese Army fought on the side of the North Koreans. The Soviets contributed military advisers to North Korea and played a significant role in the political aspect of the war but did not commit combat troops. The war lasted until an armistice was signed in 1953 (see chapter 10). Also in Asia, India received its independence from Britain in 1947 and was partitioned into two nations: Muslim Pakistan and nonsectarian but predominantly Hindu India. War between these nations broke out in 1948, the first of several during the Cold War.

The British withdrawal from the Middle East led to another partitioning of hostile, religious factions. In 1947 the United Nations voted to create two separate nations from the post–World War I British mandate in Palestine: the Jewish state of Israel and a predominately Muslim Arab state. The first of several Cold War–era Arab-Israeli wars broke out immediately following the British departure in 1948. Israel largely prevailed; however, Transjordan retained the old city of Jerusalem and much of the territory that the United Nations had designated for the separate Arab state. Annexing that territory, Transjordan changed its name to Jordan in 1949.

Containment and economic development were cornerstones of U.S. Cold War policy in the late 1940s and the early to mid–1950s, when the United States enjoyed unquestioned nuclear superiority. Containment's aim was to keep the Soviet Union within its existing spheres of influence, and it was backed up by implicit and explicit threats from the fledgling U.S. atomic arsenal. Concern over Communist insurrection in Greece led to the Truman Doctrine in March 1947 to check the Communist expansion in Europe and Asia immediately after World War II. Shortly before issuing the doctrine Truman had approved aid to Greece and Turkey. The main feature of the Truman Doctrine was the economic reconstruction of postwar Europe; its cornerstones were the Marshall Plan (1947), the Four Point Program to provide technical aid to underdeveloped countries in Asia, Africa, and Latin America (1948), and the creation of NATO (1949).

Secretary of State Marshall's plan for European recovery was one of the great successes of the Cold War and one of the greatest testimonies to the vitality and creative energy of capitalism. By promoting Western European industrial production, bolstering Western European currencies, and promoting international trade, the Marshall Plan facilitated Western Europe's surprisingly rapid recovery from the massive, widespread destruction of World War II. And by ensuring the economic stability of non–Communist governments in France, Italy, and other countries where a Communist presence was strong, the Marshall Plan helped enable friendly, procapitalist governments to remain in power. It thereby also fulfilled its Cold War objective of containing Communism. Though invited to participate in the Marshall Plan, the Soviets and their Eastern European allies rejected the offer and denounced the program.

Marshall retired as secretary of state in January 1949 because of ill health. His successor, Dean Acheson, developed the containment policy more explicitly, having been greatly influenced by George Kennan's article in *Foreign Affairs*, "The Sources of Soviet Conduct" (July, 1947). Kennan, a member of the State Department's policy-planning staff, argued that Russia sought to expand its domination by all means short of direct, superpower confrontation. He therefore recommended that the United States and its allies respond with "a long-term, patient but firm and vigilant containment of Russian expansive tendencies" and that they employ "the adroit and vigilant application of counterforce at a series of shifting geographical and political points." The Berlin airlift was the first major military application of the containment philosophy. Other important examples of containment in action were the Korean War, the 1958 intervention in Lebanon, the second Berlin Crisis, and the Vietnam War.

Chapter 4

Massive Retaliation, Second Strike, and Flexible Response (1954-69)

In 1952 Americans elected World War II hero Dwight Eisenhower president. Two months after his inauguration Stalin died and after a brief power struggle Nikita Khrushchev emerged as the dominant Soviet leader. The United States also exploded its first hydrogen bomb in 1952 and the Soviets exploded theirs in 1953. Eisenhower's basic foreign policy was to contain Communist expansion and to threaten massive retaliation against any aggressor. Articulated by Secretary of State John Foster Dulles on January 12, 1954, the policy of massive retaliation claimed that Soviet aggression against U.S. allies anywhere on the globe could be met by a nuclear response directed against the Soviet Union itself. The nuclear threat was intended to compensate for the Eastern block's numerical superiority in troops and conventional weapons. A nuclear deterrent also offered a less expensive alternative to maintaining conventional armies. Thus it was marketed in the early 1950s as "getting a bigger bang for the buck." The exchange of nuclear threats between the superpowers and their incorporation of nuclear retaliation as a cornerstone of foreign policy created one of the most intense periods of hostility during the entire Cold War (see chapter 8).

In his first term Eisenhower, a Republican, oversaw the 1953 armistice that concluded hostilities in the Korean War and left the country partitioned at the thirty-eighth parallel.

East and West Germany gained formal recognition as a sovereign countries (1954 and 1955, respectively), and first West Germany (1955) and then East Germany (1956) remilitarized. Berlin remained divided into two separate cities: east and west Berlin. Because the Soviets wanted to codify the status quo in order to legitimize and protect their gains in Eastern Europe, they recognized both

East Germany and West Germany. But the United States ultimately sought a reunified Germany and therefore refused to recognized East Germany until 1974.

Also during Eisenhower's first term, Communist nationalists under Ho Chi Minh defeated the French Army in their war to liberate Vietnam from French colonialism. The resulting 1954 Geneva Peace Accords called for the temporary creation of North Vietnam and South Vietnam, which were to be unified two years hence in national elections. Fearing Ho Chi Minh's almost certain victory, the United States refused to sign the accords and supported South Vietnam's refusal to participate in the election. The resulting de facto partition of Vietnam and the subsequent struggle for reunification waged by South Vietnamese Communist nationalists (the Vietcong) and their North Vietnamese allies became the basis of America's military involvement in Vietnam between 1961 and 1973.

In 1954 the United States covertly assisted a military coup in Guatemala. The coup overthrew the reform government of Jacobo Arbenz Guzmán who had expropriated large landholdings of the United Fruit Company and become increasingly open to Communist influence. The succeeding military dictatorship received some $90 million in U.S. aid during the rule of coup leader Colonel Carlos Castillo Armas, who imprisoned thousands of political prisoners, disenfranchised 75 percent of the voting citizenry, eliminated secret ballot elections, abolished all political parties and independent trade unions, and canceled the agrarian reform laws before his assassination in 1957. In the early 1960s the CIA used Guatemala as a base for training anti–Castro guerrillas.

In 1956 the United States refused to condone a joint British, French, and Israeli attack on Egypt or to support British and French efforts to reclaim the Suez Canal. When the USSR threatened a missile attack against France and England, however, Eisenhower informed the Soviets that such an attack would provoke a U.S. nuclear response and lead to global war. A UN armistice defused the crisis, arranging for the withdrawal of all British and French troops and leaving the United States the sole superpower in the region.

Secretary of State Dulles took a hard line against the Communist domination of Eastern Europe throughout the early 1950s. Refusing to concede a Soviet sphere of influence, Dulles advocated a policy of liberating countries under Communist rule. Eisenhower was less ideologically motivated. The ultimate test of his commitment to Dulles's liberation policy came during the 1956 Hungarian Revolution.

Ironically, the brutal suppression of the Hungarian uprising stemmed from domestic reforms in the USSR that gave Soviet citizens greater freedoms. Khrushchev implemented domestic reforms that lessened the power of the secret police (KGB), closed concentration camps and forced labor camps, restored legal procedures, and generally offered Soviet citizens greater personal freedoms, although these were still highly restricted by Western standards. However, these reforms within the Soviet Union (called de–Stalinization) and Khrushchev's 1956 rejection of Stalin's "Personality Cult" led Polish and Hungarian citizens to agitate for greater freedoms in their countries too. Their civil unrest culminated when a popular anti–Communist coalition briefly deposed Hungary's Communist regime. The new government appealed for Western support but Eisenhower respected the Soviet sphere of influence and declined to assist. Unwilling to accept this weakening of Soviet domination over its satellite states, Khrushchev suppressed the revolutionary, breakaway government by sending tanks and troops into Budapest. For Americans, however, the Hungarian Revolution reconfirmed the Soviet Union's brutal and repressive nature.

Throughout his rule (1953–64) Khrushchev vacillated between gestures of conciliation with the capitalist West and hard-line rejection of accommodation with it. Powerful, internal opposition from Communist hard-liners no doubt curbed his ability to reconcile with the West and forced him to crush resistance in client states. Khrushchev also sought to expand Soviet influence among the underdeveloped nations, especially in the Middle East, Africa, and Southeast Asia. His support of Cuba's revolutionary leader Fidel Castro, who had come to power on New Year's Day 1959, gave the USSR a base in the Caribbean, just 150 miles from the U.S. mainland. Unlike Stalin, who was not especially impressed by nuclear weapons, Khrushchev established a Soviet policy of gaining parity with or nuclear superiority over the United States. Consequently, the 1950s saw the beginnings of a nuclear arms race that continued throughout the Cold War.

The Soviets' 1957 test of an intercontinental ballistic missile (ICBM) and its launching of the first human-made space satellite, Sputnik I, changed the military terms of the Cold War. For the first time the Soviet Union showed that it had the capacity to reach the U.S. mainland with nuclear weapons. (The Soviet mainland had all along been vulnerable to U.S. nuclear air strikes from bases in Europe and Turkey.) Sputnik also undermined the conventional wisdom that asserted that the United States greatly surpassed the USSR in science and technology. Thus, the launching of Sputnik sparked a renewed interest in science and science education in America. Budgets for scientific research increased dramatically as Congress granted the National Science Foundation (NSF) increasingly larger appropriations. The science of rocketry, which the government had treated as though it still belonged to science fiction, moved to center stage with the formation of the National Aeronautics and Space Administration (NASA) in October 1958. Moreover, because Sputnik highlighted the role of science within the Cold War, it led to policies that promoted science and math education. So the effectiveness of the public schools also became a Cold War issue. Arguably, Sputnik and the Soviets' 1961 success in sending the first human into outer space (Yuri Gagarin) inspired President Kennedy's ambitious but successful program to send a person to the moon by the end of the decade.

Improvements in Soviet missile capacity and their growing nuclear capacity made the U.S. policy of massive retaliation increasingly problematic, since by 1957 the USSR could reply in kind to any American attack on its mainland.

Moreover, the USSR could also institute its own policy of nuclear retaliation against the United States for any Western offensive directed against its Eastern-block allies. The new balance of terror further undermined Dulles's dream of liberating Communist-dominated countries and more or less institutionalized Truman's containment policy (even though in 1953 the Republicans had forcefully campaigned against containment as too passive).

In the later 1950s ranking officers in the army and navy began lobbying to replace massive retaliation with a policy of "flexible response." Requiring a larger army and a greater investment in conventional weapons, flexible response was intended to give the United States more options for dealing with crises, enabling it to fight limited conventional and/or guerrilla wars without necessarily having to resort to nuclear weapons. Eisenhower resisted flexible response because he believed it was too expensive. He maintained that a healthy economy was one of the strongest defenses against Communism and feared that an arms race or other large military expenditures would weaken the economy: "To amass military power without regard to our economic capacity would be to defend ourselves against one kind of disaster by inviting another." Nonetheless, after cutting social programs and other domestic spending to pay for them, he authorized an accelerated missile program and new programs promoting science education. He also permitted a slight increase in conventional military strength during his final years in office, but he refused to increase spending for space exploration.

On the other hand, his successor, John Kennedy, a Democrat, was more willing to increase the military budget, and he and Defense Secretary Robert McNamara supported flexible response. They approved an increase of some 300,000 combat troops and expanded capabilities for airlifting American forces and equipment anywhere in the world. They also adopted recommendations to create a second-strike capacity in order to enhance the U.S. nuclear deterrent and thereby reduce the likelihood of a nuclear war. By guaranteeing that the United States would have enough remaining missiles to launch a devastating retaliatory attack in the event of a Soviet first strike, the second strike capability was intended to convince the Soviets that a first strike could not prevent their own destruction. However, the second-strike capability required replacing liquid-fuel ICBMS with solid-fuel Minuteman missiles housed in hardened underground silos and Polaris missiles on submarines. The new flexible response and second-strike policies led to a 30 percent increase in defense spending during the Kennedy administration. In Kennedy's first year he received a $6 billion increase in defense spending and, despite McNamara's substantial efforts to cut operating expenses and curtail the arms race, the defense budget rose from $43 billion to $56 billion while Kennedy was in office. The superpowers' threats to use nuclear weapons nearly became reality in the early 1960s, when the Soviets tried to alter the status quo in Berlin and Cuba. McNamara later credited flexible response for enabling Kennedy to respond to the Cuban Missile Crisis without having to resort to either a major military engagement or a nuclear war (see chapters 11 and 12).

In the immediate wake of Sputnik the USSR was perceived to have the advantage in ICBMs. This led to charges by Kennedy in the 1960 presidential campaign that a missile gap existed between the United States and Soviet Union, though within a few years it became apparent that the Soviets had never achieved superiority. In the interim Khrushchev tried to use the perception of Soviet missile superiority to compel the West to acknowledge the legitimacy of the Soviet empire in Eastern Europe. Consequently, the most unstable period of the Cold War came between November 1958, when Khrushchev issued his first ultimatum for the Western allies to evacuate West Berlin, and October 1962 during the Cuban Missile Crisis. During much of this four-year period nuclear war seemed not only possible but probable. To some it seemed inevitable. Consequently, proposals for a nuclear first strike by the United States against the Soviet Union were seriously debated throughout the country, as were the ethics of defending personal fallout shelters in the aftermath of a nuclear attack.

Despite his nuclear brinkmanship, Khrushchev accomplished relatively little from his aggressive posturing. He backed down from his ultimatums over Berlin and pulled the missiles out of Cuba, partly because by 1962 he realized that the Soviet missile and nuclear superiority had been mythical all along and that the United States was the stronger nuclear power. His international failures weakened him at home and abroad. Mao Zedong chastised him for backing down, and other Communist nations began turning to China for leadership. Khrushchev's program of de–Stalinization, his economic reforms, and his occasional willingness to seek peaceful coexistence with the West ultimately led to a major break with China, a country that advocated a traditional Marxist, revolutionary ideology viewing capitalist societies as implacable enemies. By the mid–1960s the apparent Soviet-Chinese Communist monolith had disintegrated into two separate, hostile camps.

Khrushchev's international failures undermined his position within the USSR as well. In 1964 a coup removed him from office and established Leonid Brezhnev as the new Soviet leader. A year earlier Kennedy had been assassinated and replaced by Lyndon Johnson; so within two years after the Cuban Missile Crisis both superpower leaders were gone. Their enduring legacy, however, was a 1963 nuclear test ban treaty forbidding above-ground testing of nuclear devices. The treaty ended the radioactive clouds that U.S. and Soviet explosions had sent into the atmosphere to be carried across the world. China did not participate in the treaty and it later conducted above-ground tests.

After the scare of a nuclear Armageddon occasioned by the Cuban Missile Crisis, the superpowers were less willing to risk major confrontations in Europe or in each other's immediate sphere of influence. After the mid–1960s, therefore, the Cold War battleground largely shifted to Southeast Asia, Africa, the Middle East, and Central America. In the conflicts in these areas the United States further employed its policy of flexible response and consistently avoided the nuclear option, though various ranking politicians suggested using it in Southeast Asia.

In the early 1960s the Communist Pathet Lao nearly seized control of Laos before the United States sent military aid but no combat troops to the Laotian government. A similar pattern followed in Vietnam, where Kennedy substantially increased the number of U.S. military advisers between 1961 and 1963. However, after a 1965 Vietcong attack on an American installation killed or wounded over 100 advisers, President Johnson committed ground troops, and the U.S. fighting in Vietnam began in full along with the domestic antiwar movement. Between 1965 and 1973 much of the U.S. Cold War energy and resources was devoted to the Vietnam War (see chapter 13).

In 1964 China exploded its first atomic device. Between 1965 and 1969 Mao Zedong launched the bloody first phase of his Cultural Revolution, purging his enemies in a four-year state of emergency that nearly resulted in civil war. Universities closed and students were sent to work in the fields. Many teachers and intellectuals were persecuted and/or executed. Mao emerged victorious from this power struggle in 1969. In the process he eliminated his political foes who had sought to introduce less ideologically based economic reforms as well as those who still wished to retain close ties with the Soviets. He was named supreme commander of the Army and Navy in 1970, the same year that China launched its first satellite into space.

In the strategically important Middle East, Israel's victory in its 1967 Six-Day War against a coalition of its Arab enemies not only asserted Israel as the dominant military power in the region but also solidified its affiliation with the United States and the Arab countries' alliance with the USSR. Each superpower contributed heavily to resupplying its client states' depleted military stockpiles.

In general the Soviet policy during the middle and late 1960s was to support indigenous revolutionary organizations seeking to overthrow oligarchical governments throughout the underdeveloped world. However, Brezhnev sent troops into Czechoslovakia in 1968 to crush the liberal government of Alexander Dubček, who had come to power at the beginning of the year and instituted political reforms that reduced press censorship and moved the country significantly toward democratization. Dubček's short-lived reign, often referred to as the Prague Spring, also occasioned an outburst of new literary, artistic, and cultural efforts that had previously been suppressed. After the Soviet intervention Dubček was arrested and sent to Moscow, where he was forced to consent to the cancellation of his reforms. Soon after he was removed from office and disappeared from public view.

Typically, the United States respected the Soviet sphere of influence in Eastern Europe and worked to frustrate the Communist revolutions in the Third World. Consequently, it did not move to assist Dubček when the Soviets deposed him. But the United States sent military and financial aid to sustain Asian and

Pacific Rim governments in such places as the Philippines and South Korea. Within the U.S. sphere of influence, American policy was sometimes more forceful. In 1965 Johnson sent 20,000 Marines into the Dominican Republic to restore order and protect American interests after a pro–Communist coup toppled the right-wing government that the Dominican military had installed after deposing a democratically elected government in 1963. Eventually a new right-wing government came to power.

Chapter 5

Mutually Assured Destruction and Détente (1969–79)

Since the late 1960s East-West opposition moved away from Europe and direct NATO–Warsaw Pact confrontations over such classic Cold War issues as access to Berlin, Communist oppression of Eastern Europe, and German unification. Instead, the superpowers struggled mainly through proxies in Southeast Asia, the Middle East, Africa, and Central America. This change of setting for the Cold War reduced the likelihood of direct superpower nuclear confrontation, but it also decimated the populations and undermined the governments of those countries where the proxy wars occurred: notably in Vietnam, Cambodia, Laos, Angola, Ethiopia, Afghanistan, El Salvador, and Nicaragua. Entire regions of continents were destabilized in Southeast Asia and Central America especially.

Though the superpowers did not always engineer or initiate these conflicts — which usually stemmed from local issues — they often provided military and/or economic support to one side or the other. For example, hostilities between India and Pakistan, and those between Israel and the neighboring Arab countries, stemmed from long-standing animosities, religious differences, and other provocations unrelated to the Cold War. But since the United States supported Pakistan and Israel, while the USSR supported India and the Arab nations, the Cold War deeply influenced politics and warfare in the Middle East and the Indian subcontinent. In the process the superpowers provided arsenals of sophisticated weapons and thus greatly escalated the level of violence.

Because mutual Cold War suspicions never truly ceased and because the arms race provided economic and political benefits for the superpowers, they inaugurated programs throughout the 1970s and 1980s for developing new nuclear and conventional weaponry and selling or giving weapons to underdeveloped countries. Though arms limitation and arms reduction talks regularly took place, they moved slowly and their achievements were limited. Consequently,

27

an enormous, worldwide proliferation of weaponry, both conventional and nuclear, characterizes this part of the Cold War.

The nuclear stalemate among superpowers eventually led in the late 1960s and early 1970s to a policy of détente, or peaceful coexistence, between the two hostile sides. However the coexistence was rarely friendly and more frequently distrustful and obstructionist.

Republican Richard Nixon defeated Johnson's vice president, Hubert Humphrey in the 1968 presidential election. The campaign was marked by race riots and massive, sometimes violent, anti–Vietnam War protests. Running on a law and order platform that showed little tolerance for civil disorder, Nixon also promised to achieve peace in Vietnam. In his first term he also took strong steps to reframe the terms of the Cold War.

In the popular, science-fiction "Star Trek" movie, *The Undiscovered Country*, Mr. Spock cites an old Vulcan saying, "Only Nixon could have gone to China." Nixon's undisputed Cold War credentials as an avid anti–Communist ironically gave him the political flexibility to establish new policies of détente with the USSR and the People's Republic of China (PRC). The conventional wisdom is that anyone with a soft record against Communism would have been vulnerable to charges of a sellout had he made Nixon's overtures to the Communist superpowers.

Nixon and National Security Adviser Henry Kissinger deviated from their predecessors, particularly from such earlier conservative Republicans as John Foster Dulles, in their more pragmatic, less ideological approach to the Cold War. They were willing to accept explicitly what containment had implied: that the United States and USSR each held dominion over spheres of influence created in the aftermath of World War II. Nixon's acceptance of détente — a policy formulated and implemented by Kissinger — implicitly acknowledged that Communist governments were in place in Eastern Europe and were not likely to go away.

Therefore, in 1969 Nixon redefined U.S. policy. Less willing to automatically commit U.S. resources and military aid than earlier foreign policies based on containment and flexible response, the Nixon Doctrine stated that "the United States will participate in the defense of allies and friends," but cannot and will not assume "primary responsibility" for their defense. At the same time Nixon sought to slow the pace of the nuclear arms race by initiating the Strategic Arms Limitation Talks (SALT) with USSR. The overall effect of the Nixon-Kissinger policy was to seek at least some peaceful accommodations with the Soviet Union and the PRC. The Nixon administration therefore inaugurated cultural exchanges and other forms of dialogue and interaction between the superpowers as it sought to make peaceful coexistence a way of life.

Explicit recognition of the nuclear stalemate led to new policies predicated on Mutually Assured Destruction (MAD) instead of massive retaliation, since both sides had assembled nuclear arsenals capable of destroying their opponents hundreds of times over. Massive retaliation had assumed that a nuclear war was winnable; MAD assumed that nuclear warfare was mutual suicide.

Though Nixon's policies of détente did not officially recognize all of the Communist regimes or their territorial acquisitions since World War II, it clearly eliminated Dulles's 1950s liberation policy and provided a level of de facto recognition of the Soviet occupation of Eastern Europe and its other spheres of influence. Notably, with approval from the United States and USSR, East and West Germany initiated diplomatic contacts in the late 1960s and signed a treaty granting mutual recognition in 1973. The United States acceded to East Germany's admission to the United Nations that year, and officially recognized it in 1974. During the same period West Germany signed nonaggression pacts with the USSR and Poland and improved relations with other Warsaw Pact countries.

The 1975 Helsinki Summit Conference, attended by Nixon's post–Watergate successor Gerald Ford, a Republican, represented the high point of détente. It produced accords signed by the United States, the Soviet Union, and all of the countries of Eastern and Western Europe. These agreements repudiated the use of force and respected the frontiers and territorial integrity of all European states, thereby securing the promise of peace at the cost of providing de facto recognition of the USSR's post–World War II territorial gains, something the Soviet Union had been seeking for 30 years. In repudiating force, the European countries were effectively agreeing not to wage nuclear war upon each other.

In return, the Soviets agreed to greater economic, scientific, technical, and environmental cooperation with the West and, more importantly, to the freer movement of ideas, greater access to broadcast and printed information, and the reunification of families through emigration. They also made some significant concessions to human rights. These agreements later helped make possible Poland's Solidarity movement and the internal political activity that eventually brought down the Communist governments in Eastern Europe.

Détente emphasized the need for striking a balance of power between nuclear-armed superpowers and deemphasized the picture of the Cold War as a moral struggle between forces of good and evil. Consequently, objections to Communist human rights violations sometimes interfered with U.S. attempts to reach an accommodation with the Soviets and forge a new, stabilizing balance of power in the nuclear age. The Nixon administration therefore played down human rights issues, often to the displeasure of more ideologically driven anti–Communists and advocates for Soviet Jews, who were being persecuted in the USSR and denied the right to emigrate. Ultimately, the human rights problems never vanished, and their persistence contributed to the eventual demise of détente.

Détente lasted until the late 1970s, when it broke down because neither side sufficiently desired to genuinely cooperate with the other, give up its basic objectives, or abandon its goal to achieve global dominance. Thus each side continued to pursue its own agenda and try to gain an upper hand, despite the efforts of various diplomatic agreements to limit weaponry, advance human rights, and support cultural and trade exchanges. And each side suspected the other's good faith. For instance, in 1976 the CIA, under the directorship of the future president George Bush, made a controversial and politically motivated determination that the Soviet Union was disregarding the assumptions of MAD and planning instead to prevail in any nuclear war with the West (see chapter 14).

Despite the Nixon Doctrine and other gestures to the USSR, Nixon's foreign policy also retained strong elements of containment. Nixon sustained U.S. opposition to worldwide Communist expansion, as well as U.S. commitment to its own defense and that of its Western European allies. Therefore, he continued to prosecute the Vietnam War for another four years after his election, and he continued to enhance the U.S. nuclear arsenal even while calling for strategic arms limitations talks. Continuing a long-standing U.S. Cold War policy of opposing Communist expansion within the U.S. sphere of influence, Nixon secretly supported a 1973 military coup that overthrew the freely elected, Marxist president of Chile, Salvador Allende. Allende had tried to turn Chile into a socialist state by nationalizing industries, promoting extensive land reform, and establishing closer ties with Communist countries. Allende was replaced by General Pinochet's military dictatorship, which later became notorious for its brutal and widespread human rights violations.

In Western eyes the Soviets' intensified sponsorship of populist insurgencies in underdeveloped nations and of Arab aggression defied the spirit of détente, as did its support of Egypt and Syria's surprise attack on Israel in 1973, which inaugurated the Yom Kippur War. Soviet activity in non–European regions appeared to sustain the USSR's Cold War aim to achieve worldwide Communist domination through popular revolutions. Between 1975 and 1976, for example, the Soviets directly supported pro–Communist insurgents in Angola, supplying weapons and importing 10,000 Cuban troops to ensure their victory. In 1978 Colonel Mengi Haile Mariam seized power in Ethiopia, assisted by $2 billion worth of Soviet arms, 20,000 Cuban troops, 300 tanks, and 3,000 Soviet technicians. And in 1978 the Soviets supported a coup that created a friendly government in South Yemen.

Soviet intervention in the underdeveloped world climaxed with its invasion of Afghanistan in 1979, an act that delivered the final blow to détente. President Carter, a Democrat elected in 1976, responded by restricting trade, withdrawing the SALT II Treaty from congressional consideration, and boycotting the 1980 Olympics in Moscow. Each of these acts pointedly reversed earlier attempts to foster stabilizing cooperation and exchange between the superpowers.

Ironically, the USSR's military adventure into Asia mired the Soviet Union in its own version of the Vietnam experience. Unpopular at home, the Afghanistan war failed in its primary objective to prop up a local puppet regime. Like the Americans, the Soviets withdrew after several years of guerrilla warfare. Like the Vietnam War, the Soviets' war in Afghanistan ultimately disaffected their citizens and weakened the government that had prosecuted it.

In addition to Communist insurgency and intervention in Asia and Africa, rekindled Western outrage at the Soviet record on human rights in the late 1970s and 1980s also significantly undermined détente. In very different ways both Carter and his Republican successor, Ronald Reagan, refocused attention on violations of human rights, recasting the Cold War in moral terms again as it had been depicted in the 1950s.

Détente's most lasting and perhaps most important legacy was the U.S. rapprochement with Communist China. In 1971 the United States dropped its long-standing opposition to China's admission into the United Nations, even though this entailed the simultaneous expulsion of Nationalist China, Chiang Kai-shek's government in exile on Taiwan and a Cold War ally of the United States since the 1940s. After Kissinger secretly met with Chinese leaders that year, Nixon openly visited China in February 1972 and began establishing diplomatic relationships between the two countries. On January 1, 1979, the United States reversed its long-held Cold War position recognizing Nationalist China and recognized instead the PRC and its Communist regime. Moreover, even after Communist leaders brutally suppressed the 1989 Tiananmen Square rebellion calling for democracy and greater personal freedoms, the United States retained China's most favored nation trade status throughout the duration of the Cold War and beyond. The U.S.-Chinese rapprochement of the 1970s not only reversed Mao Zedong's acrimonious posture of the 1960s, it also made China more secure from the growing possibility of a Soviet attack while placing the USSR in a more defensive position by unifying its two greatest foes.

Chapter 6

Winnable Nuclear War, the Evil Empire, and the Collapse of Communism (1980–90)

With the Soviet invasion of Afghanistan in 1979 and the election of Ronald Reagan in 1980, the Cold War atmosphere once again became highly charged. Reagan's anti–Communist credentials dated back to his efforts to rid Hollywood of Communists and Communist sympathizers during the 1940s and 1950s, when he was president of the Screen Actors Guild. As U.S. president he rejected the rapprochement between East and West that generally characterized the late 1960s and 1970s. His hard-line, ideological attacks on Communism rendered the essentially conciliatory tone of détente more acrimonious and bellicose. In fact, however, apart from ordering the Grenada invasion, Reagan never sent U.S. troops directly to fight against Communist forces.

During Reagan's first administration Cold War tensions between the United States and Soviet Union reached their highest levels since the Berlin and Cuban Missile crises of the late 1950s and early 1960s. Reagan initiated a number of policies that become collectively known as the Reagan Doctrine. Harking back to the 1950s policies of liberation advocated by John Foster Dulles, Reagan vowed to oppose Communist regimes and movements worldwide and to insist that any arms reduction agreement include reduction of Soviet conventional troops. U.S. support of rebels in Angola, Afghanistan, and Nicaragua, and U.S. intervention in the Lebanese civil war were direct results of the Reagan Doctrine.

Reagan revived the 1950s rhetoric that cast the Cold War in moral terms. He called the USSR an "Evil Empire" and denounced Communist-supported popular movements in Central America and elsewhere. During his first term Reagan increased defense spending by 40 percent, providing for the MX missile, a 600-ship Navy with new aircraft carriers, new tanks, and other conventional weapons. He replenished ammunition stocks and reinstated the B-1 bomber that Carter had canceled earlier. He also achieved the European deployment of intermediate-range, nuclear-armed Pershing and Cruise missiles, despite intense opposition by antinuclear activists in Great Britain, West Germany, and elsewhere in Western Europe.

Nineteen eighty-three was an especially tense year in the Cold War. In March Reagan initiated the highly controversial Strategic Defense Initiative (SDI), more commonly known as "Star Wars" after a popular science-fiction movie of the time. The SDI program was to provide a shield of laser-armed satellites in outer space capable of shooting down missiles targeted at American cities and defense installations. Reagan viewed SDI as an alternative to the policies of MAD, which had dominated the 1970s détente and which he believed to be highly dangerous, especially since he thought the Soviets were preparing to prevail in a nuclear war. Though SDI ostensibly violated the 1972 Anti-Ballistic Missile (ABM) Treaty, which had been a central element of the arms control process during the preceding decade, Reagan asserted that it was "consistent with our obligations under the ABM Treaty."

Many scientists remained skeptical about SDI's feasibility, though the scientific community enjoyed the additional funding for basic research that accompanied it. Other critics attacked SDI for its enormous cost, which came at the expense of social programs and/or attempts to balance the budget. And, despite Reagan's claims that SDI was to be a purely defensive system that the United States would even be willing to share with the USSR, the Soviets greatly feared its offensive capabilities. They also feared being drawn into another costly arms race that they could not afford. Moreover, the European allies were concerned that a missile shield over the United States would increase American isolationism and leave them vulnerable to a Soviet attack. When he later recognized that protecting every U.S. city was unrealistic, Reagan revised SDI's mission to that of protecting American missile sites against a first strike. The redefined mission thus echoed the second-strike capability the United States developed during the Kennedy administration, guaranteeing that a Soviet first strike could not eliminate massive American retaliation.

Some nuclear planners were also concerned that SDI might prompt the Soviet Union to launch a preemptive nuclear strike before the system could be deployed, since after the deployment the USSR would become vulnerable to an American attack. Soviet fears were exacerbated by talk from ranking Reagan administration officials who began speaking publicly of a winnable nuclear war. In 1981 Reagan approved a secret national security decision document that outlined a plan for prevailing in a protracted nuclear war. The administration adopted the position that enhanced civil defense efforts would enable civilians to survive nuclear attacks. In the words of Deputy Undersecretary of Defense T. K. Jones, "If there are enough shovels to go around, everyone's going to make it," because everyone could build primitive shelters against radioactive fallout.

"Dig a hole, cover it with a couple of doors and then throw three feet of dirt on top." Jones also predicted that the United States would be able to return to prewar economic levels in as little as two to four years if it adopted Soviet civil defense practices.

Other administration officials expressed similar sentiments during the early 1980s, including Vice President George Bush and Reagan himself. Bush and Reagan maintained that since Soviet planning was based not on MAD but on winning a nuclear war, the United States needed a policy "of that kind." Thus, during Reagan's first term public fears of nuclear war rose to levels not experienced since the Berlin and Cuban Missile crises of the late 1950s and early 1960s. The administration's suggestion that nuclear war need not result in mutually assured destruction, its introduction of SDI, Reagan's verbal attacks on the Soviet Union, and his insistence that the Communist leaders were godless monsters who were not to be trusted because they had "less regard for humanity or human beings" further increased Cold War tensions.

These actions also led the Soviets to intensify their intelligence efforts for detecting early signs of an impending Western attack and to increase their own defense budget. Their downing of a Korean passenger plane (KAL-007) that had strayed into their air space on September 1, 1983, may have resulted from their state of heightened alert and fear of an American first strike. Reagan condemned the attack as barbaric and offered it as further proof of Soviet disregard for human life. The incident increased worldwide tensions even more. On September 8 Soviet Foreign Minister Gromyko cautioned, "The world situation is now slipping toward a very dangerous precipice. Problem number one for the world is to avoid nuclear war." Two months later the Soviets feared that a NATO exercise to coordinate nuclear command procedures, Able Archer 83, might actually be preparation for a real strike against the Warsaw Pact. A flurry of coded communications between the United States and Great Britain just prior to the early November war games heightened their apprehensions, though these messages actually concerned the U.S. invasion of Grenada that occurred on October 25. During the exercise the Soviet KGB mistakenly notified its intelligence stations that American military bases had been put on alert. Neither side launched any strikes, however.

After Mikhail Gorbachev became Soviet premier in 1985 and began to introduce economic reforms and new principles of freedom (perestroika and glasnost) tension quickly began to recede. British Prime Minister Margaret Thatcher met Gorbachev shortly before he assumed power and declared, "I like Mr. Gorbachev. We can do business together." Subsequently Reagan also became more conciliatory toward him. In November 1985 Gorbachev and Reagan issued a joint statement declaring that nuclear war could never be won, must never be fought, and that neither side would seek military superiority. They were unable to reach an arms agreement during an October 1986 mini-summit in Reykjavik, Iceland, because Reagan refused to comply with Soviet demands that the United

States abandon SDI. Nonetheless, they surprised the world and their own staffs by reaching several startling agreements in principle: the elimination of all intermediate-range missiles from Europe, the elimination of all ballistic missiles over a ten-year period, and the reduction of other nuclear delivery systems, including bombers and tactical weapons. These agreements became the basis for the Strategic Arms Reduction Talks (START) which replaced the SALT talks and eventually led to the 1991 START Treaty. Moreover, in February 1987 Gorbachev dropped his demand that the United States eliminate SDI, and in December he and Reagan signed the INF Treaty to eliminate all intermediate-range nuclear weapons in Europe. The INF Treaty was the first Cold War treaty to reduce the size of superpower nuclear arsenals, and it removed the Cruise and Pershing missiles that had provoked so much domestic opposition in Western Europe and Britain. In December 1988 Gorbachev further announced his intentions to unilaterally downsize the Soviet Army by 500,000 soldiers and to withdraw Soviet troops and tanks from Eastern Europe. His economic and military reforms opened the door for change not only within the Soviet Union but throughout all Eastern Europe. Reagan met with him four times, signing an arms agreement treaty and applauding Gorbachev's reforms. These same reforms opened the door for change not only within the Soviet Union but throughout all Eastern Europe.

Once opened, the door did not close again. Gorbachev's internal reforms led to agitation throughout Eastern Europe for the same freedoms and opportunities. Similar reforms inside the Soviet Union by Khrushchev had led to uprisings in Poland and Hungary in 1956. But, unlike Khrushchev and Brezhnev, Gorbachev publicly declared that the USSR would not intervene militarily in Eastern Europe. Moreover, he curtailed other Soviet military adventurism, withdrawing Soviet troops from Afghanistan in 1989.

The iron curtain disintegrated soon after Gorbachev removed the specter of the Red Army from the internal politics of Eastern Europe, and the Cold War sped to a remarkable and almost universally unexpected conclusion. On June 5, 1989, the Solidarity trade union won general elections in Poland, and in August its nominee, Tadeusz Mazowiecki, became the first non–Communist prime minister in the Eastern bloc. The following year Solidarity's leader Lech Wałęsa was elected president.

In September 1989 Hungary opened its borders with Austria, affording 60,000 East Germans access to the West. A massive exodus of East Germans was accompanied by widespread protests in the streets. By the end of the year a new liberal cabinet was in place in East Germany led by reformer Hans Modrow. The following year East Germany reunited with West Germany, creating for the first time since World War II a single nation closely allied with the United States and its Western allies and fulfilling one of the major U.S. Cold War goals.

In October 1989 the Hungarian Communist Party dissolved and renounced Marxist-Leninism in favor of a social democracy. In November Bulgaria's

Communist government was also replaced. The Czechoslovakian Communist politburo also resigned that month, and Alexander Dubček, deposed leader of the crushed 1968 reform movement, returned to a hero's welcome. The first non–Communist government in Czechoslovakia was sworn in on December 10.

The collapse of Communism in Eastern Europe was remarkably nonviolent, except in Romania, where Communist President Nicolae Ceauşescu was overthrown by the Army and executed on Christmas Day, 1989. Moreover, the failed 1989 challenge to Communism in China also turned bloody. After initially gaining support of some of the Army, students calling for freedom in prodemocracy marches in Tiananmen Square were crushed by military intervention.

On November 10 the East Germans began to dismantle the Berlin Wall and opened access to West Germany. The most visible symbol of the Cold War was thus reduced to fragments to be cherished as souvenirs or sold for profit in capitalist markets.

The Cold War officially ended in September 1990, after Great Britain, France, the United States, and the USSR signed a peace treaty with East and West Germany. The treaty formally concluded World War II, established the withdrawal of the Soviet Army, and paved the way for German reunification. On November 17–19, 1990, leaders of all the European states, the United States, Canada, and the Soviet Union met in Paris to discuss the post–Cold War era. They signed a new charter regulating relations among all the participants, a nonaggression agreement between members of NATO and the defunct Warsaw Pact, and the Conventional Forces in Europe Treaty (CFE), which reduced the number of troops and tanks opposing each other in Europe. President Bush announced, "We have closed a chapter of history. The Cold War is over."

Chapter 7

The Aftermath
of the Cold War

The end of the Cold War did not bring the peace and stability most people hoped it would. Several traditionally hostile ethnic groups both within and outside the USSR had remained united because of the Soviet military threat. When that threat was removed they soon fractured.

On December 31, 1991, the Union of Soviet Socialist Republics dissolved, prompted by independence movements in the Baltic states that the Soviet Union had forcibly annexed after World War II. Various struggles between ethnic and nationalist groups then broke out within several former Soviet republics. Gorbachev himself fell from power after an unsuccessful coup by Communist reactionaries weakened him. Russian President Boris Yeltsin, who played a major role in defeating the hard-line Communist coup, soon challenged and defeated Gorbachev and tenuously assumed the leadership over the remnants of the USSR.

In 1992 Yugoslavia splintered into five separate republics, Serbia, Croatia, Slovenia, Bosnia-Herzegovina and Macedonia. Shortly thereafter civil war broke out among several of them, featuring World War II–style concentration camps and genocidal ethnic cleansing.

Also in 1992 Czechoslovakia splintered into two separate but not actively hostile republics, Slovakia and the Czech Republic.

With the collapse of Communism, Islamic fundamentalism became a new threat to U.S. interests in the Middle East and Asia. Hostile both to Western imperialism and Communist expansion, Islamic fundamentalism emerged in the 1980s as a strong, self-contained force, independent of the Cold War superpower struggle. Throughout the 1980s it had directly threatened some of the Soviet republics bordering the Middle East and Asia Minor, and it helped galvanize the internal opposition that ultimately defeated the Soviet-backed regime in Afghanistan.

At the same time, Muslim fundamentalism also vilified the West. In January 1979 an opposition movement inspired by Ayatollah Khomeini overthrew the pro–U.S. shah of Iran, whose family had come to power in the 1950s through a U.S.-supported coup. After President Carter agreed to shelter the exiled shah — who had been notorious for extreme human rights abuses — Iranian students invaded the U.S. embassy in Tehran, taking as hostages 66 members of the embassy's delegation, staff, and Marine guard. The Iranian students and government held 56 of them for 444 days.

Iran's hostage-taking seriously weakened the Carter presidency, absorbing much of the president's energies and attention. Moreover, his inability to free the hostages projected an image of American impotence. This image intensified after an aborted U.S. raid not only failed to rescue the hostages but also took American lives when high-tech military helicopters crashed in a desert sandstorm. Ronald Reagan successfully campaigned against Carter in 1980 by promising to reverse what he called the decline in American military power and reclaim America's ability to command worldwide respect. Iran returned the hostages on the day of Reagan's inauguration January 20, 1981.

In the 1991 Gulf War Reagan's Republican successor, George Bush, brought together a U.S.-led coalition of Western and Middle Eastern countries to wage war against another Muslim country, Iraq, after that country had invaded, captured, and occupied oil-rich Kuwait. For the first time since World War II the United States and Soviet Union allied against an aggressor, this time an Islamic nation. The war was an overwhelming military success, quickly achieving its proclaimed objective of liberating Kuwait and temporarily making Bush the most popular U.S. President during the post–World War II era. However, Iraqi President Saddam Hussein's subsequent refusal to cooperate with UN inspections to guarantee the terms of the cease-fire and his ruthless military persecution of Kurds living within Iraq significantly diminished Bush's popularity. In 1992 Democrat Bill Clinton defeated both Bush and independent Ross Perot, becoming the first Cold War Baby Boomer to become president of the United States.

Highlights of the Cold War

Chapter 8

The Bomb

The United States exploded its first atomic bomb in 1945, the Soviet Union in 1949, Great Britain in 1952, France in 1960, and the People's Republic of China in 1964. The United States tested its first hydrogen bomb in 1952, the USSR in 1953, Great Britain in 1957, China in 1967, France in 1968, and India in 1974. By the end of the Cold War Israel was believed to have secretly developed nuclear weapons too.

The Cold War stands apart from any other superpower confrontation in history in that it featured nuclear weapons. Immediately after World War II Truman favored international control of atomic energy, and his administration appointed a special committee to develop a plan. The committee report called for the United Nations to create an international atomic development agency to identify each country's holdings of raw nuclear materials and to control all fissionable material and production plants. The agency would make nuclear resources available for peaceful purposes, but it would report any country's efforts to build atomic weapons. The international community would then presumably act to forestall that possibility. The committee also recommended that the United States should cease manufacturing atomic weapons at some future date and transfer its atomic resources to the international agency in stages. However, the committee stressed that the United States should not share its knowledge about nuclear technology in the immediate future.

To make the plan more appealing to Congress, Truman asked Bernard Baruch to present it to the United Nations. But Baruch insisted on amendments that virtually assured Soviet refusal. Baruch threatened to resign if his changes were not accepted, and Truman acquiesced. The Soviets indeed vetoed the proposal in the Security Council in December 1946. The subsequent intensification of the Cold War made any further top-level efforts for international nuclear control politically impossible.

Terrifying as the bomb is, some analysts believe the presence of nuclear weaponry succeeded in keeping the Cold War largely cold. Nuclear superpowers never faced each other directly on the battlefield, though the Korean War pitted a nuclear superpower, the United States, against a nonnuclear superpower,

41

China. Moreover, many believe NATO's nuclear weapons compensated for the
Warsaw Pact's vast numerical superiority in conventional weapons, especially in
tanks. They argue that the policies of nuclear deterrence and massive retaliation
did, in fact, succeed.

Other analysts challenge the idea that the Warsaw Pact countries would have
invaded West Germany or other NATO countries, even had no nuclear deterrent
existed. They question whether the Western Europeans would have consented
even to a defensive, tactical nuclear strike on their own territory.* And they point
to the willingness of such countries as North Korea, China, North Vietnam,
and Iraq to wage war against the United States in spite of the U.S. nuclear arsenal.

Whether or not it was ever a meaningful deterrent, the bomb certainly contributed a forceful presence to the Cold War scene. For the first time in history
a virtually instantaneous, worldwide apocalypse could occur at any moment, initiated at the whim of any one of several men who could "push the button." We
should remember that all of these men were considered dangerous, unstable,
unprincipled, power-crazed, and/or insane by literally millions of people on
either side of the superpower conflict. In fact, since a completely sane and rational leader would be unlikely to order a retaliatory nuclear strike that could result
in Armageddon — while a somewhat deranged leader might — this perception of
insanity actually enhanced the credibility of nuclear deterrence, since opposing
sides had to anticipate the irrational responses of their enemies as well as the
rational ones.

Thus the bomb not only produced fear of imminent destruction by a crazed
and unpredictable power, it also created a seemingly unresolvable stalemate in
which neither side would ever be able to seize victory because the other side could
invoke its doomsday machine. In the general population the Cold War stalemate created a climate of unresolvable, ongoing stress that has probably had
more impact than we commonly acknowledge.

*The nuclear freeze movement was strongest in Western Europe, the site of the most likely
targets in a limited nuclear exchange. "Ban the Bomb" marches were commonplace. Nigel
Calder's Nuclear Nightmares presents the difference between tactical and strategic nuclear
weapons thus: "A tactical nuclear weapon is one that explodes in Germany."

Chapter 9

McCarthyism and
the Red Scare

The Red Scare produced anti–Communist fanaticism that flourished in the United States roughly between 1947 and 1960. Ironically, the Cold War — waged ostensibly to oppose Communist suppression of civil liberties — brought about one of the most politically repressive moments in the history of U.S. democracy. During the Red Scare American freedoms of expression, political activism, and press were more attacked and more restricted than at any other peacetime moment in American history. Nonetheless, though deplorable abuses occurred, the American political process did in fact ultimately reject the worst aspects of the Red Scare and the courts protected personal, political, and press freedoms to a remarkable extent during the Cold War.

Throughout the late 1940s and early 1950s various figures from the political right wing charged a growing number of American citizens with internal Communist subversion. The accused ranged from government officials and political figures — like Alger Hiss and Secretary of the Army Robert T. Stevens — to teachers, college professors, television and movie writers, actors, and ordinary citizens. Many of the victims were so-called intellectuals who had been drawn to liberal or left-wing causes during the Depression by a desire to enhance opportunities for freedom, justice, and dignified work. Thus a resurgent strain of anti-intellectualism — never long absent in American culture — was also part of the Red Scare. Since many liberal intellectuals and former and current Communist Party members were also Jewish, many historians believe that anti–Semitism also fueled the Red Scare. Red Scare rhetoric frequently attacked and denigrated homosexuals as well.

The fear of Communist espionage and so-called fifth-column actions by American citizens taking orders from Moscow escalated prior to and during the Korean War. In 1948 Whittaker Chambers accused Alger Hiss of spying for the Soviets, and in 1950 the U.S. government convicted Alger Hiss of lying about his alleged Communist affiliations and activities during the 1930s. In many ways the embodiment of Roosevelt-Truman liberalism, Hiss had been an influential figure in their administrations. A top member of the State Department with an Ivy League education, he was part of the U.S. negotiating team at Yalta and the secretary general of the inaugural meeting of the United Nations. Though the charges against him remain disputed, his perjury conviction did much to associate New Deal-Fair Deal liberalism with Communism in the mind-set of the general public. In 1951 the government also tried Julius and Ethel Rosenberg for espionage, claiming the couple had delivered atomic bomb secrets to the USSR. A year earlier the FBI had been responsible for the arrest and conviction in Great Britain of Klaus Fuchs, who had given atomic secrets to the Soviets. The Rosenbergs were convicted after a highly controversial trial and were executed in 1953, despite significant national and international protest. These events apparently supported the right-wing claim that American Communists were successfully pursuing an active and pervasive program of infiltration and subversion. The Hiss conviction also seemingly vindicated members of the House Committee on Un-American Activities (HUAC) and senators Richard Nixon and Joseph McCarthy, who had built their political careers on charges that Communists had infiltrated the Truman administration, particularly within the State Department. The Fuchs and Rosenberg convictions likewise bolstered the right-wing claim that J. Edgar Hoover's FBI was the nation's strongest defense against internal Communist subversion.

The charges in the late 1940s and 1950s of Communist infiltration of the civilian government, military, entertainment industry, universities, and other public and private institutions occasioned legislative- and executive-branch action that increasingly restricted the rights and opportunities for American Communists. In 1947 Truman barred Communists and Communist sympathizers from employment within the U.S. government, and the Taft-Hartley Act required unions to submit sworn affidavits affirming that their leadership was non–Communist. In 1950 the CIO expelled Communist-dominated unions. In the 1949 Foley Square trial the government prosecuted and convicted 11 top leaders of the Communist Party under the 1940 Smith Act on charges that they had advocated the violent overthrow of the U.S. government. Eventually, 93 Communist leaders were found guilty under the Smith Act, though some convictions were overturned in 1957 after the Supreme Court declared parts of the act unconstitutional. In 1954 Congress passed legislation revoking the U.S. citizenship of anyone convicted of conspiracy to overthrow the government by force.

The 1950 McCarran Internal Security Act established concentration camps for Communists in Pennsylvania, Florida, Oklahoma, Arizona, and California, though these were never used. The legislation also required all Communist and Communist-dominated organizations to furnish the federal government with the names of all of their members and contributors. The 1954 Communist Control Act provided strong penalties for those organizations that did not comply with the 1950 Internal Security Act, and it denied to the Communist party the "rights, privileges and immunities" of a legal organization. Though Congress outlawed the Communist Party, party membership was not made illegal. Several states followed with "little Smith acts," which denied Communist Party candidates places on election ballots and required state employees to sign loyalty oaths. Some states had anticipated the federal government. For instance, in 1949 the New York legislature ordered the dismissal of all teachers and other employees of the public school system who were Communists.

The State Department, frequently accused by McCarthy, Nixon, and others on the political right wing of being soft on Communism, banned U.S. citizens from traveling to the USSR and other iron curtain countries in 1952. It also banned from its overseas libraries all materials, including paintings, by "any controversial persons, Communists, fellow-travelers, et cetera." In 1953 McCarthy aides Roy Cohn and David Schine toured the libraries of the State Department's International Information Agency and declared that of the 2 million books on the shelves some 30,000 were by pro–Communist writers. The works of some 40 authors, including Theodore H. White and Dashiell Hammett, were removed from the shelves; some were burned, including White's best-selling *Thunder out of China,* which criticized Chiang Kai-shek and the Nationalist Chinese.

In highly publicized hearings senators and congressmen interrogated numerous witnesses about their Communist affiliations. Those witnesses who cooperated by recanting their past activities and identifying other Communist suspects were labeled friendly and were usually exculpated. In fact, several repenting ex–Communists became national celebrities and "media experts" on the Communist threat, though a relatively small number of so-called informers faced reverse discrimination and possible blacklisting. On the other hand, those witnesses who failed to renounce their earlier behavior or to give names of alleged Communist associates were labeled unfriendly. Some of these, such as the film writers known as the Hollywood Ten, were imprisoned for contempt of Congress because they refused to answer committee members' questions. Other unfriendly witnesses were stigmatized as Communist subversives, even though they had been neither formally charged with nor convicted of any illegal activity. Some individuals were blacklisted simply for protesting HUAC—an action that the political right interpreted as an attempt to disrupt the good work of the beleaguered officials trying to save the nation from Communism. As a result of the HUAC hearings into the entertainment industry in 1947, 1951–52, 1953–55, and 1957–58, hundreds of writers, actors, and directors were blacklisted.

But members of the entertainment industry were not the only ones to suffer from congressional and senatorial hearings, since the HUAC hearings and McCarthy's Government Operations Committee investigated real and/or imagined Communist threats across a broad range of public institutions. Witnesses who were unable or unwilling to clear themselves of accusations of Communist sympathies became social pariahs; some even committed suicide because of their ostracism. Many lost their jobs and were unable to obtain work within their professions for considerable periods of time, especially educators and workers in the film industry. Some went at least temporarily into voluntary exile in order to practice their professions, including screen writers Dalton Trumbo, John Lawson, and Carl Foreman, novelist Richard Wright, and performers Paul Draper and Larry Adler. Playwright Bertolt Brecht fled to East Germany almost immediately after testifying before HUAC; novelists Thomas Mann and Stephen Heym were other foreign-born writers who left the United States for fear of Cold War persecution. Historian M. I. Finley, who lost his job at Rutgers University because he had pleaded the Fifth Amendment before a government committee, moved to England, where he eventually was knighted for his work at Cambridge University. Margaret Schlauch, a distinguished linguist and literary scholar, was another prominent academic who exiled from the United States after receiving a subpoena from HUAC. An even more prominent intellectual who fell victim to charges of past Communist affiliation was J. Robert Oppenheimer, the head of the Atomic Energy Commission, who had directed the Manhattan Project that developed the atomic bomb during World War II. Like his Russian counterpart, Andrei Sakharov — the father of the Soviet atomic bomb and a human rights activist — Oppenheimer was removed from his prestigious post as a consequence of political and ideological accusations.

The Red Scare charges of Communist infiltration and subversion, though rarely substantiated, sustained a widely held public belief that treacherous subversives were routinely betraying America to the Soviets. The Red Scare reached its zenith in 1954 when McCarthy accused Secretary of the Army Stevens of concealing Communist espionage. Over the previous four years McCarthy had repeatedly attacked the State Department for harboring Communists and Communist sympathizers. But President Eisenhower had been a World War II army hero, and the U.S. military represented the most direct and powerful defense against Soviet aggression. Consequently, McCarthy's accusation was a declaration by the right wing that the national leadership entrusted with the country's defense had fallen under Communist influence. McCarthy's accusations were never sustained, but in response the Army charged that McCarthy had tried to blackmail it into commissioning David Schine, who had been drafted recently. Allegedly McCarthy had threatened to open hearings investigating Communist infiltration of the Army if Schine was not commissioned. McCarthy had, in fact, already held similar hearings in October 1953. The widely televised 1954 Army-McCarthy hearings represented a contest for power, authority, and public credibility between McCarthy's extreme right wing and Eisenhower's conservative but more centrist constituency. The showdown between the Army and McCarthy ultimately discredited McCarthy, and the Senate voted to censure him shortly thereafter for his behavior during those hearings and his mismanagement of campaign funds. Thereafter, McCarthy never commanded the same power to dominate and intimidate.

After McCarthy's censure the Red Scare diminished, though it persisted as a significant force in American political and professional life at least through the election of Democrat John Kennedy in 1960. Kennedy's so-called Camelot sought to reverse the anti-intellectualism of the Red Scare era by elevating scientists, intellectuals and other highly educated and scientifically oriented experts to positions of new authority. It also showcased the high culture of fine arts, classical music, and serious literature. However, even in the comparatively liberal 1960s and 1970s, charges of Communist sympathy were used to discredit liberals, intellectuals, antiwar advocates, feminists, civil rights advocates, and other citizens who were left of center on the political spectrum.

The Red Scare charges of widespread Communist subversion have not held up well from a historical perspective, and even the Rosenberg's complicity in atomic spying has been overstated. No evidence of Alger Hiss's alleged but never fully proven spying has as yet appeared in the Soviet files made available after the disintegration of the USSR. And during the entire Cold War no American Communist Party members were caught spying or practicing sabotage, despite their frequent depiction as Soviet agents in popular films, television, and radio shows. In spite of his accusations of widespread government infiltration, McCarthy himself never produced a single bona fide Communist on his own. And while Red Scare rhetoric employed images of burgeoning domestic Communist activity and sympathy, membership in the Communist Party in fact dramatically decreased. Indeed, by 1956 party membership had dropped from approximately 80,000 immediately after World War II to about 5,000 and so many of those were FBI agents that Director J. Edgar Hoover considered taking control of the party in 1957.

On the one hand, these facts suggest that the internal threat from Communism was never as serious as the right wing claimed, and so the Red Scare was largely an excuse for the right to launch a vicious witch hunt against the liberal proponents of the New Deal and other political enemies. On the other hand, the right wing could respond that the decline in Communist membership and the party's inability to conduct acts of sabotage simply demonstrate the success of efforts by Hoover, Nixon, McCarthy, HUAC, and other forceful anti–Communists. From this point of view the damage from the Red Scare to a relatively small number of innocents (compared to the country's population) was simply the price the nation had to pay for winning the internal battle against Communism.

Whether or not the internal threat from Communism was as significant as the right portrayed it, Red Scare–induced anxiety about subversion enabled Hoover to turn the FBI into an agency dedicated to the surveillance of suspected domestic Communists and to disrupting the work of Communist groups and operatives. The Freedom of Information Act, which Congress passed in response to the 1972 Watergate scandal, has revealed that in the process of performing their anti–Communist work the FBI and other government agencies accumulated files on literally thousands of American citizens during the Red Scare and afterward. In many instances the line blurred between a citizen's promotion of alleged Communist sympathies and his or her exercise of basic constitutional freedoms. After all, McCarthy's standard for determining when an individual was a Communist sympathizer represented only one extreme view among the many possible interpretations of a person's beliefs and behaviors. But Hoover and the FBI largely shared McCarthy's perspective, and other government police agencies employed similar standards (see chapter 14).

On the other hand, although the U.S. government did commit an alarming number of civil rights violations during the Cold War — creating a chilling effect on free speech and political activism, especially from the late 1940s through the mid–1950s — nonetheless, political protest and demonstration survived. The protest against the Vietnam War in the late 1960s, for example, compelled President Johnson to decide not to run for a second term and arguably hastened the end of that war. By contrast, in the Soviet Union mass protests were not permitted against the unpopular war in Afghanistan, a war that Soviet government officials also misrepresented to the citizenry by representing the progress in an artificially optimistic fashion.

Chapter 10

The Korean War

Japan had occupied Korea since 1905. At the Cairo Conference during World War II the United States, Great Britain, and China promised Korean independence, and in 1946 Korea was provisionally divided at the thirty-eighth parallel into two zones: U.S.-controlled South Korea and Soviet-controlled North Korea. In 1948, after the Soviet Union thwarted all UN efforts to hold elections and reunite the country under one government, two separate republics were declared. Dr. Syngman Rhee headed the pro–West South Korean government, and Kim Il Sung ruled the Communist, pro–Soviet Democratic People's Republic of Korea (North Korea). However, Sung vowed to unite the two Koreas as a single nation. Shortly thereafter, despite Rhee's earlier request for U.S. troops to remain, the United States and USSR withdrew their occupying armies.

However on June 25, 1950, North Korea launched a surprise attack against South Korea and initiated the Korean War. They captured Seoul, South Korea's capital, on June 28. On September 16 UN forces under the command of U.S. general Douglas MacArthur made a surprise landing at Inchon and on September 25 recaptured Seoul. The UN troops then pushed forward into North Korea, capturing the capital city, Pyongyang, on October 26 and driving the North Korean Army back to the Chinese border at the Yalu River. Despite U.S. government assessments that the Peoples's Republic of China (PRC) would remain out of the war and President Truman's warnings that the United States would use atomic weapons if necessary, Chinese troops crossed into Korea on November 24, driving the UN armies from the Manchurian border area. On December 24 the Chinese crossed the thirty-eighth parallel into South Korea and recaptured Seoul on January 5, 1951. At that time Truman stated that the United States would not bomb China unless Congress declared war and the United Nations authorized it. UN forces recaptured Seoul on March 14 and recrossed into North Korea on March 26. On April 11 Truman dismissed MacArthur for insubordination after the general publicly advocated extending the war to China. Matthew Ridgway replaced MacArthur. On June 13 Ridgway's troops recaptured Pyongyang, and ten days later the Soviets unexpectedly called for a cease-fire. Thereafter, both sides continued to push each other back and forth across the thirty-eighth parallel for the next two years as intermittent peace talks failed to yield results. Shortly after assuming office in 1953 President Eisenhower kept his campaign pledge to "go to Korea." He also pressured the Communist Chinese by removing the Seventh Fleet from the Formosa Straits, thereby eliminating the buffer that prevented an attack on the mainland by Chiang Kai-shek's Nationalists. He strengthened U.S. air power in Korea and announced that the United States was sending nuclear weapons to Okinawa, where they would be accessible for use in Korea. At the same time Eisenhower pressured Rhee to soften his stance and relinquish his demand that fighting resume if Korea was not unified within 90 days. On July 27, 1953, the warring parties signed an armistice that concluded the fighting but did not create a political solution.

Eisenhower's threat to employ atomic weapons to end the war has been credited for inducing North Korea to agree to the truce; however, documents released after the dissolution of the Soviet Union suggest that the armistice only became possible when Stalin's death a month earlier gave Communist negotiators the necessary authority to end the fighting. The Korean War left over 2 million people dead, including 33,629 American soldiers. After 3 years of fighting the thirty-eighth parallel still remained the demarcation line between the Koreas.

Throughout the Cold War fighting threatened to erupt again in Korea. Recently released U.S. government documents reveal that Eisenhower had been prepared in 1954 to use limited atomic bombings to stop a full-scale Chinese invasion if the PRC violated the truce and launched a massive ground offensive. The United States was also prepared to blockade China, seize offshore islands, and allow Chinese Nationalist troops to raid the mainland. In January 1968 North Korean raiders attacked Seoul and tried to kill South Korean President Park. Two days later North Korea seized the SS *Pueblo*, a U.S. spy ship that had entered its waters. Some believe North Korea timed the incident in order to siphon off U.S. military resources from Southeast Asia a week prior to North Vietnam's Tet Offensive. However, President Johnson called up 14,000 Navy and Air Force reserves instead. The United States increased its military assistance to Korea, and in March 1969 American and North Korean soldiers fired at each other across the demilitarized zone (DMZ). In October 1978 the UN military command discovered a tunnel leading from North Korea, beneath the DMZ, and 270 miles into South Korea. It was large enough to permit some 30,000 troops an hour to cross the border. North Korea denied knowledge of the tunnel, which it labeled a fabrication of American imperialists. To date, no formal peace treaty has ever been signed by the two Koreas.

Chapter 11

The Second
Berlin Crisis

The second Berlin crisis (1958–61) followed a year after the Soviet Union's launching of Sputnik and its successful testing of intercontinental ballistic missiles (ICBM's). It thus occurred while the Soviets were inaccurately believed to have missile superiority over the United States. The crisis began with Khrushchev's bellicose demand in November 1958 that the West surrender its claim to West Berlin and evacuate the city within six months. The West refused. Khrushchev later extended his deadline to permit negotiations but remained firm in his demands. After the first negotiations failed, Khrushchev visited the United States in 1959 and met personally with Eisenhower to try to settle the explosive situation. The Soviet premier's visit eased the Cold War tension temporarily, but in spring 1960 the revelation that an American U-2 spy plane had been shot down over Soviet airspace led Khrushchev to scuttle a Paris summit conference on Berlin. Tensions escalated again quickly as the United States first denied spying and then defended the practice.

In June 1961 Khrushchev met with the newly elected President Kennedy in Vienna and threatened that the allies must evacuate Berlin within six months or risk nuclear war. In response, each side employed military moves to intimidate the other.

Khrushchev's threats created a panic in East Berlin where thousands of people fled across the city to the West. In early August more than 2,000 people left in a single day. Fearful that this emigration would topple the East German regime, Khrushchev literally made Churchill's Iron Curtain metaphor concrete by ordering the Berlin Wall to be erected. The wall quickly became the Cold War's most forceful symbol.

In response to Khrushchev's ultimatum the United States increased its military presence in Europe, requested an increase in defense funding, and stressed a civil defense program. The Soviets, in turn, stepped up their rhetoric, increased their military budget, suspended plans to reduce their armed forces, issued new ultimatums, and broke a U.S.-USSR moratorium on nuclear testing about a month after putting up the wall, exploding the largest nuclear weapon ever made to that date (about 60 megatons).

The Berlin crisis peaked in October when U.S. and Soviet tanks faced each other across Checkpoint Charlie, a crossing point at the Berlin Wall. However, on October 17 Khrushchev announced that "the Western powers were showing some understanding of the situation and were inclined to seek a solution to the German problem and West Berlin." Then the crisis gradually defused as Khrushchev eased off on the deadline for the Western evacuation without actually renouncing his demands.

Chapter 12

The Cuban
Missile Crisis

The Berlin crisis fell into a tense stalemate as the superpowers failed to reach any permanent agreement. Almost exactly a year later they confronted each other again after Khrushchev placed medium and intermediate-range nuclear missiles in Cuba, about 90 miles from Key West and 150 miles from the U.S. mainland.

Khrushchev wanted to compensate for the humiliation of backing down in Berlin and placate hard-line domestic opposition inside the USSR. Moreover, he deeply resented the presence of U.S. nuclear missiles near the Soviet border in Turkey. Finally, a Soviet nuclear presence in Cuba would greatly increase its response time to prepare against a nuclear attack. From the Soviet point of view, the increased response time would lessen the likelihood of a secret, preemptive American attack on their mainland, something that vocal anti–Communists in the United States had been advocating throughout the Cold War. A nuclear arsenal in Cuba would compel the United States to strike there first, thereby giving the Soviets time to initiate their own countermeasures.

But the permanent placement of nuclear missiles in Cuba would have significantly altered the balance of power by creating a hostile nuclear presence within the American sphere of influence and placing U.S. cities under a new threat of a short-warning attack. The Kennedy administration was unwilling to accept these changes to the status quo.

The crisis itself began in mid–October 1962, when American U-2 spy planes photographed Soviet missile bases under construction in Cuba. Earlier, Khrushchev had secretly told Kennedy that he was arming Castro with short-range, surface-to-air missiles for defensive purposes. In fact, he sent 42 medium-range nuclear missiles and had ordered the delivery of an additional 24 long-range missiles, though these never arrived. He also sent over 45,000 Soviet troops and technicians and 24 surface-to-air missiles, though the extent of the Soviet ground force was unknown to Kennedy. It was clear to U.S. officials reviewing the U-2 photos that by December at least 50 strategic nuclear missiles would be operational and strongly defended.

The Soviets insisted they were supplying the island with defensive missiles, but Kennedy rejected the claim and demanded the missiles be removed. On October 22, after reviewing options to bomb or invade Cuba, Kennedy settled on an air and sea blockade to prevent further Soviet arms shipments from reaching Cuba. Documents released in 1994 show that congressional leaders were pressuring him to attack, but he rejected an air strike because the air force could not guarantee 100 percent success, and he rejected an invasion because a full invasion force had not yet been assembled. Moreover, the blockade would be less provocative for the Soviet Union. Nonetheless, Kennedy announced that any missile launched from Cuba would warrant a full-scale U.S. retaliation against the USSR, and he demanded the removal of those missiles already in place. By October 23 four of the medium-range nuclear-armed missiles were already operational.

The crisis climaxed on October 24 when missile-carrying Soviet cargo ships reached the blockade line and were stopped. The next day Kennedy cabled Khrushchev requesting the removal of the missiles already in place. Khrushchev consented, providing that the United States pledged not to invade Cuba. It was also understood that Kennedy would remove medium-range Jupiter missiles from Turkey, though Kennedy insisted that this agreement be private and omitted from the formal resolution of the Cuban Missile Crisis. Kennedy accepted Khrushchev's bargain, and the crisis ended on October 28 when the Soviets formally agreed to remove the missiles from Cuba. The United States later removed its missiles from Turkey, claiming they were obsolete.

At no point did the world ever come closer to experiencing full-scale nuclear warfare than during the four-day period between October 24 and October 28. As Secretary of State Dean Rusk stated upon learning that the Soviets were acquiescing, "We are eyeball to eyeball, and the other fellow just blinked." Khrushchev was essentially compelled to back down because of U.S. nuclear superiority. During the crisis all American missile crews were placed on maximum alert, and commands were in a state of "DefCon-2": the state of greatest combat readiness next to war itself. Some 1,500 American bombers were armed with nuclear bombs, and over 150 land-based missiles had nuclear warheads aimed at the Soviet Union. A 1989 conference in Moscow of participants in the crisis revealed that, contrary to CIA estimates of a much less potent Soviet force, 20 of the medium-range missiles in Cuba were armed with nuclear warheads and targeted for U.S. cities as far north as Washington, D.C. Moreover, the Soviet troops in Cuba were equipped with short-range, nuclear-armed artillery rockets that field commanders were authorized to use in the event of an American invasion. Robert Kennedy estimated that as many as 60 million Americans and at least as many Soviets might die in an all-out nuclear war, while Khrushchev warned his own military leaders about the possibility of 500 million human deaths.

According to recent scholarship by Richard Rhodes, Air Force Chief of Staff

General Curtis LeMay advised President Kennedy to order military action in Cuba that would provoke a Soviet response and thereby justify a preemptive nuclear attack against the Soviet Union. The goal of that strike would have been to destroy the Soviet Union's Communist system in a single blow, while the Soviet nuclear arsenal was still inferior to that of the United States. Rhodes maintains that after Kennedy rejected LeMay's proposal, LeMay and General Thomas Power, LeMay's protégé who had replaced him as commander of the Strategic Air Command (SAC), tried to provoke a military confrontation with the Soviets. While the missile crisis was ongoing, SAC carried out a previously scheduled test firing of an unarmed Atlas missile across the Pacific from California to a target in the Marshall Islands; in an unauthorized, uncoded broadcast that the Soviets doubtlessly monitored, Thomas ordered all SAC wings to "review your plans for further action," and during the height of the crisis SAC bombers deliberately flew beyond their normal fail-safe points toward the Soviet Union before turning back to their bases.

In addition to these provocations, accidents also threatened to initiate nuclear war during the crisis. Rhodes reports that at Malmstrom Air Force Base in Montana the first squadron of Minuteman I solid-fuel missiles was undergoing testing and certification prior to being deployed. As the crisis intensified, Air Force personnel working nonstop to prepare the missiles for launch had to work around equipment shortages, miswiring, wire shorts, and other problems. These difficulties required circumventing the normal safeguards against accidental or unauthorized launches. According to Scott Sagan in *The Limits of Safety,* one officer who controlled the Minutemen told him, "We didn't literally 'hot wire' the launch command system — that would be the wrong analogy — but we did have a second key.... I could have launched it on my own, if I had wanted to." An Air Force safety report after the crisis noted that "possible malfunctions of automated equipment ... posed serious hazards [including] accidental launch." Sagan also reports how an intruding bear triggered the alarm system at Volk Field in Wisconsin, causing nuclear-armed F-106 jets to scramble. Moreover, a U-2 reconnaissance plane accidentally strayed over Siberian air space, leading Khrushchev to inform Kennedy that "an intruding American plane could easily be taken for a nuclear bomber, which might push us to a fateful step." The U.S. Navy pursued Soviet submarines aggressively throughout the world and forced some to surface, despite being ordered to do so only within the quarantine area around Cuba. And on October 28 a U.S. radar tracked an ostensible missile launch from Cuba. After its predicted landing in the Tampa Bay area failed to occur, officials realized that their radar had been using a computer test tape.

The ultimate impact of the Cuban Missile Crisis was that both superpowers pulled back from nuclear brinkmanship. They accepted the stalemate in Berlin and generally sought to avoid direct military confrontations. During the Missile Crisis, one Soviet message had taken several hours to be delivered. To avoid such dangerous delays the United States and Soviet Union installed a telephone hot line directly between the White House and the Kremlin so the leaders could confer directly and expediently during future crises. As a result of the sobering implications of the Cuban Missile Crisis, the Cold War confrontations increasingly moved away from Europe, turning instead to underdeveloped countries in Southeast Asia, the Pacific, Africa, the Middle East, and Central America.

Chapter 13

The Vietnam War
and Protest

The Vietnam War must be viewed within its Cold War context. It began in the early 1960s as a classic American Cold War effort to halt Communist expansion in underdeveloped regions by supporting a local regime to oppose the Communists. By the time it ended in 1973, however, it transformed both the Cold War and the United States itself by forcing Americans to examine the assumptions behind the war and the far-reaching consequences it carried.

Prior to World War II France controlled the region of Southeast Asia called Indochina, which included Vietnam, Laos, and Cambodia. Japan conquered it during the war. Afterward the Vietminh — Vietnamese nationalists who had fought against the Japanese — demanded Vietnamese independence. But France insisted on maintaining its colonial dominance. The United States rejected appeals for aid by the Vietminh since it did not wish to undermine its ally or support a movement with Communist sympathies. Led by Ho Chi Minh, a Communist, the Vietminh took up arms to drive out the French. In 1950 France recognized a friendly, non–Communist government led by Bao Dai and located in Saigon in the south. Under the agreement Vietnam was to become an "associated state" within the French union, but France would retain control of the country's defense and finances. However, Ho Chi Minh, who was based in Hanoi in the north, declared the Democratic Republic of Vietnam (North Vietnam) and insisted that the Communist regime was the sole legitimate Vietnamese government. This dispute over which government properly represented the people of Vietnam remained at the core of the Vietnam conflict until its resolution in 1975.

In 1953, the year the Korean War ended, Secretary of State Dulles had warned of a domino effect, declaring that if Vietnam fell to the Communists the rest of Southeast Asia might soon follow. However, the French fortunes continued to fail as the Communists occupied more territory in both the north and south. During the decisive two-month battle of Dien Bien Phu in spring 1954, France appealed to the United States for assistance. Several plans were proposed, including air support for the French and atomic strikes against the Vietminh. But Army Chief of Staff Matthew Ridgway, who had commanded the UN forces in Korea, argued against intervention, claiming that "Indochina is devoid of decisive military objectives" and that intervention would "be a serious diversion of limited U.S. capabilities." He further maintained that air strikes alone would be insufficient and even atomic warfare would still require the commitment of at least 7 combat divisions, 12 if the Chinese intervened as they had in Korea. Eisenhower insisted on prior congressional approval and that of the allies. But Britain's foreign secretary Anthony Eden rejected a proposal for a joint British-American force, claiming that military support would only complicate and prolong a messy, hopeless political situation. Eisenhower then declined to provide significant assistance to the French, who lost the battle on May 7. Geneva peace talks held immediately afterward ended hostilities and set the terms for the French withdrawal from the region. The peace agreement called for Vietnam to be divided at the seventeenth parallel for two years, at which time nationwide elections were to settle the unification question in a democratic fashion. In the interim the Vietminh agreed to remove its forces from the south: something the French Army had been unable to achieve.

A participant in the Geneva talks, the United States refused to accept the agreements but agreed not to disturb them either. However Eisenhower declared that the United States would view any new Vietminh aggression in the south with concern. Bao Dai also refused to abide by the Geneva agreements as also did his successor in 1955, Ngo Dinh Diem. Consequently, neither the United States nor the Saigon government felt bound to honor the call for the 1956 elections, which never took place since U.S. and South Vietnamese officials feared a large victory for Ho Chi Minh. Instead, on October 26, 1955, Diem proclaimed a separate Republic of Vietnam (South Vietnam) with himself as president. The United States and its Western European supporters recognized Diem's government, but North Vietnam, the Soviet Union, China, and the other Communist countries continued to insist that Ho Chi Minh's government was the sole legitimate Vietnamese government, though initially China's foreign minister Zhou En-lai indicated willingness to accept a permanently partitioned Vietnam, and in 1957 the Soviet Union suggested that North and South Vietnam be admitted to the United Nations as separate states.

America's direct involvement began with the introduction of military advisers in 1955. That year North Vietnam began receiving military aid from China and the Soviet Union. In 1957 it renewed insurgent activity in the south and by 1959 it was sending cadres and weapons into South Vietnam to organize military opposition. It imposed universal military conscription in 1960, when it also formed the southern-based National Liberation Front (NLF) that the South Vietnamese derisively called the Vietcong. In the interim Diem had difficulty maintaining the support of the military and the people, especially the Buddhist majority. He squelched a coup in 1960 and brutally suppressed massive Buddhist demonstrations in 1963. A coup overthrew and murdered Diem in November 1963, three weeks before President Kennedy was assassinated.

The following decade saw considerable infighting within the South Vietnamese leadership, including a succession of military governments led by such figures as General Nguyen Khanh (1964–65), Vice Air Marshal Nguyen Cao Ky (1965–67), General Nguyen Van Thieu (1967–April 28, 1975) and General Duong Van Minh (April 28–30, 1975), who surrendered Saigon to North Vietnam's Colonel Bui Tin. Bitter internal protest against the South Vietnamese government continued throughout the war, especially among South Vietnam's Buddhist majority, whose interests were not especially served by these mostly Catholic and frequently brutal military regimes.

America initially committed military advisers and military aid to Diem to fill the vacuum in the fight against Communism created by France's exit from the region. The Vietcong continued guerrilla efforts to seize control of the south and overthrow Diem's government, and they were later supported by regular Army troops from North Vietnam. Early U.S. involvement remained at a fairly low level. However, the number of advisers leapt from 700 to 12,000 during the first 18 months of Kennedy's presidency. In 1964, in response to one authentic and one dubious attack by North Vietnamese gunboats on a U.S. destroyer in the Tonkin Gulf, Congress voted nearly unanimously to authorize President Johnson to commit U.S. forces to defend any nation in Southeast Asia against Communist aggression or subversion. The Tonkin Gulf Resolution served as Presidents Johnson and Nixon's congressional authorization to conduct the war, even though Congress repealed the resolution in 1970.

Johnson did not use his authority to strike against North Vietnam until after the 1964 presidential election when, running on a peace platform, he defeated his more hawkish Republican rival, Barry Goldwater. However, on February 7, 1965, the Vietcong attacked a U.S. transport and observation installation, killing 8 and wounding over 100 American advisers. Within hours of receiving the news Johnson authorized Operation Flaming Dart: U.S. air raids against a North Vietnamese Army camp 60 miles north of the demilitarized zone (DMZ) separating North and South Vietnam.

In March 1965 Johnson sent in two marine battalions to defend Da Nang airfield. These were the first U.S. combat troops in Vietnam. Aside from the Cambodian incursion in 1970 and the infiltration into North Vietnam and Cambodia by clandestine commando units on raids, U.S. ground troops operated solely within South Vietnam and generally respected the DMZ. However, it bombed North Vietnam from 1965 to 1968 and in 1972. Calls to expand the war to the north and to use nuclear weapons were balanced by fears that China would then enter the war and replay Korea. Growing protests by its allies also inhibited U.S. action.

In the summer of 1965 General Westmoreland requested and received 44 additional combat battalions; in October U.S. forces defeated North Vietnamese forces in the Ia Drang Valley in their first conventional confrontation of the war. By December there were 200,000 U.S. troops in South Vietnam. Johnson suspended the bombings of North Vietnam at Christmas but resumed at the end of January after failing to induce the Communists to negotiate. During 1966 America stepped up its effort, bombing oil depots near Hanoi and Haiphong Harbor and increasing the number of troops to 400,000. By the end of 1967 there were 500,000 U.S. troops serving in Vietnam and domestic opposition to the war became significant, despite government assurances that victory was close at hand.

On January 31, 1968, the Communists began their Tet Offensive in which they overran many South Vietnamese–held cities and towns and brought the war to Saigon itself, where there was intense street fighting. Commandos attacked the U.S. embassy, which was secured only after over six hours of fighting. Westmoreland's own headquarters were also attacked near Saigon Airport. Even though the Tet Offensive ultimately failed militarily for the Communists, it was probably the single most forceful event to turn U.S. public opinion against the war, as it demonstrated that the promised light at the end of the tunnel was illusory.

American troop strength peaked at 540,000 at the end of 1968. After an increasing number of his advisers expressed pessimism over prospects for an outright victory, Johnson initiated peace talks on March 31, when he also announced he would not seek reelection. He restricted bombing in North Vietnam and later imposed a full moratorium. The peace talks began in mid–May; however, North Vietnam was unwilling to settle for less than full national unification.

President Nixon, who defeated Johnson's vice president Hubert Humphrey in 1968, had campaigned on a peace platform. Both he and National Security Adviser Henry Kissinger concluded that the United States and South Vietnam could not win a limited war and that expanding the war raised too many domestic and international risks. Both also insisted that the United States must avoid the appearance of a humiliating defeat in which it would lose credibility and influence throughout the world. Thus they adopted "peace with honor" as their slogan. In August 1969 Kissinger first met secretly with a North Vietnamese negotiator, and in February 1970 he began secret talks in Paris with Le Duc Tho. However, fundamental differences in how they viewed the war kept the two sides apart. For Kissinger the Vietnam War was a conflict between two sovereign nations, while for the North Vietnamese and the NLF it was a civil war directed at reunifying the nation. According to his aide, Roger Morris, Kissinger was never able to understand North Vietnam's position. This basic difference over the very nature of the war seriously inhibited the peace negotiations. The Communists remained firm in their commitment to ultimate reunification, rejecting an early Kissinger two track proposal for a military settlement between the United States and North Vietnam and a political settlement between South Vietnam and the NLF. Thus the peace negotiations failed to show results until the very end of Nixon's first term.

As the peace talks stalled, Nixon adopted Kissinger's plan for the Viet-namization of the war in which South Vietnam assumed increasingly greater responsibility for conducting the war and U.S. troops were gradually withdrawn. Nixon reduced the number of troops to 280,000 by the end of 1970 and 140,000 by the end of 1971, when the United States announced its intention of incre-mentally turning the war over to the South Vietnamese Army. But while the number of U.S. soldiers in Vietnam diminished during Nixon's first term, Amer-ica intensified the war in other ways. In 1969 Nixon authorized secret bombing raids in Cambodia, despite official U.S. recognition of that country's sovereignty. And in 1970 he authorized a joint invasion of Cambodia by U.S. and South Viet-namese troops. Their mission was to attack Communist sanctuaries and disrupt the flow of soldiers and supplies from North Vietnam into South Vietnam through the Ho Chi Minh Trail, which passed through Cambodia. The war expanded again in 1971 when, after Congress voted to forbid sending U.S. troops into Laos or Cambodia, the United States sponsored unsuccessful South Viet-namese incursions into Laos. In 1970 Nixon permitted limited bombing of tar-gets in the north in protective reaction strikes that were made ostensibly to pro-tect reconnaissance flights. However, he did not authorize renewed massive bombings of North Vietnam until spring 1972, following a major North Vietna-mese offensive. The policy objective was to enable the United States to disen-gage from the conflict while still preserving the anti–Communist regime South Vietnam of President Nguyen Van Thieu. Kissinger maintained that U.S. cred-ibility with other countries precluded a rapid withdrawal that might undermine Thieu.

By 1972 the war had emerged as a major campaign issue and Kissinger increased his efforts to settle it. Nixon renewed the air war in the north and ordered the mining of Haiphong Harbor after North Vietnam launched a major attack across the DMZ. These efforts prevented the collapse of the South Viet-namese Army in the northern region of South Vietnam but did not succeed in forcing the North Vietnamese to make major concessions at the bargaining table. However, in October — a month before the U.S. election — Kissinger announced a major breakthrough and declared that "We believe that peace is at hand." But South Vietnam's President Thieu refused to accept the new terms and demanded 69 amendments to the agreements. After new talks between Kissinger and North Vietnamese representative Le Duc Tho broke down in December, Nixon ordered massive Christmas bombings of Hanoi and Haiphong. Nixon told the joint chiefs of staff that he was lifting the restrictions on target selections to permit the bombing of railroads, power plants, radio transmitters, and other installa-tions surrounding Hanoi, as well as docks and shipyards in Haiphong. He added, "I don't want any more of this crap about the fact that we couldn't hit this tar-get or that one. This is your chance to use military power to win this war, and if you don't, I'll hold you responsible." After 11 days of bombings the North Viet-namese returned to the bargaining table and consented to an agreement similar to the October accord. Nixon then warned Thieu, "You must decide now whether you desire to continue our alliance or whether you want me to seek a settlement with the enemy which serves U.S. interests alone." Kissinger and Le Duc Tho concluded a formal ceasefire agreement in Paris on January 8, 1973. The last U.S. troops left on March 29, 1973.

Unlike the 1954 Geneva Accords, the 1973 agreement allowed North Vietnamese troops to remain in those areas in the south where they held control. Within a year after the U.S. withdrawal hostilities resumed between North and South Vietnam. The United States continued to furnish military aid, but the amount was significantly restricted by a Congress eager to "put Vietnam behind us." Saigon fell to North Vietnamese forces on April 30, 1975.

On Veteran's Day 1982, the Vietnam War Memorial opened, commemorating the more than 50,000 U.S. soldiers and support personnel who died in the Vietnam War between 1961 and 1973. Over 3 million Americans served in Vietnam; 46,370 were killed in action and some 10,000 more died of other causes. Over 153,000 Americans were hospitalized, 1,300 soldiers were reported missing in action (MIA), and the total cost exceeded $140 billion. South Vietnam lost 400,000 soldiers killed in the war; North Vietnam lost 900,000. More than 4 million Vietnamese civilians and soldiers on both sides — about 10 percent of the total population — were killed or wounded during the U.S. era of Vietnam's war for national unification.

The size and intensity of the domestic protest against the Vietnam War significantly changed the U.S. experience of the Cold War. Throughout the late 1940s, 1950s, and early 1960s middle America had been largely unified in its support of its government's basic policy to oppose Communist expansion anywhere on the globe, a policy that reflected one of the lessons of World War II: never to allow another Munich, where British and French leaders appeased Hitler and failed to stop him when they had the chance. Moreover, despite right-wing charges of Communist infiltration of the government, most middle Americans trusted the government to act rationally and in good faith to steer the country in safe and positive directions.

However, by the late 1960s widespread antiwar sentiments had spread beyond the student ranks to middle-class America itself. This was especially true after the 1968 Tet Offensive when television pictures of enemy troops inside the American embassy belied repeated U.S. government promises that the war was almost won. Moreover, televised images of Buddhist monks setting themselves on fire to protest South Vietnamese human rights abuses undermined attempts to represent that U.S. ally as a freedom-loving democracy. So too did revelations that the South Vietnamese government placed political prisoners in tiger cages.

The Vietnam protest attacked the earlier, almost automatic acceptance of government authority as well as many of the basic assumptions behind the Cold War. In the long run these attacks did not fundamentally change America's Cold

War orientation: witness the country's enthusiastic acceptance of Ronald Reagan's hard-line, anti–Communist position during the early 1980s. During the late 1960s and early 1970s, however, the country's attitude about the Cold War was far more fragmented, nor did it ever fully return to its pre–Vietnam War unity.

The antiwar sentiment undermined many citizens' belief in the fundamental honesty and morality of their government; it also led some to question the government's commitment to such concerns as human rights, free speech, and democracy, especially in the face of government attempts to infiltrate protest groups and keep important information secret from the public. The highly moral nature of the Vietnam debate generated intense feelings that severely polarized significant elements of the citizenry. Antiwar protests became increasingly violent and confrontational as the war wore on into the late 1960s and early 1970s. Violence sometimes erupted between prowar hawks and antiwar doves, or between antiwar protesters and the police and National Guard troops charged with maintaining order. Protests to the 1970 invasion of Cambodia closed college campuses across the country as students and faculty went on strike in protest. At demonstrations at Kent State University in Ohio and Jackson State College in Mississippi protesting students were shot and killed by the National Guard and state police, and the relationship between the Nixon and his antiwar opponents became increasingly hostile. Disposed to regard the protesters as potential revolutionaries and fearful that the antiwar coalitions might cripple his presidency, Nixon and his White House aides began formulating an enemies list, and ordered the FBI, CIA, and other government agencies to maintain files on suspicious individuals as well as disrupt antiwar activities. Many of these government actions were illegal, and they were exposed during the Watergate scandal and the congressional investigations that followed.

In many instances the hawks retained the traditional Cold War view of Communism as a threat to American well-being, while doves — though not necessarily approving Communism — no longer saw it as the major threat to U.S. safety and prosperity. Hawks supported the war largely because they believed it was necessary for halting Communist expansion in Southeast Asia. They also felt that the United States should honor its commitment to the South Vietnamese people to protect them from Communist invaders who would rob them of their government, property, and freedoms. In addition, many believed that having entered a war the country should pursue it to a successful conclusion. Hawks based much of their support for the war on the domino theory that maintained that the fall of Vietnam would result in subsequent Communist takeovers in Southeast Asia and the Pacific Rim, culminating with the loss of the Philippines. The domino metaphor, drawn in part from the experience in Eastern Europe in the late 1940s, portrayed the Communist insurrections in Laos, Cambodia, Vietnam, and elsewhere in Southeast Asia as part of a concerted, monolithic, worldwide Communist offensive directed from Moscow. The domino theory thus played down the desire for social reform and national liberation by which the revolutionary factions claimed to be motivated and diminished the importance of traditional rivalries among Communist countries in the region. Put to the test after the fall of South Vietnam in 1975, the domino theory did not prove to be accurate.

Although many of the more vocal antiwar activists also espoused socialist or Communist ideology, the majority of those opposing the war did not hold such a radical viewpoint. The fuzziness of U.S. objectives, the highly televised brutality of the various corrupt and undemocratic South Vietnamese regimes that the United States propped up, and the growing willingness to view the war between north and south as being more about national unification than Communist expansionism were the primary reasons for opposing the war. In 1995 the antiwar faction received considerable vindication when former defense secretary Robert McNamara, who had been one of the chief architects of the war during the Kennedy and Johnson administrations, published *In Retrospect: The Tragedy and Lessons of Vietnam* in which he admitted the war was a mistake and U.S. policies had been muddled and improvised from the beginning. He also maintained that the United States failed to recognize the power of Ho Chi Minh's appeal to Vietnamese nationalism, and he criticized his own and President Johnson's decision to send combat troops into a country whose internal political situation was highly unstable. Twenty years after the fall of South Vietnam his book generated considerable controversy and stirred passionate feelings among Americans from every part of the political spectrum.

The Vietnam War fostered many serious divisions within the United States, often along generational lines. Together with the civil rights movement, which was concurrent with it, the war helped spawn a counterculture that rebelled not just against U.S. foreign policy but against consumer capitalism itself. In this respect the Vietnam War protest went to the heart of American Cold War ideology, which championed capitalism as the bulwark against immoral Communism. The end of the war and the economic recession of the mid–1970s led to the general decline of the anticapitalistic counterculture, which was far less evident during the last decade of the Cold War.

Chapter 14

Covert Operations:
The CIA and the FBI

The Cold War was mostly fought in three arenas: military actions in Korea, Vietnam, Grenada, and elsewhere; political actions involving negotiations, political alliances, and foreign aid; and covert actions to support friendly governments or overthrow unfriendly ones. Internally, all of the superpowers subjected suspected traitors and selected domestic political enemies to various forms of spying, harassment, and human rights violations. In the Soviet Union the Committee of State Security (KGB) conducted both foreign and domestic espionage. After Stalin's death in 1953 dissidents were less likely to be tortured or killed, though they were routinely dismissed from their positions and forced to take menial jobs. Often they were sent to forced labor camps or imprisoned in mental hospitals. In the United States responsibility for gathering intelligence abroad and conducting covert actions in foreign countries fell to the Central Intelligence Agency (CIA). The Federal Bureau of Investigation (FBI) assumed responsibility for surveillance within the United States and counterespionage against suspected domestic enemies. The activities of both organizations were restricted by law and the Constitution, but on various occasions both agencies exceeded their authority and violated legal restraints.

The CIA

President Truman disbanded the wartime, intelligence-gathering agency, the Office of Strategic Services (OSS), immediately after the conclusion of World War II. However, he soon realized that the disparate intelligence units scattered among several agencies provided conflicting information. This rendered policymaking difficult and confusing. Therefore, in January 1946 Truman issued an executive order that established a National Intelligence Authority (NIA), which contained a Central Intelligence Group (CIG) responsible for coordinating and evaluating intelligence from other units. However, because CIG personnel belonged to the

Army, Navy and State Department, the CIG could not function efficiently or independently. Thus the 1947 National Security Act eliminated the CIG and created the CIA, a new intelligence unit with its own personnel and budget. The CIA reported to the newly created National Security Council (NSC) comprised of the president and the secretaries of state, defense, Army, Navy, and Air Force. The NSC's charge was to advise on and coordinate defense and foreign policies. The CIA's mission was to advise the NSC on intelligence, collect and evaluate intelligence information related to national security, and to perform "such other functions and duties related to intelligence affecting national security" that were ordered by the NSC. The CIA assumed responsibility for supervising all intelligence activities in foreign countries. It was established solely as an intelligence gathering and processing agency and not as a policymaking body. The National Security Act further specified that the CIA would have "no police, subpoena, law-enforcement powers or internal-security functions." Admiral Roscoe H. Hillenkoetter became the agency's first director (1947–50).

After a 1948 coup brought about a Communist takeover of Czechoslovakia, the NSC feared that Communists might prevail in the upcoming Italian elections. Secretary of Defense James Forrestal had tried to raise funds from Wall Street financiers to launch a nongovernment, clandestine campaign to undermine the Italian Communists; however, Allen Dulles and others felt that a private effort would be ineffective. Instead, they promoted the creation of a special agency for carrying out clandestine operations. In the summer of 1948 the NSC authorized the CIA to conduct covert operations, with the proviso that the operations remain secret and that the government be able to plausibly deny their existence. Subsequently, the Office of Policy Coordination (OPC) was formed as a separate organization within the CIA to oversee covert operations abroad. On Dulles's recommendation his former OSS assistant Frank Wisner was chosen to head the OPC.

Later in 1948 Truman asked Dulles to chair a small committee to assess the CIA's effectiveness and recommend organizational changes. Dulles's work specialized in clandestine intelligence gathering and covert operations. One of his most significant recommendations was that the OPC be more fully integrated into the organizational structure of the CIA. In October 1950 Truman appointed General Walter B. Smith to head the CIA, and he gave Smith the recommendations from Dulles's committee. Smith invited Dulles to serve as a consultant to implement the recommendations, and Dulles soon thereafter assumed the post of deputy director of plans for the agency. In that capacity he oversaw the OPC and the agency's covert activities. The organizational recommendations he and Smith implemented in their first years defined the agency's structure for the next two decades.

In November 1951 Dulles became the CIA's deputy director and Wisner became director of plans. Believing that Eastern Europe could still be liberated and that the Soviet armies could be forced back within Soviet borders, they implemented many covert operations behind the iron curtain. In 1952 the CIA initiated a program to intercept and read mail passing between the United States and certain foreign countries. Though it clearly violated the agency's charter, this practice continued for 21 years, presumably with the unspoken approval of three postmasters general.

In 1953 the newly inaugurated President Eisenhower appointed Dulles as director of the CIA. As a public figure, the pipe-smoking Dulles projected a calm, urbane, and dignified image that became associated with the CIA. He convinced the government and the public that the work of the CIA required strict secrecy and thus managed to hide the agency from stringent congressional oversight and media inquiry. During his tenure in office, Dulles also introduced advanced technology to the CIA and relied increasingly on high-altitude U-2 reconnaissance flights to gather information.

As a member of the Eisenhower administration Dulles worked closely with his younger brother, John Foster Dulles, the secretary of state. Both men viewed the fight against Communism as a moral crusade of freedom-loving democracies against freedom-denying totalitarian regimes, and both favored policies aimed at the eventual liberation of Eastern Europe from Soviet control. However, Cold War circumstances eventually compelled both men to abandon their liberation policy and accept modified versions of Truman's containment policies.

The Eisenhower administration increasingly turned to covert actions as a tool for achieving desired political outcomes. Thus the CIA helped overthrow several left-wing governments and install governments more friendly to U.S. interests. In 1953, for instance, it helped depose Iran's prime minister Mohammad Mossadegh and restore the shah. And in 1955 it helped overthrow the leftist government of Guatemala's president Jacobo Arbenz Guzmán, who had initiated a program of land reforms that threatened the interests of the powerful, U.S.-owned United Fruit Company. The CIA both trained and supplied an Army of Guatemalan exiles and organized an Air Force staffed by American pilots to provide air cover for the revolutionary Army. When the attack appeared to be failing, Dulles convinced Eisenhower to authorize additional U.S. air support. This turned the tide of the battle, and Arbenz was forced to surrender. The right-wing Colonel Carlos Castillo Armas then came to power with CIA assistance. Elsewhere, the CIA backed other anti–Communist regimes that lacked popular support. Most significantly it helped enable South Vietnam's president Ngo Dinh Diem to consolidate control of the government, despite strong opposition from the military and important religious sects. The U.S. commitment to Diem played a major role in America's growing involvement in Vietnam, though later disaffection with Diem led the CIA and the Kennedy administration to remain silent when they learned of plans for the coup that toppled and murdered him.

Hearings by the Senate's 1975 Select Committee to Study Intelligence

Activities (the Church Committee) revealed that Dulles had authorized the assassination of Congolese leader Patrice Lumumba in 1960 and that Eisenhower may have indirectly authorized Dulles. However, Lumumba's Congolese enemies killed him before the CIA could implement its plan. The Church Committee also reported that Dulles and Eisenhower had promoted the overthrow of Rafael Trujillo, the dictator of the Dominican Republic. According to the committee, authorization for such covert operations was deliberately made vague and indirect so administration officials and the agency could maintain plausible deniability. Thus, Dulles's instructions to the CIA station in the Congo read, "We wish every possible support in eliminating Lumumba from any possibility of resuming a governmental position." Agents receiving these instructions interpreted them as a request to assassinate the leader.

A former CIA agent and a former State Department official have claimed that in 1959 Dulles altered a CIA report on Castro advising Eisenhower on the situation in Cuba. They maintained he deleted an assessment that Castro's rise to power was a natural response to the corruption of the Batista regime and replaced it with a prediction that Castro would use excessive force to consolidate his power. In response, Eisenhower authorized Dulles to begin training an Army of Guatemala-based Cuban exiles to liberate the island, and Dulles placed Richard Bissell in charge of the operation. A plan to organize an internal uprising within Cuba proved to be not feasible. Bissell also enlisted the assistance of organized crime leaders to arrange assassination attempts on Castro, but these failed. Their other options having failed, in November 1960 Bissell and Dulles advised President-elect Kennedy of the existence of the exile Army and, after assuring him an assault would succeed, recommended an assault on Cuba. In April 1961 Kennedy authorized the Bay of Pigs invasion. Dulles was out of town and Bissell oversaw the failed operation, which resulted in the death or capture of most of the invading force. In a highly controversial move Kennedy canceled a second CIA air strike intended to support the invaders. A panel headed by retired general Maxwell Taylor could not agree as to whether the plan ever had any realistic chance for success. Dulles argued that if they had followed the original plans and ordered the second air strike it might have succeeded, but Secretary of State Rusk, a former military intelligence officer, later maintained that the invasion never had "a snowball's chance in hell."

Shortly after the Bay of Pigs fiasco the president replaced Dulles with John McCone, a conservative Republican. McCone advised Kennedy during the Cuban Missile Crisis. The CIA provided the evidence confirming the presence of Soviet missiles on the island. McCone advocated a preemptive air strike to remove the missiles but Kennedy opted instead for a naval quarantine. McCone also advised Kennedy against directly supporting a coup against Diem after the South Vietnamese president brutally cracked down on Buddhists in August 1963. Instead, he recommended that the United States demand reforms but continue its support for Diem until a coup came about without direct U.S. involvement.

Kennedy adopted this policy. Later McCone unsuccessfully advised President Johnson against sending combat troops to Vietnam because he believed that they would be unable to win a war in which the soldiers were constricted by so many limitations. During McCone's tenure in office the CIA continued to illegally open the mail of U.S. citizens. It also continued its unsuccessful attempts to assassinate Castro. In fact, these attempts continued through the Nixon administration.

McCone resigned in 1965, and Admiral William Raborn, Jr., replaced him (1965–66). From 1966 to 1973 Richard Helms led the agency during the most intense period of the Vietnam War. Both the CIA and military intelligence have been criticized for exaggerating U.S. and South Vietnamese successes and understating their losses, especially during the Johnson era. The skewed information induced Johnson to believe the war was both winnable and being won. Consequently, the president dismissed advice by such prominent advisers as Dean Acheson to divorce the United States from what indeed proved to be a lost cause. Moreover, in violation of the National Security Act, the agency infiltrated antiwar groups and conducted other illegal acts of domestic espionage.

During the Nixon administration the CIA tried to prevent the election of Chile's Salvador Allende. Having failed, it then participated in the overthrow of South America's first freely elected Marxist president and helped install a brutal, right-wing military dictatorship led by General Pinochet. It also recruited and paid a private Army to fight against Communist forces in Laos. Moreover, in violation of the prohibition against domestic surveillance, the agency aided the White House's "plumbers," who spied on Nixon's political enemies and stole documents relating to Daniel Ellsberg, a government employee who had stolen and published the *Pentagon Papers*. During that time the agency also experimented on unknowing subjects with LSD and other mind-controlling drugs.

Following the Watergate scandal the CIA fell under closer scrutiny. Nixon appointed James Schlesinger to replace Helms in January 1973, but Schlesinger left the agency in June to become secretary of defense. William Colby replaced him in August and remained in office until January 1976. He resigned after revealing that the CIA still possessed a cache of poison that Nixon had ordered destroyed. 1975 Senate hearings conducted by the Church Committee revealed evidence of past illegal activities, and Congress amended the National Security Act to strengthen the prohibitions against the CIA's involvement in domestic activities.

Future president George Bush succeeded Colby and directed the CIA through the remainder of Gerald Ford's presidency. He implemented policies to improve the agency's professionalism and promoted younger personnel. He also took the unprecedented step of opening classified CIA documents to a group of conservative, antidétente foreign policy planners known as Team B. Team B succeeded in reversing the earlier agency assessment that the Soviets were seeking nuclear parity during détente, arguing instead that they were trying to achieve nuclear superiority. Team B's politicized interpretation of the data later became the operative assumption underlying the massive arms buildup and preparations for winnable nuclear war during the early 1980s. In January 1977 President Carter replaced Bush with Admiral Stansfield Turner, who directed the agency until Reagan took office in 1981. During the Ford and Carter administrations the CIA continued to gather intelligence and assist anti–Communist efforts in Africa and Asia. The CIA failed to predict the fall of the shah of Iran in 1977 and the subsequent rise of Ayatollah Khomeini's Muslim theocracy. Afterward it was largely closed off from intelligence sources in Iran and in several Arab countries where Islamic fundamentalism was becoming increasingly strong and extremist groups were holding Western hostages. Nonetheless, during the Reagan era the agency helped arm Muslim Afghani rebels in their successful fight against the Soviet-backed Communist government.

In 1981 Reagan directed the CIA to arm and organize Nicaraguan Contras trying to topple the pro–Communist Sandinistas. However, Congress opposed his efforts and in 1982 passed the first Boland Amendment, forbidding the CIA to overthrow the Nicaraguan government. Nonetheless, the covert activities continued, largely directed by the National Security Council, and in 1984 the CIA secretly mined Nicaraguan harbors: technically an act of war. When these and other illegal covert activities became publicly known, Congress passed additional Boland amendments denying government agencies funds to support "directly or indirectly military or paramilitary operations" in Nicaragua.

To bypass the Boland prohibitions on government involvement the Reagan administration, largely through high-ranking officers in the National Security Council, sought ways to channel weapons and funds to the Contras through private individuals and agencies. This privatization of the country's handling of foreign affairs led directly to the Iran-Contra Affair of 1985 and 1986. According to the reconstruction of events by the congressional committees investigating the Iran-Contra Affair an arms-for-hostages deal was originally suggested in the summer of 1985 by Israel, which acted as an intermediary in the trade in hopes of gaining improved relations with Iran, which was then fighting a war with Iraq. However, scholarship published in 1994 by former Justice Department attorney John Loftus and Mark Aarons cites new evidence claiming that Vice President Bush inaugurated the first attempt to trade arms for hostages and that Bush's first shipments through the Syrians began in 1984, more than a year before the Israelis were dragged in as scapegoats. Their book, *The Secret War Against the Jews*, documents each of the shipping manifests, bank accounts, and arms transactions, and corroborates them with cross-citations to matching entries in the diaries of Marine Lieutenant Colonel Oliver North, who was then working for the National Security Council. Despite Reagan's pledge never to swap arms for hostages, the Iran-Contra Affair involved the sale of U.S. weapons to Iran in return for the release of seven American hostages held by pro–Iranian terrorist groups in Lebanon. However, only three hostages were released, despite several transactions. The $48 million generated between September 1985 and October 1986 was diverted for various purposes, including arming the Contras ($16.5 million), running other covert operations ($1 million), establishing reserves for future operations ($4.2 million), bribing Iranian officials ($15.2 million), and paying commissions to middlemen who brokered the deals ($6.6 million). The 1987 congressional investigation revealed many top administration officials to be involved, including Reagan's national security advisers Robert McFarlane and John Poindexter and CIA director William Casey. Secretary of State George Shultz strongly opposed the scheme and was kept out of the loop of information. North controlled the funds and used them "to run the covert operation to support the Contras." According to North, Casey saw the diversion of funds as part of a more grandiose plan to create a "stand-alone," "off-the-shelf" covert capability that would extend throughout the world while evading congressional review. Casey suffered a sudden stroke just as the scandal was unfolding and died without ever testifying about it. The incident seriously undermined the administration's credibility and future effectiveness. During the 1988 presidential campaign Vice President Bush, the Republican candidate, claimed to be out of the loop when decisions were being made about the Iran-Contra deal. He thereby escaped serious political damage and easily won the election. However, new revelations by a special prosecutor a week prior to the 1992 elections hurt Bush's reelection bid, as documents showed him to be much more inside the loop than he had represented. FBI director William Webster, who had a reputation for integrity, succeeded Casey in 1987. Robert Gates served as CIA director during the Bush administration.

The CIA's Cold War performance has been praised for its intelligence-gathering accomplishments and the success of its covert operations in achieving certain U.S. political goals. After launching intelligence satellites in 1961 it was better able to assess Soviet missile capabilities and declare that the missile gap that Kennedy had campaigned on did not exist. This conclusion helped curb the arms race, as did the agency's ability to verify Soviet compliance with arms agreements. Without assurances offered by CIA verification, many arms control treaties may not have been politically viable. The agency's role in identifying the Soviet missiles in Cuba during the Missile Crisis was also crucial, though U.S. intelligence remained unaware of the full number of Soviet ground troops in Cuba while Kennedy was contemplating a full-scale invasion. Presumably, because of their secret classification, other CIA achievements remain as yet unknown to the U.S. public.

On the other hand, the agency repeatedly violated U.S. and international law, pursued political and ideological enemies, destabilized entire regions of the world, and supported repressive, nondemocratic regimes against populist movements. It may also have overstated the extent of the Communist threat and thereby fueled the Cold War and the accompanying arms race. For instance, in 1994 Turner reviewed a 1980 report the agency had generated while he was director.

It claimed that the Soviet Union then had a temporary window of opportunity to gain superiority in the arms race and thus pressured Carter to increase U.S. military capacity. In retrospect Turner pointed out that the United States had a second-strike capability to destroy 70 percent of the Soviet economy, even after a Soviet first strike. "How could we have thought we possibly needed more?" Turner also criticized the CIA's failure to forecast the shah of Iran's downfall or the collapse of the Soviet Union, and he claimed that the agency had not served Carter well.

Subject to minimal oversight and in control of vast secret budgets, the CIA was largely able to pursue its own agendas, and the information it passed on to higher authorities was sometimes skewed to reflect political biases. Critics also point to the agency's failure to adequately police its own agents. Allegations of CIA involvement with drug cartels and other criminal organizations have tarnished the agency's image, as did the revelation in 1994 that Aldrich Ames, a highly placed CIA agent, had worked for nine years as a Soviet double-agent and thrived on the agency's incredibly lax internal security. Ames's work on behalf of the Soviets, which began in 1985, resulted in the elimination, and sometimes the death, of several U.S. agents in the Soviet Union. Moreover, it induced the CIA to seriously overestimate the Soviet military capacity and fail to perceive the forthcoming collapse of the Soviet Union. Consequently, CIA reports supported the acceleration of U.S. weapons programs and distorted the strength of hard-line Communist resistance to Gorbachev's reforms. Moreover, without indicating that their sources were tainted, the CIA passed along to presidents and other top policymakers at least 95 reports that the agency knew or suspected came from Soviet agents. In December 1995 John Deutch, the CIA director during the Clinton administration, declared that this deception played "a substantial role in framing the debate" over military policy and foreign policy. Though no single weapon was developed solely as a result of these reports, Deutch maintained that "the overall effect was to sustain our view of the USSR as a credible military and technological opponent.... The net effect was that we overestimated their capability." Leaders of the Senate Intelligence Committee likewise concluded that the Pentagon used the reports "as part of an overall justification for multibillion-dollar investments in weapons systems" that increased military spending by hundreds of millions of dollars. Senator Bob Kerry, the committee's deputy chairman, speculated that this was the Soviets' intention. "We take credit for the fact that we bankrupted the Soviet Union by getting them to build more than what they needed, and I presume that they may have had the same thing in mind."

The FBI

In 1924 J. Edgar Hoover became director of the Justice Department's Bureau of Investigation, which was then only a small, investigatory agency plagued by scandals and staffed by political appointees. Hoover had earlier coordinated the so-called Palmer Raids in which thousands of alleged anarchists and Communists were rounded up, interrogated, and deported during the Red Scare of 1919–20. He insisted on hiring agents via the merit system and turned the bureau into a professional organization. After the U.S. entry into World War II President Roosevelt authorized Hoover to expand the bureau's surveillance of left- and right-wing political groups, labor unions, civil rights organizations, and the Communist Party, all of which Hoover maintained could potentially threaten the war effort. Presidential and congressional actions further authorized him to place wiretaps for national security reasons and to maintain a list of domestic Communists and Fascists for possible arrest and detention. The FBI was also responsible for checking the loyalty of federal employees. However, Hoover expanded the bureau's activities beyond those authorized by the government and, despite a pledge to discontinue and/or curtail domestic surveillance after the war, he maintained the security apparatus for monitoring groups and individuals he believed could potentially undermine the country's internal security.

During the Cold War Hoover regarded the American Communist Party as a Soviet tool dedicated to the overthrow of the U.S. government and willing to perform espionage and sabotage. The FBI thus monitored and infiltrated the Communist Party throughout the Cold War. In 1945 FBI agents arrested foreign service officer John S. Service for passing classified information to a left-wing journal, and the bureau investigated Harry Dexter White, assistant secretary of the treasury, who became the executive director of the International Monetary Fund in 1946. Hoover regarded White as the leading Communist in the U.S. government, though White died before those charges could be resolved. Alger Hiss and William Remington were among the other ranking government officials the FBI investigated for Communist espionage and/or complicity.

Hoover's 1946 testimony before Congress led to a more stringent loyalty program than originally proposed by the Truman administration. Under the tougher new rules federal employees accused of disloyalty could appeal in a hearing and have a lawyer present to represent them, but they could not confront their accusers. The FBI assumed responsibility for investigating claims of disloyalty, despite Truman's fears that this might increase the bureau's powers to a dangerously high level. In 1954 Hoover maintained that the FBI had investigated the loyalty of some 5 million federal employees. He defended the bureau against charges of a witch-hunt by pointing out that only 560 had been removed or denied employment as a result. On the other hand, some 6,000 Americans left their jobs in the private sector or withdrew their applications for federal jobs as a result of the investigations. To determine subjects' loyalty agents asked about their reading habits, their stand on civil rights and socialized medicine, and their support for former Vice President Henry Wallace, who ran for president in 1948 on the left-wing Progressive Party ticket that the American Communist Party had endorsed. In 1952 Truman expanded the FBI's wiretapping powers. However, the bureau exceeded its new authority, opening the mail of U.S. citizens and committing crimes to secure evidence against perceived enemies of the state.

During the Truman administration the FBI also cracked a Communist spy ring that had given the Soviets classified information during World War II about the atomic bomb project. The bureau thus played a major role in the arrests of Julius and Ethel Rosenberg, who steadfastly maintained their innocence, and the arrest in England of atomic scientist Klaus Fuchs, who admitted his guilt. In 1957 the FBI arrested a Soviet colonel Rudolf Abel as the head of a large spy ring, and in 1958 it uncovered another major Soviet spy operation. In the early 1950s, at Hoover's personal behest, the FBI conducted an extensive investigation of Albert Einstein but was never able to accumulate any evidence proving the scientist had been a Communist agent, despite some unsubstantiated allegations to that effect. Hoover disapproved of Einstein's liberal politics, and during World War II he had been responsible for denying the physicist a security clearance, ironically rendering him ineligible to participate in the atomic bomb project that Einstein himself had initiated in a 1939 letter to Roosevelt. Throughout the Cold War the FBI maintained files on thousands of scientists, writers, performers, professors, and other individuals who had violated no laws but employed their constitutional freedoms to express political sentiments that Hoover found objectionable and potentially treasonable.

Throughout the 1950s Hoover remained one of the most ardent and most visible anti–Communists, though he generally disassociated himself from Senator Joseph McCarthy and other promoters of the Red Scare. Hoover considered them amateurs whose theatrics hampered the real work of fighting internal subversion. As part of an ongoing effort to educate the U.S. public about the dangers of domestic Communism, Hoover had his staff ghost-write magazine articles and his 1958 book, *Masters of Deceit: The Story of Communism in America and How to Fight It. Masters of Deceit* remained in print throughout the Cold War and was often used in public school courses on Americanism versus Communism. The book asks the public to report suspicious activities to the FBI, and it suggests that readers can identify Communists and fellow travelers by their use of such phrases as "peace," "disarmament," "academic freedom," and "trade with the East." Hoover's use of mass media to educate the public later extended to television. In 1965 he endorsed ABC's "The F.B.I." which showed the bureau fighting Communist subversives as well as other public enemies. In return for the FBI's active cooperation ABC gave the bureau complete power to approve scripts, sponsorship, and personnel.

In 1956 Hoover initiated a counter-intelligence program (COINTELPRO) after federal courts made prosecuting Communists increasingly difficult under existing laws. Designed to undermine the American Communist Party, COINTELPRO involved leaking accurate and inaccurate information to the press about Communist activities, sending anonymous letters to employers of Communists demanding that they be fired, and otherwise harassing party members and disrupting their work. By 1956 party membership had dropped from 80,000 immediately after World War II to about 5,000—and so many of those were FBI agents that Hoover considered taking control of the party in 1957 by having all of his informants support one faction at the Communist Party national convention. The 1975 Church Committee revealed the COINTELPRO operations and other illegal wiretaps, burglaries, and mail openings during the Eisenhower era. The committee also reported that Hoover had informed the president, the White House staff, and the attorney general and no one had objected.

Hoover maintained his programs of domestic surveillance and harassment of political enemies throughout the 1960s. In 1961 he ordered FBI agents to initiate a disruptive program against the Socialist Workers Party, a small Trotskyite organization. He continued to believe that the civil rights movement was Communist led, and he authorized investigations of Martin Luther King, Jr., and other prominent leaders. The FBI also sent King a message suggesting that he commit suicide, and it tried to destroy his marriage by sending his wife tape-recorded evidence of his alleged affairs. During the Vietnam War the FBI infiltrated antiwar organizations, believing that these also were subversive and Communist inspired. However, feeling that the FBI was not aggressive enough, the Nixon White House encouraged the CIA to violate its charter and disrupt these groups as well.

After Hoover died in 1972, L. Patrick Gray became acting director. However, he was discredited for his role in the Watergate cover-up, which included destroying evidence. Clarence Kelley succeeded him in 1973. The Vietnam War ended that year and subsequently the bureau became less concerned with harassing political dissidents. In 1978 Carter appointed William Webster as director. Webster served until 1987, when he left to head the CIA after William Casey's death while the Iran-Contra Affair was unfolding. William Sessions succeeded him. In the late 1980s the FBI warned the CIA about Aldrich Ames's recurrent visits to the Soviet embassy, but the CIA failed to heed the warnings.

Led by the ultra-conservative Hoover for the first half of the Cold War and by other conservatives thereafter, the FBI has been criticized for its attempts to subvert the legal and legitimate activities of political opponents. It seems to have greatly exaggerated the threat to national security posed by American Communists and Communist sympathizers, thereby helping to create a climate of fear that fueled the Red Scare and justified a growing increase in FBI powers. On the other hand, the bureau's counterespionage efforts were highly successful, and it permitted few serious breaches of national security throughout the entire Cold War.

SECTION III
Chronologies

An Annotated Chronology of Important Cold War Events

I. The Pre–Cold War (1945–47)

February 4–11, 1945: The Yalta Conference convenes. (Yalta is in the Crimea in what was the USSR.) Attended by Franklin Roosevelt (United States), Winston Churchill (Great Britain), and Joseph Stalin (Soviet Union), the conference demanded Germany's unconditional surrender and mapped out the general political arrangements for the postwar world. The more significant Yalta agreements are as follows:

1. Germany was to be divided into four zones of occupation: American, French, British, and Russian.

2. The Polish Lubin government, which Stalin supported, was to be reorganized on a "broader democratic basis" to include members of Poland's London-based government in exile, which the Western Allies supported.

3. The USSR secretly agreed to enter the war against Japan within three months of Germany's surrender. In return it was promised Sakhalin, the Kurile Islands, and an occupation zone in Korea.

4. Other secret agreements disposing of Japanese holdings were as follows: Talien (Dairen) should be internationalized, Port Arthur should be restored to its status from before the 1904–5 Russo-Japanese war as a Soviet naval base, and the Manchurian railroads should be placed under joint Soviet-Chinese management. The Chinese later protested that they had not been informed of this last agreement and that their sovereignty had been compromised.

5. The United States and Great Britain agreed to recognize Outer Mongolia.

6. The Big Three — the United States, USSR, and Great Britain — would ask China and France to join them in sponsoring the founding conference of the United Nations to be convened in San Francisco on April 25, 1945. They also agreed upon the veto system for the UN Security Council, to which all five founding countries would belong. The big three also agreed to admit to the

United Nations as full voting members Ukraine and Byelorussia (now Belarus), which were in the Soviet sphere.

May 7, 1945: Germany surrenders unconditionally to the Allies.

July 17–August 2, 1945: The Potsdam Conference among the big three heads of state convenes. (Potsdam is near Berlin in the former East Germany.) The countries were represented by President Harry Truman (United States), Joseph Stalin (Soviet Union), and first Winston Churchill and then Clement Attlee, who defeated Churchill in an election for prime minister of Great Britain during the conference.

The Potsdam Conference established the terms of the postwar occupation of Germany. It divided the country into American, British, French, and Russian military zones and established a four-power Allied Control Council for settling matters concerning the whole country. It established a new system for ruling Germany aimed at outlawing the Nazi party (National Socialism), abolishing Nazi ideology, disarming Germany, and preventing it ever from becoming a military power again. The conference also called for fostering democratic ideals and introducing representative and elective principles of government in Europe. It transferred all former German territory east of the Oder and Neisse rivers to Polish and Soviet administration, pending a final peace treaty, and called for German reparations for war damages.

At Potsdam the Big Three also issued an ultimatum to Japan: either surrender unconditionally or risk total destruction. Truman was already attending the conference when he was informed of the first successful test of the atomic bomb that occurred on July 15. He did not inform Stalin.

August 6, 1945: The United States drops the first atomic bomb on Hiroshima.

August 9, 1945: The United States drops the second atomic bomb on Nagasaki.

August 14, 1945: Japan announces its surrender.

September 2, 1945: General Douglas MacArthur, commander of U.S. armed forces in the Pacific, formally accepts the Japanese surrender aboard the SS *Missouri*. MacArthur then became chief administrator of the Allied occupation of Japan, which lasted until April 28, 1952. (In 1951 Japan signed a peace treaty with most of its World War II foes; however USSR, Czechoslovakia, and Poland refused to sign; India and Burma boycotted the conference that produced the treaty.)

January 10, 1946: The UN General Assembly meets for the first time in London. On January 17 the Security Council had its inaugural meeting, and on January 29 Norwegian Trygve Lie was elected the first secretary-general.

February 14, 1946: Syngman Rhee forms the Democratic Representative Council in Seoul, South Korea. On February 19 Kim Il Sung was named chairman of the Korean People's government in Pyongyang, North Korea. Korea became provisionally divided at the thirty-eighth parallel into two zones, U.S.-supported

South Korea and Soviet-controlled North Korea. In fall 1948 they declared themselves independent sovereign nations, though North Korea's Kim Il Sung vowed to achieve the ultimate reunification of the country.

March 5, 1946: Speaking in Fulton, Missouri, Winston Churchill warns of an implacable threat to freedom that lies behind a Communist "Iron Curtain" in Eastern Europe and the USSR.

March 9, 1946: Finland elects a pro–Soviet president.

March 24, 1946: Truman threatens to send battleships to the Mediterranean if the Soviet Union does not remove its troops from Iran in accordance with the Potsdam agreements. The Soviet Union withdrew its troops in May after Iran agreed to give the USSR 51 percent of Iranian oil for the next 25 years.

May 5, 1946: A civil war in China breaks out between U.S.-backed Chinese Nationalists and Communist Chinese forces led by Mao Zedong. On August 19 Mao formally declared war on the Nationalists. Mao claimed victory and declared the People's Republic of China on October 1, 1949.

September 1, 1946: A referendum in Greece calls for the monarchy to be restored. Shortly afterward civil war broke out between royalists and Communists. The Communist Party was outlawed and political freedoms were curtailed as a result of the fighting. Under the Truman Doctrine the United States later sent military advisers and some $400 million in military and economic assistance, and the anti–Communist forces eventually prevailed in 1949.

II. Containment (1947–54)

1947–49: The East-West coalitions fall into place (see chapter 3).

January 19, 1947: Communist victories lead President Truman to declare that elections in Poland were not free or fair and thereby violated the Yalta agreements. Thereafter, the Polish government began to sovietize the country.

March 12, 1947: Truman issues the Truman Doctrine that formalizes U.S. policy to prevent Communist expansion and contain the Soviet Union within its existing spheres of influence. The main features of the Truman Doctrine were the Marshall Plan to effect the economic reconstruction of postwar Europe (1947), the Four Point Program to provide technical aid to underdeveloped countries in Asia, Africa, and Latin America (1948), and the creation of the North Atlantic Treaty Organization (NATO), an anti–Soviet military alliance (1949).

March 21, 1947: Truman requires loyalty investigations of all federal employees and forbids government employment to Communists and Communist sympathizers.

June 23, 1947: The Taft-Hartley Act becomes law over Truman's veto. It denied the facilities of the National Labor Relations Board to unions that failed to file affidavits swearing that their officers were non–Communists.

August 15, 1947: India receives its independence from Britain, and Pakistan is formed through the same agreement. Pakistan was established as a Muslim-dominated state, India as a predominately Hindu state. In late 1947 more than 500,000 people died as minority populations in each country relocated. Mohandas Gandhi, an advocate of mutual acceptance and respect between Muslims and Hindus and a major leader in the nationalist movement for independence, almost single-handedly prevented a civil war from breaking out by going on a hunger strike until violence ended in Calcutta. However, in January 1948 a Hindu fanatic assassinated Gandhi because he respected the rights and religious beliefs of Muslims.

In 1948 India and Pakistan went to war over jurisdiction in Jammu and Kashmir. During the Cold War several wars between the two countries occurred. The 1971 war, won by India, led to the autonomy of East Pakistan and the creation of a new state there, Bangladesh. In 1974 India exploded its first nuclear device.

September 1, 1947: Amid charges of voting irregularities Communists win the general elections in Hungary.

September 8, 1947: The National Security Act takes effect. Signed by Truman on July 26, the act replaced the wartime Office of Strategic Services (OSS) with the Central Intelligence Agency (CIA). It also created the National Security Council (NSC) to advise on and coordinate defense and foreign policies. The NSC was initially composed of the president and the secretaries of state, defense, Army, Navy, and Air Force.

September 22, 1947: Partly in response to the U.S. Marshall Plan, the Soviet Communist Party and Communist parties in Bulgaria, Czechoslovakia, France, Hungary, Italy, Poland, Romania, and Yugoslavia introduce the Communist Information Bureau (Cominform), which replaced the Communist International (Comintern). The political alliance served as a precursor to the 1955 Warsaw Pact, and some historians argue that its formation represented Stalin's declaration of ideological war against the West. The member countries signed the pact in December.

September 23, 1947: The head of the Bulgarian opposition party is executed and Bulgaria becomes a one-party Communist state aligned with the USSR. It nationalized industry and collectivized farms.

October 20, 1947: The House Committee on Un-American Activities (HUAC), under the chairmanship of J. Parnell Thomas, conducts its first Cold War hearings concerning alleged Communist influence within the Hollywood film industry. These hearings centered on allegations that Communist values and propaganda were being surreptitiously introduced into American films. As a result of these hearings the Hollywood Ten — mostly film writers and directors — were imprisoned for refusing to testify about their past political activities and associations, and the industry practice of blacklisting Communists and Communist sympathizers began.

December 29, 1947: Former Democratic vice president Henry Wallace declares his candidacy for president as the Progressive Party nominee. The Soviet Union and the American Communist Party endorsed him, though he never directly supported them. Wallace garnered over 1 million votes from a total of some 48 million cast in November 1948. Support for Wallace's candidacy was cited in FBI files and such blacklisting publications as *Red Channels* as an indication of a subject's possible Communist sympathies.

December 30, 1947: Romania declares itself a Communist people's republic after King Michael I and a non–Communist coalition government abdicate. Romanian industry and resources were nationalized and agriculture was collectivized.

February 16, 1948: North Korea declares itself a people's republic. It was immediately supported by the USSR. South Korea became an independent republic on August 15, and on September 9 North Korea declared itself independent. North Korean leader Kim Il Sung then vowed to unite Korea.

February 25–27, 1948: Communists seize power in Czechoslovakia through a coup by police and paramilitary "action committees" that forced the resignation of center and right-wing members of the government. This was followed by the assassination of Jan Masaryk, the Czech foreign minister who had resisted Soviet demands for Czechoslovakia to refuse U.S. aid. Masaryk's death was officially ruled a suicide.

May 14, 1948: The United Nations recognizes the state of Israel and British rule officially ends in Palestine. Israel's Arab neighbors Jordan, Lebanon, Syria, and Egypt invaded with their regular armies that same day but were repelled, except in the old city of Jerusalem. The original UN agreement had called for the formation of a separate, Palestinian state in addition to the formation of Israel. It also called for international administration of Jerusalem. After the fighting, however, a peace treaty signed in January 1949 expanded Israeli territory by about 50 percent. Jordan retained control of Old Jerusalem and refused Israelis admission to the sacred sites there. Jordan and Egypt also annexed or occupied territory that had been designated for the Palestinian state. Thus the question of an independent Palestinian homeland took a new form.

June 24, 1948: The Soviets blockade West Berlin. The United States responded with the Berlin Airlift. By spring 1949 the round-the-clock flights were averaging 8,000 tons of fuel and food supplies daily. Unable to achieve his objective of gaining control over West Berlin, Stalin lifted the blockade on May 12, 1949.

June 28, 1948: Cominform calls on the Yugoslavian Communist Party either to remove Marshal Tito or face expulsion from the alliance of Communist parties. In March Tito had responded to demands that he conform to the Soviet party line by removing Stalinists from the Yugoslavian Communist Party and purging the Army. When the Yugoslavian Communists did not eliminate Tito, the USSR withdrew military aid and expelled Yugoslavia from Cominform.

Though not falling into the Western camp, Yugoslavia maintained relations with the West and by 1951 received $150 million in U.S. civilian aid and another $60 million in arms. In 1955, however, it renewed ties with the USSR, and Cominform was dissolved as a gesture of goodwill.

July 20, 1948: Leaders of the American Communist Party are arrested under the Smith Act for conspiring to overthrow the U.S. government. They were later convicted during the Foley Square Trial of 1949 (see chapter 9).

July 29, 1948: Finland forms an all-socialist cabinet that excludes Communists. Following World War II Communists gained considerable control in Finland, capturing several high offices, briefly including that of the prime minister. Moreover, the Finns elected a pro–Soviet president in 1946. In 1947 Finland was obliged to pay $300 million in World War II reparations, cede the Karelian Isthmus and other border districts and grant a 50-year lease on the Porkkala region (near Helsinki), to the Soviet Union. On April 6, 1948, it signed a treaty of cooperation with the USSR that was extended in 1955, 1970, and 1983. However, in 1948 Communist power within Finland declined, and between 1948 and 1966 no Communists served in the cabinet.

July 30, 1948: Through their control of the ministry of the interior, Hungarian Communists arrest leading politicians, force the resignation of the president, and gain full control of the state. In 1949 Hungary was proclaimed a people's republic, characterized by nationalization of industry and resources and collectivization of farms.

August 3, 1948: Whittaker Chambers accuses Alger Hiss of being a Soviet agent. Hiss was indicted for perjury on December 15 and convicted on January 25, 1950 (see chapter 9).

August 19, 1948: Soviet troops fire upon East Berlin demonstrators protesting Soviet occupation.

November 3, 1948: In an upset victory Truman defeats Republican Thomas Dewey for the presidency. Henry Wallace, the Progressive Party candidate endorsed by the Communist Party, received slightly more than 1 million votes.

November 30, 1948: German Communists establish an independent government in Berlin's Soviet sector.

January 1, 1949: The United States recognizes the Republic of South Korea.

March 4, 1949: Stalin replaces Foreign Minister Vyachesla Molotov with Andrei Vishinsky who had presided over the notorious purges of the 1930s.

March 8, 1949: France recognizes Bao Dai as the head of a non–Communist Vietnamese government located in Saigon, in what was formerly French Indochina. In doing so France denied the claims of the Hanoi-based Vietminh under the Communist leadership of Ho Chi Minh. The Vietminh continued to fight against the French until they left Vietnam after the fall of Dien Bien Phu in 1954 (see chapter 13).

April 4, 1949: The North Atlantic Treaty Organization (NATO), a military alliance, forms to contain Communist expansion in Europe.

May 23, 1949: The Federal Republic of Germany (FRG: West Germany) proclaims its existence and designates Bonn as its capital. On August 14 West Germans elected 73-year-old Konrad Adenauer their first chancellor. He held the post through 1963.

September 23, 1949: Truman announces that the Soviet Union has exploded an atomic bomb.

September 28–October 1, 1949: The USSR, Poland, Hungary, Romania, and Bulgaria renounce their friendship and mutual assistance pacts with Yugoslavia.

October 1, 1949: Mao Zedong declares the People's Republic of China (PRC). Zhou En-lai was elected premier and foreign minister. They immediately introduced a major program of land reform, police control, and nationalization of resources and industry. In December Chiang Kai-shek established a Nationalist Chinese government on Taiwan (Formosa). By April 1950 all of mainland China was securely under Communist control. The final Communist victory set off right-wing accusations that Truman's State Department had "lost China." Though Great Britain recognized the PRC on October 26, 1949, the United States refused to do so and did not establish full diplomatic relations until 1979.

October 7, 1949: The German Democratic Republic (GDR: East Germany) proclaims its existence. The United States refused to recognize East Germany until 1974.

October 16, 1949: The three-year Greek civil war ends when Communist insurgents agree to give up their weapons.

October 26, 1949: Great Britain recognizes the People's Republic of China.

1949–50: The CIO expels unions that are Communist dominated.

February 2, 1950: France recognizes Laos and Cambodia as independent states.

February 3, 1950: Based on information uncovered by FBI interrogations of American Communists, Klaus Fuchs is arrested in Great Britain for passing information about the atomic bomb to Soviet agents. Fuchs confessed to the crime and was convicted and imprisoned. After his release in 1959 he emigrated to East Germany. He headed that country's Institute for Nuclear Physics until he retired in 1979.

February 9, 1950: Senator Joseph McCarthy first gains national prominence for a speech given in Wheeling, West Virginia, in which he claims to have a list of 205 Communists working within Truman's State Department. The State Department claimed shortly thereafter that its own internal investigations turned up no known Communists. Nonetheless, McCarthy persisted in his charges (see chapter 9).

June 16, 1950: The FBI arrests Julius and Ethel Rosenberg on charges that during 1944 and 1945 they received and passed on to Soviet agents classified information about the U.S. atomic bomb project.

June 25, 1950: In a surprise attack Communist North Koreans invade South Korea, inaugurating the Korean War (see chapter 10).

September 23, 1950: Congress overrides Truman's veto of the McCarran Internal Security Act, which establishes concentration camps for Communists in Pennsylvania, Florida, Oklahoma, Arizona, and California, though these were never used. It also required all Communist and Communist-dominated organizations to give the federal government the names of all of their members and contributors (see chapter 9).

October 21, 1950: Communist China invades Tibet. In May 1951 Tibet signed an agreement making the country a "national autonomous region" of China. Though officially under the traditional religious rule of the Dalai Lama, Tibet became politically dominated by Communist China, which soon introduced extensive land reform and reduced the power of the Dalai Lama's monastic order.

March 29, 1951: Julius and Ethel Rosenberg are convicted of conspiracy to transmit classified military information to the Soviet Union. They are sentenced to death on April 5 and executed on June 19, 1953.

August 30, 1951: The Philippines and the United States sign a mutual defense treaty.

September 1, 1951: The United States signs a mutual defense pact with Australia and New Zealand.

September 8, 1951: Forty-eight nations sign a peace treaty with Japan formally ending that part of World War II. The treaty forbade Japan to rearm and permitted the United States to station troops in Japan. Japan also signed a security treaty with the United States assuring U.S. defense of Japan in case of external attack. One long-term consequence of this arrangement was that very little of Japan's budget went for military spending during the Cold War as compared to the U.S. and USSR's military expenditure. This freed money for developing Japanese business and industry, which flourished during the Cold War.

October 19, 1951: Congress officially ends the state of war with Germany.

November 14, 1951: The United States agrees to supply Yugoslavia with military assistance.

January 10, 1952: British Prime Minister Winston Churchill agrees to allow U.S. military bases on British soil.

February 18, 1952: Greece and Turkey join NATO.

April 22, 1952: Television audiences witness the explosion of the largest atomic bomb yet to be detonated.

April 28, 1952: The U.S. occupation of Japan officially ends as Japan establishes its own government.

June 16, 1952: East Germany announces its recruitment of a "people's

Army." By December some 100,000 East Germans had joined; the Soviets provided their weapons.

October 3, 1952: Great Britain explodes its first atomic bomb.

October 31, 1952: The United States explodes its first thermonuclear device, a 12 megaton hydrogen bomb (see chapter 8).

November 5, 1952: Republican Dwight Eisenhower defeats Democrat Adlai Stevenson for the presidency.

1952–53: HUAC conducts a second and much larger set of hearings into Communist influence within the film industry. The 1951–52 HUAC hearings, under the chairmanship of John Wood, changed the focus from film content to the prestige, position, and money that the Communist Party acquired in Hollywood. In these mass hearings (HUAC called 90 witnesses in 1951, almost all of them well-known figures) people who had past Communist affiliations were compelled not only to testify about their own activities but also to name names of others who had also participated. Those who avoided cooperating with the committee often invoked the protection against self-incrimination offered by the Fifth Amendment to the U.S. Constitution. Labeled "Fifth-Amendment Communists" by McCarthy and others on the right, they typically suffered blacklisting. Testimony from cooperative, friendly witnesses produced names of literally hundreds of individuals alleged to have had past Communist affiliations (see chapter 9).

March 5, 1953: Stalin dies. Georgi Malenkov succeeded Stalin as premier until 1955 and briefly succeeded Stalin as party secretary before Nikita Khrushchev assumed that post in September 1953.

April 3–21, 1953: Roy Cohn and David Schine, aides of Senator McCarthy, take a highly publicized 17-day, 7-country tour of the State Department's European libraries, which they claim house some 30,000 books by pro–Communist writers. They removed and in some cases burned books by about 40 authors. The works of 20 other authors who had not been forthright in Senate hearings were banned, "pending further examination" (see chapter 9).

May 31, 1953: Secretary of State John Foster Dulles warns of a possible domino effect if the Communist-led Vietminh drive the French from Indochina. The domino theory, which held that the fall of one Southeast Asian country to Communism would trigger the fall of its neighbors, later became the primary justification for the Vietnam War.

June 17–July 12, 1953: Anti-Soviet uprisings in East Berlin nearly topple the East German Communist government. Martial law squelched the workers' rebellion.

June 19, 1953: Ethel and Julius Rosenberg are executed for their alleged role in an atomic spy ring. This was the first time U.S. civilians ever received the death penalty for espionage. Their widely reported deaths were both actively protested and heartily cheered.

July 27, 1953: An armistice concludes the hostilities in Korea but does not resolve the conflict or provide a mutually agreeable peace treaty. The country was partitioned at the thirty-eighth parallel, where it had been partitioned before the fighting. The war took some 2 million lives, including those of 33,629 U.S. soldiers (see chapter 10).

August 14, 1953: The Soviet Union announces that it has exploded its first thermonuclear device.

September 12, 1953: Nikita Khrushchev is named head of the Soviet Communist Party and thereby becomes the new Soviet leader.

October 13, 1953: Senator McCarthy opens hearings to investigate allegations that the U.S. Army knowingly harbored Communists at Fort Monmouth, New Jersey.

October 14, 1953: Eisenhower orders the immediate firing of any federal employee who invokes the Fifth Amendment before a congressional committee.

III. Massive Retaliation, Second Strike, and Flexible Response (1954–69)

January 11, 1954: Secretary of State Dulles announces that the U.S. defense policy is now based on instant and massive retaliation against any aggressor. The use of nuclear weapons was implied in the phrase "massive retaliation."

January 25–February 18, 1954: The Berlin Conference of Foreign Ministers meets. Representatives from the United States, Soviet Union, France, and Great Britain met to discuss German reunification. However, the attempt failed when the Soviets rejected British foreign secretary Anthony Eden's plan to hold national elections throughout the country and subsequently form a new German government. The Eden plan was the last significant attempt to reunite Germany prior to the end of the Cold War. On March 26 the Soviets recognized East Germany as a separate, sovereign state, and in 1955 they and the Western powers recognized West Germany.

March 1, 1954: Radioactive debris from nuclear testing on the Pacific Bikini atoll inadvertently falls on a Japanese fishing boat, causing radiation sickness among members of the crew, creating panic in Japan, and provoking an international incident. In 1955 the United States paid Japan $2 million in damages.

March 8, 1954: Japan and the United States sign a mutual defense agreement.

March 9, 1954: Edward R. Murrow airs "A Report on Senator Joseph R. McCarthy" on his television show, "See It Now." Primarily a collection of film clips showing the senator contradicting himself and making inaccurate statements and accusations, the show represented the first time that network television directly addressed McCarthy's reckless demagoguery. The following week the senator received free air time to respond. However, rather than address the contents of Murrow's show, McCarthy attacked the broadcaster personally, calling him a Communist and "the leader and the cleverest of the jackal pack which is always at the throat of anyone who dares expose individual Communists or traitors." Murrow's report on Senator McCarthy has since come to be regarded as one of the high points in television journalism.

March 26, 1954: The Soviet Union recognizes East Germany as a sovereign nation. The United States did not formally recognize East Germany until 1974, though the United Nations admitted it in 1973. Soviet recognition implied that the USSR had given up on creating a unified Germany that would fall under Soviet dominance.

April 22–June 17, 1954: The nationally televised Army-McCarthy hearings investigate charges that Senator Joseph McCarthy had tried to blackmail the Army into commissioning David Schine, one of his aides who had been drafted recently. Allegedly, McCarthy had threatened to conduct additional hearings investigating Communist infiltration of the Army if Schine was not commissioned. The hearings were notable because for the first time since his rise to power in 1950, McCarthy was effectively challenged and placed on the defensive. Though the Republican-dominated subcommittee ultimately exonerated McCarthy of the charges, McCarthy's outrageous performance at the investigation led directly to his debilitating censure by the Senate on December 2. The hearings were also significant because they were among the earliest congressional deliberations to receive live television coverage. (The 1950 investigation of organized crime by Senator Estes Kefauver's special committee was the first.)

May 7, 1954: The Communist-led Vietminh defeat the French Army at Dien Bien Phu, causing the French to pull out of the country. The July 20 Geneva peace agreement between France and the Vietminh called for the temporary creation of a North and South Vietnam, which were to be unified within two years through national elections and the withdrawal of Vietminh forces from South Vietnam. However, the United States and South Vietnam refused to sign the accords and the elections were never held.

June 1, 1954: J. Robert Oppenheimer loses his security clearance at the Atomic Energy Commission (AEC) despite a finding that he had been loyal in handling U.S. secrets. The AEC denied his appeal on June 29 because of alleged "fundamental defects" in his character. In 1963 Oppenheimer was "rehabilitated" when President Johnson presented him with the Fermi Award.

June 18, 1954: The CIA covertly aids a military coup in Guatemala to replace the reform government of Jacobo Arbenz Guzmán that had been becoming increasingly open to Communist influence. The United States recognized the new military government on July 13.

August 17, 1954: Eisenhower declares U.S. intentions to stop any invasion of Taiwan by Communist China. This announcement followed the sinking by the Nationalist Chinese of eight Communist gunboats off Taiwan. On September 5 the Communists attacked Quemoy, a nearby island. And on December 1 the United States and Nationalist Chinese signed a mutual security pact.

August 24, 1954: The Communist Control Act strengthens the 1950 McCarran Internal Security Act by providing severe penalties for Communist and Communist-dominated organizations that refuse to register the names of their members and supporters with the federal government. The Communist Control Act revoked the rights to collective bargaining of Communist-dominated unions, and it stripped away the "rights, privileges, and immunities" of the Communist Party as a legal organization. On August 27 Congress outlawed the Communist Party in the United States, and on September 3 Congress passed legislation revoking the U.S. citizenship of anyone convicted of conspiracy to overthrow the government by force. The Smith Act had been used to convict Communist leaders because they endorsed the teachings of Lenin, who preached the necessity of violently overthrowing governments. At this time many individual states also passed "little Smith acts," which required loyalty oaths of state employees and denied Communist candidates a place on election ballots.

September 8, 1954: The United States, Great Britain, Australia, France, New Zealand, Pakistan, the Philippines, and Thailand form the Southeast Asia Treaty Organization (SEATO) to oppose further Communist gains in Southeast Asia.

October 8, 1954: Communist-led Vietminh soldiers occupy Hanoi as the French evacuate the city in accordance with the Geneva peace agreement. Ho Chi Minh's North Vietnamese government soon introduced major land reforms, and starting in December 1955 landlords were made to stand trial before "people's tribunals."

January 28, 1955: Congress passes the Formosa Doctrine, granting the president emergency powers to protect Taiwan against a seemingly imminent Communist invasion.

February 8, 1955: Khrushchev removes Malenkov and appoints Nikolai Bulganin as Soviet premier.

February 24, 1955: Turkey and Iraq sign the Baghdad Pact, providing mutual security against Soviet expansion into Middle Eastern oil-producing regions. Pakistan, Iran, and Great Britain also joined the pact.

May 5, 1955: West Germany becomes a sovereign state and Eisenhower concludes the U.S. occupation. West Germany joined NATO shortly thereafter and received recognition by the USSR.

May 14, 1955: The Warsaw Pact for military defense is signed by Albania, Bulgaria, Czechoslovakia, East Germany, Poland, Hungary, Romania, and the USSR in response to the remilitarization of West Germany and in opposition to the NATO alliance. East Germany was remilitarized in 1956, although Soviet troops remained in East Germany.

July 1, 1955: The United States gives $216 million in aid to South Vietnam.

July 18, 1955: The first Geneva summit conference is held among leaders of the United States, the Soviet Union, France, and Great Britain. The stated aim of the conference was to reduce Cold War tensions, but a subsequent conference that fall failed to implement the directives from this summit.

October 23, 1955: A referendum in South Vietnam deposes Bao Dai and establishes the Republic of South Vietnam under the leadership of Ngo Dinh Diem.

February 1, 1956: Eisenhower and British prime minister Eden issue the Declaration of Washington, which warns Africans and Asians against seeking political or economic aid from the Soviet Union.

February 14, 1956: At the twentieth Congress of the Soviet Communist Party Khrushchev denounces the personality cult of Stalin and inaugurates de–Stalinization, bringing about a number of reforms.

March 28, 1956: The Internal Revenue Service seizes the Communist Party headquarters in several cities citing nonpayment of income taxes. When the party paid back taxes of $1,500 a week later the properties were returned.

April 18, 1956: The first steps are taken to establish an international atoms-for-peace agency in a 12-nation agreement that includes both the United States and Soviet Union.

April 26, 1956: For the first time since the beginning of the Cold War the United States eases restriction on trade with the Soviet Union and Eastern Europe.

May 21, 1956: The United States explodes the first airborne hydrogen bomb, demonstrating that it has the capacity to deliver a hydrogen bomb against an enemy.

June 28, 1956: The largest anti–Communist uprising since 1953 takes place in Poland when workers riot at an industrial fair in Poznań. In November Poland and the Soviet Union signed an agreement allowing Poland greater economic and political freedom but retaining Soviet troops on Polish soil.

July 19, 1956: The United States and Great Britain refuse to finance Egypt's proposed Aswan Dam project because of Egypt's ties with the Soviet Union.

July 20, 1956: A nationwide Operation Alert tests how federal agencies would react during a simulated atomic attack.

July 26, 1956: Gamal Nasser nationalizes the British-owned Suez Canal, proposing to use revenues from the canal to finance the Aswan Dam. Nasser also denied Israeli ships passage through the canal. He expelled British oil and embassy officials in August and increased border raids against Israeli territory.

August 16, 1956: Protestors in England stage a march against nuclear arms and the dangers of radiation.

October 23, 1956: A popular, anti–Communist Hungarian Revolution briefly overthrows the Communist government in Budapest and installs a neutral government that appeals to the United States for aid. Respecting the Soviet sphere of influence, the United States declined the appeal. On October 31 the Soviets installed Imre Nagy as the new Hungarian premier and János Kádár as first secretary. However, after Nagy declared that Hungary would leave the

Warsaw Pact and seek neutral status, Khrushchev crushed the revolution by sending tanks and troops into Budapest on November 4. Nagy and several other prominent figures were executed, and several hundred thousand Hungarian refugees fled to the West. On November 29 the United States offered political asylum to Hungarian freedom fighters, and on December 12 the United Nations voted to censure the Soviet action by a vote of 55–8.

October 29, 1956: Preempting an anticipated Egyptian attack, Israel invades Egypt and precipitates the Suez Crisis. Israel was joined shortly after by Great Britain and France, who were intent on retaking the Suez Canal that Egypt had nationalized in July. However, the United States did not support this effort. Eisenhower was angered because the allies had failed to consult with him before invading. But when the Soviets threatened a missile attack against France and England, Eisenhower declared that such an attack would provoke a U.S. nuclear response and lead to global war. A UN armistice defused the crisis, arranging for the withdrawal of all British and French troops and leaving the United States as the sole superpower in the region. The Suez Crisis also brought about further deterioration of the U.S.-French alliance.

On November 7 the United Nations achieved an armistice, replacing the British and French troops. Egypt agreed to repay the shareholders of the canal but continued to deny Israel passage. However, sunken ships and destroyed bridges kept the canal closed until March 1957.

November 6, 1956: Eisenhower defeats Adlai Stevenson again, but Democrats win a majority in both houses of Congress.

December 2, 1956: Fidel Castro lands in Cuba with a group of 82 exiles, intent on overthrowing the military regime of Fulgencio Batista. Most of the group were killed or captured, but the survivors formed the nucleus for Castro's successful revolution two years later.

December 18, 1956: Japan is admitted to the United Nations.

February 15, 1957: Hard-liner Andrei Gromyko is appointed Soviet foreign minister.

March 9, 1957: Congress approves the Eisenhower Doctrine, which announces U.S. willingness to send military and economic aid to any Middle Eastern country requesting U.S. assistance against Communism.

April 22, 1957: The U.S. Army Air Defense Command announces that New York and other major cities will soon be protected by missiles armed with nuclear warheads.

May 15, 1957: Great Britain explodes its first hydrogen bomb in the Christmas Islands. Despite earlier Soviet appeals to halt nuclear testing, the United States and Great Britain continued to test in May, June, September, and October in Australia.

June 3, 1957: The United States joins the Baghdad Pact and affirms its willingness to assist member nations in their fight to limit Communist expansion in the Middle East.

July 4, 1957: Khrushchev suppresses an internal challenge to his leadership and expels three ranking members of the Soviet Communist Party's Central Committee: Malenkov, Molotov, and Kaganovich.

August 7, 1957: Rudolf Abel is indicted spying for the Soviets. He was convicted on October 26. In 1962 the United States exchanged him for Gary Francis Powers, the U-2 reconnaissance pilot who was shot down while flying over Soviet airspace in 1960.

August 26, 1957: The USSR announces it has successfully tested an intercontinental ballistic missile (ICBM). For the first time in the Cold War the Soviet Union had the capacity to attack the United States with missiles. Because it had land-based missiles in Europe, the United States had long been able to strike the Soviet Union. The new Soviet missile capacity had the immediate effect of rendering the U.S. massive-retaliation policy problematic and creating a mistaken impression of Soviet missile superiority.

September 5, 1957: Castro leads an uprising in Cuba that Batista suppresses. Among those in the rebellion were members of the Cuban military. On October 29 Batista suspended the constitution.

October 1957: Under direction from North Vietnam, Communist insurgents in South Vietnam begin their campaign to overthrow the South Vietnamese government.

October 4, 1957: The Soviets launch Sputnik I, the first human-made satellite to orbit the earth. On November 3 they launched Sputnik II which housed Laika, the first dog in space. The Sputnik launches created a demand for advancing the U.S. space program and improving science education in American schools.

December 16–19, 1957: NATO heads of state agree to establish a European-based nuclear missile force under U.S. command.

1958–59: Cold War and Red Scare tensions abate somewhat as the United States and USSR issue voluntary moratoriums on nuclear testing, make travel easier, create cooperative arrangements within the cultural, educational, technical, sports, and scientific fields, and make various limited gestures of conciliation. In 1959 Khrushchev visited and was warmly received in the United States. But the Cold War confrontation never completely vanished. In 1958 Khrushchev initiated the Second Berlin Crisis. That year an unarmed U.S. transport plane was shot down over Soviet airspace. However, the Soviets complied with U.S. demands that the nine Americans aboard be freed. On the domestic front the Supreme Court struck down some of the most severe Red Scare legislation from earlier in the decade.

1958–62: A serious rift develops between China and the Soviet Union.

January 1, 1958: The Treaty of Rome creates the European Economic Community, commonly called the Common Market, among France, West Germany, Italy, Belgium, the Netherlands, and Luxembourg. The Common Market reduced tariffs and promoted free trade among these nations.

January 13, 1958: Some 9,000 scientists from 43 countries present a petition to the United Nations calling for an immediate international agreement to halt nuclear testing.

January 20, 1958: The Soviet Union warns the Baghdad Pact countries against introducing nuclear weapons and missile bases into their territories.

February 17, 1958: Organizers form the Campaign for Nuclear Disarmament (CND) in Great Britain. For the next six years this was a significant political force with its advocacy of unilateral nuclear disarmament.

February 22, 1958: The United States agrees to supply Great Britain with intermediate-range ballistic missiles capable of reaching the USSR.

March 27, 1958: Khrushchev replaces Bulganin as Soviet premier, while retaining his post as first secretary of the Communist Party. The Soviet Union thus returned to one-man rule for the first time since Stalin's death in 1953.

April 5, 1958: Castro declares total war against the Batista regime.

May 1958: While on a goodwill tour of South America Vice President Nixon is attacked by demonstrators in Peru and Venezuela. In response Eisenhower placed soldiers in the Caribbean on a stand-by alert to protect the vice president.

July 15, 1958: Under the Eisenhower Doctrine U.S. Marines go to Lebanon to support the presidency of Camille Chamoun, whose pro–West policies had sparked rebellion in Beirut and Tripoli. Following a UN resolution and the succession of General Fouad Chehab to the Lebanese presidency, the Marines departed on August 13.

August 23, 1958: Communist China begins bombarding Quemoy and Matsu, contested islands off of Taiwan. In response on August 27 the United States dispatched an aircraft carrier and four destroyers to defend them, and on September 7 the U.S. Navy escorted Nationalist Chinese ships carrying weapons to fortify the islands. On September 11 Eisenhower declared the U.S. determination to defend Quemoy and Matsu by force if necessary. The Communists resumed shelling on October 20, but the situation died down over the next few months. The degree to which the United States would be willing to defend these islands later became an issue in the 1960 Nixon-Kennedy presidential debates.

November 4, 1958: The United States, Soviet Union, and Great Britain agree to a voluntary moratorium on nuclear testing.

November 27, 1958: Khrushchev initiates a Second Berlin Crisis by demanding that Western troops evacuate West Berlin and leave it as a demilitarized free city. NATO rejected this demand on December 16 and a tense four-year U.S.-USSR stand-off began (see chapter 11).

December 17, 1958: Due to the failure of his economic programs in the Great Leap Forward, Mao Zedong steps down as China's head of state. Moderate reformer Liu Shaoqi succeeded him.

December 31, 1958: After losing a series of battles to Castro, Batista flees from Cuba on New Year's Eve.

January 1, 1959: Castro enters Havana and takes control of the Cuban government, establishing his own totalitarian regime. He officially became premier of Cuba on February 2, and in April he took an 11-day tour of the United States and Canada. Initially perceived by many Americans as a liberator overthrowing a corrupt dictatorship, Castro alienated U.S. sympathies by consolidating military power, conducting wholesale arrests, executing Batista supporters, collectivizing agriculture, expropriating the holdings of all native and foreign industries, and promoting close ties with Communist countries. In 1961 he openly declared himself a Marxist-Leninist and denounced U.S. imperialism. His rise to power spawned an exodus of middle- and upper-class Cubans to the United States in the early 1960s and led to the creation of a Cuban enclave in Miami.

January 27–28, 1959: The Soviet Communist Party denounces the revisionist movement led by Yugoslavia's Marshal Tito.

March 13–27, 1959: China crushes a rebellion in Tibet and forces the Dalai Lama to flee to India, where he receives political asylum.

March 14, 1959: By refusing to put 33 percent of France's Navy under NATO command, president De Gaulle begins the gradual French withdrawal from NATO. The United States transferred 200 aircraft from France to bases in West Germany and Great Britain.

May 11–August 5, 1959: At the Foreign Ministers' Conference in Geneva representatives from the United States, the Soviet Union, France, and Great Britain fail to produce a mutually acceptable plan for German reunification.

July 21, 1959: The U.S. National Academy of Sciences and its Soviet counterpart agree to exchange information and organize joint forums for scientists of both nations.

July 23, 1959: Vice President Nixon opens the American National Exhibition in Moscow. He and Khrushchev held their "Kitchen Debate," when they argued about the relative merits of Communist and capitalist economies.

August 4, 1959: Laos declares a state of emergency after the Pathet Lao launches a campaign to win back northern provinces they had lost two years earlier. The Pathet Lao was a Communist guerrilla movement backed by China and North Vietnam. Eisenhower gave economic aid but refused to send military assistance, hoping instead that the United Nations could resolve the situation.

August 21, 1959: The Baghdad Pact changes its name to the Central Treaty Organization (CENTO) and expresses concern over Communist sympathies in Iran.

September 15, 1959: Khrushchev visits the United States in a moment of lessening tensions over the Berlin crisis. In addition to conferring with Eisenhower on September 25 — when they claimed to reach new understandings on Berlin and other problem areas — Khrushchev also visited and was warmly received in several U.S. cities.

December 12, 1959: The United Nations adopts a resolution drafted by the United States and Soviet Union promoting the peaceful use of outer space.

December 19, 1959: At a meeting in Paris the Western leaders agree to invite Khrushchev to attend a summit conference in April 1960 in hopes of defusing the Berlin situation.

January 6, 1960: Cuba expropriates property belonging to the Manati Sugar Company, a U.S.-owned corporation. In response the State Department terminated aid to Cuba on May 27.

January 14, 1960: The Soviets reduce their armed forces by about 33 percent, down 1,200,000 troops from the previous 3,623,000.

February 13, 1960: France explodes its first nuclear device, despite objections from the United States and the United Nations.

March 15–16, 1960: Syngman Rhee wins reelection in South Korea. However, after massive protests that the elections were dishonest, Rhee declared martial law on April 18. Subsequently, police killed 30 protestors. After a week of rioting Rhee resigned on April 27 and went into exile. He was temporarily replaced by Chang Myun (Dr. John M. Chang) who formed a Second Republic of Korea. In May 1961 General Park Chung Hee deposed Chang in a bloodless coup.

May 5, 1960: Soviets shoot down an American U-2 spy plane flying over Soviet airspace and capture the pilot alive on May 5. (In 1962 they exchanged the pilot, Gary Francis Powers, for convicted Soviet spy Rudolf Abel.) In response to the U-2 spy flight Khrushchev scuttled a Paris summit meeting with Great Britain, France, and the United States scheduled for May 14.

May 8, 1960: Cuba and the Soviet Union renew diplomatic ties.

May 8, 1960: Leonid Brezhnev becomes president of the Soviet Union.

May 14, 1960: A Paris summit conference among leaders from the United States, Great Britain, France, and the Soviet Union collapses after only three hours. The summit had been called to address the growing Berlin crisis but instead of subsiding, tensions over Berlin intensified. Khrushchev walked out on the meeting as a protest to American aerial spying over the Soviet Union, which became irrefutable after the Soviets shot down a U.S. U-2 reconnaissance plane in their airspace on May 5. Some historians believe Khrushchev was under pressure from hard-liners at home not to make concessions to the Western allies and that he used the U-2 incident as an excuse for canceling the summit.

May 26, 1960: Mass demonstrations in Tokyo protest the 10-year extension of a U.S.-Japanese security treaty signed in January.

June 30, 1960: After Belgian rule in the Congo collapses, the Republic of the Congo is declared with Patrice Lumumba as premier and Joseph Kasavubu as president. However, on July 6 the Army mutinied against Lumumba and on July 11 the province of Katanga declared its independence under the leadership of Moise Tshombe.

July 12, 1960: Khrushchev declares his willingness to support any Cuban effort to expel the United States from its naval base in Guantánamo Bay. On November 1 Eisenhower declared his intention to defend the base.

August 7, 1960: Castro nationalizes all U.S.-owned property in Cuba in retaliation for "U.S. economic aggression." In response the United States imposed a trade embargo against Cuba on October 19, and it recalled its ambassador the next day.

September 8, 1960: East Germany impedes access to East Berlin by requiring entry permits for West Berliners.

November 9, 1960: Democrat John Kennedy defeats Republican Vice President Nixon to become the youngest man ever elected U.S. president. This was the closest presidential race in 76 years, as Kennedy won by about 120,000 votes out of some 68 million cast. Kennedy's election signaled an abatement of the Red Scare.

November 17–December 7, 1960: Eisenhower orders a special naval patrol in the Caribbean to prevent a Communist takeover in Guatemala or Nicaragua.

December 20, 1960: North Vietnam forms the National Liberation Front (NLF) in South Vietnam to prosecute the war for national unification. Anti-Communist South Vietnamese derisively called the NLF "Vietcong."

January 3, 1961: The United States cuts diplomatic ties with Cuba.

January 25, 1961: A bloodless coup in El Salvador overthrows a left-leaning junta.

April 12, 1961: Soviet cosmonaut Yuri Gagarin becomes the first human to orbit the earth.

April 17, 1961: Kennedy approves Cuban expatriates' Bay of Pigs invasion that the CIA had planned and prepared for during the Eisenhower administration. But the invasion devolved into a fiasco in which most of the 1,500 liberating expatriates were killed or captured and imprisoned. In a controversial decision while the fighting was in progress, Kennedy canceled a second CIA air strike after deciding the mission was doomed. On April 20 Castro announced "total victory." A subsequent panel failed to agree whether the invasion plan ever had a serious chance for success. Not only was the invasion a military failure, but it lent credibility to Castro's claims of U.S. imperialism and U.S. intentions to overthrow him by invasion. The Bay of Pigs debacle also contributed significantly to the strong disaffection that Cuban-Americans in the Miami enclave felt for the Democratic Party throughout the entire Cold War. In December 1962 Castro released 1,113 of the captured invaders in exchange for food and medicine raised by private donations within the United States.

May 5, 1961: U.S. astronaut Alan Shepard becomes the first American to be launched into space, though John Glenn was the first American to orbit the earth (February 20, 1962).

June 3, 1961: Kennedy and Khrushchev meet to discuss the Berlin Crisis. Khrushchev personally delivered an ultimatum to Kennedy, insisting that the allies evacuate Berlin within six months or risk nuclear war. In response each side initiated military moves to intimidate the other. The crisis intensified throughout the summer and early fall (see chapter 11).

July 12, 1961: The United States launches its Midas III satellite, which assumes a near-polar orbit in order to detect Soviet missile launches with infrared radiation detection devices. The satellite made it possible for the CIA to conclude that no "missile gap" existed between the Soviets and United States.

August 17–18, 1961: The East German government builds the Berlin Wall to stem the flow of emigrants to West Berlin. In early August more than 2,000 people left in a single day. Fearful that this emigration would topple the East German regime, Khrushchev literally made Churchill's iron curtain metaphor concrete by closing the border between East and West Berlin on August 13 and then ordering the Berlin Wall to be erected. The wall became the most forceful symbol of the Cold War.

August 31, 1961: Ending a voluntary moratorium that had lasted since 1958, the Soviets resume nuclear testing as the Berlin crisis further intensifies. They exploded a 60 megaton device: the largest ever tested to that date. In response Kennedy resumed U.S. underground nuclear tests that did not issue radioactive fallout. However, in the spring of 1962 Kennedy authorized the resumption of nuclear testing in the atmosphere.

October 17, 1961: After U.S. and Soviet tanks face each other across Checkpoint Charlie, a crossing point at the Berlin Wall, the Second Berlin crisis abates when Khrushchev announces, "the Western powers were showing some understanding of the situation and were inclined to seek a solution to the German problem and West Berlin." He subsequently eased off from his ultimatum for the Western evacuation of Berlin by December 31 without actually renouncing his demands.

December 9, 1961: The Soviet Union breaks off relations with Albania.

December 11, 1961: Kennedy increases U.S. military support to South Vietnam by sending as military advisers 2 helicopter companies with 400 soldiers.

April 25, 1962: The United States resumes above-ground nuclear testing in response to over 50 Soviet tests during the fall of 1961.

May 6, 1962: Parts of Laos fall to the Communist Pathet Lao, prompting the United States to send forces to Thailand to prevent a complete takeover of the country. A July 23 Geneva peace agreement established a coalition government in Laos and officially ended a civil war dating from 1959 between the pro-U.S. Laotian Army and North Vietnamese–backed Pathet Lao guerrillas. However, the fighting resumed in 1963 and continued periodically until the Pathet Lao's final victory in 1975.

June 16, 1962: Secretary of Defense McNamara announces that the United States is replacing its strategy of massive retaliation with one of "flexible response."

June 27, 1962: Kennedy declares that the United States would respond to a Communist Chinese assault on the islands Quemoy and Matsu that surround Taiwan.

September 2, 1962: The Soviet Union agrees to deliver weapons to Cuba to help it defend itself from "threats from aggressive imperialist elements."

September 24, 1962: Relations between Yugoslavia and the USSR improve as President Brezhnev visits Yugoslavia. In December Tito visited Moscow.

October 14–28, 1962: The Cold War reaches its high point as the United States and USSR nearly initiate all-out nuclear warfare during the Cuban Missile crisis (see chapter 12).

December 18–21, 1961: The United States and Great Britain agree to arm Britain with U.S. Polaris nuclear missiles.

1962–64: Mao Zedong reenters Chinese politics as head of the Socialist Campaign Movement whose mission is to lead the country back to the true path of Communism. He allied with the minister of defense and prepared to move against his domestic rivals who advocated economic reforms. He also attacked Khrushchev's more liberal policies, accusing him of "revisionism" and chiding him for backing down in Berlin and Cuba.

January 22, 1963: France and West Germany sign a pact pledging cooperation on foreign policy, defense, and cultural matters.

June 26, 1963: Kennedy is greeted by cheering crowds during a visit to Berlin where he proclaims that he, too, is a Berliner.

August 5, 1963: The United States, Great Britain, and USSR sign a nuclear test ban treaty forbidding atmospheric (above-ground) testing of nuclear devices. Such testing had, during the past 18 years, been sending clouds of radioactive dust around the world with increasing frequency. Kennedy considered this treaty to be the greatest achievement of his presidency.

August 30, 1963: The United States and USSR establish a hot-line communications link to avert accidental war.

October 15, 1963: After serving as West German chancellor since the country's inception in 1949, Konrad Adenauer resigns. Ludwig Erhard succeeded him.

November 1–2, 1963: The United States tacitly supports the overthrow and assassination of the corrupt South Vietnamese ruler, Ngo Dinh Diem and endorses a government led by the coup that usurped him.

November 22, 1963: Lee Harvey Oswald, acting alone or in collaboration with others, assassinates President Kennedy in Dallas. Vice President Lyndon Johnson assumed the presidency.

December 1963: The number of U.S. military advisers in South Vietnam has risen from 685 at the beginning of 1962 to about 16,000.

January 20, 1964: The United States and USSR agree to reduce their production of enriched uranium and plutonium over the next few years.

January 27, 1964: France establishes diplomatic relations with Communist China. Soon afterward Nationalist China breaks off its relations with France.

January 30, 1964: A military coup replaces the South Vietnamese government. General Nguyen Khanh emerged as leader.

June 3, 1964: President Park Chung Hee imposes martial law in South Korea following riots protesting his repressive rule.

August 7, 1964: Congress, in response to one authentic and one dubious attack by North Vietnamese gunboats on a U.S. destroyer in the Tonkin Gulf, passes the Tonkin Gulf Resolution voting nearly unanimously to authorize Johnson to commit U.S. forces to defend any nation in Southeast Asia against Communist aggression or subversion.

October 15, 1964: A coup engineered by Leonid Brezhnev and other conservatives removes Khrushchev from power. Brezhnev emerged as Communist Party leader and the chief figure in Soviet politics until his death in November 1982. Aleksei Kosygin became Soviet premier.

October 16, 1964: China explodes its first atomic bomb and then calls for an international summit to ban nuclear weapons and destroy nuclear stockpiles.

November 3, 1964: Johnson defeats Republican Barry Goldwater for the presidency in a landslide victory.

January 4, 1965: In his State of the Union address Johnson encourages trade with Eastern Europe.

January 27, 1965: South Vietnamese military leaders withdraw their support from the government and seize power. After a brief provisional government Nguyen Cao Ky becomes premier of the military regime on June 19.

February 7, 1965: In South Vietnam the Communist Vietcong attack an American transport and observation installation, killing 8 and wounding over 100 American advisers. Within hours, Johnson authorized Operation Flaming Dart: U.S. air raids against a North Vietnamese Army camp 60 miles north of the dividing line between North and South Vietnam. In March Johnson sent in 2 marine battalions to defend Da Nang airfield: the first U.S. combat troops in Vietnam.

April 28, 1965: Johnson sends 20,000 Marines into the Dominican Republic after a pro–Communist coup topples the civilian government. On May 29 peace-keeping soldiers from the Organization of American States (OAS) replaced many of the U.S. troops, whose number had peaked at 30,000. Negotiations in June led to elections in June 1966, which finally ended the crisis. The American-backed candidate, Joaquín Balaguer, won.

July 28, 1965: Johnson orders an immediate buildup of U.S. forces in Vietnam from 75,000 to 125,000 and announces that the call for the military draft will be doubled.

September 2, 1965: Mao Zedong launches the Cultural Revolution in China, purging his enemies in a brutal four-year state of emergency, the first phase of which lasts until 1969.

September 20, 1965: The U.S. House of Representatives approves the use of force by any American nation to prevent a Communist takeover.

October 18–21, 1965: Massive anti–Vietnam War demonstrations are held in the United States.

February 21, 1966: De Gaulle calls for the dissolution of NATO. On March 10 he announced France's intention to withdraw its forces from the integrated NATO military command and ordered all U.S. and NATO troops from French soil. On July 1 France withdrew all of its NATO troops, and NATO headquarters moved to Brussels. Nonetheless, De Gaulle proclaimed his willingness to adhere to the NATO mutual defense pact in the event of an unprovoked attack against alliance members.

March 11, 1966: Following weeks of anti–Communist demonstrations, Indonesian president Sukarno assigns political powers to the Army, though he nominally retains the title of president. The next day Indonesia banned the Communist Party.

March 26, 1966: Rallies against the Vietnam War are held in the United States and throughout the world on the International Day of Protest.

April 10, 1966: South Vietnamese Buddhist leaders declare war on the military government of South Vietnam.

June 29, 1966: For the first time U.S. planes bomb North Vietnam's two major cities, Hanoi and Haiphong. Great Britain disassociated itself from the bombing of civilian centers.

January 1, 1967: The number of U.S. troops in South Vietnam reaches 380,000.

January 10, 1967: Johnson introduces a 6 percent surcharge on taxable income to pay for the Vietnam War. On August 3 he raised it to 10 percent.

February 22, 1967: Indonesian President Sukarno surrenders all of his remaining powers to the military. On March 12 General Suharto became acting president.

April 1, 1967: Under intense U.S. pressure to hold democratic elections, South Vietnam forms a new constitution. It held elections in the fall.

April 15, 1967: Over 100,000 demonstrators protest the Vietnam War before the UN headquarters in New York.

June 5–10, 1967: Israel wins the Six-Day War against Egypt, Jordan, and Syria. It occupied the Gaza Strip, the Sinai Peninsula of Egypt, and Syria's Golan Heights, and took the West Bank and Arab sector of Jerusalem from Jordan. It later annexed the old city of Jerusalem.

On November 22 a UN resolution called for Israel to withdraw from the territories it had occupied. The resolution also declared the right of all states to live in peace within secure and recognized boundaries and to enjoy freedom of navigation through international waterways (an Egyptian blockade of an Israeli port was one of the major causes of the war). The United Nations also called for a resolution to the Arab refugee problem (that is, the Palestinians).

Arab leaders meeting earlier in Khartoum had adopted a policy of no peace, no negotiations, and no recognition of the state of Israel, thereby rejecting Israeli calls for direct peace negotiations, secure and recognized boundaries, and the right of passage through the Red Sea and Suez Canal.

One outcome of the war was that the Arab states turned increasingly to the Soviet Union for support and rearmament, and Israel became more closely aligned with the United States.

June 17, 1967: China explodes its first hydrogen bomb.

October 8, 1967: Argentinean-born Cuban revolutionary Che Guevara is killed following his capture by the Bolivian Army.

January 4, 1968: Some 486,000 U.S. troops are now in Vietnam.

January 5, 1968: Reformer Alexander Dubček becomes first secretary of the Czechoslovakian Communist Party.

January 21, 1968: North Korean raiders attack Seoul and attempt to kill South Korean President Park. On January 30 the United States promised to increase military assistance to South Korea.

January 23, 1968: The U.S. intelligence ship SS *Pueblo* is captured by North Koreans after it strays within North Korean territorial waters. One U.S. crewman was killed and 3 were injured when the ship was seized and its captain and crew of 81 men were captured. The incident led Johnson to call up 14,000 Navy and Air Force reserves in order to reinforce the U.S. military presence in Korea without decreasing troop strength in Vietnam, and the incident led to renewed tensions between the United States and North Korea during 1968. Some believe the North Koreans coordinated the incident with Vietnamese Communists who were preparing the Tet Offensive for the following week. They suggest that the North Vietnamese were hoping to siphon off U.S. troops to Korea just prior to their offensive. The crew of the *Pueblo* was released in December after the United States simultaneously admitted and denied responsibility for the incident. The ship was never returned.

January 31, 1968: The North Vietnamese Army and Vietcong partisans initiate the Tet Offensive during a cease-fire for the Tet holiday, temporarily capturing Hue and other South Vietnamese cities and towns, and even briefly occupying the U.S. embassy in Saigon. Television coverage of the Tet Offensive did much to undermine public confidence in government claims that the United States and South Vietnam were winning the war and that there was a "light at the end of the tunnel." Consequently, a growing "credibility gap" developed between what the government claimed and what the public believed.

March 16, 1968: American soldiers under the command of Lt. William Calley kill some 347 unarmed South Vietnamese men, women, and children in the My Lai massacre. The American public did not learn of this for over a year. Calley was court-martialled and found guilty, but his conviction was later overturned.

April 4, 1968: Civil rights leader Martin Luther King is assassinated in Memphis, Tennessee. FBI Director Hoover had accused King of Communist affiliations.

April 5, 1968: Czechoslovakia's First Secretary Dubček introduces his Action Program that brings freedom of the press and allows for minority views to be expressed within the Communist Party. These reforms introduced a brief period of relative political and artistic freedom known as the Prague Spring.

May 13, 1968: The United States and North Vietnam initiate peace talks in Paris.

June 5, 1968: Senator Robert Kennedy, the brother of the late President John Kennedy, is assassinated after winning the Democratic presidential primary in California.

June 11, 1968: East Germany announces that West Germans will need visas to cross East Germany in order to enter West Berlin and that West Berliners will need visas to cross into West Germany. The Western powers protested.

June 27, 1968: Czech intellectuals appeal to quicken the pace of democratization.

July 1, 1968: Sixty-two nations, including the United States, Great Britain, and the Soviet Union, sign a nuclear nonproliferation treaty.

July 15, 1968: Czech military leaders demand equality with the Soviet Union within the Warsaw Pact, but the next day they are rebuffed by a joint letter from the USSR, East Germany, Hungary, Bulgaria, and Poland. On July 18, however, Yugoslavia expressed its full support for Czech liberalization.

August 16, 1968: Czechoslovakia and Romania sign a 20-year friendship treaty.

August 20–21, 1968: The Soviet Union, East Germany, Poland, Bulgaria, and Hungary send troops and tanks into Czechoslovakia to crush Dubček's liberal government. Dubček and other leaders were arrested. On August 24 the Soviet Union vetoed a resolution by the UN Security Council condemning the invasion. On October 4 the new Czech leaders agreed to dismantle Dubček's liberal programs and allow Warsaw Pact troops to be stationed indefinitely in Czechoslovakia. In November Brezhnev issued the Brezhnev Doctrine to justify the invasion.

August 25, 1968: France explodes its first hydrogen bomb.

September 12, 1968: Albania formally withdraws from the Warsaw Pact.

October 31, 1968: Johnson halts the bombing of North Vietnam, but the Paris peace talks are postponed indefinitely because South Vietnam refuses to negotiate if the Communist National Liberation Front (NLF) participates.

November 5, 1968: Former Vice President Richard Nixon, a Republican, defeats Democratic Vice President Hubert Humphrey in the presidential election. Earlier in the year incumbent President Johnson had declined to seek nomination for reelection, largely because of the intense public protests against the Vietnam War. Democrats Robert Kennedy and Eugene McCarthy had challenged Humphrey for the nomination by running on antiwar platforms; Nixon also ran as a peace candidate.

On the evening that Robert Kennedy won the crucial Democratic California primary, he was assassinated. His murder eliminated the strongest antiwar challenge to Humphrey. Antiwar protestors later demonstrated during the 1968 Democratic convention in Chicago, disrupting Humphrey's nomination.

The protestors were ultimately attacked by the police in what a grand jury later ruled "a police riot." Viewers across the nation watched police assault television commentators inside the convention hall.

Culminating three years of race riots, civil unrest, and political assassinations (including the killings of Martin Luther King and Malcolm X), the chaotic Democratic convention symbolized the divisiveness within the country and the apparent breakdown of order that the Vietnam War had spawned. Many feel that it contributed significantly to Nixon's narrow victory over Humphrey. The FBI file on singer/activist John Lennon shows that the Nixon administration feared a similar occurrence at the 1972 Republican Convention on Miami Beach and took steps to avoid it.

November 12, 1968: Brezhnev issues the Brezhnev Doctrine three months after the Warsaw Pact invasion of Czechoslovakia. The doctrine, which attempted to justify that invasion, acknowledged respect for the sovereignty of Communist-ruled countries but added that "when internal and external forces that are hostile to socialism try to turn the development of some socialist country toward the restoration of a capitalist regime...[it becomes] a common problem of all socialist countries."

IV. Mutually Assured Destruction and Détente (1969–79)

March 2, 1969: Troops from Communist China and the Soviet Union fire on each other over a disputed border on the Ussuri River. On March 16 similar clashes occurred, and on June 10 and July 8 the Soviet Union sent tanks, armored cars, gunboats, and planes into Chinese territory. The conflict crested on August 13 when Soviet troops crossed the Sinkiang border and heavy fighting produced numerous casualties.

March 11, 1969: North Korean and U.S. troops exchange fire across the Korean demilitarized zone.

April 1, 1969: After purging his enemies, Mao Zedong reasserts his Communist Party leadership by serving as chairman of the Ninth Communist Party Congress. On October 1 he addressed a crowd of 500,000 and thereby ended rumors of his ill health. In 1970 he was named supreme commander of the Army and Navy. Mao's consolidation of power concluded the first phase of the Cultural Revolution that had begun in 1966.

April 17, 1969: Dubček is officially deposed as Czech leader and replaced by hard-liner Dr. Gustav Husák. In late September a more conservative cabinet was installed and Dubček was expelled from the Communist Party presidium. He was expelled from the party in June 1970.

July 8, 1969: Nixon begins the Vietnamization of the Vietnam War, reducing the number of U.S. troops and gradually giving more of the responsibility for fighting the war to South Vietnam.

July 20, 1969: Astronaut Neil Armstrong becomes the first human to step foot on the moon; Edwin "Buzz" Aldrin, Jr., is the second as the Apollo 11 mission achieves Kennedy's dream to send a person to the moon by the end of the decade.

July 25, 1969: Nixon proclaims the Nixon Doctrine in which the United States withdraws its willingness to assume primary responsibility for the defense of nations besieged by Communism.

August 8, 1969: The United States and West Germany establish a telephone hot line between the heads of state.

September 1, 1969: Colonel Muammar Qaddafi leads a rebellion in Libya and establishes the socialist Libyan Arab Republic.

September 3, 1969: North Vietnam's leader Ho Chi Minh dies.

October 21, 1969: Willy Brandt becomes chancellor of West Germany. Brandt went on to play a major role in creating the East-West détente by forging more friendly relations with Eastern Europe.

November 17, 1969: Nixon initiates Strategic Arms Limitation Talks (SALT I) with the USSR.

November 24, 1969: The Nuclear Nonproliferation Treaty is ratified in ceremonies in Washington and Moscow. West Germany signed the treaty on November 28. The treaty went into effect on March 5, 1970, at which time 45 countries had ratified it.

February 1, 1970: West Germany and the Soviet Union agree that a West German firm will build a pipeline to the USSR in exchange for German access to Soviet natural gas resources. The pipeline from the Ukraine to West Germany opened on October 1, 1973.

February 20, 1970: Kissinger and North Vietnam's Le Duc Tho begin secret peace negotiations in Paris.

March 19, 1970: Willy Brandt and Willi Stoph meet in East Germany, the first time the heads of East and West Germany have met since the inception of those countries.

March 26, 1970: U.S., French, Soviet, and British leaders meet in West Berlin to discuss problems concerning Berlin. This was the first such meeting since the Second Berlin Crisis.

April 19, 1970: Communist forces capture a town 20 miles from Phnom Penh, the capital of Cambodia. Cambodian Premier Lon Nol personally appealed to Nixon for military assistance.

April 24, 1970: China launches its first satellite into outer space.

April 30, 1970: A combined U.S. and South Vietnamese force attacks Communist bases in Cambodia, setting off widespread, massive antiwar demonstrations throughout the United States. Many university campuses closed down in protest.

May 2, 1970: Nixon resumes the bombing of North Vietnam for the first time since November 1968.

May 4, 1970: National Guardsmen kill four students and wound nine others at Kent State University in Ohio. The governor had called in the National Guard in response to massive antiwar protests; however, most of those killed were not involved in the demonstrations. Eight guardsmen were tried and acquitted for the shootings, though the victims' families later received compensation from the state, which acknowledged that the tragedy "should not have occurred." The Kent State Massacre highlighted a series of violent confrontations during the late 1960s and early 1970s between antiwar protestors and police and National Guardsmen.

May 14, 1970: State police kill 2 students and wound 11 others at the all-black Jackson State University in Mississippi where antiwar rallies were occurring. Following reports that students were harassing white motorists, about 40 police lined up facing demonstrators and opened fire at a distance of some 50 feet. The President's Commission on Campus Unrest later charged the police with "unreasonable, unjustified overreaction."

May 20, 1970: Kosygin acknowledges that the Soviet Union is providing extensive aid to the Arab nations to enable them to defend "legitimate national rights."

May 24, 1970: Laotian government troops begin a major counterattack in response to recent gains by North Vietnamese and Pathet Lao armies in Laos.

October 24, 1970: In Chile, Marxist candidate Salvador Allende is elected president, thereby becoming the first freely elected Marxist in the Western hemisphere. His attempts to nationalize industry and implement land reforms met with limited success due to opposition within his coalition government.

November 6, 1970: Italy establishes diplomatic relations with China and cuts ties with Nationalist China in Taiwan.

November 25, 1970: North Vietnam boycotts the Paris peace talks in response to heavy U.S. bombardments in Laos, Cambodia, and North Vietnam.

December 7, 1970: West Germany and Poland agree on a border along the Oder-Neisse line.

December 20, 1970: Following massive riots in Gdansk in response to rising food costs, Polish First Secretary Gomułka and other key members of the government resign.

January 31, 1971: Telephone service is established between East and West Berlin for the first time in 19 years.

February 8, 1971: Supported by U.S. aircraft, South Vietnam launches an offensive into Laos to cut North Vietnamese supply lines. They withdrew their troops on March 24.

February 11, 1971: Sixty-three nations sign a treaty banning nuclear weapons from being installed on the seabed in international waters.

April 7, 1971: Nixon announces the reduction of U.S. troops by another 100,000 in Vietnam.

April 10, 1971: A U.S. table tennis team arrives in China to play a series of matches. For the first time since the Communist takeover in 1949 the U.S. press was allowed into China.

April 23, 1971: Antiwar protesters begin a week of demonstrations in Washington, D.C.

May 27, 1971: Egypt and the Soviet Union sign a 15-year friendship treaty. On June 9 Israel requested increased military aid from the United States to match the Soviet arms buildup in Egypt.

August 18, 1971: New Zealand and Australia announce that they will withdraw their combat troops from Vietnam by the end of the year.

August 21, 1971: At Malta's request NATO moves its naval headquarters from Malta to Naples.

September 3, 1971: France, Great Britain, the United States, and the Soviet Union sign the Quadripartite agreement on Berlin, permitting travel from West Germany through East Germany to West Berlin but allowing the Berlin Wall to stand and the border between East and West Berlin to remain closed.

November 12, 1971: Nixon announces the withdrawal of an additional 45,000 soldiers from Vietnam and declares that the United States will no longer play an offensive role in the war. Nixon continued gradually withdrawing troops throughout 1972, while simultaneously intensifying the air war in hopes of winning North Vietnamese willingness to negotiate a mutually satisfactory end to the war. The antiwar protests continued in the United States.

October 25, 1971: The People's Republic of China is admitted to the United Nations as the sole legitimate government of China. Simultaneously, the Republic of China, Chiang Kai-shek's Nationalist government in exile, was expelled.

1972–75: U.S. presidents Nixon and Ford hold a total of five summit talks with Soviet Premier Brezhnev, indicating a new willingness of the two countries to work out some basic agreements. These talks focused mostly on arms control, though Ford's Helsinki agreements also addressed human rights, and other summits expanded trade and cultural exchange as a bridge for stability and peace.

1972–73: As part of Chancellor Willy Brandt's *Ostpolitik* (Eastern policy), West Germany signs a series of treaties improving relations with East Germany, the Soviet Union, Romania, and Czechoslovakia. Brandt also promoted the ultimate reunification of a single, independent Germany.

January 25, 1972: Nixon reveals that Kissinger has been conducting secret peace negotiations with North Vietnamese leaders.

February 21–27, 1972: Nixon and Kissinger travel to China and meet openly with Mao Zedong and Zhou En-lai. U.S.-Chinese relationships improved after this point, and the two countries became trading partners. The U.S.-Chinese alliance put new pressures on the Soviet Union, which had been at odds with its Communist ally since the late 1950s.

March 13, 1972: Great Britain and China resume diplomatic relations after 22 years.

May 22, 1972: Nixon begins a week-long visit to the USSR, becoming the first U.S. president to visit that country. On May 26 he and Brezhnev signed a Strategic Arms Limitation Treaty (SALT I).

June 17, 1972: A security guard catches five men breaking into the Democratic Party National Committee offices in the Watergate complex in Washington, D.C. Their arrest initiated the two-year constitutional crisis popularly labeled "Watergate."

September 29, 1972: Japan and China sign an accord that technically ends a state of war dating back to 1937. They establish diplomatic relations and Japan severs relations with Nationalist China.

October 3, 1972: The United States and USSR sign SALT accords limiting submarine-carried and land-based missiles. The agreements also featured an Anti-Ballistic Missile (ABM) treaty, which greatly restricted the development of defensive missiles.

October 8, 1972: A month before the U.S. presidential election Kissinger and Le Duc Tho reach a breakthrough in their Vietnam peace negotiations. Soon after Kissinger announced, "We believe that peace is at hand." But South Vietnam's President Thieu refused to accept the new terms and demanded 69 amendments to the agreements. The peace process again stalled.

November 7, 1972: Incumbent President Nixon, running a law and order campaign, defeats Democratic peace candidate George McGovern in a landslide victory.

November 21, 1972: The discussions known as SALT II begin to further limit nuclear weapons production.

November 24, 1972: The United Nations grants East Germany observer status: the same status held by West Germany.

November 24, 1972: Finland becomes the first Western nation to formally recognize East Germany and establish diplomatic ties with both East and West Germany. The USSR had recognized both Germanys since the mid–1950s.

December 18, 1972: Nixon orders intense Christmas bombings of Hanoi and Haiphong and the mining of North Vietnamese harbors "until such time as a settlement is arrived at." The widely criticized bombings lasted 11 days, after which the North Vietnamese returned to the bargaining table and an agreement similar to the October accord was reached.

January 17, 1973: President Ferdinand Marcos permanently reinstates martial law in the Philippines and proclaims a new constitution in which he achieves near dictatorial powers.

January 27, 1973: United States and North Vietnam sign a formal cease-fire in Paris officially concluding the Vietnam War. Nixon immediately ended the very unpopular military draft.

February 21, 1973: A cease-fire between the Laotian government and the Pathet Lao ends 20 years of war. On September 14 a coalition government was established. But the fighting resumed in 1974 and Laos fell to the Communists in 1975.

March 29, 1973: The last U.S. troops leave South Vietnam. Over 3 million Americans served in Vietnam and more than 50,000 Americans were killed between 1961 and 1973. Some 4 million Vietnamese on both sides were also killed or wounded, about 10 percent of the total population.

May 19, 1973: The USSR and West Germany sign a ten-year agreement allowing for economic, industrial, and technical cooperation.

June 22, 1973: While visiting the United States, Brezhnev signs a pact aimed at avoiding nuclear war.

June 25, 1973: Former White House counsel John Dean testifies that President Nixon tried to cover up the Watergate affair.

July 21, 1973: Despite international protests, France begins a series of nuclear tests in the South Pacific.

September 11, 1973: A U.S.-backed military coup overthrows Chile's Marxist president, Salvador Allende. A brutal military dictatorship led by General Pinochet Ugarte assumed power.

September 18, 1973: Both East and West Germany become full members of the United Nations.

October 6, 1973: Egyptian and Syrian troops, with Soviet support, attack Israel on the Jewish holy day Yom Kippur. After initial success crossing the Suez canal the Egyptians were beaten back and badly defeated in their own territory, as were the Syrians. UN cease-fires on October 22, 23, and 25 established UN buffer zones between Israel and the other two nations.

In order to reduce U.S. support of Israel, the Arab countries embargoed oil shipments to the United States, causing long lines for much higher-priced gasoline. The increase in oil prices ended the era of economic growth and prosperity that typically characterized the Vietnam era and introduced a period of high inflation.

February 6, 1974: The U.S. House of Representatives votes to hold an impeachment investigation on charges that Nixon helped cover up the Watergate investigation. On July 30 the Judiciary Committee voted to recommend that the House impeach the president.

March 1974: North Vietnam resumes military initiatives in South Vietnam.

April 2, 1974: France's President Georges Pompidou dies in office. Elections to replace him on May 27 gave Valéry Giscard d'Estaing a narrow victory over socialist candidate François Mitterrand.

May 6, 1974: Willy Brandt resigns as West Germany's chancellor following the arrest for espionage of a highly placed close friend within his administration. Helmut Schmidt succeeded him.

May 18, 1974: India explodes its first nuclear device.

August 9, 1974: Richard Nixon resigns from the presidency after the bilateral House Judiciary Committee recommends that the House of Representatives vote to impeach him. Vice President Gerald Ford assumed the presidency and soon after pardoned Nixon for all federal crimes he "committed or may have committed."

September 4, 1974: The United States recognizes East Germany.

November 23, 1974: Brezhnev and Ford begin two days of talks at Vladivostok in the USSR. They tentatively agreed to limit offensive strategic weapons over the next ten years.

April 17, 1975: The Khmer Rouge, under Pol Pot, conclude a five-year Cambodian civil war by capturing the capital city, Phnom Penh. On January 5, 1976, they introduced a new constitution and renamed the country Democratic Kampuchea. The simultaneous Communist victories in neighboring Southeast Asian countries may have initially seemed to bear out the domino theory. But soon the Communist neighbors were at war with each other, and in 1979 Vietnam overthrew Pol Pot.

April 30, 1975: South Vietnam falls to North Vietnam, and Vietnam is unified under Communist rule. This North Vietnamese victory concluded a war of national liberation extending back to 1941 when Ho Chi Minh formed the Vietminh to fight both French colonialism and Japanese occupation. It also concluded Ho's war for unification, dating back to 1954 when the Geneva Agreement partitioned the country after the Vietminh defeated the French at Dien Bien Phu. The two Vietnams were officially reunited on July 2, 1976, when a single socialist republic was declared.

May 12, 1975: A Cambodian naval vessel fires upon the *Mayaguez*, a U.S. cargo ship sailing from Hong Kong to Thailand. The Cambodians then seized the ship and crew. After Cambodian and Chinese officials ignored U.S. diplomatic notes requesting the release of the *Mayaguez* and its crew, President Ford ordered a company of Marines stationed on the aircraft carrier *Coral Sea* to rescue them. He also ordered air strikes against an airfield in Cambodia. The rescue mission was successful and the initial report of minimal casualties generated an enthusiastic response among the U.S. public, which had witnessed the demoralizing U.S. evacuation from Vietnam two years earlier and the fall of both South Vietnam and Cambodia only weeks before. However, when later reports showed that 41 Americans were killed, presumed dead, or missing in action, Congress called for an investigation by the Government Accounting Office. That election-year investigation concluded that Ford had failed to exhaust diplomatic channels before ordering the military rescue. Ford dismissed the report as partisan politics.

July 17, 1975: The U.S. Apollo 18 and the Soviet Soyuz 19 space capsules link in outer space in the first joint space venture between the two superpowers.

July 30, 1975: The Helsinki Summit Conference attended by Ford produces accords signed by the United States, Soviet Union, and all of the countries of Eastern and Western Europe. These renounced the use of force to settle disputes among European countries and recognized existing post–World War II national boundaries as "inviolable." The latter had been one of the main Soviet Cold War objectives. The accords also promoted Western objectives of improved trading opportunities, cultural exchange, and adherence to human rights.

August 23, 1975: The Communist Pathet Lao forces gain control of Laos, ending a civil war dating back to 1953. Long-standing beneficiaries of North Vietnamese support, the Pathet Lao established the Lao People's Democratic Republic on December 3.

1975–76: The Soviets directly support the pro–Communist Popular Movement for the Liberation of Angola (MPLA) during the Angolan Civil War. The USSR supplied weapons and imported 10,000 Cuban troops to ensure an MPLA victory. In June 1976 the United States vetoed Angola's request for admission to the United Nations because Cuban soldiers were still stationed in the country.

January 8, 1976: Chinese Prime Minister Zhou En-lai dies at age 78 and Hua Guofeng succeeds him. Following Zhou's death the radical Gang of Four assumed considerable influence over the aging Chairman Mao. At their behest Mao purged Zhou's moderate protégé, Deng Xiaoping, in April.

February 24–March 5, 1976: The twenty-fifth Soviet Communist Party Congress convenes and Brezhnev declares that the Soviet Union will continue to support détente but will also continue its struggle against capitalism.

May 28, 1976: The United States and USSR sign a five-year treaty restricting the size of underground nuclear tests and permitting U.S. on-site inspections of Soviet tests.

June 29, 1976: Communist Party leaders from 29 European countries meet in East Berlin. They voted to permit greater independence of each national Communist party in a move intended to lessen Soviet dominance.

September 9, 1976: Mao Zedong dies. The radical Gang of Four, which included his wife Jiang Qing, initially replaced him but in October they were deposed by a more moderate coalition. Prime Minister Hua Guofeng then became Communist Party chairman in addition to prime minister. However, by 1977 Deng Xiaoping emerged as China's strongest leader.

October 10, 1976: Castro holds elections in Cuba for the first time since he came to power in 1959. The ballot was highly restricted and Castro prevailed.

November 2, 1976: Democrat Jimmy Carter defeats incumbent Ford for the presidency.

December 9, 1976: NATO rejects a Warsaw Pact proposal that each side renounce first use of nuclear weapons.

January 31, 1977: The Czech government declares illegal a demand by Czech intellectuals to implement human rights in compliance with the 1975 Helsinki Agreements.

February 3, 1977: Colonel Mengistu Mariam seizes power in Ethiopia assisted by $2 billion worth of Soviet arms, 20,000 Cuban troops, 300 tanks, and 3,000 Soviet technicians. On May 6 Ethiopia and the Soviet Union signed a pact that reversed Ethiopia's previous dependence on the United States and brought it in closer economic and political alignment with the USSR.

February 17, 1977: Carter provokes Soviet accusations of meddling with their internal affairs when he sends a personal letter to Soviet dissident Andrei Sakharov. The letter asserted that human rights were a "central concern" of his administration.

April 28, 1977: Cuba and the United States sign a fishing rights agreement after holding their first formal talks since Castro took power in 1959.

June 16, 1977: Brezhnev becomes Soviet president as well as first secretary of the Communist Party.

September 7, 1977: Bitterly opposed by right-wing politicians, Carter signs two Panama Canal treaties allowing Panama to take full control of the canal by 1999 and ensuring that the canal will remain permanently neutral.

November 4, 1977: Meeting in Yugoslavia, representatives of 14 Western countries call on the Soviet Union and its allies to recognize human rights.

April 27, 1978: The Soviets assist a pro–Communist coup in Afghanistan.

June 26, 1978: Communists in the ruling coalition of South Yemen carry out a successful armed coup and sign a 20-year defense pact with the Soviet Union.

September 5–17, 1978: Carter brokers the Camp David Accords between Egypt and Israel, establishing "A Framework for Peace in the Middle East." Egypt agreed to recognize Israel's right to exist in exchange for return of captured territories. Provisions were made to increase trade, travel, and cultural exchange between the two countries. On November 5 the Arab League denounced the accords and offered $50 billion to Egypt if it would renounce them. However, President Sadat refused.

September 27, 1978: France joins the UN disarmament committee after refusing to participate since 1960.

October 27, 1978: The UN military command in South Korea discovers an invasion tunnel leading from North Korea under the demilitarized zone and 270 miles into South Korea. The tunnel was large enough to permit 30,000 armed troops per hour to enter into South Korea. North Korea denied knowledge of the tunnel, maintaining it was a fabrication of U.S. imperialists.

November 3, 1978: Vietnam and the United States sign a friendship treaty calling for economic, scientific, and technical cooperation.

January 1, 1979: The United States and China establish formal relations, and the United States and Nationalist Chinese on Taiwan sever relations.

January 7, 1979: The Vietnamese invade Cambodia, replacing the radical Communist, pro–Chinese Khmer Rouge government with a Communist, pro–Soviet regime. Under the leadership of Pol Pot the Khmer Rouge had exterminated some 2 million Cambodians, including many middle-class and educated citizens. A 1989 UN report stated that Pol Pot's violations of human rights were "the worst to have occurred anywhere in the world since Nazism."

January 16, 1979: After domestic rebellion and worldwide protests against his repressive rule, the shah of Iran flees the country. Islamic fundamentalist Ayatollah Khomeini assumed power three weeks later, and March elections converted the country into a Muslim theocracy hostile to both the United States and the USSR.

January 29, 1979: China's deputy prime minister Deng Xiaoping visits the United States and advises of Chinese plans to attack Vietnam in reprisal for Vietnamese raids over the previous six months.

February 17, 1979: In response to Vietnam's border raids against China and its attack on Cambodia, China initiates a brief border war with Vietnam. Chinese forces withdrew on March 16.

May 3, 1979: Margaret Thatcher is elected prime minister of Great Britain, becoming the first female prime minister in Europe. She remained in power through 1990.

July 17–19, 1979: A popular insurrection in Nicaragua deposes the Somoza dictatorship. Pro-Communist Sandinistas came to power in a five-man junta dominated by Daniel Ortega.

June 18, 1979: Carter and Brezhnev sign the SALT II Treaty in Vienna. However, Carter withdrew the treaty from Senate consideration following the Soviet invasion of Afghanistan on December 25.

October 1, 1979: Panama takes control of the American Canal Zone. The United States had controlled the strip of Panamanian soil for 70 years.

October 16, 1979: A military coup in El Salvador leads to a civil war between right-wing oligarchs who control the government and left-wing rebels. Carter initially supported the new government but withdrew support because of extreme human rights violations. Carter resumed military aid at the end of his term, and presidents Reagan and Bush supported the El Salvador government throughout their presidencies.

October 26, 1979: South Korea's President Park is assassinated by his head of intelligence. Prime Minister Choi Kyu Ha is elected president on December 6.

November 4, 1979: Iranian students invade the U.S. embassy in Tehran, taking as hostages 66 members of the embassy's delegation, staff, and Marine guard. The Iranian students and government held most of the hostages for 444 days. The United States responded by establishing a general embargo on trade and financial transactions and freezing all Iranian assets in U.S. banks. Included in this embargo was a ban on all arms trade and shipments to Iran.

November 21, 1979: Following rumors that the United States had supported an attack on the holy mosque at Mecca, widespread anti–American rioting breaks out in Pakistan. The United States subsequently evacuated all nonessential personnel from its embassies in ten Muslim countries and the State Department warned Americans to avoid traveling to Islamic countries in the Persian Gulf and Middle East.

December 12, 1979: NATO votes to deploy intermediate-range, nuclear-armed Cruise and Pershing II missiles in Western Europe in response to Soviet deployment of SS-20 intermediate-range missiles.

December 23, 1979: The Czech government convicts six leading dissidents on charges of subversion. Among them was playwright and future president of Czechoslovakia, Václav Havel.

December 25, 1979: The Soviets invade Afghanistan in order to prop up the regime they had installed there. By January 8, 1980, the Soviet Army controlled most of the country. On January 14 the United Nations voted overwhelmingly to demand the immediate withdrawal of all foreign troops, but the Soviet Union did not abide by the vote. This direct use of force involving Soviet soldiers effectively ended détente, provoking Carter to withdraw the SALT II Treaty from Senate consideration, boycott the 1980 Moscow Olympic games, and cancel grain sales to the Soviet Union.

V. Winnable Nuclear War, the Evil Empire, and the Collapse of Communism (1980–90)

February 5, 1980: China attends the Geneva disarmament conference for the first time.

April 4, 1980: The Mariel boatlift begins after 25 Cubans seek political asylum in the Peruvian embassy in Havana and set off a massive wave of emigration from the island. Castro allowed boats from the United States to pick up people from Cuba, though he also insisted that criminals and mentally ill patients be taken too. During the boatlift over 100,000 Cuban refugees came to south Florida.

April 7, 1980: Carter severs diplomatic relations with Iran.

April 24–25, 1980: An attempt by U.S. commandos to free the Iranian hostages fails when American helicopters break down in a desert sandstorm. Eight soldiers died in the effort, and Secretary of State Cyrus Vance, who had opposed a rescue operation, resigned in protest.

May 4, 1980: Yugoslavia's Marshal Tito dies. A collective rotating presidency replaced him.

August 11, 1980: China orders the removal of most public portraits, slogans, and poems of Mao Zedong.

August 24, 1980: The Polish government, which had been presiding over a failing economy, negotiates a settlement with the Solidarity trade union providing the right of workers to unionize, reducing working hours, and permitting greater freedom for news media.

Threatened by this liberalization, Brezhnev had Polish General Wojciech Jaruzelski seize control of the Polish government and declare martial law in December 1981. Jaruzelski arrested Solidarity leader Lech Wałęsa and 14,000 other trade unionists, but Solidarity continued as a significant force throughout the decade. The union achieved official recognition during the liberalization of 1989 when its nominee was named prime minister in a coalition government with the Communists. Wałęsa was elected president in 1991.

November 20, 1980: In China the radical Gang of Four who had influenced Mao during his final year stands trial for treason. Among the convicted is Jiang Qing, Mao's widow.

September 22, 1980: Iraq invades Iran, initiating an eight-year war that featured Iraq's use of chemical weapons and produced casualties exceeding those in World War I. The warring countries agreed upon a cease-fire in 1988. Throughout much of the war the United States supported Iraq in limited ways because Iraq was curbing Iran's Islamic fundamentalism, a growing force that threatened to destabilize such pro–West Arab governments as Saudi Arabia, Kuwait, and Egypt.

November 4, 1980: Republican Ronald Reagan defeats incumbent Jimmy Carter for the U.S. presidency. Iran released the remaining 52 hostages on inauguration day, January 20, 1981.

February 9, 1981: Polish Prime Minister Jozef Pinkowski resigns after five months of civil unrest. Defense Minister General Jaruzelski succeeded him.

May 10, 1981: François Mitterrand is elected the first socialist president of France since the establishment of the Fifth Republic in 1958.

August 7, 1981: Approximately 1 million members of the Polish Solidarity trade union go on strike in protest against food shortages and the economic crisis.

October 18, 1981: Greece elects its first socialist government under the leadership of Andreas Papandreou.

December 12, 1981: The Solidarity trade union calls for a day of national protest in Poland.

December 13, 1981: General Jaruzelski imposes martial law in Poland, bans Solidarity, and arrests its leader Lech Wałęsa. Jaruzelski then announced he had formed a Military Council of National Salvation to run the country. In response Solidarity called for a referendum on replacing the government. In December the United States imposed economic sanctions on Poland and the Soviet Union in protest. Great Britain, Belgium, Japan, and Canada followed suit in 1982.

December 1981: The United States grants $161 million in economic and military assistance to El Salvador in order to combat leftist guerrillas.

December 1981: Reagan directs the CIA to arm and organize Nicaraguan exiles who were attempting to overthrow the Communist Sandinista regime. These exiles became known as Contras.

February 11, 1982: Under socialist leadership France nationalizes 5 groups of major industries and 39 banks.

March 11, 1982: Great Britain announces its decision to purchase the U.S. Trident missile system to replace its obsolete Polaris missiles.

May 18, 1982: Brezhnev calls for an immediate freeze on strategic nuclear weapons and for new arms limitation talks, which begin on June 29.

May 30, 1982: Spain joins NATO.

September 1–12, 1982: The twelfth Congress of the Chinese Communist Party restructures the constitution and elects Deng Xiaoping chairman of the new Central Advisory Commission.

November 10, 1982: Brezhnev dies. Another elderly member of the conservative, hard-line old guard, Yuri Andropov, replaced him on November 12 as the Community Party's general secretary. Brezhnev's death initiated a three-year period of aging, infirm, and unstable Soviet leadership as Andropov died on February 9, 1984, and his successor, Konstantin Chernenko, died on March 10, 1985.

November 12–14, 1982: The first fully operational flight of the U.S. space shuttle *Columbia*. On November 28, 1983, *Columbia* carried the European-made Spacelab into orbit.

November 22, 1982: Reagan announces his decision to deploy the controversial MX intercontinental ballistic missile.

December 12, 1982: Over 20,000 British women surround the Greenham Common Air Base to peacefully protest the installation of U.S. Cruise missiles.

December 21, 1982: Reagan reluctantly signs into law the Intelligence Authorization Act, which contains the first Boland Amendment forbidding the covert use of funds to overthrow the Nicaraguan government.

1983: Reagan initiates a number of policies that become collectively known as the Reagan Doctrine. Reagan vowed to oppose Communist regimes and movements worldwide and to insist that any arms reduction agreement include reduction of Soviet conventional troops.

March 23, 1983: Reagan proposes the Strategic Defense Initiative (SDI) and begins speaking publicly of winnable nuclear war. SDI — popularly known as "Star Wars" — proposed to provide a shield against missile attacks by using laser-armed satellites in space to shoot down incoming intercontinental ballistic missiles (ICBMs). Though Reagan claimed SDI would exist solely for defensive purposes, the Soviets feared its first-strike capabilities.

April 5, 1983: France expels 47 Soviet diplomats and nationals whom it accuses of spying.

June 16, 1983: Andropov is elected president of the Soviet Presidium.

July 21, 1983: Poland lifts martial law and declares an amnesty for political prisoners.

August 4, 1983: Italy elects its first socialist prime minister, Bettino Craxi, who heads a coalition government.

September 1, 1983: A Soviet jet shoots down a civilian South Korean passenger plane that has drifted off course and into Soviet airspace. The downing of KAL Flight 007 provoked international outrage and brought Cold War tensions to a level not seen since the Cuban Missile Crisis. On September 8 Soviet

Foreign Minister Gromyko cautioned, "The world situation is now slipping toward a very dangerous precipice. Problem number one for the world is to avoid nuclear war."

October 23, 1983: A terrorist car bomb in Beirut, Lebanon, kills 241 American servicemen who had been sent there as peacekeepers in accordance with the Reagan Doctrine.

October 25, 1983: Reagan orders a full-scale military invasion the Caribbean island, Grenada. The massive invasion encountered minimal resistance, mostly from armed construction workers, and quickly deposed Grenada's pro–Communist government.

October 31, 1983: Scientists from the United States, the Soviet Union, and other nations meet in Washington, D.C., at the World after Nuclear War Conference where they warn that a "nuclear winter" might follow a large-scale nuclear war.

November 14, 1983: The first U.S. Cruise missiles arrive in England. The next day women led violent protests outside the Greenham Common Air Base where the missiles were stationed.

November 22, 1983: U.S.-Soviet arms limitation negotiations break down, and the Soviet Union announces its intention to increase its nuclear forces.

January 1984: The CIA secretly mines harbors in Nicaragua. Technically an act of war, this action provoked Congress in April to limit U.S. involvement in Nicaragua. Between 1984 and 1986 Congress passed a series of Boland amendments denying government agencies funds to support "directly or indirectly military or paramilitary operations" in Nicaragua.

To bypass this prohibition on government involvement the Reagan administration, largely through high-ranking officers in the National Security Council, sought ways to channel weapons and funds to the Contras through private individuals and agencies. This privatization of the country's handling of foreign affairs led directly to the Iran-Contra scandal of 1986, which debilitated the administration during its final year.

February 9, 1984: Soviet Premier Yuri Andropov dies; Konstantin Chernenko, another elderly hard-liner, replaces him as general secretary on February 13 and becomes president of the Supreme Soviet on April 11.

November 6, 1984: Reagan is overwhelmingly reelected, defeating Carter's vice president, Democrat Walter Mondale.

December 19, 1984: Great Britain agrees to hand over control of Hong Kong to China in 1997.

March 10, 1985: Chernenko dies and Mikhail Gorbachev succeeds him as general secretary on the next day. On July 2 Andrei Gromyko became president. Gorbachev initiated two programs of domestic reforms: glasnost (openness: permitting greater individual freedoms and greater freedom of press) and perestroika (restructuring: permitting initial movement toward a more free-market type economy).

March 12–April 23, 1985: The United States and Soviet Union initiate a new round of arms reduction talks (START) in Geneva.

May 1, 1985: The United States imposes a total trade and financial embargo on Nicaragua.

June 12, 1985: The House of Representatives votes to provide $27 million dollars in nonmilitary aid to assist the Contras in their effort to depose the pro–Communist government in Nicaragua.

September 13, 1985: Great Britain expels 25 Soviet diplomats and officials accused of belonging to the KGB. The next day the USSR expelled 25 British officials and further expulsions followed.

November 19–21, 1985: In Geneva Reagan and Gorbachev hold their first of five summit meetings. They agreed in principle to a 50 percent reduction in nuclear weapons and suggested an interim agreement on intermediate-range nuclear forces (INF). They also issued a joint statement declaring that nuclear war could not be won and must never be fought, and they vowed that neither side would try to achieve nuclear superiority. They disagreed over Reagan's SDI, which Gorbachev strongly opposed, but Reagan left the summit declaring that the summit represented a "fresh start" in superpower relations.

January 28, 1986: The space shuttle *Challenger* explodes upon take-off, killing all aboard including Christa McAuliffe, a teacher who had been chosen to be "the first citizen in space." The launch was televised live and witnessed by millions. The disaster marked the beginning of a series of serious setbacks that plagued NASA through the end of the Cold War.

February 15, 1986: President Marcos is declared winner of the presidential elections in the Philippines, despite widespread allegations that he rigged the election. Following massive protests and defections from the Army, Marcos fled, and on March 25, Mrs. Corazon Aquino, the widow of his major political opponent, was sworn in as president under a new provisional constitution.

February 24–March 6, 1986: The Congress of the Soviet Communist Party approves major changes to the membership of the Central Committee and Politburo and rejects outmoded thinking from the past.

March 12, 1986: A public referendum leaves Spain in NATO but removes it from the NATO military command structure and retains a ban on nuclear weapons on Spanish soil.

March 16, 1986: Right-wing Jacques Chirac is elected by a narrow majority as France's prime minister, ending five years of socialist leadership. He and socialist President Mitterrand then entered an uneasy collaboration as rulers of the country.

March 24, 1986: Following alleged Libyan attacks on U.S. aircraft, U.S. warplanes bomb targets in Libya. The Soviet Union called the action a threat to world security. On April 15 the United States attacked terrorist bases near Tripoli and Benghazi, and Libya retaliated with missiles directed at radar installations on the Italian island of Lampedusa. However, these failed to strike their targets.

May 19, 1986: China and Taiwan hold their first face-to-face talks since the founding of the People's Republic of China in 1949.

September 13–20, 1986: The Soviet Union requests affiliation with GATT (General Agreement on Tariffs and Trade), the international organization that regulates much of the world's economy.

September 22, 1986: The Stockholm Security Conference concludes the first conventional arms agreement since World War II. The participating 35 nations also agreed to notify each other when significant military exercises would take place and to grant participatory countries the right to inspect them.

October 11–12, 1986: Reagan and Gorbachev meet in Reykjavik, Iceland, where the Soviets surprise U.S. negotiators by offering widespread proposals to reduce strategic weapons by 50 percent and eliminate intermediate-range nuclear forces (INF). The Soviets also wanted confirmation of the Anti-Ballistic Missile (ABM) treaty that would have stopped or seriously limited the development of SDI. However, Reagan refused to yield on this point.

November 3, 1986: A Lebanese newspaper reports that in 1985 the United States had secretly sold arms to Iran in return for Iran's promise to release American hostages held by terrorist groups in Lebanon. On November 13 Reagan admitted conducting a secret arms deal with Iran, and on November 25 national security adviser John Poindexter and Lieutenant Colonel Oliver North were dismissed. This trade later became known as the Iran-Contra Affair since much of the profit from the Iranian arms sales was eventually diverted, with some detours and siphoning along the way, to the Nicaraguan Contras.

During the 1988 presidential election Vice President George Bush, the Republican candidate, claimed to be "out of the loop" when decisions were being made about the Iran-Contra deal. He thereby escaped serious political damage and won the election. However, new revelations by a special prosecutor a week prior to the 1992 elections hurt Bush's reelection bid, as documents showed Bush to be much more inside the loop than he had represented.

February 28, 1987: Gorbachev drops his demand that the United States eliminate the SDI as part of an agreement to eliminate intermediary nuclear weapons in Europe. This resolved the only remaining outstanding difference over the INF Treaty that was signed on December 8.

March 1, 1987: The socialist government of Bettino Craxi resigns after three and a half years in power. It was the longest-lasting Italian government during the Cold War.

March 19, 1987: In Czechoslovakia Gustav Husák announces economic and political reforms similar to those Gorbachev is introducing within the Soviet Union.

June 11, 1987: Conservative Margaret Thatcher wins reelection, becoming the first British prime minister in 160 years to win election to a third term.

June 21, 1987: Reforms in the Soviet Union allow voters in some local elections to choose from more than one candidate for the first time.

June 28, 1987: After three weeks of rioting South Korea releases 534 political prisoners and agrees to hold the first direct presidential election in 16 years. On December 16 Roh Tae Woo won by a substantial majority.

August 7, 1987: The presidents of Guatemala, Honduras, El Salvador, Nicaragua, and Costa Rica sign an agreement intended to bring peace to Central America.

October 10, 1987: Poland introduces major economic changes in which the government agrees to surrender some of its controls on wages and prices. In a November 29 referendum 44 percent of those voting endorsed the government, but 33 percent of the eligible voters did not cast ballots.

December 8, 1987: Gorbachev and Reagan sign the INF Treaty to eliminate all intermediary-range nuclear missiles in Europe. This was the first Cold War agreement between the superpowers to actually reduce nuclear arsenals instead of merely limiting their growth.

January 29, 1988: Angolan-Cuban talks begin with U.S. participation. On December 22 Angola, South Africa, and Cuba signed an agreement granting Namibia independence from South Africa and providing for the withdrawal of Cuban troops. Namibia officially became independent on January 1, 1989.

February 8, 1988: Gorbachev announces that Soviet troops will begin withdrawing from Afghanistan on May 15, subject to the conclusion of a peace agreement between Pakistan and Afghanistan that was signed on April 14 with Soviet and U.S. participation. Gorbachev promised to complete the troop removal by February 15, 1989.

March 16, 1988: Gorbachev proposes a U.S.-Soviet freeze on naval forces in the Mediterranean, but the United States responds by reiterating its support of its NATO allies.

March 23, 1988: Leaders of the Nicaraguan government and rebel Contras sign a 60-day cease-fire agreement. The talks concluded on June 9 without an agreement and the fighting resumed.

May 8, 1988: Mitterrand is reelected as France's president, provoking the resignation of right-wing Prime Minister Chirac on May 10. Michel Rocard replaced Chirac.

May 29, 1988: Reagan begins a four-day visit to Moscow and supports Gorbachev's reforms.

June 28-July 1, 1988: The Communist Party approves six resolutions for Gorbachev's economic reforms known as perestroika.

August 26, 1988: The Soviet Union announces plans to increase agricultural efficiency by leasing land to private individuals.

August 31, 1988: Following two weeks of strikes Solidarity leader Lech Wałęsa meets with the Polish interior minister. This was Wałęsa's first official meeting with the Polish government since Solidarity was outlawed in 1981. After the meeting Wałęsa called for an end to the strikes.

September 21, 1988: The Soviet Union declares a state of emergency in the Nagorno-Karabakh region as ethnic clashes intensify.

September 30, 1988: Gorbachev consolidates his power as opponents of his reforms are voted out of office and Gorbachev is appointed president of the Soviet Union while retaining his position as general secretary of the Communist Party.

November 8, 1988: Vice President George Bush defeats Democrat Michael Dukakis for the presidency.

December 7, 1988: In an address to the United Nations Gorbachev announces plans to unilaterally reduce Soviet armed forces by 500,000 troops and cut conventional arms.

January 11, 1989: Cuba begins withdrawing troops from Angola. On June 22 the Marxist Angolan government agreed to a cease-fire with guerrilla forces.

March 26, 1989: The Soviet Union holds its first democratic elections as citizens elect representatives to the Congress of People's Deputies.

April 13, 1989: Congress votes to provide the Nicaraguan Contras with food, clothes, and medicine to support them through the elections scheduled for February 1990.

April 18–June 4, 1989: Inspired by Gorbachev's visit to Beijing, Chinese students protest in prodemocracy marches in Tiananmen Square. On May 13 3,000 students began a hunger strike and demanded the resignation of Deng Xiaoping. On May 20 the government imposed martial law. The internationally televised protest gained world attention and the support of some Army units, but on June 4 the Army crushed it. Public executions of protest leaders began on June 10.

May 25, 1989: The newly elected Congress of People's Deputies elects Gorbachev president of the Soviet Union.

June 4, 1989: Solidarity wins the first partially democratic elections in Poland, and on August 24 its nominee, Tadeusz Mazowiecki, becomes the first non–Communist prime minister in the Eastern bloc.

August 7, 1989: The leaders of Costa Rica, El Salvador, Guatemala, Honduras, and Nicaragua sign the Latin Accord, which declares that by December 8 Nicaraguan Contra armies based in Honduras must be disbanded. The United States denounced this decision.

September 10, 1989: Hungary opens its borders with Austria, affording 60,000 East Germans access to the West. On October 18 the East German Communist Party removed Erich Honecker, its hard-line leader for the past 18 years. Egon Krenz replaced him. As the exodus of East Germans to West Germany intensified demands for radical changes in the East German government also increased. On November 7 Prime Minister Willi Stoph stepped down, and most of the Politburo resigned the next day. On November 9 the government removed virtually all restrictions on travel from East Germany to West Germany. It opened the Berlin Wall on November 10, permitting free travel between East and West

Berlin for the first time since 1961. On December 3 Krenz and the entire Polit-buro and Central Committee resigned following revelations of widespread cor-ruption. By the end of the year a new liberal cabinet was in place in East Ger-many, led by reformer Hans Modrow. Huge crowds demanded the dissolution of the Communist Party and the reunification of Germany, which followed on October 3, 1990.

October 19, 1989: The Hungarian Parliament legalizes opposition politi-cal parties and concludes more than 40 years of single-party rule by the Com-munists. It calls for multiparty elections in 1990. On October 23, the thirty-third anniversary of the Hungarian Revolution, a new Hungarian Republic was declared. The Hungarian Communist Party dissolved and renounced Marxist-Leninism in favor of a social democracy.

October 25, 1989: Yugoslavia's Communist Party endorses free elections, political pluralism, labor unions, and greater individual freedoms. On Janu-ary 22, 1990, the party voted overwhelmingly to abandon the one-party sys-tem.

November 10, 1989: East Germany dismantles the Berlin Wall and opens access to West Germany.

November 10, 1989: Bulgaria's Todor Zhivkov resigns. The long-established president and head of the Communist Party was later expelled from the party. Demonstrations on November 17 demanded democracy and freedom, and on February 1, 1990, the Communist leadership resigned to permit a broad-based coalition government.

November 15, 1989: Solidarity leader Lech Wałęsa asks the United States for economic assistance similar to that provided by the Marshall Plan in the late 1940s to stabilize European governments vulnerable to Communist takeover.

December 7, 1989: Czechoslovakia's Prime Minister Ladislav Adamec resigns after a coalition of non–Communist parties demands his resignation. Marian Calfa replaced him and announced his intention to form a multiparty system. President Husák resigned on December 10, and on December 28 Alex-ander Dubček, who had been deposed following the 1968 Prague Spring, was elected chairman of the Czech Parliament. On December 29 Václav Havel, a prominent playwright, philosopher, and government protestor, became presi-dent.

December 22, 1989: Romania's Communist President Nicolae Ceauşescu is overthrown by the Army and executed on Christmas Day along with his wife after being hastily convicted of genocide and gross misuse of power.

January 1, 1990: After a 30-year absence Cuba is given a seat in the UN Security Council.

February 24, 1990: Lithuania holds genuine multiparty elections, the first in the USSR since 1917.

February 26, 1990: In a closely monitored presidential election in Nic-aragua, non–Communist coalition leader Violeta Barrios de Chamorro defeats the ruling Marxist Sandinista leader, Daniel Ortega. The transfer of power was relatively smooth and nonviolent. The Sandinistas retained considerable power, especially over the military.

February 26, 1990: President Havel announces that the Soviet Union will withdraw all of its troops from Czechoslovakia by July 1991.

March 11, 1990: Lithuania declares its independence from the Soviet Union and elects Vytautas Landsbergis as its leader.

March 25, 1990: Estonia's Communist Party votes to separate from the Soviet Communist Party within six months.

April 30, 1990: Fourteen months after crushing the Tiananmen Square demonstrations the Chinese government lifts martial law.

May 4, 1990: Latvia's Parliament votes for independence from the Soviet Union.

July 6, 1990: NATO agrees to redefine its military strategy in order to facilitate Soviet approval for a united Germany.

August 2, 1990: Iraq invades Kuwait and annexes it on August 8. This provoked the 1991 Gulf War.

August 23, 1990: The Republic of Armenia declares its independence from the Soviet Union.

September 12, 1990: World War II officially concludes as Great Britain, France, the United States, the Soviet Union, and East and West Germany sign the Treaty on the Final Settlement with Respect to Germany. The peace treaty paved the way for German unification on October 3 and arranged for the removal of Soviet troops from Eastern Europe: one of the West's primary objectives since the beginning of the Cold War.

September 24, 1990: The Soviet Parliament gives Gorbachev near-dictatorial powers so he can handle every aspect of reform.

October 3, 1990: East and West Germany unite into a single Germany. It remains a NATO country with its capital in Bonn, the capital site of the former West Germany. This fulfills a major, long-standing U.S. Cold War objective. On December 2 the Christian Democratic Party won the first nationwide elections since Hitler came to power in 1933, and Helmut Kohl became the first chancellor of reunited Germany.

November 17–19, 1990: Leaders of all the European states, the United States, Canada and the Soviet Union meet in Paris. They signed a new charter regulating relations among all the participants and a nonaggression agreement between members of NATO and the Warsaw Pact (the latter being dissolved in 1991). They also signed the Conventional Forces in Europe Treaty (CFE), which reduced the number of troops and tanks opposing each other in Europe. President Bush announced, "We have closed a chapter of history. The Cold War is over."

VI. The Aftermath of the Cold War (1990–92)

December 9, 1990: Solidarity's Lech Wałęsa is elected president of Poland.

January 16–February 28, 1991: A U.S.-led coalition of Western and Middle Eastern countries wages the short but successful Gulf War against Iraq after that country invaded, captured, and occupied oil-rich Kuwait. The Gulf War was the first major post–Cold War U.S. military action, and it was supported by the Soviet Union.

February 20, 1991: The first steps are taken toward the breakup of Yugoslavia when Slovenia votes to give local laws precedence over federal laws. Croatia enacted similar legislation the next day.

April 4, 1991: The Soviet Parliament learns that the nation faces imminent economic collapse since 15 Soviet republics have not made their payments to the central budget.

April 9, 1991: Georgia proclaims its independence from the Soviet Union.

June 3, 1991: Gorbachev and regional leaders rename the USSR the Union of Soviet Sovereign Republics.

June 4, 1991: Albania's Communist government collapses following a 20-day general strike. A coalition government led by Communist Ylli Bufi replaced it, but that government fell in December. Elections in March 1992 brought in a totally non–Communist government under the leadership of Sali Berisha.

June 27, 1991: Heavy fighting breaks out in Slovenia as Yugoslavian tanks enter the breakaway republic. The Yugoslavian Army withdrew on June 30.

July 1, 1991: The Warsaw Pact dissolves by mutual consent of the six participatory nations.

July 29, 1991: U.S. and Soviet arms negotiators agree to reduce long-range nuclear weapons.

August 19, 1991: A coup led by Communist hard-liners in the USSR places Gorbachev under house arrest in his holiday villa. Boris Yeltsin, the president of the Republic of Russia, led populist opposition that toppled the coup on August 21 and restored Gorbachev to power. Thereafter, however, Yeltsin's power increased as Gorbachev's waned. On August 23 Yeltsin banned the Communist Party and seized its assets, and on August 24 he recognized the independence of the Baltic States. The Ukraine declared its independence on August 24 as well.

August 25, 1991: Gorbachev resigns as head of the Soviet Communist Party and the party prepares to dissolve.

September 9, 1991: Macedonia declares its independence from Yugoslavia.

December 8, 1991: The Soviet republics form the Commonwealth of Independent States.

December 25, 1991: Gorbachev resigns as president of the Soviet Union and is not replaced. The Republic of Russia occupied the offices of the Soviet Union.

December 31, 1991: The Union of Soviet Socialist Republics officially dissolves, prompted by independence movements in the Baltic States, areas that the USSR had forcibly annexed after World War II. Various struggles between ethnic and nationalist groups then erupted within several of the former Soviet republics.

February 29, 1992: Bosnia-Herzegovina declares independence from Yugoslavia. Bosnian Serbs declared a separate state and fighting soon broke out within Bosnia. Serbia occupied what remained of Yugoslavia after Slovenia, Croatia, Macedonia, and Bosnia-Herzegovina had asserted their independence.

April 7, 1992: The European Community and the United States recognize Bosnia-Herzegovina as a sovereign state. This triggered a civil war led by ethnic Serbs living within Bosnia who feared domination by ethnic Croats and Muslims. They were assisted by armies from neighboring Serbia who besieged Sarajevo and began a genocidal policy of ethnic cleansing, in which Croats and Muslims were killed or removed from their lands. In March 1993 Bosnian Croats rebelled against the Muslim-led Bosnian government, initiating a one-year civil war. Meanwhile, despite periodic cease-fires, the civil war with Bosnia Serbs continued into 1995 and became one of the greatest challenges for NATO and Europe in the early days of the new world order following the Cold War. However, after Croatia entered the war in late 1995 — placing Bosnian Serbs on the defensive for the first time — peace talks among Bosnian, Serbian, and Croatian leaders began in Dayton, Ohio. These resulted in a U.S.-brokered peace treaty that was signed in Paris on December 14, 1995, calling for a force of 60,000 NATO troops under U.S. command to enter Bosnia as peacekeepers. The United States committed some 25,000 soldiers to the peacekeeping force.

August 26, 1992: Czechoslovakia declares it will break up into two separate but not hostile republics. On September 3 the new constitution for the Slovak Republic was signed, and the Czech Republic and the Slovak Republic became independent states on January 1, 1993.

November 3, 1992: Democrat "baby boomer" Bill Clinton defeats Bush, becoming the first U.S. president born after World War II.

A Chronology of Superpower and Allied Leadership

Great Britain

1940–45:	Winston Churchill (Conservative)
1945–51:	Clement Attlee (Labour)
1951–55:	Winston Churchill (Conservative)
1955–57:	Anthony Eden (Conservative)
1957–63:	Harold Macmillan (Conservative)
1963–64:	Alec Douglas-Home (Conservative)
1964–70:	Harold Wilson (Labour)
1970–74:	Edward Heath (Conservative)
1974–76:	Harold Wilson (Labour)
1976–79:	James Callaghan (Labour)
1979–90:	Margaret Thatcher (Conservative)
1990– :	John Major (Conservative)

France

1945–46: Charles De Gaulle

1946–58: During the Fourth Republic (1947–58) a succession of coalition governments came to power and the leadership was mercurial. The first government was led by Socialist Vincent Auriol. Georges Bidault (Mouvement Republicain Populaire) and Maurice Thorez (Communist Party) dominated French politics in the late 1940s, and Jules Moch and Robert Schuman wielded power in the early 1950s. Communists were excluded from the cabinet by the mid–1950s. Between the French defeat at Dien Bien Phu in 1954 and the collapse of the Fourth Republic during the Algerian crisis in spring 1958, Pierre Mendès-France (1954–55), Edgar Faure (1955-56),

Guy Mollet (1956-57), Maurice Bourgès-Maunoury (1957), Félix Gaillard (1957-58), and Pierre Pflimlin (1958) headed coalition governments.

1958–69: Charles De Gaulle (Gaullist Party). He was named premier with power to rule by decree for six months following the collapse of the Fourth Republic and was inaugurated president of the Fifth Republic in January 1959.

1969–74: Georges Pompidou (Gaullist Party)

1974–81: Valéry Giscard d'Estaing (Independent Republican Party)

1981–95: François Mitterrand (Socialist)

Nationalist China

(Single-party rule)

1949–75: Chiang Kai-shek

1975–88: Chiang Ching-kuo

1988– : Lee Teng-hui

People's Republic of China

(Single-party Communist rule)

1949–76: Mao Zedong

1959–68: Liu Shaoqi (head of state; Mao remained party chairman)

1976– : The Gang of 4

1977– : Deng Xiaoping

Union of Soviet Socialist Republics

(Single-party Communist rule, Party Secretaries)

1929–53: Joseph Stalin

1953–64: Nikita Khrushchev

1964–82: Leonid Brezhnev

1982–84: Yuri Andropov

1984–85: Constantin Chernenko

1985–91: Mikhail Gorbachev

United States of America

1945–53: Harry Truman (Democrat)

1953–61: Dwight Eisenhower (Republican)

1961–63: John Kennedy (Democrat)
1963–69: Lyndon Johnson (Democrat)
1969–74: Richard Nixon (Republican)
1974–77: Gerald Ford (Republican)
1977–81: Jimmy Carter (Democrat)
1981–89: Ronald Reagan (Republican)
1989–93: George Bush (Republican)
1993– : Bill Clinton (Democrat)

West Germany

1949–63: Konrad Adenauer (Christian Democrat)
1963–66: Ludwig Erhard (Christian Democrat)
1966–69: Kurt Kiesinger (Christian Democrat)
1969–74: Willy Brandt (Social Democrat)
1974–82: Helmut Schmidt (Social Democrat)
1982– : Helmut Kohl (Christian Democrat; Kohl became the first chancellor of reunified Germany in 1990)

U.S. Presidential Administrations and Soviet Leadership

	President	Sec. of State	Others	Soviets
1945	Truman	Byrnes	Kennan (State Dept.)	Stalin
1946			Baruch (UN)	
1947		Marshall		
1948				
1949	Truman	Acheson		
1950				
1951				
1952				
1953	Eisenhower	J. F. Dulles	Allen Dulles (CIA)	Khrushchev
1954				
1955				
1956				
1957	Eisenhower	J. F. Dulles	Allen Dulles (CIA)	
1958				
1959		Christian Herter		
1960				
1961	Kennedy	Rusk	Bundy (NSC) McNamara (DOD)	
1962				
1963	Johnson	Rusk	McNamara (DOD)	

	President	Sec. of State	Others	Soviets
1964				Brezhnev
1965	Johnson	Rusk	McNamara (DOD)	
1966				
1967				
1968			Clifford (DOD)	
1969	Nixon	Rogers	Kissinger (NSC)	
1970				
1971				
1972				
1973	Nixon	Kissinger	Kissinger (NSC)	
1974	Ford	Kissinger		
1975			Scowcroft (NSC)	
1976				
1977	Carter	Vance	Brzezinski (NSC)	
1980		Muskie		
1981	Reagan	Haig	Weinberger (DOD)	
1982		Shultz		Andropov
1983				
1984				Chernenko
1985	Reagan	Shultz		Gorbachev
1986				
1987				
1988				
1989	Bush	Baker	Scowcroft (NSC)	
1990				

Leaders of the Western Allies

	Britain	France	W. Germany	Nationalist China
1945	Attlee	De Gaulle		
1946				
1947		Fourth Republic (a series of coalition governments 1947–58)		
1948				
1949			Adenauer	Chiang Kai-shek
1950				
1951	Churchill			
1952				
1953				
1954				
1955	Eden			
1956				
1957	Macmillan			
1958		De Gaulle (Fifth Republic)		
1959				
1960				
1961				
1962				
1963	Douglas-Home		Erhard	

	Britain	France	W. Germany	Nationalist China
1964	Wilson			
1965				
1966			Kiesinger	
1967				
1968				
1969		Pompidou	Brandt	
1970	Heath			
1971				
1972				
1973				
1974	Wilson	Giscard d'Estaing	Schmidt	
1975				Chiang Ching-kuo
1976	Callaghan			
1977				
1978				
1979	Thatcher			
1980				
1981		Mitterrand		
1982			Kohl	
1983				
1984				
1985				
1986				
1987				
1988				Lee Teng-hui
1989				
1990	Major			

Leaders of the Soviet Union and the People's Republic of China

	Soviet Union	People's Republic
1945	Stalin	
1946		
1947		
1948		
1949		Mao Zedong
1950		
1951		
1952		
1953	Khrushchev	
1954		
1955		
1956		
1957		
1958		
1959		Liu Shaoqi (head of state through 1968; Mao remained party chairman)
1960		
1961		
1962		

	Soviet Union	People's Republic
1963		
1964	Brezhnev	
1965		
1966		
1967		
1968		
1969		Mao Zedong
1970		
1971		
1972		
1973		
1974		
1975		
1976		Gang of 4
1977		Deng Xiaoping
1978		
1979		
1980		
1981		
1982	Andropov	
1983		
1984	Chernenko	
1985	Gorbachev	
1986		
1987		
1988		
1989		
1990		

SECTION IV

Prominent Cold War Figures

Biographies of
U.S. Political Figures

Acheson, Dean (1893–1971) Secretary of state, 1949–53. The son of an Episcopal bishop, Acheson grew up in New England where he attended the prestigious Groton Preparatory School and Yale University. He graduated from Yale in 1915, served in the Navy during World War I, and then returned to New England where he received a law degree in 1918. He served as secretary to Supreme Court Justice Louis Brandeis for two years before joining the renowned law firm of Covington and Burling in 1921. In 1933 President Roosevelt appointed him undersecretary of the treasury, but Acheson resigned six months afterward as a protest to Roosevelt's reduction of the gold content in the U.S. dollar: an act he considered reckless and unconstitutional. Prior to World War II Acheson chaired a committee to study the operation of the government's administrative offices and helped formulate Roosevelt's constitutional justification for the lend-lease program with Great Britain. Subsequently, Roosevelt asked Acheson to serve as assistant secretary of state for economic affairs, a post he held from 1941 to 1944. In addition to his continued work on the lend-lease program, Acheson played an active role in preparing for the postwar era. He helped organize the United Nations Relief and Rehabilitation Agency (UNRRA), the World Bank, the International Monetary Fund, and the Food and Agriculture Organization.

After Roosevelt's death in 1945 Truman appointed James Byrnes secretary of state, and Byrnes appointed Acheson as undersecretary. During Byrnes's frequent trips abroad, Acheson served as acting secretary of state. In that capacity he gave the president daily briefings on foreign affairs and thereby developed a close relationship with him. Acheson's primary duties as undersecretary involved Western Europe's economic recovery. He advocated extended financial support for UNRRA and Great Britain and, because he considered Poland's economy to be important to the overall redevelopment of Europe, Acheson endorsed a controversial loan to the new Polish government, which was already being called a Soviet puppet.

In the years immediately following World War II Acheson also became deeply involved with atomic energy. Unlike Byrnes and Secretary of Navy James V. Forrestal, who believed the atomic bomb gave the United States a crucial edge over the Soviet Union, Acheson initially favored international control of the bomb and the international development of peaceful uses for atomic energy. With atomic scientist Leo Szilard he warned against a suicidal arms race that would necessarily ensue after the Soviets developed their own nuclear weapons, as they inevitably would in the absence of international restraints. Consequently, along with Roosevelt's Secretary of War Henry Stimson, Acheson called for the exchange of atomic information among the United States, Great Britain, and the USSR and the eventual international control of atomic material.

In early 1946 he chaired a committee whose charge was to prepare a plan for submission to the United Nations. Other committee members included J. Robert Oppenheimer, who had overseen the development of America's atomic bomb, and David Lilienthal, who chaired the Tennessee Valley Authority. The committee report called for the United Nations to create an international atomic development agency to identify each country's holdings of raw nuclear materials and control all fissionable material and production plants. The agency would make nuclear resources available for peaceful purposes but report the efforts by any country to make atomic weapons. The international community would then presumably act to forestall that action. Acheson's committee also recommended that the United States cease manufacturing atomic weapons at some future date and transfer its atomic resources to the international agency in stages. However, the committee stressed that the United States should not release information about nuclear technology in the immediate future. The committee recommendation was passed on to the U.S. representative to the UN Atomic Energy Commission, Bernard Baruch, who effectively killed it by appending demands that the Soviets would be certain to refuse. The Soviets vetoed the Baruch Plan in December 1946. However, the plan's insistence on international inspections of nuclear facilities remained the cornerstone of U.S. policy on nuclear disarmament throughout much of the Cold War.

In the immediate aftermath of World War II Acheson favored a policy of conciliation with the USSR. However, by the spring of 1946 Soviet actions in Turkey, Iran, and the eastern Mediterranean led him to reverse his position and support George Kennan's recommendation that the United States should try to contain Communist expansion throughout the world. Much of his subsequent work as undersecretary and then as secretary of state was dedicated to pursuing this containment policy. In 1947 Acheson helped formulate the Truman Doctrine aimed at containing the USSR within its existing sphere of influence. The doctrine's main feature was the economic reconstruction of postwar Europe, and its cornerstones were the Marshall Plan, which Acheson helped formulate; the Four Point Program to provide technical aid to underdeveloped countries in Asia, Africa, and Latin America; and the creation of the North Atlantic Treaty Organization (NATO), an anti–Soviet military alliance.

Acheson became secretary of state at the beginning of 1949, after George Marshall stepped down due to poor health. His appointment was generally well received both domestically and in Europe. He was well regarded for his intellect, style, mental discipline, and commitment to work against Communist expansion. As secretary he pictured the superpower confrontation as a matter of power politics and did not believe in formulating policies according to abstract principles of morality or internationalism. He felt such idealistic motivations would compel the United States to avoid its responsibilities as a superpower to exercise power in order to create and sustain world order. He also believed that negotiation with the Soviet Union was futile since that nation was unwilling to bargain in good faith. Thus Acheson increasingly came to view the world as divided into distinct Eastern and Western spheres of influence.

Acheson worked to establish the Federal Republic of Germany (West Germany; FRG) which he helped bring into the Western, anti–Communist alliance and whose eventual rearmament he promoted. He also promoted a massive U.S. military buildup to counter the Communists, and he advocated that the United States should be willing to assume unilateral responsibility for the defense of the non–Communist world. Though Truman initially resisted his call to increase the annual military budget to $35 billion — or 20 percent of the gross national product — the president supported the military increase after the outbreak of the Korean War in 1950. During his first year as secretary, Acheson declined to aid Chiang Kai-shek, who was in the process of losing the Chinese civil war to Communist forces under Mao Zedong. In a 1949 White Paper on China Acheson stated that Chiang lacked the support of the Chinese people and that the United States would be unwise to waste its resources propping him up or to intervene militarily on his behalf. A month later the Communists assumed complete control of the Chinese mainland and established the People's Republic of China (PRC). Chiang's defeat allowed Acheson's right-wing critics to charge him and his State Department with "selling out" China, and in 1950 Senator Joseph McCarthy claimed to have names of highly placed Communists within the State Department. Acheson defended his aides in congressional hearings, but the fierce right-wing attack that persisted throughout his term in office compelled him to reject his original plan to recognize the PRC. Instead, he agreed to provide economic aid to Chiang's government in exile on Taiwan (then called Formosa) but he refused to commit the United States to its military defense, especially since the island held no strategic value.

In a January 1950 address Acheson indicated that the U.S. defense perimeter in Asia included Japan, the Ryuku Islands, and the Philippines. When, six months later, the North Korean Communists launched a surprise attack on South Korea, Republican Senator Robert Taft and other critics of the Truman administration charged that by failing to publicly include Korea in his list of crucial countries Acheson had signaled a tacit U.S. willingness to permit the Communist invasion. Acheson responded to the North Korean attack by advocating U.S.

military intervention. He believed the USSR was behind the North Korean action, that it was probing for weaknesses in the Western alliance, and that the United States must deny the Soviets victory by standing up to Communist aggression throughout the world. He thus coordinated the political efforts that brought about the U.S. "police action" in Korea, lobbying Congress and the United Nations and working with diplomats from nonaligned countries. Along with General Douglas MacArthur he advocated liberating North Korea after the military situation in South Korea stabilized. However, both men seriously under-estimated the Chinese resolve to attack if the UN forces crossed the thirty-eighth parallel into North Korea, and they were caught off guard when the Chinese entered the war in November 1950. Unable to negotiate a suitable peace treaty, Acheson resisted calls from leading Republicans to extend the war to China. A truce was not negotiated until shortly after Eisenhower took office in 1953. Despite these setbacks in Korea, however, Acheson continued to follow a con-tainment policy in Asia. Thus he supported the French in their fight against Viet-namese nationalists under the Communist leadership of Ho Chi Minh.

In 1952 the Republican Party platform criticized Acheson's containment philosophy as insufficient and, led by John Foster Dulles, it called for a new lib-eration policy to free Eastern Europe from Soviet control. It also attacked Ache-son's view of power politics as amoral, and members of the extreme right wing accused him and other members of the State Department of being traitors. In response Acheson rejected the liberation policy as unrealistic unless the United States was willing to commit to another major European war, and he pointed to the successes of the Truman administration's containment policies: Western Europe remained politically and economically strong and within the U.S. camp, and the NATO alliance assured its protection against military aggression. Through-out the 1950s Acheson criticized Dulles's foreign policy after Dulles became Eisenhower's secretary of state. Specifically, he attacked as irresponsible and unre-alistic Dulles's call for a moral crusade against Communism, and he denounced Eisenhower's reliance on nuclear weapons. Later he advised presidents Kennedy and Johnson, urging Johnson to deescalate the Vietnam War in 1968.

Baker, James A., III (1930–)   White House chief of staff, 1981–85; secretary of the treasury, 1985–88; secretary of state, 1989–92; and White House chief of staff, 1992. Born in Houston to a prominent Texan family, Baker grad-uated from Princeton in 1952 and then served in the Marine Corps for two years. In 1957 he received his law degree from the University of Texas and began prac-ticing law. He helped manage the unsuccessful 1970 senatorial campaign of Republican Congressman George Bush, a longtime friend. As finance chairman for the Texas Republican Party Baker campaigned for President Nixon's reelec-tion in 1972. In 1975 President Ford appointed him undersecretary of com-merce, but Baker resigned soon afterward to manage Ford's unsuccessful presi-dential campaign. In 1980 he earned praise for almost engineering a major upset when he managed Bush's campaign for the Republican nomination against heavily favored Ronald Reagan.

Reagan appointed Baker White House chief of staff, and Baker earned a reputation for his skill in managing disputes within the White House as well as those between the administration and Congress. He played a large role in winning passage of Reagan's 1981 supply side tax and budget package. In 1985 Reagan appointed Baker secretary of the treasury. His plan to stimulate the economies of developing nations failed, but by devaluing the dollar he temporarily helped them alleviate their debt. Baker had written a college thesis on how Great Britain used international institutional affiliations to extend its political influence during the early days of the Cold War, despite its waning economic power. He tried to accomplish something similar for the United States, establishing the 1985 Plaza and Louvre Agreements to provide a more unified approach to the world economy. These agreements enabled the Western banks to manage exchange rates and the orderly decline of the dollar. While retaining U.S. leadership in NATO, he established the North Atlantic Consultive Council that included parts of Eastern Europe. His attempts to establish an Asian-Pacific institution to stabilize the regional economy failed due to disagreements over Hong Kong's colonial status and difficulties over Taiwan. Nonetheless, Baker supported the Asia-Pacific Economic Cooperation Process, which included China, Hong Kong, and Taiwan. He described his ultimate goal as follows:

> [I]magine a fan spread wide, with its base in North America, and radiating west across the Pacific. The central support is the U.S.-Japan alliance, the key connection for the security structure and the new Pacific partnership we are seeking. To the north, one spoke represents our alliance with the Republic of Korea. To the south, others extend to our treaty allies ... the Philippines and Thailand. Further south, a spoke extends to Australia. ... Connecting these spokes is the fabric of shared economic interests now given form by the Asia-Pacific Economic Cooperation Process. ... Similarly, the emerging North American Free Trade Area will support both APEC and the global, multilateral systems for trade and financial flows.

Baker resigned in 1988 to manage Bush's successful presidential campaign. President-elect Bush then appointed him secretary of state. During his confirmation hearings Baker further stressed the need for international alliances:

> We enter a new era characterized especially by the greater strength of our friends. We live in a world of increasingly influential allies whose cooperation is essential if we are to surmount common problems. There are new global dangers, such as terrorism, the international narcotics trade, and the degradation of the world's environment, that cannot be managed by one nation alone — no matter how powerful. The realities will not permit a blind isolationism or a reckless antagonism.

In that spirit Baker helped forge the international alliance that prosecuted the 1991 Gulf War against Iraq and managed to secure assistance in financing the war from Japan and other allies who did not commit troops. Baker's most notable achievement as secretary of state was his proposal for a comprehensive peace plan in the Middle East that helped lead to direct and eventually fruitful talks between Israel and the hostile Arab nations. He responded slowly and cautiously to the events of 1989 and 1990 that brought about the collapse of Communism in the Soviet Union and Eastern Europe, and he received criticism for not supporting Soviet Premier Boris Yeltsin more vigorously. Due to disarray in the White House, Baker took a leave of absence from the State Department to become White House chief of staff in the summer of 1992. He also managed Bush's unsuccessful campaign for reelection.

Baruch, Bernard M. (1870–1965)   Presidential adviser and representative to the UN Atomic Energy Commission, 1946–47. Born in Camden, South Carolina, the son of a German-Jewish doctor and a Portuguese-Jewish mother from a prominent South Carolina family, Baruch graduated from City College in New York in 1889. Afterward he went to work for the Wall Street brokerage house of A. A. Housman and Company where he quickly rose from office boy to broker to partner. A millionaire by the age of 30, he retired from the firm to establish his own business in industrial development. Baruch strongly supported President Woodrow Wilson, who appointed him to regulatory agencies preparing for possible U.S. entry into World War I. When the United States entered the war in 1918, Wilson named Baruch chairman of the War Industries Board, where he had vast powers for mobilizing the country. In that capacity he became known as the second most powerful man in the United States. A strong Democratic supporter, Baruch secretly advised Republican presidents during the 1920s. Upon his 1932 election Franklin Roosevelt offered to appoint Baruch secretary of the treasury, but the financier declined. Instead, he unofficially advised the president on politics and the economy until Roosevelt's death in 1945.

In 1946 President Truman asked Baruch to serve as the U.S. representative to the UN Atomic Energy Commission, which — less than a year after the atomic bombings of Hiroshima and Nagasaki — was considering plans for international control of atomic energy. A committee chaired by Undersecretary of State Dean Acheson had prepared a U.S. plan. Other committee members included J. Robert Oppenheimer, who had overseen the development of America's atomic bomb, and David Lilienthal, who chaired the Tennessee Valley Authority. The committee report called for the United Nations to create an international atomic development agency to identify each country's holdings of raw nuclear materials and control all fissionable material and production plants. The agency would make nuclear resources available for peaceful purposes but report any country's efforts to make atomic weapons. The international community would then presumably act to forestall that action. Acheson's committee also recommended that the United States should cease manufacturing atomic weapons at some future date and transfer its atomic resources to the international agency in stages. However, the committee stressed that the United States should not release information about nuclear technology in the immediate future. To make the plan more appealing to Congress, the Truman administration asked Baruch to present it to the UN Atomic Energy Commission.

However, Baruch demanded the right to change details of the proposal. Specifically — because he feared Soviet vetoes in the Security Council could impede the work of a UN atomic agency — he demanded that vetoes be prohibited on votes concerning atomic energy. Moreover, he insisted that the plan establish fixed penalties for illegal possession and/or use of atomic bombs or other atomic material. Acheson and his supporters complained that the Soviets would never accede to Baruch's changes, but Baruch threatened to resign if his terms were not included, and Truman acquiesced. Acheson's forecast proved accurate. Baruch submitted the amended plan in June 1946, and in December the UN Atomic Energy Commission unanimously recommended that the Security Council adopt it. Abstaining were Poland and the Soviet Union, which had condemned the plan as an attempt to weaken the Security Council and instead insisted on immediately destroying all atomic weapons. At this time only the United States possessed them. When the plan went to the Security Council for consideration, the Soviets vetoed it. The subsequent intensification of the Cold War in 1947 and 1948 made further top-level efforts for international control of atomic energy politically impossible. Lilienthal had earlier described Baruch as "about the vainest old man I have ever seen," and Truman later maintained that Baruch revised the atomic energy plan mainly to gain greater public recognition. However, the plan's insistence on international inspections of nuclear facilities remained the cornerstone of U.S. policy on nuclear disarmament throughout much of the Cold War.

Though Baruch supported Truman's 1948 election bid and formulated some of the strategy that helped the president become elected, he disapproved of Truman's deficit spending and promoted a balanced budget instead. Their conflicting views intensified just prior to the election, and Baruch's role in Truman's administration diminished greatly. For instance, Truman rejected Baruch's call for a balanced budget and wage and price controls during the Korean War. In 1952 Baruch finally broke with the Democratic Party and supported Dwight Eisenhower for president. He continued to advise U.S. presidents until his death in 1965.

Brzezinski, Zbigniew (1928–   )   National security adviser, 1977–81. The son of a Polish diplomat, Brzezinski was born in Warsaw but lived in France and Germany before settling in Montreal in 1938. He received a bachelor's degree from McGill University in 1949 and a master's degree in economics and political science in 1950. Harvard awarded him a Ph.D in 1953, and he taught there until 1960 when he joined the faculty at Columbia. In 1961 he became director of Columbia's newly created Institute on Communist Affairs. During the 1960s he predicted that the emerging postindustrial, high-tech culture in the United States, Europe, and Japan would diminish tensions between capitalist and Communist countries but increase the differences between industrialized and underdeveloped nations. He advised President-elect Kennedy on foreign affairs and was a strong proponent of the Vietnam War during the Johnson and Nixon administrations, arguing that it was necessary for creating a stabilizing balance of power in Asia. Johnson appointed him to the State Department's Policy Planning Council in 1966, and he assumed responsibility for Vice President Hubert Humphrey's foreign policy positions during the 1968 presidential campaign.

President Carter named Brzezinski national security adviser in 1977, and Brzezinski held the post throughout the Carter years, during which he competed with Secretary of State Cyrus Vance for influence in formulating foreign policy. They differed most strongly in their positions regarding the Soviet Union. Brzezinski advocated a hard line, opposing Soviet attempts to extend their influence throughout the world, even at the expense of nuclear arms control. Vance, on the other hand, favored continuing the détente initiated by presidents Nixon and Ford and pursued arms limitation. For this reason Vance urged a more tolerant response to the 1978 Soviet-backed coup in Ethiopia, while Brzezinski argued that "Soviet leaders may be acting merely in response to an apparent opportunity, or the Soviet action may be part of a wide strategic design. In either case, the Soviets probably calculate, as previously in Angola, they can later adopt a more conciliatory attitude and that the U.S. will simply again adjust to the consolidation of Soviet presence in yet another African country."

In 1979 Vietnam invaded Cambodia and installed a pro–Soviet regime, and in December 1979 the Soviets invaded Afghanistan to prop up the government they had helped place in power. Vance urged a degree of restraint, while Brzezinski again promoted a hard line. He argued that the Soviet Union was deploying "a two-pronged offensive strategy, one pointing through Afghanistan at the Persian Gulf and one through Cambodia at the Straits of Malacca." Carter sided with Brzezinski and used the Afghanistan invasion as an occasion to end détente. He withdrew the SALT II Treaty from Senate consideration, canceled a grain sale to the Soviet Union, and backed Afghani rebels fighting against the Soviets.

The National security adviser and secretary of state also differed in their response to the 1979 crisis in Iran. Brzezinski wanted to inform the shah that the United States would tolerate military suppression of rebellious dissidents, while Vance disagreed. Consequently, the shah received ambiguous messages about U.S. intentions. After the shah was overthrown and Islamic fundamentalists seized the U.S. embassy, taking 66 hostages, Brzezinski and Vance again disagreed on how the United States should respond. Brzezinski favored a military rescue while Vance advocated diplomatic measures. Carter initially followed Vance's advice, but after five months he authorized a rescue attempt. However, a sandstorm debilitated the American helicopters and the mission failed. Eight soldiers died in the attempt and Vance resigned in protest. The hostages were finally released on the day Carter left office, and Brzezinski returned to private life: teaching, lecturing, and writing about foreign policy.

Bundy, McGeorge (1919–1996)   Special assistant to the president for national security affairs, 1961–66. Born in Boston into a prominent New England family, Bundy was the son of Harvey Bundy, an associate of former Secretary of State and Secretary of War Henry L. Stimson. Stimson proved to be a role model, making Bundy aware of the power of his social class and the importance of disinterested service for the public good. In 1941 Bundy graduated first in his class from Yale. During World War II he helped plan the invasions of Sicily and France as an officer in the Army. After leaving the service in 1946 he helped Stimson write his autobiography and in 1948 went to work for the government agency responsible for implementing the Marshall Plan. He resigned shortly afterward to serve as foreign policy adviser to the presidential campaign of Republican nominee Thomas Dewey. After Truman defeated Dewey, Bundy joined the prestigious Council on Foreign Relations as a policy adviser. In 1949 he joined the faculty at Harvard, where he taught a course in modern foreign policy that embodied Stimson's basic outlook. He rose rapidly at Harvard and in 1953 became dean of the College of Arts and Sciences. In that position he became known for his diplomatic skills and his ability to work through the bureaucracy.

Though he supported Eisenhower during the 1950s, Bundy backed Kennedy after the Republicans nominated Nixon in 1960. Impressed by Bundy's handling of a campaign committee of scientists and professionals, Kennedy offered to appoint him to various positions in the State and Defense departments. Bundy declined those but accepted the designation of special assistant for national security affairs, more commonly known as national security adviser. In that capacity he collected information from the departments of State and Defense and from the intelligence agencies, consolidated it, and presented it to the president. He thus controlled the nature and flow of information reaching Kennedy and thereby helped determine the president's view of world events, which in turn shaped administration policies. Especially after the Bay of Pigs fiasco in April 1961, Kennedy turned increasingly to an inner circle of advisers that included Bundy. Bundy reorganized Kennedy's staff and gathered a group of scholars and intellectuals at the White House. These came to play a significant role in determining foreign policy. During the Cuban Missile Crisis Bundy served as one of the president's closest advisers, and he organized the meetings of Excom, a special panel composed of veteran diplomats who advised Kennedy and helped win congressional support for the administration's response to the crisis. On October 17, 1962, when most of the president's advisers favored an air strike against the missile sites, Bundy held out in favor of a diplomatic solution. Two days later, however, he supported an air strike. Kennedy ultimately settled upon a naval quarantine, which proved to be a successful strategy.

Bundy also advised Kennedy on the growing U.S. involvement in Vietnam. In August 1963, after harsh crackdowns on Buddhist dissidents by South Vietnam's President Ngo Dinh Diem, the Kennedy administration wanted to disassociate from Diem but could not agree on how to do it. Roger Hilsman recommended withdrawing U.S. support to Diem in hopes of prompting a coup, while Defense Secretary Robert McNamara advocated retaining support but demanding reforms from Diem. Bundy recommended a compromise position that Kennedy accepted. The United States would retain support and demand reforms but at the same time be willing to exercise its option not to inform Diem about plans for any coup that promised to succeed. It would, however, notify Diem of any plans that had "poor prospects for success." On November 1, with U.S. knowledge but not its direct support, South Vietnamese generals killed Diem and overthrew his regime. Exactly three weeks later Kennedy was assassinated.

Bundy stayed on to advise Lyndon Johnson and helped convince the president to send U.S. Marines to the Dominican Republic in 1965. That year he also advocated bombing North Vietnam, a policy that Johnson also adopted. He left the administration in 1966 because of personality differences with the president and assumed the presidency of the Ford Foundation. After the 1968 Tet Offensive Bundy spoke out in favor of deescalating the war. Bundy's younger brother, William, also held high posts in the Kennedy and Johnson administrations and influenced U.S. policy in Southeast Asia.

Bush, George H. (1924–   )   Republican congressman 1967–71; director of the CIA, 1975–77; vice president, 1981–89; and U.S. president, 1989–93. The son of Republican Senator Prescott Bush, George Bush was born in Milton, Massachusetts. He attended the Phillips Academy and joined the U.S. Naval Reserve upon graduating in 1941. He fought during World War II and in 1943 became the youngest pilot in the Navy. After the war Bush attended Yale University and graduated in 1948. He went to work in the oil industry and in 1954 founded the highly successful Zapata Off-Shore Company, which made him a millionaire. While supporting Barry Goldwater for president, Bush won the Texas Republican Senate nomination but lost the general election in 1964. In 1966 he won election to the House of Representatives and was reelected in 1968. His district was one of Houston's most affluent. He served on the House Ways and Means Committee, taking conservative positions and supporting the oil industry. He also supported environmental legislation and President Johnson's civil rights legislation. In 1970 Bush ran for the Senate but conservative Democrat Lloyd Bentsen defeated him. Subsequently, President Nixon appointed him U.S. ambassador to the United Nations. He supported the Middle East peace proposals initiated by Secretary of State William Rogers and urged concerted world action against the narcotics trade. In 1971 he led the unsuccessful U.S. effort to have the People's Republic of China (PRC) admitted to the United

Nations under a "two Chinas" plan that would also retain the membership of non–Communist Nationalist China in the General Assembly. The PRC was ultimately admitted and Nationalist China was expelled. Bush also defended the administration's support of Pakistan during its December 1971 war with India, but in May he offered U.S. relief aid to Bangladesh. That month he also defended the U.S. blockade of North Vietnam before the United Nations.

After the 1972 elections Nixon named Bush chairman of the Republican National Committee. He set out to broaden the party by appealing more to workers and ethnic groups but quickly he became distracted by the ongoing Watergate scandal that dominated much of Nixon's second term. Bush did not directly involve the party in defending the president; nonetheless, his effectiveness in promoting party goals suffered from the scandal. Following Nixon's resignation Bush accepted an appointment by President Ford to lead the U.S. Liaison Office in the PRC. He impressed the Chinese with his friendliness and informality, touring Beijing on a bicycle and hosting hot dog and hamburger parties in the U.S. compound. He also helped host Ford's state visit to China in 1975.

In November 1975 Ford appointed Bush director of the CIA, and he held the post through the remainder of Ford's presidency. Bush implemented policies to improve the agency's professionalism and promoted younger personnel. He also took the unprecedented step of opening classified CIA documents to a group of conservative, anti-détente foreign policy planners known as Team B. Team B succeeded in reversing the earlier agency assessment that the Soviets were seeking nuclear parity during détente, arguing instead that they were trying to achieve nuclear superiority. Team B's politicized interpretation of the data later became the operative assumption underlying the massive arms build-up and preparations for winnable nuclear war during the early 1980s, when Bush was vice president.

Bush contended for the Republican vice presidential nomination in 1976 but Ford chose Senator Robert Dole instead. After Ford's defeat in the general election Bush returned to private life, serving as chairman of the First National Bank of Houston. In 1980 he challenged front-runner Ronald Reagan for the presidential nomination but lost in a surprisingly close contest. Reagan named him as his running mate, and Bush served as vice president from 1981 to 1989. During that time he supported the president and cultivated ties to right-wing Republicans who were suspicious of his commitment to the conservative cause. Though he maintained that he had been "out of the loop," a 1992 special prosecutor's report concluded that Bush had been involved in the Iran-Contra scheme that sold U.S. arms to Iran in return for promises to free American hostages in Lebanon and then illegally diverted the profits from the arms sales to support the anti–Communist Nicaraguan Contras and conduct other covert activities. Bush's role in Iran-Contra had not been established in 1988 when he defeated Democrat Michael Dukakis for the presidency. However, the long-awaited special prosecutor's report, issued just prior to the 1992 election, contributed to Bush's loss to Bill Clinton.

In his first year in office Bush ordered an invasion of Panama that led to the ouster and arrest of President Manuel Noriega whom the United States accused of promoting drug smuggling. Though not directly linked to the Cold War, the invasion established Bush's willingness to employ military force to achieve U.S. goals. The Bush administration continued to support the right-wing military dictatorship in El Salvador in its civil war against pro–Communist populists; that war finally concluded in 1991 with a negotiated peace settlement. Bush also maintained a hard line against Castro in Cuba. In February 1990 Violeta Barrios de Chamorro defeated the ruling Marxist Sandinista leader, Daniel Ortega, in Nicaragua in an internationally supervised election and concluded the civil war between the ruling pro–Communist Sandinistas and U.S.-backed Contras. The transfer of power was relatively smooth and nonviolent, though the Sandinistas retained considerable power, especially over the military.

Bush had campaigned by taking a hard line against Soviet Premier Gorbachev declaring, "Gorbachev is not a freedom-loving friend of democracy, but an orthodox, committed Marxist," and later claiming "the jury is still out on the Soviet experiment [with reforms]." Shortly after Bush's inauguration National Security Adviser Brent Scowcroft publicly accused Gorbachev's reforms of being "a peace offensive" designed to make "trouble within the Western alliance."

Despite this initial skepticism, the quickly spreading collapse of Communism in Eastern Europe and the Soviet Union forced Bush to reevaluate and offer greater support to Gorbachev. Following Gorbachev's declaration before the United Nations in December 1988 that the USSR would no longer base policy on ideology and that it would renounce force and unilaterally reduce its military strength in Europe, the Soviet Union assented to radical changes behind the iron curtain. During the summer of 1989 Gorbachev and Bush engaged in secret dialogues to arrange a summit meeting, and the Soviets assured the Americans that they would not intervene in Eastern Europe.

Soon after Gorbachev made his position public the Communist empire quickly collapsed. In June 1989 the Solidarity trade union won general elections in Poland, and its nominee became the first non–Communist prime minister in the Eastern bloc. The following year Solidarity's leader Lech Wałęsa was elected president. In September 1989 Hungary opened its borders with Austria, affording 60,000 East Germans access to the West, and in October the Hungarian Communist Party dissolved and renounced Marxist-Leninism in favor of a social democracy. On November 10 East Germany dismantled the Berlin Wall and opened access to West Germany. By the end of the year a new liberal cabinet was in place in East Germany. Also in 1989 Bulgaria's Communist government was replaced; the Czechoslovakian Communist Politburo resigned and was replaced by a non–Communist government; Romanian Communist President

Nicolae Ceauşescu was overthrown by the Army and executed on Christmas Day; and the Soviets completed their withdrawal of troops from Afghanistan, thereby reversing the action that had destroyed détente ten years earlier. Thus despite Bush's doubts, the United States was on the verge of achieving one of its most central Cold War objectives: "Germany whole and free in a Europe whole and free."

By 1990 Bush and Gorbachev had come to some basic agreements. Both wanted to preserve political stability during these times of immense change. Both accepted the internal changes within the Warsaw Pact countries but recognized the Soviets' need for security. They agreed that for the sake of stability the Warsaw Pact and NATO should be continued, if only temporarily, and both recognized the need for each side to retain their armies in Europe during the period of transition. In September 1990 Great Britain, France, the United States, and the Soviet Union signed a peace treaty with East and West Germany officially concluding World War II and establishing the withdrawal of the Soviet Army from Eastern Europe. They thus realized the objectives of Eisenhower's Secretary of State John Foster Dulles who had advocated a "liberation policy" some 35 years earlier. On October 3 East and West Germany united into a single Germany with its capital in Bonn, the capital site of the former West Germany. This fulfilled another major long-standing U.S. Cold War objective. And on November 17–19 leaders of all the European states, the United States, Canada, and the Soviet Union met in Paris where they signed a new charter regulating relations among all the participants, a nonaggression agreement between members of NATO and the defunct Warsaw Pact, and the Conventional Forces in Europe (CFE) Treaty, which reduced the number of troops and tanks opposing each other in Europe. President Bush announced, "We have closed a chapter of history. The Cold War is over."

In the aftermath of the Cold War Bush and Gorbachev worked together to promote world stability and begin to establish a new world order. In July 1991 the Warsaw Pact dissolved, and shortly thereafter Bush traveled to Moscow where he and Gorbachev signed the Strategic Arms Reduction Treaty (START). This was the first Cold War treaty to reduce long-range nuclear stockpiles instead of merely limiting their growth. Afterward Bush flew to Kiev in support of Gorbachev's efforts to hold the Soviet Union together. He warned the citizens of the Ukraine, "Freedom is not the same as independence," and "Americans will not support those who seek independence to replace a far-off tyranny with a local despotism." However, Bush declined to grant Gorbachev the massive amounts of economic aid the Soviet leader insisted he needed to maintain stability and which he had counted on in return for concessions on arms control and for withdrawing Soviet troops from Afghanistan. Politically weakened at home, Gorbachev was imprisoned during an August coup led by Communist hard-liners. Efforts by Russian President Boris Yeltsin foiled the bloodless coup and Gorbachev returned to power, dissolving the Communist Party a week later.

However, the coup weakened Gorbachev's effectiveness, and Yeltsin assumed political dominance in the rapidly deteriorating Soviet Union, which dissolved later that year. In 1992 former President Nixon criticized the Bush administration for its lukewarm support of Gorbachev and Yeltsin, claiming that it was "failing to seize the moment to shape the history of the next half-century."

In addition to his policies in Eastern Europe, Bush tried to improve relations with China, offering most favored nation trade status, offering to sell military planes, and largely ignoring the 1989 uprising in Tiananmen Square in which the Army routed students demanding democratic freedoms. That year he also authorized aid to Vietnam in return for its assistance in accounting for over 2,000 U.S. soldiers missing in action during the Vietnam War. In early 1991 Bush assembled the first Cold War military alliance in response to Iraq's annexation of oil-rich Kuwait. Supported by the Soviet Union, the U.S.-led alliance quickly drove back the Iraqi troops. The war was an overwhelming military success, quickly achieving its proclaimed objective of liberating Kuwait and temporarily making Bush the most popular U.S. president during the post–World War II era. However, Iraqi President Saddam Hussein's subsequent refusal to cooperate with UN inspections to guarantee the terms of the cease-fire and his ruthless military persecution of Kurds living within Iraq significantly diminished Bush's popularity, as did a declining economy and preelection revelations that Bush had lied about his role in the Iran-Contra scandal. He thus lost his 1992 reelection bid to Democrat Bill Clinton.

Byrnes, James F. (1879–1972) Secretary of state, 1945–47. Born in Charleston, South Carolina, the son of Irish immigrants, Byrnes was apprenticed as a law clerk at age 14. He was admitted to the South Carolina bar in 1903. In 1908 he ran successfully for court solicitor and was elected to the U.S. House of Representatives in 1910. He served in the House until 1925 and was elected to the Senate in 1930. An initial supporter of Franklin Roosevelt's New Deal during the 1930s, Byrnes withdrew his support as Roosevelt's policies became more radical. Nonetheless, he approved of the president's foreign policy. Roosevelt appointed Byrnes to the Supreme Court in 1941, but Byrnes resigned 16 months later to head the wartime Office of Economic Stabilization. In 1943 he became head of the Office of War Mobilization where he supervised the production of war and consumer goods. Known as the "assistant president on the home front," Byrnes earned respect for his administrative ability and his ability to work with the bureaucracy responsible for running the domestic war effort. Byrnes accompanied Roosevelt to the Yalta Conference in April 1944 and helped win congressional approval for the postwar plan that implicitly acknowledged spheres of influence but insisted upon free elections and representative governments in Eastern Europe. Unable to choose between Byrnes — who enjoyed support from conservative Democrats — and incumbent Vice President Henry Wallace — who was favored by the Party's left wing — Roosevelt selected compromise candidate Harry S. Truman for his running mate in the 1944 election. The ticket won and when Roosevelt died in April 1945 Truman became president. Truman appointed Byrnes secretary of state in July.

The two men did not work easily together, but initially they shared the same foreign policy objectives: to sustain the wartime alliance and inhibit the Soviets' attempts to take full control of Eastern Europe. Neither man viewed the Soviets as ideologues bent on world conquest. Instead, they regarded Stalin as a fellow politician willing to negotiate a political arrangement. Disregarding the Soviet Union's insistence that it must have secure borders with Eastern Europe, Truman and Byrnes promoted the revitalization of Germany, the founding of democratic governments in Germany and Eastern Europe, and the eventual evacuation of Soviet troops from occupied European territories.

Byrnes played a major role at the Potsdam Conference in August 1945 at which the so-called big three — the United States, Great Britain, and the Soviet Union — set policies for controlling Germany during the occupation. They agreed to foster democratic ideals and introduce representative and elective principles of government in Germany. The Soviets reluctantly acceded to the economic redevelopment of the Germany that Truman and Byrnes believed was crucial to the revitalization and security of Europe. Stalin also agreed to restrict Soviet reparation claims on West German goods. Left unrestricted, reparation claims could have seriously impeded Germany's economic recovery. In return for Stalin's concessions Byrnes and Truman consented to the transfer of part of eastern Germany to Poland where it fell under Soviet control pending a final peace treaty (which was not signed until 1990).

After the United States concluded the war against Japan by dropping atomic bombs on Hiroshima and Nagasaki, Byrnes believed that the atomic bomb would also "make Russia more manageable in Europe." However, at the September 1945 London Conference of Foreign Ministers he found that the Soviets seemed unimpressed by America's atomic monopoly. The Soviets demanded U.S. recognition of the governments they had imposed in Romania and Bulgaria. In return Byrnes acknowledged that the United States would tolerate governments friendly to the Soviet Union but insisted that they should be democratically elected. The two sides reached an impasse, and Byrnes became discouraged about Soviet willingness to reach political compromises. He warned, "We are facing a new Russia, totally different than the Russia we dealt with a year ago. ... Now that the war was [*sic*] over they [are] taking an aggressive attitude and stand on political and territorial questions that [is] indefensible."

Despite his growing pessimism, Byrnes went to Moscow in November for further negotiations. He agreed to recognize the Soviet-controlled regimes in Bulgaria and Romania in return for broader representation within those governments. Angered by Byrnes's refusal to keep him informed during the conference and by the secretary's announcement of the agreement before reporting to him, Truman disassociated himself from Byrnes who, he claimed, had "lost his nerve at Moscow." Republican Senator Arthur Vandenberg, a vocal critic of the administration's foreign policy, termed the agreement "one more typical American give away."

Truman also was at odds with Byrnes over the question of atomic energy. Truman favored international control and had stated his position in October 1945, while Byrnes still viewed the U.S. atomic monopoly as a useful political weapon. Despite his objections, Byrnes asked Undersecretary Dean Acheson to chair a committee to prepare a plan for international control. However, when the administration submitted the plan to Bernard Baruch to present before the United Nations, Baruch effectively killed the proposal by insisting on changes the Soviets were sure to find unacceptable. The Soviets vetoed the amended plan in December 1946.

As the USSR continued to make gains in postwar Eastern Europe in 1946, Truman and Byrnes gradually assumed a harder line against the Communists. In February 1946 George Kennan wrote his detailed "Long Telegram" analyzing U.S. policy toward the USSR, and Truman made it the intellectual basis for subsequent Soviet policy. Departing from Byrnes's earlier view that the Soviets were pragmatic politicians who sought to achieve their goals primarily through diplomacy, the Long Telegram maintained that Soviet foreign policy was predicated on the Communist ideological belief that conflict between Communism and capitalism was historically inevitable. Consequently, Kennan argued that Stalin would consolidate his power at home and insulate the Soviet Union by surrounding it with allied client states. Being too weak to attack the West militarily, the Soviets would attempt to isolate the United States through the political subversion of capitalist countries. Byrnes thus adopted a policy of "patience with firmness" in which the United States would negotiate with the USSR but would expect any further concessions to come from the Soviets. When Soviet troops occupied part of Iran in early 1946 in a dispute over oil rights, Byrnes applied diplomatic pressure until the two countries reached a formal agreement and the Soviets withdrew their soldiers. That summer at the Paris Peace Conference Byrnes became convinced that the Soviets would not honor their Potsdam commitment to create an independent and democratic Germany. Consequently, the administration moved toward establishing a separate, democratic West German government rather than allow a single Soviet-dominated German state. A few months later Byrnes announced, "If complete unification cannot be secured, we shall do everything in our power to secure maximum possible unification. ... We do not want Germany to become a satellite of any power. Therefore, as long as there is an occupation Army in Germany, American armed forces will be part of that occupation Army." This early, firm position on Germany became one of the cornerstones of U.S. policy throughout the Cold War.

Discouraged by accusations that he was a Communist appeaser and increasingly uncomfortable with Truman's civil rights policies — which the segregationist Byrnes believed to be too liberal — Byrnes resigned in January 1947. Truman appointed former General George Marshall to replace him. In 1950 Byrnes was elected governor of South Carolina while running on a states' rights platform. His administration improved state mental health facilities and passed legislation directed at halting activities of the Ku Klux Klan. On the other hand, he took measures to forestall anticipated federal efforts to integrate South Carolina schools. The National Association for the Advancement of Colored People (NAACP) challenged the school policy, and the Supreme Court considered the case along with others in its 1954 Brown versus the Board of Education ruling that struck down public school segregation. Byrnes led an unsuccessful fight against the decision. He retired from public life in 1955, unable to succeed himself as governor.

Carter, James E., Jr. (Jimmy; 1924–   )   U.S. president, 1977–81. Born in Plains, Georgia, to a Baptist farming family, Carter attended Georgia Southwestern College and the Georgia Institute of Technology before receiving an appointment to the U.S. Naval Academy at Annapolis. He graduated in 1946 and in 1948 joined the submarine fleet. He served as an officer on conventional submarines before entering Admiral Hyman Rickover's new nuclear submarine program in the early 1950s. After his father died in 1953, Carter resigned from the Navy and returned to Plains to manage the family farm and general store. He served as a Democratic senator in the Georgia legislature from 1963 to 1967 but lost the party's nomination for governor in 1966. In 1967 he became a "born again" Christian, a spiritual transformation that he considered among the most profound developments in his life. He was elected governor in 1970. During his term in office he pursued a moderate agenda, hiring more women and blacks in government, reorganizing the state bureaucracy, and instituting zero-based budgeting. He introduced a "sunshine law" to allow greater public access to government meetings and promoted proenvironmental legislation. He also supported anticrime measures, including capital punishment and stiff penalties for drug dealers. He unsuccessfully sought the 1972 Democratic nomination for vice president. However, in 1976 he won the Democratic nomination for president and narrowly defeated incumbent President Gerald Ford who had assumed office after President Nixon resigned due to the Watergate scandal. Carter's campaign attacked the Republican Party's record of political corruption. He promised never to lie to the American public and to conduct his administration within a moral framework of action. The chief domestic issues during Carter's presidency were the economy and the energy crisis. However, lack of support from the Democratic Congress prevented him from enacting much of the legislation he proposed.

Carter's Cold War policy was greatly influenced by National Security Adviser Zbigniew Brzezinski. Carter continued the détente initiated by presidents Nixon and Ford but took a more forceful stand on human rights. He strengthened relations with China, establishing formal relations on New Year's

Day 1979, and severing relations with the Nationalist Chinese on Taiwan. He also pursued arms limitation negotiations, and in June 1979 signed a new Strategic Arms Limitation Agreement (SALT II) with Soviet Premier Brezhnev.

Having reached its zenith with the 1975 Helsinki Accords, détente began to seriously deteriorate shortly afterward as the Soviets intensified their efforts to gain power and influence in Africa and Asia. They directly supported a pro–Communist revolutionary group during the Angolan Civil War and imported arms and Cuban soldiers to ensure their victory. In 1977 Colonel Mengistu Mariam seized power in Ethiopia assisted by $2 billion worth of Soviet arms, 20,000 Cuban troops, 300 tanks, and 3,000 Soviet technicians; in 1978 Communists in the ruling coalition of South Yemen carried out a successful armed coup; and in 1978 the Soviets assisted a coup in Afghanistan that brought an unpopular Communist regime to power.

On Christmas Day 1979 the Soviets invaded Afghanistan in order to prop up the government they had installed. That action not only scuttled the SALT II agreement — Carter withdrew the treaty from Senate consideration — it also ended détente. The Soviet invasion also prompted Carter to boycott the 1980 Moscow Olympic games and cancel a major grain sale to the USSR. Moreover, he supported Afghani rebels fighting against the Communists. This was the first time during the Cold War that the United States openly supported surrogate armies against Soviet troops. He also issued the Carter Doctrine that asserted "An attempt by any outside force to gain control of the Persian Gulf region will be regarded as an assault on the vital interests of the United States of America and such assault will be repelled by any means necessary, including military force."

Concerned about the deterioration of NATO forces during the early and mid–1970s, Carter supported NATO plans to station an additional 35,000 U.S. soldiers in Europe and deploy the intermediate-range, nuclear-armed Cruise and Pershing missiles. Furthermore, he reinstituted draft registration in 1980, increased the defense budget by 5 percent, and projected additional increases through 1985. Thus his policies anticipated President Reagan's defense buildup in the early 1980s.

Carter's greatest diplomatic achievement came in 1978 when he brokered the Camp David Accords between Egypt and Israel. These ended a 29-year state of war and established "A Framework for Peace in the Middle East." Egypt agreed to recognize Israel's right to exist in exchange for return of captured territories. Provisions were made to increase trade, travel, and cultural exchange between the two countries.

On January 1, 1979, Carter officially recognized the People's Republic of China (PRC). Shortly thereafter Vietnam invaded Cambodia, replacing the pro–Chinese Khmer Rouge government with a Communist, pro–Soviet regime, and in response China initiated a brief border war with Vietnam. Chinese Deputy Minister Deng Xiaoping informed Carter beforehand of his country's plans to attack Vietnam; he also suggested a loose anti–Soviet alliance between the United States and China.

The last two years of Carter's presidency also saw important developments in Central America and the Caribbean. In March 1979 Marxists seized power on the island of Grenada and established ties to Cuba and the USSR, which gave the new government a limited number of weapons. In July a popular insurrection in Nicaragua deposed the Somoza dictatorship and pro–Communist Sandinistas assumed power. In an attempt to keep Nicaragua from "turning to Cuba and the Soviet Union," Carter maintained diplomatic relations with the new regime but was unable to achieve his goal of establishing a middle ground between pro–Cuban populist revolutionaries and right-wing, military dictatorships loosely affiliated with the United States. Later that year a military coup in El Salvador spawned a civil war between right-wing oligarchs — who controlled the government — and left-wing rebels. Carter initially supported the new government but withdrew support because of extreme human rights violations. However, he resumed military aid at the end of his term. The situation in El Salvador further complicated Carter's efforts to establish a viable diplomatic arrangement with neighboring Nicaragua.

The most severe blow to the Carter presidency also came in 1979, following the fall of the shah of Iran whose family had come to power in the 1950s through a U.S.-supported coup. The Ayatollah Khomeini, an Islamic fundamentalist, created a theocracy shortly afterward. Carter agreed to shelter the exiled shah — who had been notorious for human rights abuses — so Iranian students invaded the U.S. embassy in Tehran taking as hostages 66 members of the embassy's delegation, staff, and Marine guard. Carter responded by freezing Iranian assets, imposing economic sanctions, and attempting to use diplomacy to gain the hostages' release, but these efforts did not succeed. In April 1980 he ordered a military rescue operation, but a sandstorm debilitated the American helicopters and the mission failed. Eight soldiers died in the attempt and Secretary of State Cyrus Vance, who had opposed the mission, resigned in protest. Carter appointed Senator Edward Muskie to replace him. Carter's aid Hamilton Jordan later wrote, "The hostage crisis had come to symbolize the collective frustration of the American people. And in that sense, the president's chances for reelection probably died on the desert of Iran with eight brave soldiers." The crisis was a major issue during the 1980 presidential campaign, and the hostages were released on the day that Ronald Reagan replaced Carter. In return for their release the United States unfroze the Iranian assets and provided medical supplies to Iran, which had recently entered a war with Iraq. The Reagan campaign team was later accused of undermining Carter's negotiations in order to deprive the president of a diplomatic success prior to the election, but these charges were never proven.

Carter left office with the lowest presidential popularity rating ever recorded. However, he later revived his standing through his good offices as a peace negotiator. During the later days of the Cold War he helped end civil wars in Ethiopia and Nicaragua. In 1994 he defused a growing crisis by obtaining a North Korean commitment not to develop nuclear weapons, and he forestalled a U.S. invasion of Haiti by negotiating a dramatic last-minute settlement in which Haitian military leaders agreed to surrender power and leave the country. U.S. warplanes had already left their bases to implement the attack when the settlement was announced. At the end of the year he tried to negotiate a settlement of the civil war in Bosnia. The former president also became known for his work with Habitat for Humanity in which he personally helped build low-cost housing for poor Americans.

Cohn, Roy (1927–86)   A U.S. lawyer and top assistant to Senator Joseph McCarthy. The brilliant son of a New York State Supreme Court judge, Cohn entered Columbia University at age 16 and received his LL.B when he was 20. After being admitted to the New York state bar in 1948 he was hired as an assistant U.S. state attorney. A specialist in prosecuting cases involving subversive activities, Cohn participated in the perjury case against William Remington, who had been accused of passing information to the Communists by former party member Elizabeth Bentley. He also served as a staff lawyer in the trial of Julius and Ethel Rosenberg, who were convicted of spying for the Soviets. In 1951 Cohn transferred to Washington, D.C., where he served briefly as a special assistant to the U.S. attorney general. In that capacity he drew up the perjury indictment against Owen Lattimore whom Senator Joseph McCarthy had earlier accused of heading a ring of subversives within the Acheson State Department. Cohn's later probe of UN employees suspected of subversion again called him to McCarthy's attention, and McCarthy hired Cohn as chief counsel to the Permanent Investigations Subcommittee of the Senate Government Operations Committee 1953–54, which the senator chaired. Cohn worked closely with McCarthy, who once asserted that Cohn was "as indispensable as I am." Known for his arrogant style, sharp mind, and photographic memory, Cohn acquired a reputation for interrogating witnesses relentlessly and scornfully. His detractors considered him a bullying thug who disregarded the ethics of his profession: much as they depicted Senator McCarthy himself.

In April 1953 Cohn and another McCarthy aide, David Schine, took a highly publicized 17-day, 7-country tour of the State Department's European libraries, which they claimed housed some 30,000 books by pro–Communist writers. They removed and in some cases burned books by about 40 authors. Notable among the objectionable authors were detective writer Dashiell Hammett, and Theodore H. White, whose best-selling *Thunder Out of China* was among those burned, presumably because it criticized the ignorance and corruption of Chiang Kai-shek, the U.S.-backed, anti–Communist leader of the Chinese government-in-exile. The works of 20 other authors who had not been forthright in Senate hearings were banned "pending further examination."

President Eisenhower responded shortly thereafter by publicly warning against book burners.

When Schine was drafted into the Army in the fall of 1953, Cohn and McCarthy used their influence to try to have him commissioned as an officer and to obtain other special treatment for him. Their efforts ultimately led to McCarthy's political downfall. In 1954, when McCarthy's committee was investigating charges of Communist subversion within the Army, the Army accused McCarthy and Cohn of political extortion: threatening to discredit the Army unless Schine received preferential treatment. In turn, McCarthy maintained that the Army was using Schine as a "hostage" to impede his investigation. These charges led to the Army-McCarthy hearings conducted by the Investigations Subcommittee. Cohn, who had temporarily removed himself as counsel, was seen waving a folder labeled "Jackson" and threatening to attack opposition Senator Henry Jackson. Later, despite Cohn's counsel to the contrary, McCarthy recklessly accused a member of the law firm of Army counsel Joseph Welch. The resulting televised confrontation between Welch and McCarthy contributed significantly to the senator's fall from power. The committee's Republican majority report criticized Cohn for being "unduly aggressive and insistent," while the Democratic minority claimed he had "misused and abused the powers of his office and brought disrepute to the Committee." Cohn had already resigned under pressure by time the report was issued in August.

He subsequently went into private practice in New York where he invested in many corporations and promoted championship boxing matches between Sonny Liston and Floyd Patterson. In 1963 a grand jury indicted him for perjury and conspiracy in a stock fraud case, but he was acquitted after a mistrial. In 1968 he published *McCarthy*, a defense of the senator. He died of complications from AIDS in 1986.

Dulles, Allen W. (1893–1969)   Deputy director of the Central Intelligence Agency (CIA), 1951–53; and director 1953–61. Dulles was born in Watertown, New York. His father was a Presbyterian minister and his uncle, John Welsh, served as the envoy to England during the administration of Rutherford B. Hayes. His younger brother, John Foster Dulles, served as Eisenhower's secretary of state while Allen headed the CIA during the 1950s. After attending private schools in New York and Paris, Dulles graduated from Princeton University in 1916. That year he entered the diplomatic corps, and during World War I he joined the American legation at Bern, Switzerland as an intelligence officer. He attended the Paris Peace Conference in 1919 where he helped establish the frontiers of Czechoslovakia and worked on the terms of the peace settlement for Central Europe. At the conference he supported closer ties between Germany and the United States in order to deal with possible threats posed by the newly created Communist government in Russia. Afterward Dulles served in Berlin and Istanbul before returning to Washington, D.C., where he served as chief of the State Department's Near Eastern Division. In 1926 he received his LL.B degree from George Washington University and resigned to join the international law firm of Sullivan and Cromwell, in which his brother was senior partner. As a result of his legal work he established connections with powerful political and industrial figures in Europe, especially in Germany. During World War II he served as chief of the Office of Strategic Services (OSS) in Bern and received credit for several intelligence successes, including infiltration of the German intelligence organization. In 1945 he helped negotiate the German surrender in Italy.

After the fall of Germany Dulles headed the OSS in Berlin. He believed initially that the U.S.-USSR wartime alliance could be sustained, but his experiences with Soviet occupying forces quickly made him skeptical about Soviet intentions. After the Japanese surrender Dulles returned to his law practice in New York but retained his ties with government. In 1946 he advocated a largely independent, "de–Prussianized," "de–Bismarckized" Germany, and throughout the formative years of the Cold War he maintained that a restored, economically viable Germany was necessary for resisting the increasingly aggressive Soviet actions in Europe.

President Truman disbanded the OSS immediately after the war's conclusion. However, he soon realized that the disparate intelligence units scattered among several agencies provided conflicting information. This rendered policymaking difficult and confusing. Therefore, in January 1946 Truman issued an executive order that established a National Intelligence Authority (NIA). The NIA contained a Central Intelligence Group (CIG) responsible for coordinating and evaluating intelligence from other units. However, because CIG personnel belonged to the Army, Navy, and State Department, Dulles maintained that it could not function efficiently or independently. He testified before Congress that a new intelligence unit should be created with its own personnel and budget. It should supervise all intelligence activities in foreign countries and have access to all intelligence relating to foreign countries. Dulles proposed that the new organization should be the recognized agency for dealing with the intelligence agencies of other countries and that legislation should be passed to punish personnel who breached security. Dulles further insisted that the head of the new agency should be a civilian and that the agency should be divorced from policymaking. "It should try to get at the hard facts on which others must determine policy."

In 1946 Dulles helped draft the National Security Act, which Congress passed in 1947. The act replaced the CIG with the CIA, which reported to the newly created National Security Council (NSC), composed of the president and the secretaries of state, defense, Army, Navy and Air Force. The NSC's charge was to advise on and coordinate defense and foreign policies. The CIA's mission was to advise the NSC on intelligence, collect and evaluate intelligence information related to national security and perform "such other functions and duties related to intelligence affecting national security" that were ordered by the NSC. The National Security Act specified that the CIA would have "no police, subpoena, law-enforcement powers, or internal-security functions."

Like Secretary of State George Marshall, Dulles concluded that the United States must send massive amounts of economic aid to Europe in order for the European countries to avoid social, economic, and political chaos that would render them vulnerable to Communist takeovers and Soviet domination. Shortly after Marshall announced his plans for the European Recovery Program in June 1947, Dulles became consultant to the Herter Commission that traveled to Europe to gather information and make recommendations to Congress about European aid. He later served on the Committee on the Marshall Plan to Aid European Recovery, and in 1948 he advocated continuing the Marshall Plan for four more years and arming friendly nations for their defense against Communist forces.

After a 1948 coup brought about a Communist takeover of Czechoslovakia, the NSC feared that Communists might prevail in the upcoming Italian elections. Secretary of Defense James Forrestal had tried to raise funds from Wall Street financiers to launch a nongovernment, clandestine campaign to undermine the Italian Communists; however, Dulles felt that a private effort would be ineffective. Instead he promoted the creation of a special agency for carrying out clandestine operations. In the summer of 1948 the NSC authorized the CIA to conduct covert operations, with the proviso that the operations should remain secret and that the government should be able to plausibly deny their existence. Subsequently, the Office of Policy Coordination (OPC) was formed as a separate organization within the CIA to oversee covert operations abroad. On Dulles's recommendation his former OSS assistant Frank Wisner was chosen to head the OPC.

Later in 1948 Truman asked Dulles to chair a small committee to assess the CIA's effectiveness and recommend organizational changes. Dulles's work specialized in clandestine intelligence gathering and covert operations. One of his most significant recommendations was that the OPC be more fully integrated into the organizational structure of the CIA. In October 1950 Truman appointed General Walter B. Smith to head the CIA and gave him the recommendations from Dulles's committee. Smith invited Dulles to serve as a consultant to implement the recommendations, and Dulles soon thereafter assumed the post of deputy director of plans for the agency. In that capacity he oversaw the OPC and the agency's covert activities. The organizational recommendations he and Smith implemented in their first years defined the CIA's structure for the next two decades.

In November 1951 Dulles became the CIA's deputy director and Wisner became director of plans. Believing that Eastern Europe could still be liberated and that the Soviet armies could be forced back within Soviet borders, they implemented many covert operations behind the iron curtain. In 1952 the CIA initiated a program to intercept and read mail passing between the United States and certain foreign countries. Though it clearly violated the CIA's charter, this practice continued for 21 years, presumably with the unspoken approval of three postmasters general.

In 1953 the newly inaugurated President Eisenhower appointed Dulles director of the CIA. As a public figure, the pipe-smoking Dulles projected a calm, urbane, and dignified image that became associated with that agency. He convinced the government and the public that the work of the CIA required strict secrecy and thus managed to hide the agency from stringent congressional oversight and media inquiry. For instance, by appealing to the need for secrecy he forestalled a Senate investigation by Senator Joseph McCarthy while McCarthy was at the height of his power. McCarthy had wanted to look into allegations about one of the CIA's employees, William Bundy.

As a member of the Eisenhower administration Dulles worked closely with his younger brother, John Foster Dulles, the secretary of state. Both men viewed the fight against Communism as a moral crusade of freedom-loving democracies against freedom-denying totalitarian regimes, and both favored policies aimed at the eventual liberation of Eastern Europe from Soviet control. However, Cold War circumstances eventually compelled both men to accept modified versions of Truman's containment policies. The liberation of iron curtain countries by means that were short of all-out war had become an increasingly unrealistic goal by the mid–1950s, especially after Eisenhower refused in 1956 to support the provisional anti–Communist government in Budapest that briefly seized power during the Hungarian Revolution.

The Eisenhower administration increasingly turned to covert actions as a tool for achieving desired political outcomes. Thus Dulles's CIA helped overthrow several left-wing governments and install governments more friendly to U.S. interests. In 1953, for instance, it helped depose Iran's Prime Minister Mohammad Mossadegh and restore the shah. And in 1955 it helped overthrow the leftist government of Guatemala's President Jacobo Arbenz Guzmán, who had initiated a program of land reforms that threatened the interests of the powerful, American-owned United Fruit Company. The CIA both trained and supplied an Army of Guatemalan exiles and organized an Air Force staffed by U.S. pilots to provide air cover for the revolutionary Army. When the attack appeared to be failing, Dulles convinced Eisenhower to authorize the use of additional U.S. planes. These turned the tide of the battle and Arbenz was forced to surrender. The right-wing Colonel Carlos Castillo Armas then came to power with CIA assistance. Elsewhere the CIA backed other anti–Communist regimes that lacked popular support. Most significantly it helped enable South Vietnam's President Ngo Dinh Diem to consolidate control of the government, despite strong opposition from the military and important religious sects. The U.S. commitment to Diem played a major role in the growing U.S. involvement in Vietnam.

Hearings by the Senate's 1975 Select Committee to Study Intelligence Activities (the Church Committee) revealed that Dulles had authorized the assassination of Congolese leader Patrice Lumumba in 1960 and that Eisenhower may have indirectly given his authorization. However, Lumumba's Congolese enemies killed him before the CIA could implement its plan. The Church Committee also reported that Dulles and Eisenhower had promoted the overthrow of Rafael Trujillo, dictator of the Dominican Republic. According to the committee, authorization for such covert operations was made deliberately vague and indirect so that the agency could maintain plausible deniability. For example, Dulles's instructions to the CIA station in the Congo read, "We wish every possible support in eliminating Lumumba from any possibility of resuming a governmental position."

A former CIA agent and a former State Department official have claimed that in 1959 Dulles altered a CIA report on Castro, advising Eisenhower on the situation in Cuba. They maintained he deleted an assessment stating that Castro's rise to power resulted naturally from the Batista regime's extensive corruption and replaced it with a prediction that Castro would use excessive force to consolidate his power. In response Eisenhower authorized Dulles to begin training an Army of Guatemala-based Cuban exiles to liberate the island, and Dulles placed Richard Bissell in charge of the operation. A plan to organize an internal uprising proved to be not feasible. Bissell then enlisted the assistance of organized-crime leaders to arrange assassination attempts on Castro, but these failed. Dulles's complicity in this underworld plot remains uncertain; Bissell claimed that he had informed Dulles of his plans to employ known criminals. Their other options having failed, in November 1962 Bissell and Dulles advised President-elect Kennedy of the existence of the exile Army and recommended an assault on Cuba. In April 1961, Kennedy authorized the Bay of Pigs invasion. Dulles decided not to cancel a long-standing speech in Puerto Rico on the day of the invasion because he did not want to raise any unnecessary suspicions. Thus Bissell oversaw the failed operation, which resulted in the death or capture of most of the invading force. In a highly controversial move Kennedy canceled a second CIA air strike intended to support the invaders. A panel headed by retired General Maxwell Taylor could not reach an agreement as to whether the plan ever had any realistic chance for success. Dulles argued that if they had followed the original plans and ordered the second air strike it might have succeeded. Shortly after the Bay of Pigs fiasco the president replaced Dulles, who returned to his private law practice. He later served on the Warren Commission that investigated the Kennedy assassination, and in 1964 he served as President Johnson's special emissary to evaluate "law observance problems" in Mississippi after the disappearance of three civil rights workers there.

Dulles, John Foster (1888–1959) A U.S. diplomat; senator; and secretary of state in the Eisenhower administration, 1953–59. A graduate of Princeton University (1908), Dulles also attended the Sorbonne in Paris and received his law degree from George Washington University in 1911. During World War I he served as legal counsel to the War Trade Board and advised President Wilson during the Versailles Treaty negotiations that ended that war. From 1946 to 1948 and in 1950 Dulles served as U.S. delegate to the United Nations. During that period he was also a special adviser to the secretaries of state George Marshall and Dean Acheson at the councils of foreign ministers in London (1945), Moscow (1947), and Paris (1949). He briefly served as a U.S. senator in 1949, filling an open seat in New York, but he lost in the general election that fall. As U.S. ambassador he helped negotiate the 1951 peace treaty with Japan that formally ended World War II in the Asian theater.

Following Eisenhower's 1952 election Dulles was appointed secretary of state. Eisenhower, who once called him "the wisest, most dedicated man that I know," gave Dulles considerable latitude in formulating U.S. foreign policy throughout the 1950s, one of the most critical periods in the Cold War. Dulles took a very hard line against international Communism which he believed to be a unified, monolithic, and immoral force dedicated to world conquest. In contrast to the Truman administration's containment policy, which George Kennan had devised in order to limit Communist domination to those nations which the Communists had secured after World War II, Dulles advocated a liberation policy to eventually free countries under Communist rule, especially those in Eastern Europe. However, Eisenhower's refusal to intervene in the 1956 Hungarian Revolution demonstrated the limits of this liberation policy.

Dulles also believed the United States had to be prepared to go to the brink of war in order to halt the spread of Communism around the world. He credited this brinkmanship for ending the Korean War, forestalling a Chinese invasion of the islands of Quemoy and Matsu in the Formosa Strait, and settling the Indochina War between the French and Vietnamese Communists, though the United States and South Vietnam refused to sign the 1954 Geneva accords calling for the temporary partition of Vietnam and nationwide elections in 1956.

On January 11, 1954, Dulles announced a nuclear-based U.S. defense policy predicated on instant and massive retaliation against any aggressor at any target the United States deemed appropriate. Developed at a time when the United States had unquestioned nuclear superiority, massive retaliation maintained that the United States could respond with a nuclear attack against the USSR if that country were to attack a U.S. ally anywhere in the world. One attraction of this policy for Eisenhower was that it was more cost efficient than conventional defenses, thereby giving the United States "a bigger bang for the buck." However, as the Soviet Union developed its own nuclear arsenal and intercontinental ballistic missiles during the late 1950s, massive retaliation became an increasingly problematic strategy, since the USSR could adopt a similar policy directed against the United States.

Dulles saw the importance of cultivating allies among underdeveloped African and Asian countries as a Cold War strategy. In his first year in office he not only visited European capitals but also spent three weeks in Southeast Asia and the Middle East. One consequence of his trip was a policy predicated on even-handedness to both Israel and the Arab nations. In 1955 he devised a plan to promote stability in the Middle East by developing water resources to provide arable land for 900,000 Arab refugees from Israel. In 1956 he successfully argued against U.S. support of the French-British-Israeli invasion of Egypt after that country seized the Suez Canal, because he feared that U.S. approval would alienate anti–Israeli Arab countries as well as other underdeveloped nations leery of military intervention by former colonial powers. In 1957 Dulles also encouraged Eisenhower to support the rights of black school children seeking to attend white schools in Little Rock, Arkansas, because he wanted to defuse criticism of U.S. racism, which the Communists were using to turn underdeveloped countries against the United States. That year Dulles also played a major role in formulating the Eisenhower Doctrine, which expressed U.S. willingness to send military and economic aid to any Middle Eastern country requesting assistance against Communism. In 1958 the president invoked that doctrine to send U.S. Marines to Lebanon to support the presidency of Camille Chamoun whose pro–West policies had sparked rebellion in Beirut and Tripoli.

Dulles feared the Communists were trying to gain control of the world's "rice bowl" in Thailand, Indochina, Burma, and Malaya, in order to gain power over India and Japan. Consequently, he played a major role in forming the Southeast Asia Treaty Organization (SEATO) among the United States, Great Britain, Australia, France, New Zealand, Pakistan, the Philippines, and Thailand to oppose further Communist gains in Southeast Asia. He also helped form the Baghdad Pact, which later evolved into the Central Treaty Organization (CENTO). In addition to the defensive purposes these organizations proclaimed, they also had the effect of surrounding the USSR with hostile forces.

Throughout Dulles's tenure as secretary of state, the United States and USSR maneuvered both politically and sometimes militarily to resolve the fate of Germany, which had been divided after World War II. In 1954, in response to the remilitarization of West Germany and in opposition to the North Atlantic Treaty Organization (NATO) alliance, the USSR recognized East Germany as a sovereign country. In 1955 West Germany gained recognition from both superpowers and joined NATO shortly thereafter. However, hoping to achieve the eventual unification of a neutral or pro–West Germany, Dulles argued against U.S. recognition of East Germany. In fact, the United States did not formally recognize East Germany until 1974. In 1958 the Soviets inaugurated a three-year-long Berlin Crisis by demanding that Western troops evacuate the city. However, Dulles fell ill from cancer in April 1959 and was forced to resign while the crisis was still ongoing. Christian A. Herter replaced him.

Eisenhower, Dwight D. (1890–1969) U.S. president, 1953–61. Born in Abilene, Kansas, to a working-class family of Swiss descent, Eisenhower graduated from West Point in 1915. He served as a tank instructor in World War I and during the 1920s he attended the Army's Command and General Staff School and its War College. In 1932 he graduated from the Army Industrial College. During the 1930s Eisenhower served as personal assistant to General Douglas MacArthur and assistant military adviser to the Philippines. Soon after the United States entered World War II he became chief of operations for General George Marshall. His work greatly impressed President Roosevelt, who chose Eisenhower over many more senior generals to assume command first of U.S. forces in Europe and then of all Allied forces in Europe. Roosevelt and Marshall valued him especially for his administrative capabilities and his diplomatic skills, which helped hold together the anti–Fascist alliance. Eisenhower commanded the Allied invasions of North Africa (1942) and Sicily and Italy (1943). In 1944 he oversaw the Normandy invasion that led to the fall of Germany in 1945. After the war he succeeded Marshall as Army chief of staff, a position he held until assuming the presidency of Columbia University in 1948. During this time he resisted overtures from both political parties to run for president. In 1951 President Truman appointed Eisenhower commander of the forces then being assembled by the newly created North Atlantic Treaty Organization (NATO).

Fearful that the Republican Party would back highly conservative Senator Robert Taft, whose ideologically based foreign policies Eisenhower believed would undermine U.S. interests, Eisenhower ran for and received the Republican presidential nomination in 1952. To attract the party's right-wing constituency he nominated California Senator Richard Nixon as his vice presidential running mate, and the Eisenhower-Nixon ticket went on to win easily over the Democratic nominee, Adlai Stevenson. However, despite a personal landslide for the Eisenhower, the Republicans gained only a small majority in the House of Representatives and an even split with the Democrats in the Senate. Thus Eisenhower had to achieve a significant degree of consensus during his first administration, something he was temperamentally disposed to do anyway since he believed the presidency should be largely above partisan politics. In his domestic agenda he promoted limited government and a sound economy, believing that a healthy, unrestricted economy provided the best basis for a socially, politically, and militarily strong United States. Most of his cabinet appointments came from the upper managerial positions in big business, though his conservative secretary of state, John Foster Dulles, had been a lawyer and career diplomat.

Throughout his presidency, and especially during his first term, Eisenhower had to appease the ultra-conservative right wing of the Republican Party, which insisted on a uniform hard line against all real and/or imagined Communist initiatives. Thus in the 1952 campaign Eisenhower chose Nixon for vice president and declined to defend his mentor, five-star General George Marshall, against charges of Communist sympathy. The right wing compelled Eisenhower to take an inflexible stand against the Chinese Communists and unsuccessfully opposed his nomination of Charles Bohlen as Soviet ambassador because Bohlen had followed the Truman-Acheson policy of appeasement. This group also tried to limit the president's powers to make treaties but narrowly failed. Under prodding by right-wing Senator Joseph McCarthy, the Eisenhower administration tightened internal security restrictions on federal employees, enabling the government to fire individuals because they had questionable associates or suspicious personal habits. This eventually permitted the FBI to determine subjects' loyalty by asking about their reading habits, their stand on civil rights and socialized medicine and their support for former vice president Henry Wallace, who ran for president in 1948 on the left-wing Progressive Party ticket. Despite international appeals from such figures as Albert Einstein and Pope Pius XII, Eisenhower declined to intervene in the decision to execute Julius and Ethel Rosenberg after their controversial conviction as atomic bomb spies. And under rightwing pressure Eisenhower upheld the Atomic Energy Commission's decision to suspend the security clearance of J. Robert Oppenheimer, who had headed the U.S. program to develop the atom bomb during World War II. As the head of the AEC from 1946 to 1952, Oppenheimer had angered the right by promoting international control of atomic energy and opposing for moral and scientific reasons the development of hydrogen bombs. Right-wing accusations that Oppenheimer had had Communist associations during the 1940s led to his dismissal from the AEC.

During Eisenhower's presidency and afterward, liberals and moderates criticized Eisenhower for failing to oppose McCarthy, whom the president personally detested. In a 1953 investigation of State Department libraries McCarthy's aides Roy Cohn and David Schine burned books by authors they considered pro–Communist, and Eisenhower shortly afterward denounced book burners in a public speech at Dartmouth College. He also described another McCarthy aide's allegation that Communists had infiltrated the Protestant clergy as "generalized and irresponsible." In 1954 he supported Army Secretary Robert Stevens's refusal to testify before McCarthy's Senate committee after McCarthy had attacked Stevens. The confrontation between McCarthy and the Army eventually led to the senator's downfall later that year, but Eisenhower did not play a major role in the Senate vote to censure him.

Though he believed government should play a limited role in domestic policy, Eisenhower advocated an activist foreign policy. He and John Foster Dulles worked closely together until Dulles's death in 1959. Dulles was more ideologically driven than the pragmatic Eisenhower. While Dulles viewed the Cold War as a moral crusade against the tyranny of Communism in its enslavement of Eastern Europe, Eisenhower regarded the struggle more as a matter of power politics. And though he authorized covert CIA operations directed at driving the Soviets from Eastern Europe, Eisenhower refused to risk a major military confrontation to implement Dulles's liberation policy. His reticence to use military force to achieve Cold War objectives in Europe became evident during 1953 when Eisenhower declined to assist the anti–Communist populist movement that had spawned a general strike in East Berlin and threatened to topple East Germany's Communist government. Nor did he support the anti–Communist forces in Hungary in 1956 when they briefly overthrew the Soviet-backed government and appealed to the United States for protection. In each instance Eisenhower refused to authorize military aid or U.S. military action, and in each case Soviet Premier Khrushchev ordered tanks into the key cities and crushed the rebellions. Eisenhower's basic foreign policy was to retain peace while containing Communism and increasing U.S. influence abroad. He favored reducing Cold War tensions and restricting the arms race: "This is not a way of life at all, in any true sense. Under the cloud of threatening war, it is humanity hanging from a cross of iron."

Wishing to avoid outright warfare, the Eisenhower administration increasingly turned to covert actions as a tool for achieving desired political outcomes. Thus the CIA helped overthrow several left-wing governments and install governments more friendly to U.S. interests. In 1953, for instance, it helped depose Iran's Prime Minister Mohammad Mossadegh and restore the shah. And in 1955 it helped overthrow the leftist government of Guatemala's President Jacobo Arbenz Guzmán, who had initiated a program of land reforms that threatened the interests of the powerful, American-owned United Fruit Company. The CIA both trained and supplied an Army of Guatemalan exiles and organized an Air Force staffed by U.S. pilots to provide air cover for the revolutionary Army. When the attack appeared to be failing, CIA director Allen Dulles convinced Eisenhower to authorize the use of additional U.S. planes. These turned the tide of the battle, and Arbenz was forced to surrender. The right-wing Colonel Carlos Castillo Armas then came to power with CIA assistance. During the Eisenhower years the CIA also helped enable South Vietnam's President Ngo Dinh Diem to consolidate power, despite strong opposition from the military and important Vietnamese religious sects. The U.S. commitment to Diem played a major role in the growing U.S. involvement in Vietnam, though the number of American military advisers remained small while Eisenhower was in office.

The Korean War was still in operation during the 1952 election season, and Eisenhower had promised during the campaign that "I will go to Korea." Prior to his inauguration he traveled to South Korea to meet with President Syngman Rhee. After entering office he pressured the Communist Chinese by removing the Seventh Fleet from the Formosa Straits, thereby eliminating the buffer that prevented an attack on the mainland by Chiang Kai-shek's Nationalists. He also strengthened U.S. air power in Korea and announced that the United States was sending nuclear weapons to Okinawa, where they would be accessible for use in Korea. At the same time Eisenhower pressured Rhee to soften his stance and relinquish his demand that fighting would resume if Korea was not unified within 90 days. In July 1953, after the death of Stalin made new political accommodations possible, the warring parties signed an armistice that concluded the fighting, but they never obtained a political solution.

In 1954, despite Dulles's warning that a French defeat in Indochina (Vietnam, Laos, and Cambodia) could produce a domino effect in which other Southeast Asian countries would fall to Communist insurgency, Eisenhower declined to send substantial military assistance to save the surrounded French Army at Dien Bien Phu. He feared becoming deeply involved in another land war in Asia and accepted the advice of the joint chiefs of staff that air power would ultimately require ground troops. Eisenhower also resisted requests to employ nuclear bombs. That year Eisenhower also restrained the Taiwan-based Nationalist Chinese who wanted to bomb the mainland in retaliation for Communist shelling of the islands of Quemoy and Matsu. Instead, John Foster Dulles negotiated a defense treaty guaranteeing U.S. protection of Taiwan (Formosa) in return for Chiang Kai-shek's agreement not to attack the mainland without U.S. consent. In 1955 Congress passed the Formosa Resolution, which empowered the president to take whatever action he felt was necessary to defend Taiwan. Eisenhower then indicated U.S. willingness to employ nuclear weapons if the United States became involved in an Asian war. Shortly afterward the Chinese Communists reduced their shelling and indicated their willingness to negotiate a solution. However, due to pressure from the Republican Party's highly pro–Chiang right wing, Eisenhower refused to negotiate with the Communists and firmly opposed Communist China's admission to the United Nations.

In the 1956 Suez Crisis Eisenhower again declined to support the French. In July Egyptian President Gamal Nasser nationalized the British-owned Suez canal and denied Israel passage through it. He later expelled British oil and embassy officials and increased border raids on Israeli territory. On October 29, preempting an anticipated Egyptian attack, Israel invaded Egypt; it was joined shortly after by Great Britain and France, who were intent on retaking the canal. Eisenhower was angered because the allies had failed to consult with the United States before invading, and he refused to support their effort. However, when the Soviets threatened a missile attack against France and Great Britain, Eisenhower declared that such an attack would provoke a U.S. nuclear response and lead to global war. A UN armistice defused the crisis, arranging for the withdrawal of all British and French troops and leaving the United States as the sole superpower in the region. Another consequence of the Suez crisis was the further deterioration of the U.S.-French alliance.

Because he believed so strongly that a healthy economy was necessary to U.S. strength, Eisenhower worked to hold down the defense budget. "This country could choke itself to death piling up military expenditures, just as surely as it can defeat itself by not spending for protection." His administration, therefore, turned to a defense program centered around nuclear weapons, which were far more cost effective than maintaining conventional armies. Thus Eisenhower promoted the hydrogen bomb, which was developed in 1953 because it promised to give "a bigger bang for the buck." In 1956 Eisenhower reduced the military by 25 percent. Most of the reductions cut the Army and Navy's conventional forces. At the same time the Air Force, which was responsible for delivering a nuclear attack, received a spending increase.

The reconfigured, nuclear-dependent military was more suited to the administration's policy of massive retaliation that Dulles had announced in early 1954. Massive retaliation claimed that Soviet aggression against U.S. allies anywhere on the globe could be met by a nuclear response directed against the Soviet Union itself. The nuclear threat was intended to compensate for the Eastern block's numerical superiority in troops and conventional weapons. On the other hand, at a Geneva summit meeting in July 1955 Eisenhower proposed his "atoms for peace" plan aimed at reducing the possibility of nuclear war.

In September 1955 Eisenhower suffered a mild heart attack. Although he recovered quickly, his doubts about his own health made him reconsider plans to run for a second term. However, after receiving encouragement from friends, the Republican Party, and public opinion polls, he sought and won reelection, again handily defeating Stevenson. Once again, however, his personal popularity did not affect the congressional races, and the Democrats maintained control of Congress.

Tensions in the Middle East continued after the Suez crisis. In 1957 the president issued the Eisenhower Doctrine announcing U.S. willingness to send military and economic aid to any Middle Eastern country requesting U.S. assistance against Communism. In July 1958 he invoked the doctrine by sending U.S. Marines to Lebanon to support the pro–U.S. President Camille Chamoun against popular uprisings that threatened to topple his government. Following a UN resolution and the succession of General Fuad Chehab to the Lebanese presidency, the Marines departed in the fall.

In 1958 the Chinese Communists resumed shelling Quemoy and Matsu. Initially, Eisenhower took a hard-line position and in September asserted U.S. willingness to defend the islands. But he was unable to win support either at home or abroad and had to adopt a more moderate stand. Dulles declared that the United States had no obligation to defend the islands and that Chiang's decision to place a large garrison on them was "rather foolish." The Communists subsequently reduced their attacks.

In 1958 Khrushchev initiated the Second Berlin Crisis by demanding that the Western allies evacuate the divided city within six months. The West refused and the possibility of a superpower military confrontation increased substantially. Khrushchev later extended his deadline to permit negotiations but remained firm in his demands. After the first negotiations failed, Khrushchev visited the United States in 1959 and met personally with Eisenhower to try to settle the explosive situation. The Soviet premier's visit eased the Cold War tension temporarily, and the leaders signed a treaty establishing Antarctica as a nuclear-free zone. But in the spring of 1960 the revelation that an American U-2 spy plane had been shot down over USSR airspace scuttled a Paris summit conference on Berlin just as it began. Tensions escalated again quickly as the

United States first denied spying and then defended the practice after the Soviets produced the pilot, who was still alive. The Berlin Crisis continued beyond Eisenhower's term in office and did not conclude until 1961, when the Communists erected the Berlin Wall and U.S. and Soviet tanks confronted each other across the line dividing East and West Berlin.

In 1957, shortly after successfully testing an intercontinental ballistic missile (ICBM), the Soviets launched Sputnik, the first human-made satellite to orbit the earth. Eisenhower did not regard these developments too seriously, though the Soviet ICBM capability had long-term implications for massive retaliation since it gave the USSR the capacity to respond in kind. However, others throughout the country responded with greater alarm. Democratic senators John Kennedy and Stuart Symington charged, inaccurately, that the United States had fallen behind and allowed a missile gap to grow between the superpowers. Led by General Maxwell Taylor and Admiral Arleigh Burke, the Army and Navy criticized Eisenhower's continued reliance on the nuclear arsenal in light of the Soviets' increasing nuclear parity and called instead for a substantial buildup of conventional forces capable of fighting limited wars throughout the globe. Kennedy later adopted those recommendations when, as president, he replaced massive retaliation with Defense Secretary McNamara's policy of flexible response. Members of Congress and the public also called for greater federal expenditures for science and science education and for a commitment to eventual U.S. superiority in outer space.

Concerned about the economic consequences of such programs and not wanting to overreact to the new Soviet missile capacity, Eisenhower maintained that the United States should remain calm and not "mount our charger and trot to ride off in all directions at once." He created the new position of special assistant to the president for science and technology, and supported new government initiatives to encourage citizens to pursue careers in science. His 1958 budget also called for increased spending on an accelerated missile program and programs involving science education. To pay for these he reduced other social programs, warning "to amass military power without regard to our economic capacity would be to defend ourselves against one kind of disaster by inviting another." Nonetheless, in 1958 Congress appropriated more than he requested, and the resulting $12.5 billion deficit was the largest during Eisenhower's two terms. Eisenhower remained unconvinced that space flight would ever become practical or useful; consequently, he was reluctant to fund it generously. He sought to reserve space solely for peaceful exploration and turned down recommendations that missile and satellite programs be combined. Despite protests from the Army, he placed the space program within the civilian-run National Aeronautics and Space Administration (NASA), which his administration created in 1958.

In his final two years in office Eisenhower refused to increase spending for space and missile programs, though he acceded to moderate increases in other forms of military spending. With Dulles's death in May 1959, Eisenhower assumed greater responsibility for foreign policy and became less fettered by conservative ideological constraints against peaceful coexistence with the Soviets. Declaring "There is no place on this earth to which I would not travel...[to] promote the general cause of world peace," he began a series of goodwill visits to Latin America, Africa, and Asia. After Castro began to reveal his Communist inclinations shortly after assuming power in 1959, Eisenhower initiated steps to oppose him. He restricted Cuban sugar imports, and in March 1960 he authorized the CIA to begin training an Army of Cuban exiles for an invasion aimed at overthrowing Castro. These plans later manifested as the failed Bay of Pigs invasion, which took place during Kennedy's third month in office. Other, more constructive programs also influenced Kennedy's Latin American policy. The 1960 Act of Bogota, which enjoyed support from all Latin American countries but Cuba, provided health services, housing and educational facilities, and agricultural support. It became the foundation for Kennedy's Alliance for Progress.

Domestically, Eisenhower favored a restricted role for the federal government. Consequently, he did not propose many social initiatives. However, having learned during World War II of the importance of a good road system for military defense, Eisenhower initiated the 1956 Interstate Highway Act that began the interstate highway system. The interstate highways went on to radically change U.S. commerce and dwelling habits. Partly because he favored limiting federal involvement in domestic issues and partly because he did not believe that "legislation alone could institute instant morality," Eisenhower did not take a strong role in promoting civil rights. Perceiving civil rights to be more a matter of education than legislation, he did not vigorously enforce the 1954 Brown versus the Board of Education ruling calling for integrated public schools. However, he sent federal troops to Little Rock in 1957 when Arkansas Governor Orval Faubus challenged the federal government's primacy over states' rights by refusing to desegregate schools there. Eisenhower also supported and signed voting rights legislation.

Eisenhower accepted the Republican Party's nomination of Nixon in 1960 but did not warmly endorse it. At the same time Nixon, wanting to establish his own identity, asked Eisenhower to forego active campaigning on his behalf. Thus Eisenhower largely remained apart from the 1960 campaign until the final week before the election. His election-night appeal to West Coast voters may have enabled Nixon to win California, but Kennedy, who had refrained from attacking the popular president during the campaign, won the election. In his farewell address in January 1961 Eisenhower warned of the growing "military-industrial complex" that had joined "an immense military establishment and a large arms industry. ... The total influence — economic, political, even spiritual — is felt in every city, every state house, every office of the federal government." He cautioned against "the disastrous rise of misplaced power" that could "endanger our liberties or our democratic processes."

After leaving office Eisenhower retired to a farm near Gettysburg, Pennsylvania. He continued to oppose increases in defense spending and called for smaller troop commitments to NATO. He supported President Johnson's policies for Vietnam and frequently advised Johnson. Denying that he had "never really liked or supported or really believed in" his former vice president, Eisenhower supported Nixon against Johnson's vice president Hubert Humphrey in 1968. He suffered a heart attack three weeks before the election and died in March 1969.

Ford, Gerald R. (1913–   ) Republican Congressman, 1949–73; vice president, 1973–74; and U.S. president, 1974–77. Born in Omaha, Nebraska, Ford grew up in Grand Rapids, Michigan. He was an all-star football player at the University of Michigan and graduated from Yale Law School in 1941. During World War II he served in the Navy and afterward practiced law in Grand Rapids. With the support of Senator Arthur Vandenberg, Ford ran for Congress in 1948 and defeated an incumbent, isolationist congressman for the Republican nomination. He then easily won the general election. Over the next 25 years Ford won reelection 12 times by majorities of over 60 percent. He consistently supported conservative domestic policies and an active foreign policy. During the 1950s he supported Eisenhower's internationalism. Unlike the president, he also favored large defense budgets. He opposed most of the social programs sponsored by the Kennedy and Johnson administrations and was tepid on civil rights. After the Kennedy assassination he served on the Warren Commission and later defended its conclusion that Lee Harvey Oswald had been the sole assassin. As the Vietnam War escalated he frequently criticized Johnson for not prosecuting it more vigorously. When Nixon came to power in 1969 Ford championed the new administration. He supported Nixon's 1969 request to appropriate funds for a defensive antiballistic missile system (ABM) and attacked opponents who, he claimed, favored unilateral disarmament "in the face of a serious threat from the Soviet Union." He also supported Nixon's conduct of the Vietnam War and declared that demands for an immediate U.S. withdrawal were "tantamount to surrender." He opposed all congressional efforts to cut spending for the war, set a timetable for U.S. withdrawal, or limit the president's authority to wage war. Conversely, he supported the intense bombings of North Vietnam and the mining of its harbors.

On October 10, 1973, Vice President Spiro Agnew resigned after working out a plea bargain that enabled him to plead no contest to tax evasion and avoid prosecution on multiple charges of extortion, bribery, and conspiracy. Nixon chose Ford to replace him and congressional confirmation hearings began on October 12. Ford promised to make all of his finances available and vowed not to run for president in 1976. The Watergate scandal had by then already become serious, and when asked if, in the event of Nixon's resignation, he would try to stop an investigation, Ford answered that the public would not stand for it.

Eventually, Congress approved him overwhelmingly and he assumed office on November 20. The new vice president spent much of his time defending Nixon and dismissing charges stemming from Watergate. However, Nixon resigned after a House subcommittee voted to recommend impeachment proceedings against him, and on August 9, 1974, Ford was sworn in as the thirty-eighth president.

Ford pledged to operate an administration committed to "openness and candor," but his credibility suffered a severe setback when he pardoned Nixon a month later for any and all federal crimes he may have committed in office. In so doing Ford not only enabled Nixon to avoid prosecution, he also stifled any further revelations of illegal government conduct that might have surfaced in a court trial. The pardon, which may have been part of a deal worked out in advance of Nixon's resignation, caused a public furor and seriously harmed Ford during the 1976 election. He tried to balance the presidential pardon by also granting limited amnesty for Vietnam-era draft evaders and military deserters. The program required two years of alternate service for draft evaders and established a clemency board to review the cases of deserters. It was attacked by prowar partisans as too lenient and by antiwar elements as insufficient. When the program expired in 1975 only about 15 percent of those eligible had participated.

Though most of his efforts centered on such domestic matters as reviving the economy and establishing an energy program in response to the 1974 Arab oil boycott, Ford made some significant contributions to U.S. foreign policy. He retained Nixon's activist Secretary of State Henry Kissinger, though he restricted Kissinger's powers somewhat. Ford supported Kissinger's attempts to forge a détente with the Soviets and authorized him to travel to the USSR in October 1974 to finalize preparations for a new arms limitation agreement. In November Ford traveled to Vladivostok, Siberia, where he and Soviet Premier Brezhnev signed a controversial agreement to place a ceiling on the number of multiple warhead missile systems (MIRVs) each country could possess. The MIRV agreement later came under attack by conservatives, including Defense Secretary James Schlesinger whom Ford replaced shortly thereafter. Ford and Brezhnev also announced plans for new Strategic Arms Limitation Talks (SALT II) in January. However, the SALT II negotiations were not completed during Ford's presidency.

Ford supported Kissinger's shuttle diplomacy in the Middle East, which was directed at forging peace agreements between Israel and its Arab enemies. These efforts provided the groundwork for the separate peace established between Israel and Egypt during the Carter administration.

In the wake of post–Watergate revelations of abuses by the CIA, including attempts to assassinate foreign leaders and conduct other illegal operations, Ford appointed a commission to investigate U.S. Cold War intelligence activities. Chaired by Vice President Nelson Rockefeller, the commission concluded that abuses had occurred but that they were not widespread or overly serious. Nonetheless, a Senate committee chaired by Frank Church conducted its own hearings and revealed more extensive evidence of illegal clandestine activities. Congress then enacted greater restrictions on and oversight of intelligence activities. Over Ford and Kissinger's objections it also voted to eliminate funding for covert CIA operations in Angola's civil war.

Congress also rejected Ford's 1975 requests for military aid to South Vietnam after Communist troops renewed the fighting in Vietnam and Cambodia, in violation of the 1973 peace agreements that ended U.S. participation in the Vietnam war. Congress did appropriate emergency funds for evacuating U.S. personnel from the American embassy in Saigon. Shortly afterward Communist forces concluded the wars by capturing the capital cities in South Vietnam and Cambodia. Ford blamed Congress for the Communist victories but admitted that the end of the fighting "closes a chapter in the American experience." However, less than a month later Cambodian Communists captured a U.S. merchant ship, the *Mayaguez*, and imprisoned its American crew. Calling the seizure an act of piracy, Ford ordered a military operation that succeeded in releasing the crew but incurred heavy casualties among the rescuing forces. Congress subsequently called for an investigation by the Government Accounting Office. The election-year investigation concluded that Ford had failed to exhaust diplomatic channels before ordering the military rescue. However, Ford dismissed the report as partisan politics.

In July 1975 Ford participated in a summit conference in Helsinki, Finland. The high point of détente, the Helsinki Conference produced accords signed by the United States, the Soviet Union, and all of the countries of Eastern and Western Europe. These agreements repudiated the use of force and respected the frontiers and territorial integrity of all European states, thereby securing the promise of peace at the cost of providing de facto recognition of the USSR's post–World War II territorial gains, something the Soviet Union had been seeking for 30 years. In repudiating force the European countries effectively agreed not to wage nuclear war upon each other. In return the Soviets consented to greater economic, scientific, technical, and environmental cooperation with the West and, more importantly, to the freer movement of ideas, greater access to broadcast and printed information, and the reunification of families through emigration. They also made some significant concessions to human rights. These agreements later helped make possible Poland's Solidarity Movement and the internal political activity that eventually brought down the Communist governments in Eastern Europe. However, Ronald Reagan and other conservatives attacked the agreement during the 1976 Republican primaries, arguing that it had doomed Eastern Europe to perpetual Soviet domination. Nonetheless, Ford edged out Reagan for the party's presidential nomination. However, he narrowly lost the general election to Jimmy Carter, who capitalized on voter disaffection due to Watergate and the Nixon pardon.

Haig, Alexander M. (1924–   )   Assistant to the president; supreme allied commander of NATO; and secretary of state, 1981–82. Born in Bala-Cynwyd, Pennsylvania, to a professional-class family, Haig attended Notre Dame for two years before being accepted into West Point in 1944. Though he graduated in the bottom third of his class, he nonetheless advanced rapidly after graduating. During the 1940s and 1950s he served in Japan, Korea, and Vietnam as well as in the Pentagon. In 1961 he received a master's degree in international relations from Georgetown University. On the recommendation of the Army's general counsel Joseph Califano, Secretary of the Army Cyrus Vance appointed Haig as his military assistant. During the Vietnam War, Haig commanded an infantry battalion. After his return to the United States he was promoted to colonel and later appointed deputy commandant of cadets at West Point.

During the transition between the Johnson and Nixon administrations, Califano, who was then Johnson's domestic adviser, recommended Haig to Henry Kissinger, who was to be Nixon's national security adviser. Impressed by what Califano called "one of the new breed of sophisticated Army officers," Kissinger made Haig his military assistant at the National Security Council (NSC). While serving at the NSC Haig earned a reputation for his competence, efficiency, and meticulous staff work. He reorganized the NSC staff to improve internal communications, prepared a daily summary for the president, acted as liaison between the Pentagon and State Department, and ran NSC meetings in Kissinger's absence. In 1970 he became deputy assistant to the president.

That year Haig made a series of trips to Vietnam to furnish Nixon with a first-hand assessment of the war. During the final year of peace negotiations he served as Nixon's primary diplomatic courier to South Vietnam's President Thieu and played a major role in convincing Thieu to accede to the cease-fire accord that Kissinger had negotiated with Le Duc Tho. Haig also helped prepare for Nixon's 1972 visit to China. In recognition of Haig's service Nixon promoted him to the rank of four-star general in 1972 and appointed him Army vice chief of staff, selecting him over 240 more senior officers.

This appointment removed Haig from the White House just as the Watergate cover-up was beginning and he was not implicated in the scandal. However, after the president's chief advisers H. R. Haldeman and John Ehrlichman resigned in April 1973 Haig returned as assistant to the president. In accepting a permanent White House appointment Haig had to resign from the Army, but he felt called upon to sacrifice his promising military career in order to serve the president. He thus joked that he was a "historical phenomenon — the first active-duty general who had to retire from military service to enter combat." Replacing Haldeman as chief of staff, Haig restored calm to the chaotic White House staff and made Nixon more accessible. For instance, he no longer required cabinet officials to go through the chief of staff to report to the president. In October 1973 he helped convince Vice President Spiro Agnew to plea bargain rather than provoke a constitutional crisis over his anticipated indictment for corruption.

As the Watergate crisis deepened Nixon turned increasingly to Haig for advice. Haig counseled the president not to resign after John Dean testified that Nixon had recommended offering hush money to the Watergate burglars and again after revelations of a White House taping system. However, after the Supreme Court ordered the release of White House tapes containing conclusive evidence of Nixon's involvement in the cover-up, Haig helped arrange the transfer of power from Nixon to Vice President Gerald Ford. During the first week of August 1974 Haig functioned as an unofficial "acting president." He remained as chief of staff after Ford took office on August 9. However, because he was so closely associated with Nixon he proved an embarrassment to the new administration, despite his competent job performance. Thus Haig resigned in late September.

Soon afterward Ford recalled Haig to active military service and rewarded him for his political service by naming him supreme allied commander in Europe, the most prestigious foreign military appointment available. He assumed command of NATO forces in December 1974 and retained the post until 1979. Serving during the middle and final period of U.S.-Soviet détente, Haig considered his chief goal to be convincing the "allies to remain equipped and trained to fight even as the U.S. itself [was] beginning to debate the importance of its own military commitment in Europe." Considered a hard-liner during the Carter presidency in the late 1970s, Haig advocated increasing military preparedness and upgrading weapons systems.

In 1981 newly inaugurated President Reagan appointed Haig secretary of state, and Haig promoted the Reagan administration's arms buildup, its hard line against the Soviet Union, and its abandonment of mutually assured destruction (MAD) in favor of a policy of limited and winnable nuclear war. He refused to renounce first use of nuclear weapons and testified before Congress that NATO had a contingency plan for a "demonstration" nuclear explosion should the Soviets launch a conventional attack. Haig was frequently involved in disputes with critics within and outside of the administration, and his declaration that he was "in charge" after a 1981 assassination attempt on Reagan spurred charges of arrogance and delusions of power. He resigned abruptly in June 1982 after a series of fights with the White House staff and was replaced by George Shultz. In 1988 Haig ran unsuccessfully against Vice President George Bush for the Republican nomination.

Hammer, Armand (1898–1990)   A U.S. businessman. Born in New York City, Hammer studied at the Columbia College of Physicians and Surgeons. Although he performed well in medical school, Hammer turned to business and quickly became successful. He earned his first $1 million before receiving his medical license. In 1921, four years after the Russian Revolution, he visited the Soviet Union and began a lucrative trade exchanging U.S. wheat for Soviet furs, precious stones, and caviar. He also served as an agent for other Western countries doing business in the Soviet Union, and amassed an important collection of Soviet art. Hammer retired in 1956, but in 1957 he accepted the presidency of Occidental Petroleum Corporation, which he saved from near bankruptcy. By 1975 it had become the eleventh largest oil company in the country.

Hammer contributed to and benefited from the U.S.-Soviet détente of the late 1960s and 1970s. His business contacts with the USSR enabled him to broker commercial exchanges between the two countries, giving the Soviets access to U.S. technology, and the Americans entry to a vast, new business market. In 1974 he completed a $20 billion deal to provide U.S. equipment and technical assistance for a fertilizer complex that Occidental Petroleum was to build in the USSR.

Hammer's art dealings promoted cultural exchange between the superpowers. In 1973 he arranged for a U.S. showing of 48 post–Impressionist paintings from the Soviet Union, and he arranged another exchange of art for the U.S. Bicentennial in 1976. He viewed his business and art dealings with the USSR as an important step for achieving peace between the Cold War antagonists. In the 1980s he extended his efforts to Communist China, where he contracted to build the world's largest open-pit coal mine.

Hammer became implicated in the 1972 Watergate scandal and in 1976 pleaded guilty to making and concealing illegal contributions to Nixon's reelection campaign. Noting Hammer's advanced age and bad health, the judge fined him $3,000 and placed him on probation for one year in lieu of sentencing him to jail.

Hiss, Alger (1904–   )   A top-ranking member of the State Department and president of the Carnegie Endowment for International Peace, 1946–49. Born in Baltimore, Hiss was raised by his mother after his father committed suicide when he was two. As an undergraduate he excelled at Johns Hopkins University, where he was elected president of the student government. He received his law degree from Harvard Law School in 1929. Professor Felix Frankfurter, later a Supreme Court Justice, recommended Hiss to Justice Oliver Wendell Holmes as law secretary. After serving in that prestigious position for a year Hiss practiced law until 1933, when he joined President Franklin Roosevelt's New Deal administration. His first post was in the legal division of the Agricultural Adjustment Administration (AAA), where he unsuccessfully tried to add protection for sharecroppers and tenant farmers to the standard contract the government used with farmers. Hiss became identified with a group of reformers within the AAA who were later purged, after he had left to become legal assistant to the Nye Committee that was investigating the weapons industry. In 1935 he joined the Justice Department and assisted Solicitor General Stanley Reed in his unsuccessful attempt to defend the constitutionality of the AAA. Between 1936 and 1945 Hiss held a number of government jobs before becoming director of the Office of Special Political Affairs. In that capacity he played a major role in creating the United Nations. In February 1945 he accompanied Roosevelt to the Yalta Conference to advise the president on matters relating to the United Nations. He served as executive secretary to the Dumbarton Oaks Conference that established the framework for the United Nations, and he was later elected temporary secretary-general. As its principal adviser, he accompanied the U.S. delegation to the first session of the General Assembly in 1946. At the end of that year he resigned from the State Department to become president of the Carnegie Endowment for International Peace, whose mission was to foster efforts to eliminate war. During his two-and-one-half-year tenure in that office Hiss's policy objectives coincided with those of the United Nations.

In August 1948 Whittaker Chambers, a former Communist then working as a senior editor for *Time* magazine, testified before the House Committee on Un-American Activities (HUAC) that he, Hiss, and other members of Roosevelt's liberal administration had belonged to the same underground Communist cell in Washington, D.C. Hiss was the most senior and most prominent of those Chambers named. Two days later Hiss appeared before the committee and denied ever belonging to the Communist Party or any of its front organizations. He also denied knowing anyone named Whittaker Chambers. In a subsequent special session of HUAC Hiss met Chambers. He testified that Chambers resembled a journalist he had known between 1934 and 1935 under the name of George Crosley and that he had sublet his apartment to Crosley and lent him money that had never been repaid. Chambers admitted that he had used the name Crosley but had gone by the first name of Carl, not George. Chambers agreed to take a lie detector test but Hiss refused. No test was administered.

On August 25 Hiss and Chambers delivered their conflicting stories before HUAC in a televised session. On the one hand, Chambers testified that the head of the Washington, D.C., cell had introduced them in 1934, that Hiss had paid his party dues to him, and that he had last met Hiss in 1938 when he tried to persuade Hiss to renounce Communism. On the other hand, Hiss called Chambers a "self-confessed liar, spy and traitor," maintaining that he had met "George Crosley" as a journalist writing about issues relating to the Nye Committee. He stated that the only money he had ever given to Crosley was about $30 in personal loans, and that after 1935 he had never seen Crosley again prior to his HUAC testimony. Hiss also challenged Chambers to repeat his accusations outside of the committee hearing so Hiss could sue him for slander. Two days later Chambers complied, stating on "Meet the Press" that "Alger Hiss was a Communist and may still be one." After being criticized for his delay, Hiss filed a $75,000 legal suit for slander.

Until this point in the proceedings Chambers had only accused Hiss of Communist membership and willingness to promote the Communist agenda within Roosevelt's administration. However, after Hiss filed for slander, Chambers escalated his charges, claiming that Hiss had also been guilty of passing classified State Department documents to the Soviet Union. In particular, Chambers produced four 1938 memoranda in Hiss's handwriting summarizing confidential information and 65 pages of retyped State Department documents that Chambers claimed Hiss had given to him. Chambers maintained that he had kept these documents in order to forestall attempts by Communists to kill him after he left the party; the State Department documents were his "life preserver," which he had saved to prove the existence of the spy ring should anything happen to him. Chambers further claimed that he had previously withheld the espionage charges in order to protect Hiss, but that he now needed to convince the world that he was being truthful about his earlier charges.

In December 1948 Chambers responded to a HUAC subpoena by submitting five roles of microfilm that he had concealed the day before inside a carved-out pumpkin at his farm in Maryland. Republican Congressman Richard Nixon, a member of HUAC, arranged for extensive press coverage of the theatrical retrieval of the microfilm from its bizarre hiding place, and the Hiss case became an even greater public drama and spectacle. Two roles of the microfilm contained classified State Department material that Hiss had initialed. President Truman denounced the HUAC probe as a deliberate, political distortion and a Republican "red herring." In return Nixon criticized Truman for his flagrant "flouting of the national interests of the people."

Shortly after the HUAC revelations a New York grand jury heard extensive testimony from both Chambers and Hiss. Because the statute of limitations for espionage had expired, Hiss was immune from being charged with spying. However, on December 15 the grand jury indicted Hiss for perjury, alleging that he had lied when he claimed he had not seen Chambers since 1937 and that he had never given Chambers classified information. In May 1949 Hiss underwent his first perjury trial. The prosecution established that the retyped State Department documents had been typed on the Woodstock typewriter Hiss owned during the 1930s. In turn, Hiss claimed that he and his wife had given the typewriter away in December 1937 and that someone else must have subsequently acquired it and typed the 1938 documents on it. Moreover, Hiss's lawyer tried to undermine Chambers's credibility, forcing him to admit that he had lied on several past occasions, including when he told a grand jury in October 1948 that he had no knowledge of any espionage activities. The defense also brought in several eminent character witnesses, among them Supreme Court justices Frankfurter and Reed. Under cross-examination Hiss acknowledged several discrepancies between his testimony at the trial and his statements made to the FBI and before HUAC. This trial ended in July in a hung jury; the jurors split 8–4 in favor of conviction.

In the second trial, which lasted from November 1949 to January 1950, the prosecution introduced another witness who testified that she knew Hiss to be a Communist during the 1930s, and the defense presented testimony by two psychiatrists who labeled Chambers as having a "psychopathic personality." However, neither psychiatrist had ever directly examined Chambers. The defense also tried to show that Chambers could have acquired the classified documents from other sources in the State Department. And it raised the possibility that Chambers might have procured the typewriter from the people to whom Hiss had donated it and retyped the documents himself in order to incriminate Hiss. The jury was unconvinced, and it found Hiss guilty on both counts of perjury. Judge Henry Goddard sentenced him to 5 years in federal prison, which he began serving in March 1951 after his appeals were turned down. He was released in 1954 after serving over two-thirds of his sentence. Disbarred and unable to practice law, Hiss initially worked for a manufacturer of women's hair accessories before spending 15 years selling office supplies in New York. The Massachusetts bar readmitted him in 1975.

Coming in the formative days of the Cold War, when Communists were seizing control of Eastern Europe and China and the Soviets were testing their first atomic bombs, the Hiss case acquired immense significance that far exceeded the individuals involved. A New Deal liberal, Hiss had been a member of the Washington, D.C., elite that, as a class, fell under attack from right-wing anti–Communists. The right believed that many of the highly educated, highly placed, and well-credentialed liberals occupying important positions during the early days of the Cold War were either outright Communist agents or, in their well-intentioned but misguided liberalism, Communist dupes. Thus they claimed that the recent worldwide Communist successes stemmed from treason by members of the liberal ruling class. As Nixon put it, "Hiss was clearly the symbol of a considerable number of perfectly loyal citizens whose theaters of operation are the nation's mass media and universities, its scholarly foundations, and its government bureaucracies. They are of a mindset, as doctrinaire as those on the extreme right, which makes them singularly vulnerable to the Communist popular front appeal under the banner of social justice. In the time of the Hiss case they were 'patsies' for the Communist line." Hiss's conviction thus provided the right with credible evidence that its view of internal subversion was accurate and not paranoid, as its opponents charged. It is certainly no coincidence that Senator Joseph McCarthy initiated his anti–Communist crusade less than a month after Hiss's conviction, accusing the State Department of harboring over 200 known Communists. Hiss's conviction also lent credence to right-wing charges that the United Nations was a Communist instrument and that an ailing Roosevelt had sold out to Stalin at the Yalta Conference, since Hiss had played a significant role in each. The jury's conclusion that Hiss had been a spy also hovered over the trial of accused atomic bomb spies Julius and Ethel Rosenberg, which took place less than 6 months later. And throughout the Cold War defenders of the right-wing viewpoint pointed repeatedly to the Hiss case as proof not only that highly placed Communist agents worked in the government and influenced U.S. policies, but also that liberals were suspect, untrustworthy, and capable of selling out their country in a naive but dangerous attempt to achieve social justice.

On the other hand, liberals and other Hiss defenders maintain that Chambers's accusations were fraudulent and that the right-wing prosecution and persecution of Alger Hiss was part of a deliberately manipulated Republican attempt to discredit Roosevelt's liberal New Deal policies and undermine Truman's Democratic administration. Some maintain that the FBI, whose director was the ultra-conservative J. Edgar Hoover, manufactured the evidence showing that the typewriter used to type the documents had been Hiss's. Others point to how the Hiss case helped inflame the Red Scare, in which the right succeeded in purging many of its liberal political foes from positions of authority. Whether or not the Hiss case was concocted for this reason, it certainly contributed to that end.

The Hiss case also played a large role in promoting the career of then Congressman Nixon, who had been one of Hiss's most ferocious attackers. According to Robert Stripling, who had been HUAC's legal counsel, "It was a personal thing." Stripling believed Nixon bore a personal animosity toward Hiss, whose upper-class polish contrasted with Nixon's more modest background and demeanor. Nixon later wrote in *Six Crises*, "I received considerable credit for spearheading the investigation which led to Hiss's conviction. Two years later I was elected to the U.S. Senate and two years after that General Eisenhower introduced me as his running mate to the Republican national convention as 'a man who has a special talent and ability to ferret out any kind of subversive influence wherever it may be found, and the strength and persistence to get rid of it.'"

No consensus has yet been reached on Hiss's guilt or Chambers's veracity. Hiss continues to proclaim his complete innocence. In 1957 he presented his account, *In the Court of Public Opinion*. Chambers, who died in 1961, wrote his autobiography, *Witness*, in 1952. In 1978 historian Allen Weinstein wrote his controversial study, *Perjury: The Hiss-Chambers Case*, which concluded that Hiss had indeed passed along secret documents to Chambers. On the other hand, to date no documents released from Russia after the breakup of the Soviet Union, including those from the Communist Party archives, have shown that Hiss participated in a spy ring or had other Communist affiliations.

In addition to the case's theatrics and sensational charges, the Hiss-Chambers conflict enacted a class power struggle that took place throughout the Cold War and underlay part of the Red Scare. In their personal appearance, manner of speech, and virtually every other way of being Hiss and Chambers contrasted each other greatly. They clearly came from different social backgrounds and represented differing interests and beliefs. Refined, articulate, well dressed, and at ease in the courtroom, Hiss projected an image of upper-class sophistication. On the other hand, the nervous, overweight Chambers dressed indifferently and spoke melodramatically, without Hiss's polish or self-assuredness. Since the judgment largely depended upon which man was personally more credible and trustworthy, the Hiss case also came to embody the ongoing clash for respect, authority, and power between Hiss's Eastern establishment elite and Chambers's more conservative, less urbane middle class. Apart from the particulars in the case, in choosing whom to believe the American public was also choosing which group it most trusted to guide the nation through the Cold War.

Hoover, J. Edgar (1895–1972) Director of the Federal Bureau of Investigation (FBI), 1924–72. Born and raised in Washington, D.C., the son of a government bureaucrat, Hoover worked his way through George Washington University Law School. He graduated in 1916 and joined the Justice Department as a clerk. In 1919 he became assistant to Attorney General A. Mitchell Palmer and assumed responsibility for coordinating the so-called Palmer raids in which thousands of alleged anarchists and Communists were rounded up, interrogated, and deported during the Red Scare of 1919–20. In 1921 he became assistant director of the Justice Department's Bureau of Investigation, which was then only a small, investigatory agency plagued by scandals and staffed by political appointees. In 1924 Hoover consented to become director, but only if he could hire agents via the merit system. Attorney General Harlan Fiske Stone agreed, and Hoover began transforming the bureau into a highly professional organization. He established a national fingerprint file in 1925, a major crime laboratory in 1932, and a sophisticated training school for FBI agents and local police in 1935. Throughout the 1930s the FBI achieved growing national prominence as Hoover's government agents apprehended several of the country's most notorious criminals, including John Dillinger, "Baby Face" Nelson, "Ma and Pa" Barker, and "Pretty Boy" Floyd.

In 1936 President Roosevelt authorized the FBI to investigate espionage and sabotage, and Hoover used that authority to maintain a watch on both political extremes. He also monitored Roosevelt's political enemies, including Wendell Willkie, John L. Lewis, and isolationists Charles Lindbergh and Senator Burton Wheeler. Eventually, even Vice President Henry Wallace and Roosevelt's wife Eleanor, both of whom had connections to the left, fell under FBI surveillance. Throughout his tenure as director, Hoover had his agents perform similar political favors for other U.S. presidents from both parties. After the U.S. entry into World War II Roosevelt authorized Hoover to expand the bureau's surveillance of left- and right-wing political groups, labor unions, civil rights organizations, and the Communist Party, all of which Hoover maintained could potentially threaten the war effort. Presidential and congressional actions further authorized him to place wiretaps for national security reasons and to maintain a list of domestic Communists and Fascists for possible arrest and detention. Hoover was also responsible for checking the loyalty of federal employees. However, he expanded the bureau's activities beyond those authorized by the government and, despite a pledge to discontinue and/or curtail domestic surveillance after the war, he maintained the security apparatus for monitoring groups and individuals he believed might undermine the country's internal security.

During the Cold War Hoover regarded the American Communist Party as a Soviet tool dedicated to the overthrow of the U.S. government and capable of espionage and sabotage. In the late 1940s the bureau arrested some prominent members of the Truman administration, among them Alger Hiss, William Remington, and Foreign Service officer John S. Service. It also investigated Harry Dexter White, assistant secretary of the treasury, who became the executive director of the International Monetary Fund in 1946. Hoover regarded White as the leading Communist in the U.S. government, though White died before those charges could be resolved. The FBI also cracked a spy ring that, during World War II, had passed secrets about the atomic bomb project to the Soviets. Klaus Fuchs and Julius and Ethel Rosenberg were among those convicted. In 1957 the FBI arrested Soviet Colonel Rudolf Abel as the head of a large spy ring, and in 1958 it uncovered another major Soviet spy operation.

Hoover's 1946 testimony before Congress led to a more stringent loyalty program than originally proposed by the Truman administration. The FBI assumed responsibility for investigating claims of disloyalty, despite Truman's fears that this might increase the bureau's powers to a dangerously high level. In 1954 Hoover maintained that the FBI had investigated 5 million federal employees. To determine subjects' loyalty agents asked about their reading habits, their stand on civil rights and socialized medicine, and their support for former Vice President Henry Wallace, who ran for president in 1948 on the Progressive Party ticket and received the Communist Party's endorsement. In 1952 Truman expanded the FBI's wiretapping powers; however, Hoover exceeded his new authority, opening the mail of U.S. citizens and conducting burglaries to secure evidence against perceived enemies of the state.

Throughout the 1950s Hoover remained one of the most ardent and most visible anti–Communists, though he generally disassociated himself from Senator Joseph McCarthy and other prominent advocates of the Red Scare. Hoover considered them amateurs whose theatrics hampered the real work of fighting domestic subversion. As part of an ongoing effort to educate the U.S. public about the dangers of domestic Communism, Hoover had his staff ghost-write magazine articles and his 1958 book, *Masters of Deceit: The Story of Communism in America and How to Fight It. Masters of Deceit* remained in print throughout the Cold War and was often used in public school courses on Americanism versus Communism. The book asks the public to report suspicious activities to the FBI and suggests that readers can identify Communists and fellow travelers by their use of such phrases as "peace," "disarmament," "academic freedom," and "trade with the East." Hoover's use of mass media to educate the public later extended to television. In 1965 he endorsed ABC's "The FBI," which showed the bureau fighting Communist subversives as well as other public enemies. Hoover not only permitted the producers to film some background scenes at the FBI headquarters in Washington, D.C., and to open and close each episode with a shot of the FBI seal, he also inaugurated each new season with a personal appearance.

In return for the FBI's active cooperation ABC gave the bureau complete power to approve scripts, sponsorship, and personnel. Each episode concluded with an expression of gratitude to "J. Edgar Hoover and his associates for their cooperation in the production of this series."

In 1956 Hoover initiated COINTELPRO after the federal courts made prosecuting Communists increasingly difficult under existing laws. An operation designed specifically to undermine the American Communist Party, COINTELPRO involved leaking accurate and inaccurate information to the press about Communist activities, sending anonymous letters to employers of Communists demanding that they be fired, and otherwise harassing party members and disrupting their work. A 1975 Senate committee headed by Frank Church revealed the COINTELPRO operations and other illegal wiretaps, burglaries, and mail openings during the Eisenhower era. The committee also reported that Hoover had informed the president, the White House staff, and the attorney general, and no one had objected. Hoover maintained his programs of domestic surveillance and harassment of political enemies throughout the 1960s. During his tenure in office the FBI maintained files on thousands of scientists, writers, performers, professors, and other individuals who had violated no laws but employed their constitutional freedoms to express political sentiments that Hoover found objectionable and potentially treasonous.

Hoover continued to believe that the civil rights movement was Communist led, and he authorized investigations of Martin Luther King, Jr., and other prominent leaders. During the Vietnam War he had the FBI infiltrate antiwar organizations, believing that these, too, were subversive and Communist inspired.

Jackson, Henry M. (1912–83)   A Democratic congressman, 1941–53; and senator, 1953–83. Born in Everett, Washington, "Scoop" Jackson won his first public election at age 23 and was elected to the U.S. House of Representatives at age 28. He joined the Senate the same year that Eisenhower became president. Jackson generally took liberal Democratic positions on domestic issues and a hard line against Communism in foreign affairs. He opposed President Kennedy's creation of the Arms Control and Disarmament Agency in 1961 and was skeptical of the administration's other efforts to control the arms race. As a member of the Armed Services Committee Jackson endorsed the U.S. Cold War policy of containing Communist expansion and supported large defense expenditures throughout his Senate career. He was nicknamed the senator from Boeing because his support for a strong military often benefited the aircraft manufacturer from his home state. At Jackson's insistence additional safeguards were added to the 1963 nuclear test ban treaty, whose passage was possible only with his support. He supported the Vietnam War and favored expanding the Pentagon's military options and taking an even more aggressive position than Johnson and Nixon's policies of limited war allowed.

In 1968 Jackson turned down President-elect Nixon's offer to name him defense secretary, fearing that the appointment would limit future political aspirations. Jackson ran for the Democratic presidential nomination in 1972, hoping to attract moderate and conservative members of the party. Moreover, his record of support for labor, industry, the military, and Israel promised to attract a range of special interest groups. However, antiwar sentiment distanced him from the liberal wing of the party, and George Wallace's entry into the election siphoned off many conservative voters. He finished second to George McGovern after Senator Hubert Humphrey withdrew from the race. Nixon defeated McGovern in a landslide, and Jackson and Humphrey went on to help return the Democratic Party to a more moderate orientation.

Jackson opposed the U.S.-Soviet détente engineered by Nixon and national security adviser Henry Kissinger. He criticized the treaty in 1972 that came from the Strategic Arms Limitation Talks (SALT I), arguing that it gave the Soviets some strategic advantages and that "agreements are likely to lead to an accelerated technological arms race with greater uncertainties, profound instabilities and considerable costs." He refused to vote for the treaty until an amendment gave hard-line instructions to the negotiators, and insisted that U.S. intercontinental nuclear capability never become smaller than that of the Soviets. In 1973 Jackson struck a further blow against détente by charging that a 1972 sale of U.S. grain to the Soviet Union had given excessive profits to grain exporters and excessively low prices to the Soviets, while the U.S. taxpayers suffered higher prices, depletion of grain reserves, and a crisis in the livestock industry. His committee report in August 1974 declared that the deal had been the "great grain robbery." He succeeded in temporarily halting grain shipments in October 1973.

Jackson consistently supported Israel since its creation in 1948. Throughout the 1970s he spoke out repeatedly on behalf of Soviet Jews whose human rights were being denied in the USSR and whose attempts to emigrate were stifled. In 1974 he introduced the Jackson-Vanik Amendment to the East-West Trade Relations Act. Seventy-five senators cosponsored the amendment, which barred the Soviet Union from most favored nation designation as long as it inhibited emigration. The Soviets denounced the amendment as interference in its internal affairs. Nonetheless, Kissinger subsequently won a Soviet commitment to allow 45,000 Jews to emigrate each year. However, Jackson thought the number was too small and opposed the bill until receiving additional assurances. The trade bill passed in December 1974, as amended by Jackson. But the Soviets found the amendment unacceptable and canceled the treaty the following month. Throughout the 1970s the trade bill and the Jackson-Vanik Amendment plagued détente, giving the Soviets a basis to charge that the United States had failed to honor its promises to increase East-West trade and providing anti–Communists with an opportunity to point out yet another example of Soviet tyranny. After the treaty was scuttled Soviet-Jewish emigration fell to 14,000 in 1975. It continued to follow the ebbs and flows of détente throughout the Ford and Carter presidencies, rising to 51,000 after Carter signed a wheat deal and began the SALT II negotiations and then dropping again after the Soviet invasion of Afghanistan. Ultimately, by remaining intransigent on the human rights issue that Kissinger and Nixon had preferred to smooth over as a matter of expediency, Jackson highlighted a basic U.S.-Soviet disagreement that détente was never able to resolve or overcome.

Jackson again sought the Democratic nomination in 1976, but after winning the New York primary he fell behind to Jimmy Carter and dropped from the race, running instead for reelection to the Senate. He won handily and remained in the Senate until his death in 1983.

Johnson, Lyndon B. (1908–73)   Democratic congressman; senator; and U.S. president, 1963–69. Born in Stonewall, Texas, to a family of cattle speculators, Johnson graduated from Southwest Texas State Teachers College in 1930. The following year he served as secretary to a Texas congressman, and while in Washington, D.C., he impressed Texas Representative Sam Rayburn who encouraged Johnson to enter politics. In 1934 he married Claudia Alta Taylor, better known as "Lady Bird." In 1935 President Roosevelt appointed him Texas state administrator of the National Youth Administration, and his experience in that position provided Johnson with a political base to run successfully for Congress in 1937. Initially a strong supporter of Roosevelt, Johnson began to distance himself from the New Deal in 1938. World War II interrupted his political career while Johnson served in the Navy. In 1948 he won a Senate seat with a margin of only 87 votes out of 1 million cast. Almost 30 years later a Texas voting official claimed that he had certified enough fictitious ballots to swing the election to Johnson.

Johnson had powerful friends in Congress, including House Speaker Rayburn and Democratic Senator Richard Russell. In 1953 the Democrats voted him minority leader, and after the Democrats regained control of the Senate in 1954 he became majority leader. Despite a massive heart attack in 1955, he was able to retain his leadership position within the Senate, and Johnson earned a reputation as a powerful and effective politician who understood the intricacies of the legislative process. He sought the presidential nomination in 1960 but declined to enter the primaries, hoping that either Senator John Kennedy or Senator Hubert Humphrey would drop out of the race or that a deadlocked convention would turn to him. However, Kennedy received the nomination on the first ballot. To appeal to a more conservative constituency Kennedy chose Johnson for his running mate, a selection that is credited with helping Kennedy narrowly defeat incumbent Vice President Richard Nixon. As vice president, Johnson chaired the National Aeronautics and Space Council and made several trips throughout the world. Otherwise, he was — by his own assessment — ineffectual. When Kennedy was assassinated on November 22, 1963, Johnson was sworn in as president aboard the presidential jet, Air Force One. The quick and smooth transition of power was intended to reassure the distraught country and make clear to U.S. enemies that although Kennedy was dead the power structure remained intact.

Johnson quickly moved Kennedy's civil rights program through Congress, presenting the legislation as a memorial to the dead president. In July 1964 he signed the Civil Rights Act after using his influence to end a filibuster by Southern senators. In 1965 he also won passage of the Voting Rights Act, which enfranchised some 3.5 million black citizens. Johnson also endorsed Kennedy's $11 billion tax cut intended to stimulate the economy and inaugurated antipoverty legislation that later became the basis of his War on Poverty. As the sitting president, Johnson received the 1964 Democratic nomination, and he selected Humphrey as his running mate. He easily defeated the ultraconservative Republican candidate Senator Barry Goldwater, whom Johnson represented as a warmonger anxious to involve the country in a nuclear war. By contrast, Johnson presented himself as a peace candidate and steadfastly proclaimed that he would not involve U.S. combat troops in the intensifying war in Vietnam: "We are not about to send American boys nine or ten thousand miles away from home to do what Asian boys ought to be doing for themselves." Johnson's landslide victory also spurred important Democratic wins in the House and Senate, giving liberals and moderates control of the presidency and Congress for the first time since the Roosevelt era.

Despite his campaign promises, Johnson quickly became enmeshed in foreign crises. In January 1964 Panama suspended diplomatic relations with the United States after widespread riots calling for local control of the Panama Canal. But Johnson took a hard line, demanding that civil order be restored before negotiations could begin. In April 1965 he sent 30,000 U.S. Marines to the Dominican Republic after the ruling military junta was threatened by Communist-backed insurgents. The military action alienated some liberals, especially Senator J. William Fulbright who chaired the Foreign Relations Committee and later became a leading critic of Johnson's Vietnam War policies.

More than any other Cold War crisis, the Vietnam War came to dominate the Johnson presidency. The roots of the U.S. involvement dated back to January 1955, about eight months after Vietnamese nationalists under Communist leader Ho Chi Minh defeated the French at Dien Bien Phu. Fearing Ho's almost certain election, the United States and South Vietnam refused to sign the 1954 Geneva peace settlement that temporarily partitioned the country into North and South Vietnam but called for national elections to unify the nation in 1956. Instead the United States slowly began propping up a series of unpopular minority-led regimes in the south to fight against the Communists. As early as 1953 Secretary of State John Foster Dulles had warned of a domino effect, claiming that if Vietnam went Communist the other countries in Southeast Asia would soon follow. Thus the initial U.S. involvement in Vietnam was a classic case of Cold War containment of Communist expansion. When Kennedy took office in 1961 some 700 U.S. military advisers were training and providing limited assistance to South Vietnamese government troops fighting North Vietnamese armies and their South Vietnamese sympathizers, the Vietcong. At the time of Kennedy's death 15,000 military advisers were in the country. Johnson accepted the domino theory and shortly after assuming office told Henry Cabot Lodge, the U.S. ambassador to South Vietnam, "I am not going to be the President who saw Southeast Asia go the way of China."

Johnson, who retained Kennedy's Secretary of State Dean Rusk and Defense Secretary Robert McNamara, appointed General Maxwell Taylor to replace Lodge in June 1964. In August North Vietnamese gunboats attacked a U.S. destroyer in the Tonkin Gulf and Congress voted nearly unanimously to authorize Johnson to commit U.S. forces to defend any nation in Southeast Asia against Communist aggression or subversion. The Tonkin Gulf Resolution served as presidents Johnson and Nixon's congressional authorization to conduct the war, though Congress repealed the resolution in 1970.

Johnson did not use his authority to strike against North Vietnam until after the 1964 presidential election, though Daniel Ellsberg's *Pentagon Papers* reveal that he had decided to attack North Vietnam as early as October. In February 1965 the Vietcong attacked an American transport and observation installation, killing 8 and wounding over 100 American advisers. Within hours of receiving the news Johnson authorized U.S. air raids against a North Vietnamese Army camp 60 miles north of the dividing line between North and South Vietnam. In March Johnson sent in 2 Marine battalions to defend Da Nang airfield. These were the first U.S. combat troops in Vietnam. That summer General Westmoreland, whom Johnson had appointed a year earlier to command the U.S. forces, requested and received 44 additional combat battalions; and in October U.S. forces defeated North Vietnamese forces in the Ia Drang Valley in their first conventional confrontation of the war. By December there were 200,000 American troops in South Vietnam. During 1966 America stepped up its effort, bombing oil depots near Hanoi and Haiphong Harbor and increasing the number of troops to 400,000. By the end of 1967 some 500,000 American troops were serving in Vietnam and domestic opposition to the war had become significant, despite administration assurances that victory was close at hand. At the same time hawkish critics complained about policy restrictions that kept the United States from invading North Vietnam or attacking North Vietnamese bases and supply lines in Cambodia. Wanting to avoid Chinese entry into the war, Johnson pursued a policy of limiting the ground war to South Vietnam.

On January 31, 1968, the Communists began their Tet Offensive. They overran many South Vietnamese–held cities and towns and brought the war to Saigon itself, where there was intense street fighting. Commandos even occupied the U.S. embassy, which was secured only after over six hours of fighting. Westmoreland's own headquarters were also attacked near Saigon Airport. Even though in the long run the Tet Offensive failed militarily, it was probably the single most forceful event to turn U.S. public opinion against the war, as it demonstrated that the administration's oft-proclaimed "light at the end of the tunnel" was illusory.

By the end of 1968 American troop strength peaked at 540,000. To pay for the war Johnson reduced his antipoverty program in 1965 and introduced a 10 percent income tax surcharge in 1967. To secure the surcharge he agreed to placate conservatives by cutting additional social programs at home. Thus Johnson's vision of a "Great Society" became one of the war's casualties. Moreover, the combined costs of the war and his social programs brought about spiraling inflation that continued to affect the economy into the 1970s. As the war dragged on its financial cost, poorly defined objectives, and lack of success provoked strong antiwar sentiments. Peace rallies and demonstrations grew larger, more frequent, and more widely televised. Though Johnson had entered the war partly for moral reasons — to defend Southeast Asia against Communist tyranny — he found himself cast as a moral villain as the war got out of hand and television coverage showed South Vietnamese civilians suffering at the hands of U.S. soldiers and the U.S.-backed government in Saigon. Protesters standing outside the White House chanted such slogans as "Hey, hey, L.B.J./ How many kids did you kill today?" In 1968 antiwar candidate George McGovern further shocked Johnson when he ran against the president for the Democratic nomination and polled well in the New Hampshire primary. Three days later Robert Kennedy emerged as an even more formidable peace candidate.

During the 1968 Tet Offensive Johnson replaced McNamara with Clark Clifford, who wanted to deescalate the war, and in March he replaced Westmoreland with General Creighton Abrams. After assembling a group of advisers including Lodge, Dean Acheson, George Ball, and General Matthew Ridgway, Johnson decided to deescalate and begin negotiations with the North Vietnamese. On March 31 Johnson announced a unilateral cessation of air and naval bombardment of North Vietnam and invited the North Vietnamese to seek a peace agreement. He also declared his decision not to seek reelection. Three days later the United States and North Vietnam agreed to initiate peace talks that opened in May. During the presidential campaign Johnson supported Humphrey, who gained the Democratic nomination but lost the election to Nixon. After Nixon's inauguration Johnson retired to Texas where he died in 1973.

Kennan, George (1904–)   A U.S. diplomat and architect of Truman's containment policy of limiting the spread of Communism to those nations already under its control. A graduate of Princeton University (1925), Kennan entered the Foreign Service and served in Central and Eastern Europe in the late 1920s and early 1930s. Expecting that the United States would eventually grant official recognition to the Soviet government, the State Department sent Kennan to the University of Berlin to study Russian language and culture. He served in the first U.S. embassy in Moscow from 1933 to 1936. Appalled by Stalin's repressive regime, Kennan adopted a strong anti–Communist position that became the basis for his later policy suggestions.

Kennan was subsequently stationed in Prague and Berlin, where the Nazis interned him shortly after the declarations of war between Germany and the United States following the Japanese attack on Pearl Harbor. He was released in May 1942, after which he joined the U.S. embassy in Portugal. In 1943 he became a member of the European Advisory Commission in London and helped formulate plans for the fate of postwar Germany. In 1944 he became an adviser to the U.S. ambassador to the USSR, Averell Harriman. Throughout the war Kennan took a strong anti–Soviet position, arguing against forming a close alliance with the USSR because "to welcome Russia as an associate in the defense of democracy would invite misunderstanding." In 1944, after the Soviets had expelled the German invaders, he urged the cessation of the lend-lease program and a "full-fledged and realistic political showdown with the Soviet leaders." To compel them to withdraw their armies from Eastern Europe, he recommended cutting off economic aid to the Soviets. However, although he believed that over the long run the Soviets would be unable to maintain their control over Eastern Europe, he argued unsuccessfully that in the immediate postwar environment both superpowers should recognize and respect each other's spheres of influence.

After the war the U.S.-Soviet alliance quickly crumbled, and in February 1946 Kennan wrote his detailed, carefully worked out Long Telegram, analyzing U.S. policy toward the USSR. Truman made it the intellectual basis for his subsequent Soviet policy, and the secretary of the Navy made it required reading for ranking military officers. The Long Telegram maintained that Soviet foreign policy was predicated on the Communist ideological claims that conflict between Communism and capitalism was historically inevitable. Consequently, Kennan argued that Stalin would consolidate his power at home and insulate the Soviet Union by surrounding it with allied client states. Being too weak to attack the West militarily, the Soviets would attempt to isolate the United States through the political subversion of capitalist countries.

In July 1947 Kennan introduced his containment theory in a *Foreign Affairs* article entitled "The Sources of Soviet Conduct." This article, which appeared anonymously under the signature "Mr. X," described the rationale behind Soviet foreign policy and anticipated future Soviet moves. In Kennan's view the Soviet threat was primarily political not military. He believed that by firmly halting any new Soviet aggression the West could ultimately induce the USSR to accept the status quo. At that point international tensions would subside and the internal Soviet police state would become less severe. Consequently, he recommended "a long-term patient but firm and vigilant containment of Russian expansive tendencies through…the adroit and vigilant application of counterforce at a series of constantly shifting geographical and political points, corresponding to the shifts and maneuvers of Soviet policies."

Though many who were influenced by this article believed counterforce suggested military action, Kennan maintained in later articles and speeches that he had never conceived containment primarily in military terms. Instead, he felt the economic development of Western Europe and Japan would provide the best buffer against Soviet expansion. He had already taken steps along those lines in April 1947 when, as head of the State Department's policy planning staff, he provided the draft that became the basis for the Marshall Plan, the program for European recovery put forth by Secretary of State George Marshall. Kennan described a two-staged recovery. In the first the United States would accept primary responsibility for addressing Europe's immediate needs. In the second the Europeans would become responsible, with minimum U.S. assistance. Kennan also stressed the necessity for an economically strong but militarily disarmed Germany. And he recommended that all nations, including the USSR, be invited to participate in the recovery plan but that the conditions be severe enough to ensure that the Soviet Union would decline. The Marshall Plan became one of the great successes of U.S. Cold War policy.

However, after Marshall resigned in 1949 due to ill health, Kennan clashed frequently with his successor, Dean Acheson. Frequently under attack from the political right for being soft on Communism, Acheson advocated a more forceful military posture vis-à-vis the Soviets, while Kennan retained his belief that the conflict was fundamentally political and economic. Consequently, Kennan questioned the need for the creation of the North Atlantic Treaty Organization (NATO) in 1949. He believed that a military alliance predicated on conventional weapons would be "obsolete in the nuclear age." Also, Acheson favored a strong role for Germany in NATO , while Kennan maintained that superpower tensions would subside if both the United States and USSR withdrew their troops and permitted the development of a neutral, demilitarized nation. Finally, though Kennan supported the initial U.S. intervention in South Korea after the North Korean invasion in 1950, he disagreed with Acheson's support of the U.S. plan to invade North Korea. Kennan predicted, correctly, that such action would provoke the Chinese Communists to enter the war.

In 1951 Kennan resigned in order to join the Institute for Advanced Studies at Princeton. However, Truman appointed him ambassador to the USSR in 1952. That experience proved frustrating since Acheson's State Department failed to seek out his advice. Moreover, Kennan disliked living in Stalin's police state, which he publicly likened to his experience in a Nazi internment camp. The Soviets subsequently declared him *persona non grata* for his remarks.

When the Eisenhower administration came to power in 1953 the new secretary of state, John Foster Dulles, declined to offer Kennan a new post, and Kennan retired temporarily from diplomacy. During the Eisenhower years he returned to Princeton where he attacked Dulles's policy of massive retaliation and his depiction of the Cold War as a moral crusade. In 1957 Kennan gave a series of lectures on the BBC calling for a reassessment of U.S. policy toward the

Soviet Union. He maintained that since Stalin's death in 1953 the Soviet leaders had become more liberal domestically and more inclined to negotiate with the United States rather than seek military resolutions. Kennan, therefore, suggested that the United States could use the threat of arming Germany with nuclear weapons to win the simultaneous U.S. and Soviet disengagement from Europe. Acheson and Henry Kissinger severely criticized the lectures, but Senator John Kennedy called them brilliant and stimulating. In 1959 Kennan reiterated his attack on the massive retaliation policy, advocating instead that the United States and the USSR abolish nuclear weapons and that the United States rely on conventional weapons for its defense. When Kennedy became president in 1961 he appointed Kennan ambassador to Yugoslavia. Later Kennan became a prominent critic of the Vietnam War.

Kennedy, John F. (1917–63)   Democratic congressman; senator; and U.S. president, 1961–63. Born in Brookline, Massachusetts, to a wealthy and powerful Irish-American family, Kennedy graduated from Harvard in 1940. His father was ambassador to Great Britain in the Roosevelt administration and Kennedy spent part of his youth in England and Europe. His observations inspired his senior thesis, which he later published as the best-selling book, *Why England Slept*. During World War II he commanded a Navy torpedo boat and injured his back when a Japanese vessel rammed and sank his boat. His subsequent heroic exploits became highly publicized during his presidential campaign. Kennedy won election to Congress in 1946 and generally voted in harmony with other Northern liberals. However, he created some controversy in 1949 when he criticized the Truman State Department for allowing China to fall to Mao Zedong's Communists. In 1952 he narrowly defeated incumbent Senator Republican Henry Cabot Lodge. In his freshman year as senator he married Jacqueline Lee Bouvier. In 1954 he entered the hospital for back surgery and thereby avoided the vote to censure Republican Senator Joseph McCarthy, who was a fellow Catholic and a family friend, despite his fierce antiliberalism. While recovering from his operation Kennedy wrote *Profiles in Courage*, a bestseller about seven U.S. politicians who adhered to their principles, despite the political costs. The book garnered widespread publicity for Kennedy and helped further his aspirations for national office. In 1956 Kennedy gave the nominating speech for Democratic presidential nominee Adlai Stevenson and unsuccessfully sought the vice presidential nomination.

In 1960 the Democrats nominated Kennedy for president and Senate majority leader Lyndon Johnson for vice president. Kennedy tried to defuse the issue of his Catholicism by proclaiming his belief in the absolute separation of church and state. He and his opponent, Vice President Richard Nixon, shared similar views on many issues. Both believed that foreign policy was the dominant issue, and both supported a strong Cold War stand against Communist expansion. Nixon took a slightly more aggressive position in asserting the need to defend the Nationalist Chinese island outposts, Quemoy and Matsu, and Kennedy attacked the Eisenhower administration's failure to take stronger action against Castro in Cuba. Kennedy also charged that Eisenhower had permitted the Soviets to gain superiority in intercontinental ballistic missiles (ICBMs) and that a dangerous missile gap was growing between the two superpowers. After Kennedy's election the missile gap proved to be an illusion. On domestic issues Kennedy vowed to "get the country moving again" and spoke in favor of civil rights. He gained popularity among black voters during the campaign when he made a sympathetic telephone call to the wife of Rev. Martin Luther King, Jr., after officials in Georgia arrested the civil rights leader. Kennedy's brother, Robert, later helped arrange for King's release. The 1960 election featured the first televised debates between presidential candidates, and these are often credited for providing Kennedy with his small margin of victory. Kennedy's poise, charm, energy, and youthful good looks contrasted against Nixon's obvious discomfort with the television medium, his weariness after a recent hospitalization, and his more sinister appearance under the television lights. Kennedy won the election by slightly more than 100,000 votes, the narrowest margin in the twentieth century. He carried fewer states than Nixon but won more votes in the electoral college.

Believing that handling the Cold War was his foremost task, Kennedy wanted to exert substantial personal control over foreign policy. Therefore, he passed over such likely candidates for secretary of state as Stevenson and Chester Bowles in favor of the more obscure Dean Rusk. Rusk acquiesced to Kennedy's desire to control policy and conceived his role more as a presidential adviser than a policymaker. Especially after the Bay of Pigs fiasco early in his administration, Kennedy turned increasingly toward an inner circle of trusted advisers for policy advice. Among these were McGeorge Bundy, General Maxwell Taylor, and Secretary of Defense Robert McNamara, all of whom were known for their exceptional intellectual prowess. Indeed, the Kennedy administration became known for bringing intellectuals into high positions of government and high culture to the White House under the supervision of the first lady. On the other hand, having barely won the election and without a strongly Democratic or liberal Congress, Kennedy also tried to win a middle ground and appease some of his opponents by appointing conservative Republicans to key positions. For instance, he retained J. Edgar Hoover as director of the FBI and later replaced CIA Director Allen Dulles with another conservative, James McCone. Even McNamara had been a Republican and the newly appointed president of Ford Motor Company before joining the administration.

Accepting the advice of Taylor and McNamara, Kennedy quickly began to reverse Eisenhower's nuclear-dependent policy of massive retaliation in favor of flexible response, which would allow the United States to respond to conventional and guerrilla warfare without being compelled to resort to nuclear weapons or all-out warfare. He also adopted recommendations to create a second-strike capacity in order to enhance the U.S. nuclear deterrent and thereby reduce the likelihood of a nuclear war. By guaranteeing that the United States would have enough remaining missiles to launch a devastating retaliatory attack in the event of a Soviet first strike, the second strike capability was intended to convince the Soviets that striking first could not prevent their own destruction. For Eisenhower one of the attractions of massive retaliation had been that it was cost-efficient; it gave "a bigger bang for the buck." Flexible response, on the other hand, required an increase of some 300,000 combat troops and significantly enhanced capabilities for airlifting U.S. forces and equipment anywhere in the world. Moreover, the second-strike capability required replacing liquid-fuel ICBMs with solid-fuel Minuteman housed in hardened underground silos and Polaris missiles on submarines. Implementing these new policies required a 30 percent increase in defense spending during the Kennedy administration. In Kennedy's first year in office he received a $6 billion increase in defense spending, and, despite McNamara's substantial efforts to cut operating expenses and curtail the arms race, the defense budget rose from $43 billion to $56 billion while Kennedy was president.

The Bay of Pigs invasion of Cuba was the first major Cold War crisis for Kennedy. The CIA had organized and trained a Guatemala-based Army of Cuban exiles during the Eisenhower administration in hopes of deposing Castro. After failed attempts to foment a popular revolt on the island and assassinate the Cuban leader, in late 1960 the CIA advised the president-elect of its plans to launch an invasion. (The CIA continued its attempts to assassinate Castro through the Kennedy, Johnson, and Nixon administrations.) No U.S. troops were to be directly involved but U.S. aircraft would provide air cover. Dulles personally assured Kennedy that the attack would overthrow Castro. Kennedy authorized the mission in April, but the surprise air strike by the CIA's obsolete B-26 bombers failed to destroy the Cuban fighters on the ground. The Cuban jet trainer aircraft then shot down the B-26s and sank the exiles' ammunition supply ship. Convinced that the battle was lost, Kennedy refused to authorize a second air strike. Taylor chaired a special panel to investigate the fiasco. Dulles maintained that the invasion might have succeeded had Kennedy permitted the second air attack, but the panel was not able to agree about that assessment. The panel did recommend that the CIA be allowed to conduct further covert operations but that the agency should not launch major paramilitary operations unless these could be plausibly denied. Not only was the Bay of Pigs a military failure, it lent credibility to Castro's claims of U.S. imperialism and intentions to overthrow him by invasion. The Bay of Pigs debacle also contributed significantly to the strong disaffection for the Democratic Party felt by the politically influential Cuban enclave in Miami throughout the entire Cold War, since they blamed the invasion's failure on Kennedy's refusal to authorize the second air strike.

Also in early 1961 a civil war in Laos between Soviet-supported Communist nationals and the U.S.-backed Laotian government led Kennedy to resist against a Communist takeover in that country. However, after meeting with NATO leaders prior to his summit conference with Khrushchev, Kennedy forewent a U.S. military commitment and settled for a short-lived negotiated settlement.

Kennedy accepted the Cold War premise of containment and felt it was necessary to avert a Communist takeover in Vietnam in order to prevent a domino effect in which the rest of Southeast Asia would soon fall to Communism. In the fall of 1961 he sent Taylor and Walt Rostow to Vietnam to report on the situation, and they recommended sending more military advisers and increasing military support to the regime of South Vietnamese President Ngo Dinh Diem. Throughout his presidency Kennedy increased the U.S. military presence in Vietnam but never authorized combat troops. By the end of 1963 the number of advisers had risen from 700 to 15,000. In August 1963 the administration became alarmed at Diem's brutal crackdown against dissident Buddhists and his overall ineffectiveness in leading the war against the Communists. Though the administration did not actively contribute to the coup that overthrew and killed Diem in November, it declined to advise Diem of its knowledge about the planned coup and quickly supported the new regime that replaced him.

The Second Berlin Crisis had begun in 1958, when Khrushchev issued an ultimatum insisting that the Western allies were to evacuate the city within six months. The West refused. Khrushchev later extended his deadline to permit negotiations but remained firm in his demands. The situation vacillated between hot and cold through 1961, when Kennedy took office. In June Kennedy and Khrushchev met in Vienna, and Khrushchev personally delivered a new ultimatum that the allies must evacuate Berlin within six months or risk nuclear war. In response each side employed military moves to intimidate the other. In July Kennedy called up 250,000 reservists to active duty, received another increase in his military budget from Congress, and produced plans for a massive civil defense program to protect Americans in the event of a nuclear war. The situation escalated in August when the Soviets built the Berlin Wall to keep East Berliners from fleeing to the West. A month later they broke a U.S.-USSR moratorium on nuclear testing, exploding the largest nuclear weapon ever made to that date: a 60 megaton bomb. The Berlin crisis peaked in October when U.S. and Soviet tanks faced each other at Checkpoint Charlie, a crossing point at the Berlin Wall. Then the crisis gradually defused when Khrushchev backed away from the deadline for the Western evacuation of Berlin without actually renouncing his demands. In June 1963, 18 months after the crisis had ended, Kennedy traveled to Berlin where he declared, "I am a Berliner." His show of U.S.-German unity made him very popular in Germany and further underscored the U.S. resolve not to permit Soviet control of a unified Germany: one of the primary U.S. objectives throughout the Cold War.

The Cuban Missile Crisis began almost exactly one year after the peak of the Berlin Crisis and the two were related. Khrushchev needed to compensate for the humiliation of backing down in Berlin and to placate hard-line domestic opposition inside the USSR. Therefore, in 1962 he ordered the introduction of medium- and intermediate-range nuclear missiles in Cuba, 90 miles from Key West and 150 miles from the mainland.

The crisis itself began in mid–October 1962 when American U-2 spy planes photographed Soviet missile bases under construction. Earlier Khrushchev had secretly told Kennedy that he was arming Castro with short-range, surface-to-air missiles for defensive purposes. Kennedy rejected the claim and demanded the missiles be removed. On October 22, after reviewing options to bomb or invade Cuba, Kennedy settled on an air and sea blockade to prevent further Soviet arms shipments from reaching Cuba. He announced that any missile launched from Cuba would warrant a full-scale U.S. retaliation against the USSR and demanded the removal of those missiles already in place.

The missile crisis climaxed on October 24 when missile-carrying Soviet cargo ships reached the blockade line and were stopped. The next day Kennedy cabled Khrushchev requesting the removal of the missiles already in place. Khrushchev consented, provided that the United States pledged not to invade Cuba. It was also understood that Kennedy would remove medium-range Jupiter missiles from Turkey, though Kennedy insisted that this agreement be private and omitted from the formal resolution of the Cuban Missile Crisis. Kennedy accepted Khrushchev's bargain, and the missile crisis ended on October 28 when the Soviets agreed to remove the missiles from Cuba. The United States later removed its missiles from Turkey, claiming they were obsolete. Kennedy's handling of the crisis received widespread praise as the United States achieved its objective of removing the missiles without having to engage in warfare. For McNamara it demonstrated the effectiveness of having a flexible response. Rightwing critics, however, charged that by obtaining the U.S. pledge not to invade Cuba and by securing the removal of the Jupiter missiles Khrushchev gained major concessions without giving up anything. Khrushchev's hard-line, domestic foes viewed the situation differently, and his backing down before the Americans helped provoke the coup that removed him from power a year later.

The ultimate impact of the Cuban Missile Crisis was that both superpowers pulled back from nuclear brinkmanship. They accepted the stalemate in Berlin and generally sought to avoid direct military confrontations. They installed a telephone hot line directly between the White House and the Kremlin so the leaders could confer directly and expediently during future crises.

The Cuban Missile Crisis may also have provoked Kennedy and Khrushchev to reopen negotiations on a nuclear test ban treaty. Though unable to resolve differences over on-site inspections of underground tests, Kennedy and Khrushchev eventually agreed upon a limited nuclear test ban that forbade atmospheric testing. Kennedy considered the 1963 Nuclear Test Ban Treaty his greatest accomplishment in office. It not only put an end to the radioactive clouds that circled the earth after each test, it also reduced worldwide fears of an imminent nuclear war.

On November 22, 1963, while in Dallas for a political trip, Kennedy was assassinated. Although a commission headed by Supreme Court Justice Earl Warren ruled that Lee Harvey Oswald had acted alone, many have disputed that conclusion and point to various conspiracy theories.

Kissinger, Henry A. (1923–   )   Special assistant to the president for national security affairs, 1968–75; and secretary of state, 1973–77. Born in Fürth, Germany, Kissinger and his Orthodox Jewish family fled from the Nazis in 1938, going first to England and then to the United States. He worked in a shaving brush factory while pursuing studies in accounting at City College in New York. In 1943 he was drafted into the Army where he did intelligence work. After the war he served as a district administrator in occupied Germany. In 1946 he enrolled at Harvard and received his B.A. summa cum laude in 1950 and his Ph.D in 1954. His doctoral thesis, which later appeared as a book, studied the relatively long period of European peace in the nineteenth century following the defeat of Napoléon. Kissinger attributed the political stability to the efforts of the conservative Austrian Prince Metternich who, unencumbered by bureaucracy or public opinion, skillfully employed personal and secret negotiations and occasional threats of military force to maintain order among the European states. Kissinger's dissertation later reflected his own approach to politics when he came to power.

In 1954 Kissinger joined the Council on Foreign Relations' efforts to explore foreign policy alternatives to massive retaliation. The project's final report in 1957 accepted Eisenhower's premise that the Soviets were trying to expand Communist influence and undermine stability of Western countries, but recommended policies based on the limited use of nuclear weapons instead of massive retaliation. Kissinger also criticized a program in 1957 of BBC radio broadcasts by George Kennan, Truman's foreign policy adviser who had formulated the idea of containment. Kennan maintained that since Stalin's death in 1953 the Soviet leadership had become more liberal domestically and more inclined to negotiate with the United States rather than seek military resolutions. Kennan, therefore, suggested that the United States could use the threat of arming Germany with nuclear weapons to win the simultaneous U.S. and Soviet disengagement from Europe. From 1956 to 1961 Kissinger directed a special project by the Rockefeller Brothers Fund to study the major foreign and domestic problems before the United States. Entitled *The Necessity for Choice: Prospects for American Foreign Policy*, the final report discounted prospects for peaceful coexistence among the superpowers and recommended a strategy centered around tactical nuclear weapons for use in limited warfare. It also recommended expanding the civil defense system and increasing defense spending. These recommendations coincided with policies then being undertaken by the new Kennedy administration.

While serving on this project, Kissinger also joined the faculty of Harvard where he achieved the rank of professor in 1962.

From 1959 to 1969 he directed Harvard's Defense Studies Program and served as consultant to the Arms Control and Disarmament Agency from 1961 to 1967. In the early 1960s he was also an adviser to the National Security Council (NSC). During the late 1960s Kissinger served as a consultant to the State Department for whom he traveled to South Vietnam. Though he concluded that a U.S. victory in Vietnam was impossible, Kissinger maintained that the war was necessary to contain Communism and that the United States would lose credibility if it withdrew dishonorably from South Vietnam. When he joined the Nixon administration he tried to implement a new strategy calling for the Vietnamization of the war: the gradual replacement of U.S. soldiers by South Vietnamese troops. Nixon initiated this in 1969. However, Kissinger was unable to implement other elements of the plan that recommended troop withdrawals on both sides, an international peacekeeping force, internationally monitored free elections, and negotiations for the reunification of Vietnam.

Though Kissinger had campaigned for Nelson Rockefeller during the 1968 Republican nomination, Nixon appreciated his work and, prior to the general election, Nixon's aides induced Kissinger to serve as the Republican Party's foreign policy consultant. After the election Nixon appointed Kissinger to head the NSC and offered him the position of special assistant to the president for national security affairs (national security adviser). Kissinger's initial low opinion of Nixon changed as the men worked together. Whereas Kissinger had earlier regarded Nixon as an opportunist with no deep sense of history, he recognized that they shared similar views on foreign policy, the limits to U.S. power, and the insidious nature of bureaucracy. Both desired greater flexibility, more thorough planning, and a more clearly defined foreign policy. They each wanted the United States to maintain an active role in international affairs while recognizing that the U.S. public was tiring of the Cold War in general and the Vietnam War in particular.

They also agreed that President Johnson had overly delegated authority and had been ill served by the government bureaucracy that shaped his view of world events by controlling the information he reviewed. Therefore, Nixon charged Kissinger, as head of the NSC, with coordinating the information and recommendations coming from several departments. Kissinger also presented sets of options for dealing with specific foreign policy problems. Because information passed from the departments of Defense and State through the NSC en route to the president, Kissinger became a more powerful figure than either Secretary of State William Rogers or Secretary of Defense Melvin Laird.

By 1969 Kissinger did not accept the myth of a worldwide, monolithic, Soviet-run, Communist conspiracy, but he did believe that the USSR retained desires for expanding and undermining the West. Preferring for the Soviet Union and the United States to work together as two responsible countries dedicated to maintaining a stabilizing balance of power, Kissinger established policies of linkage in which concessions on certain issues by one side would bring accommodations by the opposite side on different issues. In particular, he pressured the Soviets to induce North Vietnam to negotiate an acceptable end to the war in return for Soviet access to U.S. technology.

In 1969 Nixon and Kissinger redefined U.S. foreign policy in the Nixon Doctrine. Less willing to automatically commit U.S. resources and military aid than earlier policies based on containment and massive retaliation, the Nixon Doctrine stated that "the U.S. will participate in the defense of allies and friends," but cannot and will not assume "primary responsibility" for their defense. At the same time Nixon and Kissinger sought to slow the pace of the nuclear arms race. The overall effect of their policy was to seek at least some peaceful accommodations with the Soviet Union and the People's Republic of China (PRC). Many of these efforts came to fruition during the early 1970s when the Nixon administration inaugurated trade, cultural exchanges, and other forms of dialogue and interaction between the superpowers.

Explicit recognition of the nuclear stalemate led to new policies predicated on mutual assured destruction (MAD) instead of massive retaliation, since both sides had assembled nuclear arsenals capable of destroying their opponents hundreds of times over. Massive retaliation had assumed that a nuclear war was winnable; MAD assumed that nuclear warfare was mutual suicide. Shortly after assuming office Kissinger ordered a study on the relative strength of the United States and the Soviet Union. Based on that report he recommended that Nixon should approve the nuclear nonproliferation treaty that the Johnson administrated had negotiated. He also concluded that Nixon's campaign pledge to achieve "clear-cut military superiority" was unrealistic, and he induced the president to change the goal to guaranteeing "sufficient military power to defend our interests and to maintain ... commitments." He also continued the Strategic Arms Limitation Talks (SALT) that Johnson had initiated as a means for easing the arms race, but he pursued these more slowly. Kissinger upset members of Congress and outraged the Soviets when he supported the development of an antiballistic missile (ABM) system and multiple-head intercontinental ballistic missiles (MIRV). But subsequent negotiations led to 1974 treaties barring ABMs and limiting MIRVs.

Ending the unpopular and increasingly divisive Vietnam War was a high priority for the first Nixon administration. Both Nixon and Kissinger agreed that the United States and South Vietnam could not win a limited war and that expanding the war raised too many domestic and international risks. Both also insisted that the United States must avoid the appearance of a humiliating defeat in which it would lose credibility and influence throughout the world. Thus they adopted "peace with honor" as their slogan, and Kissinger began pursuing negotiations that Johnson had initiated in 1968. However, Kissinger's basic view of the war differed sharply from that of North Vietnam or the National Liberation

Front (NLF), which represented South Vietnamese nationalists who were also fighting for the country's unification. The 1954 Geneva accords between the defeated French and the victorious government in North Vietnam had called for the temporary partition of Vietnam followed by national elections in 1956 to unify the country. However, the United States and the Saigon-based Vietnamese government that America recognized had refused to sign the accords, and in 1955 South Vietnam declared itself a separate republic. The United States and its Western allies recognized South Vietnam, but North Vietnam, the PRC, the Soviet Union, and the Warsaw Pact countries did not. Thus, for Kissinger the Vietnam War was a conflict between two sovereign nations, while for the North Vietnamese and the NLF, also known as the Vietcong, it was a civil war directed at reunifying the nation. According to his aide Roger Morris, Kissinger was never able to understand North Vietnam's position. This fundamental difference over the very nature of the war seriously inhibited the peace negotiations. The Communists remained firm in their commitment to ultimate reunification, rejecting an early Kissinger two-track proposal for a military settlement between the United States and North Vietnam and a political settlement between South Vietnam and the NLF. Thus the peace negotiations failed to show results until the very end of Nixon's first term.

As the peace talks stalled Nixon adopted Kissinger's plan for the Vietnamization of the war, in which South Vietnam assumed increasingly greater responsibility for conducting the war and U.S. troops were gradually withdrawn. The policy objective was to enable the United States to disengage from the conflict while still preserving the anti–Communist regime of South Vietnamese President Nguyen Van Thieu. Kissinger maintained that U.S. credibility with other countries precluded a rapid withdrawal that might undermine Thieu. Thus between 1969 and 1972 Nixon withdrew 555,000 troops from Vietnam while continuing massive air attacks. In 1969, with Kissinger's approval, Nixon authorized secret bombing raids in Cambodia, despite official U.S. recognition of that country's sovereignty. And in 1970 Kissinger approved the U.S. invasion of Cambodia: an act that provoked the resignation of all but one of his aides. During this period Kissinger became increasingly estranged from the academic community and liberals and moderates who had looked to him to quickly end the war. He also alienated members of Congress by invoking executive privilege to avoid testifying before the elected representatives. He gained a reputation for arrogance and for being "the second most powerful man" in the country, and he increasingly became a target for antiwar activists.

By 1972 the war had emerged as a major campaign issue and Kissinger increased his efforts to settle it. Nixon intensified the air war and ordered the mining of Haiphong Harbor after North Vietnam launched a major attack across the demilitarized zone that separated it from South Vietnam. These efforts prevented the collapse of the South Vietnamese Army in the northern region of South Vietnam but did not succeed in forcing the North Vietnamese to make major concessions at the bargaining table. However, in October — a month before the U.S. election — Kissinger announced a major breakthrough and declared, "We believe that peace is at hand." But South Vietnam's President Thieu refused to accept the new terms and demanded 69 amendments to the agreements. After new talks between Kissinger and North Vietnamese representative Le Duc Tho broke down in December Kissinger approved Nixon's plan to order massive Christmas bombings of Hanoi and Haiphong. After 11 days of bombings the North Vietnamese returned to the bargaining table and accepted an agreement similar to the October accord. Nixon then warned Thieu, "You must decide now whether you desire to continue our alliance or whether you want me to seek a settlement with the enemy which serves U.S. interests alone." In January 1973 all of the parties accepted a new peace agreement, and the last U.S. combat troops left Vietnam on March 29. In October Kissinger and Le Duc Tho shared the Nobel Peace Prize. However, unlike the 1954 peace accords, the 1973 agreement permitted the North Vietnamese armies to remain in southern regions they already controlled, and by the next year the war had begun anew. On April 30, 1975, Saigon fell to the Communists. Cambodia also fell under Communist rule that month.

If their Vietnam policy was their most unpopular Cold War position, Kissinger and Nixon's decision to ease East-West tensions and promote a new era of détente earned them the most praise. By 1969 Mao Zedong had completed the first stage of his Cultural Revolution and consolidated power in China. Though a long-standing opponent of Chinese Communism, Nixon perceived that China was ready to assume an important leadership role in the world. Moreover, he and Kissinger realized that a U.S.-Chinese alignment would further pressure the Soviets. Thus in July 1971, three months before the PRC replaced Taiwan in the United Nations, Nixon authorized Kissinger to fly secretly to Peking to arrange a presidential visit. Kissinger thereby became the first U.S. official to enter China since the formation of the PRC in 1949. He forged a cordial, personal relationship with Chinese Premier Zhou En-lai. And as a major concession to the Chinese he indicated that the United States would regard Taiwan, which housed the opposition Nationalist Chinese government, as part of China. Kissinger also laid the groundwork for Nixon's historic visit in 1972, after which the United States reduced its troop strength in Taiwan.

Largely under Kissinger's influence U.S.-Soviet relations also improved considerably during the Nixon era. Initially, Kissinger took a hard line against the Soviets. In 1970, over the objections of Secretary of State Rogers, Kissinger directed a series of U.S.-Israeli military moves to prevent pro-Soviet Syria from overthrowing Jordan's pro-Western King Hussein. He also warned the USSR not to build a nuclear submarine base in Cuba, since the United States would regard this as a violation of the agreement that had concluded the 1962 Cuban Missile Crisis. The Soviets stopped the construction.

In 1972 Kissinger began to implement his plans more fully for a superpower détente. In addition to helping arrange the rapprochement with China, he traveled secretly to Moscow to prepare for a May summit meeting between Nixon and Soviet Premier Brezhnev, and gain Soviet assistance in pressuring North Vietnam over the Paris peace talks. He did not succeed in pressuring North Vietnam, but the summit played a large role in Kissinger's plans for détente, and Nixon signed agreements that created cultural, scientific, environmental, and trade exchanges, as well as the SALT I Treaty that limited specified defensive weapons. In September Kissinger negotiated a large grain sale that Democratic Senator Henry Jackson and other opponents of détente later attacked. In October Nixon and Brezhnev signed an ABM Treaty in hopes of reducing the arms race. And in 1973 Brezhnev visited the United States and signed a pact aimed at avoiding superpower confrontations that could lead to a nuclear war.

In 1971 Kissinger promoted an unpopular tilt toward the Muslim military dictatorship in Pakistan during its war with India, the world's largest democracy. He adopted the position partly to reward Pakistan for its efforts in helping the United States establish relations with China. When Soviet-supported India won the war and established the independent country of Bangladesh, Kissinger considered resigning. Records from secret meetings about the war were leaked to the press, purportedly by White House aides John Ehrlichman and H. R. Haldeman, who allegedly were jealous of Kissinger's stature and influence with the president.

In May 1973 Nixon appointed Kissinger as secretary of state, though he retained his position as national security adviser. Kissinger sought the post to guarantee his control over foreign affairs while the Watergate crisis was making the president increasingly desperate. Nixon hoped the appointment would strengthen his administration, and Kissinger believed it would give him greater leverage over his new White House rivals, Secretary of the Treasury John Connally and Chief of Staff Al Haig, who had replaced Haldeman. Kissinger also maintained that as secretary of state he would no longer need to rely so much on secret diplomacy.

Overcoming reluctance by Defense Secretary James Schlesinger who feared a threatened Arab oil boycott, Kissinger convinced Nixon to support Israel during the Yom Kippur War of October 1973. The U.S. aid has been credited with enabling the Israelis to reverse initial Egyptian gains and force the Arabs and their Soviet sponsor to seek a truce. Kissinger flew to Moscow where he was authorized to sign any agreement in Nixon's name. Though Kissinger felt the Soviet role in the war violated the spirit of détente, he and Brezhnev negotiated an arrangement calling for direct Egyptian-Israeli talks. Shortly afterward, however, in response to provocative Soviet military moves that Kissinger claimed were designed to help the Arabs, Kissinger convinced Nixon to order a worldwide nuclear alert. A crisis was averted when the United Nations worked out a cease-fire and established a peacekeeping force in the region. Critics have accused Kissinger of deliberately overreacting to the Soviet actions in order to distract domestic attention from the growing Watergate crisis.

Two weeks later, in an effort to weaken Egyptian ties with the USSR, the United States and Egypt restored diplomatic relations that had been broken since the 1967 Arab-Israeli War. Kissinger's subsequent shuttle diplomacy helped lay the foundation for the separate peace established between Israel and Egypt under the auspices of President Carter. Kissinger also negotiated a disengagement settlement between Israel and Syria, though the two countries remained hostile. On the other hand, the U.S. support for Israel provoked the threatened oil boycott that Schlesinger had feared. By using his influence to keep Israel from obtaining a complete victory, Kissinger sought to make the embargo temporary as well as to create circumstances more favorable to an eventual Middle East peace. Lasting from December 1973 to March 1974, the boycott created an energy crisis in the United States that quadrupled oil prices, worsened the trade deficit, stimulated inflation, and created a worldwide recession later in the year.

Also in 1973 Kissinger secretly supported a military coup that overthrew the freely elected Marxist president of Chile, Salvador Allende. Allende had tried to turn Chile into a socialist state by nationalizing industries, promoting extensive land reform, and establishing closer ties with Communist countries. He was replaced by General Pinochet's military dictatorship, which later became notorious for its brutal and widespread human rights violations. Kissinger's willingness to sacrifice human rights concerns for achieving political goals occasioned considerable criticism during the 1970s. He was, for instance, prepared to tolerate the persecution of Soviet Jews in order to obtain the 1974 East-West Trade Relations Act. However, Senator Jackson amended the legislation to bar the Soviet Union from most favored nation designation as long as it inhibited Jewish emigration. Kissinger won a Soviet commitment to allow 45,000 Jews to emigrate each year, but Jackson thought the number was too small. The Soviets denounced what they considered interference in their internal affairs and eventually canceled the amended agreement. Throughout the 1970s the trade bill and the Jackson-Vanik Amendment plagued détente, giving the Soviets a basis to charge that the United States had failed to honor its promises to increase East-West trade and providing anti–Communists an opportunity to point out yet another example of Soviet tyranny.

Though Kissinger's diplomatic accomplishments received widespread praise in the United States, many of the Western allies resented his failure to consult or involve them in the process, and this caused the alliance to deteriorate. He was criticized for his secrecy, and the European allies did not support his plans for treating Europe as a single region in terms of energy, military, monetary, and commercial issues. They also feared that a separate peace between the United States and USSR would leave them vulnerable to Soviet aggression. Moreover, they regarded as reckless Kissinger's threats to occupy Arab oil fields if the Arab nations refused to cooperate on petroleum exports. U.S.-European relations remained uneasy while Kissinger remained in office.

During the Watergate affair Kissinger admitted that he had approved wire-tapping government employees and newsmen to stem information leaks, but claimed that FBI Director J. Edgar Hoover and Attorney General John Mitchell had assured him the wiretaps were legal. His role in the overthrow of Allende and in the 1969 secret bombings of Cambodia also became public, and he became perceived as someone just as likely to employ covert operations to achieve his objectives as anyone else in the scandal-tainted administration. In June 1974 Kissinger threatened to resign because it was not "possible to conduct the foreign policy of the United States under these circumstances when the character and credibility of the Secretary of State is at issue." He demanded that the Senate Foreign Relations Committee investigate the charges against him, but when he was cleared of wrongdoing the case against Nixon appeared even stronger. Though he had never been Nixon's close friend, Kissinger tried to comfort the president in his final days in office by reminding him that he would be remembered for his accomplishments, especially in foreign affairs. Shortly before resigning Nixon reportedly asked Kissinger to kneel beside him and pray. Nixon resigned on August 9, 1974.

The Watergate affair crippled Kissinger's ability to promote détente in late 1973 and 1974, since the Soviets were reluctant to deal with a government that appeared on the verge of collapse. After Nixon left Kissinger remained as secretary of state in the Ford administration. Domestic opposition from Jackson and other conservatives slowed détente, and Kissinger began receiving criticism from the right that he was selling out to the Soviets; some extremists called him the "Jewish Communist." At the same time liberals continued to oppose his disregard of human rights. Schlesinger accused Kissinger of making too many concessions and allowing the Soviets too many MIRVs, and in the political fallout of that debate Schlesinger was removed as secretary of defense. To appease the conservatives, Ford also removed Kissinger as head of the NSC but appointed a successor who supported Kissinger.

The 1975 Helsinki Summit Conference represented the high point of Kissinger's détente. It produced accords signed by the United States, the Soviet Union, and all of the countries in Eastern and Western Europe. These agreements repudiated the use of force and respected the frontiers and territorial integrity of all European states, thereby securing the promise of peace at the cost of providing de facto recognition of the USSR's post–World War II territorial gains, something the Soviet Union had been seeking for 30 years. In repudiating force the European countries were effectively agreeing not to wage nuclear war upon each other. In return, the Soviets agreed to greater economic, scientific, technical, and environmental cooperation with the West and, more importantly, to the freer movement of ideas, greater access to broadcast and printed information, and the reunification of families through emigration. They also made some significant concessions to human rights. These agreements later helped make possible Poland's Solidarity Movement and the internal political activity that eventually brought down the Communist governments in Eastern Europe.

In 1975 Kissinger began to change U.S. policy in Africa, which had traditionally supported white, minority governments. He denounced apartheid in South Africa and implied support for Namibia's independence. He sought increased aid for drought relief and construction projects within Africa. He withdrew U.S. support of the white-supremacist regime in Rhodesia and helped pressure Rhodesian Prime Minister Ian Smith to end white rule and create a coalition government that would include moderate blacks. His support for Turkey during its 1975 invasion of Cyprus prompted a contentious Congress to enact legislation forbidding military aid to Turkey because it was using U.S. weapons for nondefensive purposes.

During the 1976 Republican primaries Ronald Reagan attacked Kissinger for caving in to the Soviets. Reagan charged that the Helsinki agreements doomed Eastern Europeans to permanent Soviet domination, and he accused Kissinger of favoring revolutionaries in Rhodesia over a legitimate government. Reagan also objected to Kissinger's acceptance of Communist China and his efforts to negotiate the return of the Panama Canal to the Panamanians. After Ford defeated Reagan for the Republican nomination, Democratic nominee Jimmy Carter attacked Kissinger's approach to foreign policy, which he described as based on "the assumption that the world is a jungle of competing national antagonisms where military muscle and economic muscle are the only things that work."

LeMay, Curtis (1906–90)   A U.S. Air Force general and Air Force chief of staff, 1961–65. Educated at Ohio State University's School of Engineering, LeMay was commissioned as a second lieutenant in the Army Air Corps in 1930. He rose steadily through the ranks, becoming a major general in 1937. During World War II he helped formulate tactics in the European theater and planned the B-29 firebombings of Tokyo in the final months of the war. Afterward he headed the U.S. Air Force in Europe and helped direct the Berlin Airlift of 1948–49. In the fall of 1948 he returned to the United States to head the Strategic Air Command (SAC), a position he retained even after his promotion to Air Force vice chief of staff in 1957.

A passionate defender of SAC, LeMay successfully staved off attempts to reduce its funding. Throughout the 1950s he warned of a "bomber gap" between the United States and USSR and predicted that the United States would become increasingly vulnerable to a Soviet attack unless "we continue to improve the combat capacity, readiness, and security of our air power." He also sought the development of reliable intercontinental ballistic missiles (ICBMs), and some of his statements gave credence to the loudly proclaimed but erroneous assertion in the late 1950s that the Soviet Union had acquired missile superiority. In 1957 he warned that by 1959, unless the Air Force received greater funding for expanding and upgrading its bomber fleet, the United States would lose its lead in air power. That situation would "invite a cataclysmic preemptive strike by the superior Communist intercontinental ballistic missile force at some future date." He opposed diverting money from the Air Force to the Army, whose overriding concern was for conventional, not nuclear, warfare. When asked how effective bombers would be in a guerrilla war — such as the later Vietnam War proved to be — he replied, "I do not understand why a force that will deter a big war will not deter a small war too, if we want it to and say it will."

In 1961 LeMay was promoted to Air Force chief of staff. In that position he opposed Defense Secretary Robert McNamara's preference for unmanned missiles over manned bombers. According to recent scholarship by Richard Rhodes, during the 1962 Cuban Missile Crisis LeMay advised President Kennedy to order military action in Cuba that would provoke a Soviet response and thereby justify a preemptive nuclear attack against the Soviet Union. The goal of that strike, which SAC would have spearheaded, was to destroy the Soviet Union's Communist system in a single blow. Rhodes maintains that after Kennedy rejected LeMay's proposal LeMay and General Thomas Power, LeMay's protégé who replaced him as commander of SAC, tried to provoke a military confrontation with the Soviets. While the missile crisis was in progress, SAC carried out a previously scheduled test firing of an unarmed Atlas missile across the Pacific from California to a target in the Marshall Islands; in an unauthorized, uncoded broadcast that the Soviets doubtlessly monitored, Thomas ordered all SAC wings to "review your plans for further action," and during the height of the crisis SAC bombers deliberately flew beyond their normal fail-safe points toward the Soviet Union before turning back to their bases. Rhodes argues that LeMay's intention was to instigate a war with the Soviets while the United States still enjoyed significant nuclear superiority.

Fearing that LeMay might become a significant political threat upon his retirement, high-ranking officials in both the Kennedy and Johnson administrations repeatedly extended his tour of duty at the Pentagon. When he did retire in 1965 LeMay publicly criticized the Johnson administration for restricting the bombing raids over North Vietnam. LeMay advocated that the United States "bomb them back to the Stone Age." In 1968 he ran for vice president on George Wallace's American Independent Party ticket. During the campaign LeMay criticized Johnson's decision to halt the bombing of North Vietnam, promising that, if elected, he would reinstate the bombing and use nuclear weapons if necessary. The Wallace-LeMay ticket garnered 13.4 percent of the popular vote.

MacArthur, Douglas (1880–1964)   A U.S. Army general and commander of UN forces in Korea, 1950–51. Born in Little Rock, Arkansas, the son of a Union Army general, MacArthur attended West Point, where he graduated first in the class of 1903. After serving in several Army posts throughout the country he fought in World War I. He received 13 decorations and 7 citations for bravery and in 1918 achieved the rank of brigadier general. He then served as superintendent of West Point from 1919 to 1922 before being reassigned to the Philippines. In 1930 he became a four-star general and the youngest Army chief of staff in history, and then from 1935 to 1941 he served as military adviser to the Philippines. Four months prior to the Japanese attack on Pearl Harbor he was promoted to commander of Army forces in the Far East. After the U.S. entry into the war in December 1941, MacArthur led the fight against the Japanese attack on the Philippines. However, in March President Roosevelt ordered him to evacuate to Australia, where he became commander of the Allied forces in the Southwest Pacific. Upon his evacuation MacArthur forecast, "I shall return," which he succeeded in doing in 1944. Shortly afterward he was promoted to five-star general and in April 1945 he took command of all Army forces in the Pacific. As supreme commander of the Allied Powers in the Pacific MacArthur accepted the Japanese surrender aboard the U.S. battleship *Missouri* that August.

Following the cessation of hostilities, President Truman appointed Mac-Arthur to administer the U.S. military occupation of Japan. In theory, occupation policies were to be determined by a Far Eastern Commission composed of representatives from 11 nations who had fought together against Japan. In practice, however, MacArthur largely ignored the commission and directives from Washington, D.C., preferring to rely on his own judgment and that of his military advisers. As military governor he sought to eliminate all forms of Japanese militarism that had been responsible for Japan's prosecution of the war. He also sought to introduce political, economic, and social reforms that would help effect Japan's transition to a democratic society. MacArthur rapidly disarmed the Japanese military, destroyed the war industries, and conducted trials for war crimes. Nonetheless, the Japanese generally regarded him as fair and he acquired their respect. In 1947 Japan adopted a new constitution containing a number of democratic rights, including the freedoms of speech and press. It also renounced Japan's right ever to wage war and banned the creation of military forces. Thereafter, MacArthur administered the occupation in harmony with the new constitution. He decentralized the police force and school system and broke up large landholdings and some large industrial combines. MacArthur had originally advocated a three-year occupation, but failure among the victorious Allies to agree upon a Pacific peace treaty led to its prolongation. After Chinese Communists gained control of mainland China in 1949 the Soviets opposed full Japanese recovery. Following the outbreak of the Korean War in 1950 MacArthur convinced the Japanese government to restrict Communist activities and establish a 75,000-man police reserve to guard against sabotage. In 1951, shortly after Truman fired MacArthur for insubordination, the United States concluded a separate peace treaty with Japan, thereby ending the military occupation.

After the Korean War began MacArthur charged that the Truman administration had ignored his warnings of an impending North Korean invasion. Truman appointed him commander in chief of UN armies in Korea. Initially, the outnumbered UN troops were driven back and pinned within the Pusan perimeter. However, MacArthur planned a daring and successful landing behind enemy lines at Inchon on September 15, 1950, and then took the offensive. Confident that Communist China would not enter the war MacArthur predicted final victory by the new year. However, in late November, while the UN armies were well into North Korea, Chinese armies invaded and eventually drove the outnumbered UN troops back to the thirty-eighth parallel that divided the two Koreas. Arguing that "there is no substitute for victory," MacArthur advocated expanding the war by bombing Chinese supply depots in Manchuria and destroying bridges over the Yalu River that separates China from North Korea. Truman and Secretary of Defense George Marshall disagreed, preferring to fight a limited "police action" rather than provoke an all-out war that might eventually involve the Soviets. MacArthur's public criticism of administration policy angered Truman. On April 5, 1951, Representative Joseph Martin read on the floor of Congress a letter MacArthur had written to him objecting to the administration's pursuit of a limited war. Truman regarded the letter as an act of insubordination and fired MacArthur on April 11. The controversial dismissal provoked a congressional inquiry. Senator Joseph McCarthy, who had suggested that MacArthur retire when the general ran against McCarthy's political ally Harold Stassen in 1948, now declared "the son of a bitch [Truman] should be impeached." Nonetheless, Truman weathered the storm. Despite MacArthur's immense popularity on his return from Korea and his dramatic farewell appearance before Congress soon after, he was unable to remain a major political player. In 1952 he gave the keynote address at the Republican National Convention, but his bid for the Republican nomination that year was squelched by another World War II military hero, Dwight Eisenhower. MacArthur subsequently became chairman of the board for the Remington Rand Corporation. In 1962 Congress ordered that a gold medal be struck to commemorate his service to his country. He died two years later.

McCarran, Patrick A. (1876–1954)   A Democratic senator from Nevada, 1933–47, and 1949–53. Born in Reno, Nevada, McCarran graduated from the University of Nevada in 1901, after which he began ranching and studying law in his spare time. Between 1903 and 1932 he established a law practice, won a six-year term on the Nevada Supreme Court, and tried unsuccessfully to secure the Democratic nomination for the U.S. Senate. In 1932 the Democrats nominated him and McCarran defeated the popular Republican candidate, Tasker Oddie. Though he benefited from the Democratic landslide that accompanied Franklin Roosevelt's presidential victory, McCarran soon helped lead the conservative anti–New Deal contingent within the Senate, and he successfully fought against Roosevelt's 1937 attempt to increase the number of Supreme Court justices. A staunch Catholic, McCarran supported Franco's anti–Communist dictatorship and promoted closer relations between the United States and Spain. Coming from a state rich in silver, McCarran was known for his persistent lobbying for higher silver prices.

During the Cold War McCarran led a coalition of conservative Democrats and Republicans who passed a number of anti–Communist bills. In 1947 he introduced legislation that permitted the State Department to fire employees whose actions it considered detrimental to national interests. McCarran's proposed 1950 Internal Security Act required the registration of Communist and Communist-front groups, even those that were legally established; it extended the statute of limitations and intensified the penalties for espionage and sedition; and it enabled the Justice Department to deport or detain aliens believed to be subversive and to bar them from immigration. Concerned that McCarran's bill would require cumbersome regulations and undermine constitutional freedoms, a group of liberal senators tried to preempt the legislation with a substitute bill that would establish concentration camps for Communists in the event of a national emergency. However, a series of conservative parliamentary maneuvers incorporated the substitute bill within the original, and the amended McCarran Internal Security Act passed both houses of Congress by substantial margins. According to the New York Times, several opponents of the bill voted for it because it was "too risky politically to vote against anti–Communist legislation in this election year." Truman vetoed the legislation and spoke forcefully against it; however, Congress overrode the veto. Subsequently, Communist and Communist-dominated organizations were required to provide the federal government the names of all of their members and contributors, and concentration camps were established in Pennsylvania, Florida, Oklahoma, Arizona, and California, although these were never used.

Concerned that internal Communist subversion stemmed from immigration from Communist-dominated regions, McCarran helped write a displaced persons bill in 1948 that permitted 200,000 World War II refugees to immigrate to the United States. Critics charged that the legislation discriminated against Jews and Catholics from Eastern Europe, but McCarran succeeded in blocking reforms until 1950. The 1952 McCarran-Walter Act overhauled U.S. immigration, naturalization, and nationality laws, eliminating race as a criterion but retaining restrictions on national origin. It also expanded the grounds for excluding and deporting aliens. The act relied on the 1920 census for allocating immigration quotas. Critics complained that the 32-year-old census reflected a disproportionately smaller number of Asians and Eastern, Central, and Southern Europeans since most of the immigrants from those regions had arrived since 1920. In reply McCarran warned against "opening the gates to a flood of Asiatics." Truman charged that the act would "intensify the repressive and inhumane aspects of our immigration procedures" and so vetoed the bill. In return McCarran claimed that Truman's veto conformed to the Communist Party line and that it was "one of the most un–American acts I have ever witnessed in my public career." Congress overrode Truman's veto.

Though McCarran supported the Marshall Plan, the formation of the North Atlantic Treaty Organization (NATO), and other aspects of the Truman Doctrine intended to fight the spread of Communism in Europe, he criticized the administration for failing to adequately support Chiang Kai-shek in China. Like Senator Joseph McCarthy, McCarran attacked the State Department, which he claimed was composed of "desk-bound intellectuals" whose statesmanship was characteristic of a "psychopathic ward." In 1949 and 1950 he succeeded in gaining military loans for Chiang's Nationalists, whom Mao Zedong's Communist armies drove from the Chinese mainland onto the island of Taiwan (Formosa) in 1949.

In 1951, as chair of the newly formed Internal Security Subcommittee, McCarran began investigating Communist influence within unions and inside the entertainment and communications industries. The committee also investigated alleged subversion by U.S. citizens employed by the United Nations and conducted hearings into Communist influences within colleges and universities. The committee became best known for its renewed accusations against Professor Owen Lattimore, a China scholar who had supported agrarian reform and attacked Chiang for being corrupt and insufficiently democratic. In 1950, in cooperation with a powerful right-wing, pro–Chiang China lobby, McCarthy had accused Lattimore of being pro–Communist and sabotaging U.S. aid to Chiang's Nationalist government. However, although McCarthy labeled Lattimore the top Soviet espionage agent in the United States and introduced unsubstantiated testimony from former ranking members of the U.S. Communist Party, a Senate panel cleared the professor after finding no evidence that Lattimore had ever been a Soviet agent. But in 1951 McCarran's committee renewed the investigation and recommended that Lattimore be indicted for possible perjury since the professor had been "for some time, beginning in the middle of the 1930s a conscious, articulate instrument of the Soviet conspiracy." A grand jury indicted Lattimore on five counts, but after three years a federal court dismissed most of the charges as vague, and the Justice Department withdrew the rest. Nonetheless, McCarran remained one of McCarthy's few Democratic supporters, and he unsuccessfully fought the Senate's attempts to censure McCarthy in 1954. McCarran died shortly afterward of a heart attack suffered while addressing a political rally in Nevada.

McCarthy, Joseph R. (1909–57) A Republican senator from Wisconsin, 1947–57. One of the most powerful and most feared politicians during the early 1950s, McCarthy grew up on his father's farm in northwestern Wisconsin. He left school after the eighth grade to become a chicken farmer; however, he returned at age 19 and completed 4 years of high school work in a single year. He then attended Marquette University where he received his law degree in 1935. Unable to thrive in private practice, McCarthy began a career in politics. He ran unsuccessfully as a Democratic candidate for county attorney in 1936 but was elected circuit court judge in 1939, when he ran as a Republican.

When World War II broke out McCarthy waived his deferment and enlisted in the Marines. Stationed on the Solomon Islands, McCarthy briefed and debriefed combat pilots and went along as an observer on a limited number of missions. Afterward those flights became the basis for the nickname he gave himself for his political campaigns, "Tail Gunner Joe." In 1944, while still serving in the military, McCarthy ran against incumbent Senator Alexander Wiley and two other candidates for the Republican nomination, disregarding Marine Corps regulations forbidding active duty Marines from seeking public office or making political speeches. McCarthy came in second to Wiley and increased his standing among Wisconsin Republicans. In 1946 McCarthy narrowly won the Republican nomination after defeating Senator Robert La Follette, Jr., McCarthy attacked the incumbent for his Progressive Party past, his ties to organized labor, and his prewar isolationism, which McCarthy contrasted to an inflated account of his own wartime service. McCarthy then defeated the Democratic nominee and entered the U.S. Senate in 1947.

McCarthy's ferocious and vindictive anti–Communism first surfaced in his fierce antiunion stance. In 1946 he called on President Truman to draft striking mine workers into military service and then court-martial them if they refused to return to work. The following year he tried unsuccessfully to amend the Taft-Hartley Act to require union leaders to notify employers of any members belonging to Communist associations and to approve the firing of these workers. McCarthy's anti–Communism also dictated his positions on foreign policy. He supported Truman's developing containment policies, which included the Marshall Plan, foreign aid for Greece and Turkey to forestall Communist takeovers in those countries, and the formation of the North Atlantic Treaty Organization (NATO), an anti–Soviet military alliance of Western European democracies.

However, McCarthy claimed that Truman's State Department under George Marshall and Dean Acheson had not done enough to support Chiang Kai-shek in his unsuccessful fight against Mao Zedong's Chinese Communists. Moreover, he charged that the State Department's failures in China stemmed from treason: that ranking members of the State Department were Soviet agents. He first made these accusations on February 9, 1950, in a speech before a Republican women's group in Wheeling, West Virginia. Holding up a copy of a 1946 letter, McCarthy declared, "I have here in my hand a list of 205" members of the Communist Party who, although known to the State Department "nevertheless are still working and shaping the [department's] policy." McCarthy's charges created an immediate furor. When Democrats demanded proof, McCarthy further obfuscated the issue by revising and rerevising the number of alleged Communists on his list. In one case it was 57, in another 207. Despite these inconsistencies, however, McCarthy's accusations were taken seriously and the Senate appointed a Foreign Relations Subcommittee to investigate. Chaired by Democrat Millard Tydings, the committee tried unsuccessfully to discredit McCarthy, partly because the Truman administration initially refused to surrender its loyalty files on government employees. Testifying before the committee, McCarthy named ten people from his list, including ambassador at large Philip Jessup and China scholar Owen Lattimore, who was then a professor at Johns Hopkins University. McCarthy charged that Jessup had "an unusual affinity" for Communist causes and that Lattimore was the Soviet Union's top espionage agent in the United States. Former top-ranking American Communists Louis Bundenz and Freda Utley supported McCarthy's claims. All of the accused protested their innocence, and the committee ultimately exonerated them. None was ever found guilty of treason. Republican Senator Patrick McCarran later reopened hearings into Lattimore, and his committee recommended that the professor be indicted for perjury. However, subsequent grand jury indictments were eventually either rejected by a federal court as too vague or dropped by the Justice Department. Although Tydings's committee officially labeled McCarthy "a fraud and a hoax," the Wisconsin senator repeated his charges on radio and television. When called upon to produce his evidence he refused, adding new accusations instead. McCarthy emerged from the controversy as a chief spokesman for the anti–Communist sentiment then growing within the country and as a powerful and prominent member of the Republican Party.

The Tydings committee reported its findings in June 1950. That same month Communist North Korea launched a surprise attack against South Korea and inaugurated the Korean War. McCarthy reluctantly supported the U.S. intervention on South Korea's behalf, but blamed the war on earlier policies made by "that group of Communists, fellow travelers and dupes in our State Department." When Truman fired General Douglas MacArthur for insubordination, McCarthy declared that "the son of a bitch [Truman] should be impeached."

In November 1950, less than six months after the Tydings committee dismissed McCarthy as a hoax, Republican John Butler defeated Tydings. Although most political observers had expected the Democratic incumbent to win easily, McCarthy campaigned hard for Butler, and this upset further enhanced McCarthy's standing among Republicans. Voters also unseated several other critics of McCarthy in the 1950 elections, including majority leader Scott Lucas whose opponent was closely identified with McCarthy. In 1951 the Senate Rules Committee's Subcommittee on Privileges and Elections denounced McCarthy's role in the Tydings-Butler election.

Shortly thereafter, Democratic Senator William Benton asked that the Rules Committee consider whether McCarthy should be expelled from the Senate for his attacks on Secretary of Defense George Marshall. McCarthy had accused Marshall of virtual treason for his earlier role in determining U.S. policy toward China. The engineer of the highly successful Marshall Plan for European economic recovery, Marshall had been the much respected Army chief of staff during World War II, and McCarthy's claims that the architect of the victory over Germany was "an instrument of the Soviet conspiracy" who had an "affinity for Chinese Reds" outraged the former general's supporters. The Democratic leadership moved slowly on Benton's request, until new accusations against the State Department provoked majority leader Ernest McFarland to have the Subcommittee on Privileges and Elections formally commence hearings on Benton's motion. However, the committee did not issue its report until January 1953. It criticized McCarthy for several offenses, including questionable financial dealings with lobbyists, but did not recommend any actions be taken against him. As with the earlier reprimand by Tydings's committee, these criticisms did little to undermine McCarthy's support. Between February 1950, when he gave the speech in Wheeler, West Virginia, and December 1954, when the Senate finally voted to censure him, McCarthy remained virtually impervious to attacks by his critics.

McCarthy won reelection in 1952. The same elections brought a Republican, Eisenhower, to the White House and a Republican majority to the Senate. Thus in January 1953 McCarthy became chairman of the Government Operations Committee, the Senate's permanent subcommittee for investigations. He used this position to conduct hearings into alleged domestic Communist subversion in a wide number of areas. Despite the fact that a Republican administration was now in power, McCarthy continued his attacks on the State Department. In 1953 he expanded them to the Army, charging that it had attempted to conceal Communist subversive activity at the Fort Monmouth Army Signal Corps Center, and accusing the Army of "Communist coddling" when it approved the routine promotion at Camp Kilmer of a captain with somewhat left-wing sympathies, Irving Peress. He accused Peress's commander, World War II hero General Ralph Zwicker, of being "a disgrace to the uniform" and attacked Secretary of the Army Robert Stevens so savagely that Stevens offered to resign.

However in April 1954 the Army charged that McCarthy was trying to blackmail it by threatening to conduct further investigations unless it commissioned his aide, David Schine, who had recently been drafted. The Senate opened new televised hearings to investigate the Army's charges. Even though the Republican-controlled committee ultimately exonerated McCarthy, the widely viewed hearings led to his political downfall. The U.S. public saw McCarthy's bullying style, his threats, his incessant use of points of order and points of personal privilege to confuse his opponents, and his incoherent rambling. The carefully controlled, soft-spoken manner of Army counsel Joseph Welch — a Republican lawyer from a well-established Boston law firm — further contrasted McCarthy's unrestrained emotion. The hearings climaxed when Welch challenged McCarthy's aide, Roy Cohn, to provide the FBI with the names of the Communists and possible spies whom Cohn and McCarthy had alleged were at Fort Monmouth. As Welch implored Cohn to give the names "before the sun goes down," McCarthy interrupted with an unrelated accusation: "I think we should tell Mr. Welch that he has in his law firm a young man named Fisher who has been for a number of years a member of an organization named as the legal bulwark of the Communist Party [Fisher had once belonged to the National Lawyers

Guild].... Mr. Welch, I just felt that I had a duty to respond to your urgent request that before sundown, when we know of anyone serving the Communist cause, we let the agency know.... I have been rather bored with your phony requests to Mr. Cohn here that he personally get every Communist out of government before sundown."

Welch replied, "Until this moment, Senator, I think I never really gauged your cruelty or your recklessness. Fred Fisher is starting what looks to be a brilliant career with us. Little did I dream you could be so reckless and so cruel as to do an injury to that lad. I fear he shall always bear a scar needlessly inflicted by you.... Let us not assassinate this lad further, Senator. You have done enough. Have you no sense of decency, sir, at long last? Have you no sense of decency."

Shortly after the Army hearings concluded McCarthy wanted to open his own hearings into alleged Communist infiltration of the CIA and nuclear power plants, but Eisenhower squelched the CIA investigation. McCarthy's conduct at the Army hearings, along with questionable financial dealings and other improprieties, provoked the Senate to censure him on December 2. Though McCarthy remained in the Senate until his death in 1957, after this censure he ceased to be a significant force in U.S. politics.

McNamara, Robert S. (1916–   )   Secretary of defense, 1961–68. Born in San Francisco to a middle-class family, McNamara grew up in Oakland. He excelled academically throughout his school years and graduated from the University of California at Berkeley. In 1939 he received an M.B.A. from Harvard Business School, where he began teaching in 1940. Rejected for military service at the beginning of World War II because of poor eyesight, McNamara taught Army Air Corps officers how to use statistical techniques that were necessary for war planning. He later went to England to help direct the planning and logistics for bomber operations and in 1943 entered the Army Air Corps with the rank of captain. By the end of war he won promotion to lieutenant colonel and received praise for his assessments of the effects of B-29 bombing raids on Japan. After the war McNamara went to work for Ford Motor Company and in 1960 became the first person outside the Ford family to become the company's president.

Shortly thereafter President-elect Kennedy, on the recommendation of financier Robert Lovett, offered McNamara his choice of secretary of the treasury or defense. McNamara chose the latter because he believed it offered the greater challenge. He quickly reorganized the Defense Department to permit greater central authority. Departing from earlier defense secretaries who primarily mediated among the armed services, he diminished the power of the secretaries of the Army, Navy and Air Force and increased his own. He also created several new civilian-run departments to coordinate the services. And he formed the Defense Intelligence Agency to assemble and evaluate military intelligence from all three services and the Defense Supply Agency to cut costs by purchasing standard equipment for all of the services. McNamara tried to merge the

National Guard and the Army Reserves into a single system, but conservative opposition in Congress defeated his efforts.

In the interest of further reducing costs McNamara approved a planning programming budgeting system (PPBS) to eliminate duplication and waste and allow cost-efficiency comparisons in comparable weapons systems under development by different services. Thus the Defense Department could more accurately compare the Navy's Polaris missile, the Air Force's Minuteman, and the proposed RS-70 bomber, a jet favored by Air Force Chief of Staff Curtis LeMay that McNamara refused to fund, despite congressional appropriations. He also vetoed construction of nuclear power plants on Navy vessels. In 1964 he abruptly canceled the nuclear Skybolt missile that Great Britain had expected to use for its defense. The cancellation produced tensions between the two allies and contributed to the fall of Britain's Conservative government that year.

McNamara tried to resist the growing arms race arguing, "The military feels it has to have every bright shiny new gadget that comes along no matter how much it costs. I think we ought to buy what we need." Moreover, he claimed that since the Soviets would eventually counter any system the United States developed, U.S. national security would ultimately not be enhanced. He thus argued against an antiballistic missile (ABM) system and supported the 1963 nuclear test ban treaty, which he hoped would generate arms limitations talks between the superpowers.

On the other hand, McNamara believed that nuclear deterrence required the United States to be able to absorb a Soviet first strike and retain enough of a missile force to retaliate effectively. He argued that a second-strike capability would give the United States greater latitude in responding to an ambiguous Soviet threat and thereby reduce the risk of being pressured into starting a nuclear war. To ensure a second-strike nuclear capability he replaced the U.S. fleet of vulnerable, liquid-fuel intercontinental ballistic missiles (ICBMs) with solid-fuel Minuteman housed in hardened underground silos and Polaris missiles on nuclear submarines. He also called for increased construction of fallout shelters to reduce the loss of life in the event of a nuclear war.

McNamara believed Eisenhower's policy of massive retaliation to be outmoded and favored developing a flexible response capability to respond to guerrilla or conventional warfare without having to resort to nuclear weapons. He thus gained approval to increase the U.S. armed services by 300,000 troops. And to make the U.S. fighting forces more mobile he greatly enlarged the military's capacity to airlift troops throughout the world. McNamara regarded the Cuban Missile Crisis as a prime example of the success of his flexible response strategy. He supported the naval quarantine method in favor of other proposals for air strikes or an invasion. The quarantine enabled the United States to secure the removal of the Soviet nuclear-armed missiles without resorting to warfare. To pay the costs of the second-strike and flexible response capabilities McNamara won a 20 percent increase in the defense budget between 1960 and 1964.

Under Kennedy the Defense Department assumed primary responsibility for handling the situation in Vietnam. At the end of 1961 some 2,000 U.S. military advisers were training South Vietnamese military personnel and operating aircraft and communications facilities. After visiting Vietnam in 1963 McNamara and General Maxwell Taylor advised Kennedy that the U.S. military role could be expected to conclude by 1965. At that time approximately 15,000 military advisers were in the country. When other members of the administration wanted to disassociate from Ngo Dinh Diem after the South Vietnamese president brutally cracked down on Buddhist dissidents in August 1963, McNamara favored retaining support for Diem but demanding reforms. Shortly afterward a coup assassinated Diem and replaced his regime, and the United States quickly recognized the new leadership. Three weeks later Kennedy was assassinated. McNamara continued in the cabinet as President Johnson's defense secretary. Soon after Kennedy's assassination McNamara determined that a greater U.S. commitment to Vietnam was necessary. Believing that "it is a very important war, and I am pleased to be identified with it and do whatever I can to win it," he successfully recommended that President Johnson send in combat troops in 1965 and bomb North Vietnam. Over the next two years he received conflicting advice from his military staff, who favored heavy, widespread bombing of the North, and his civilian advisers, who believed that the bombing was ineffective and inhumane. By the time he stepped down from office in early 1968 he had lost confidence in the probable success of the war and come close to an emotional breakdown. Over 500,000 U.S. troops were then serving in Vietnam and the war was costing $2.5 billion a month.

After leaving office McNamara became president of the World Bank, a U.S.-supported organization formed to lend money to underdeveloped nations. After maintaining an almost 30-year silence about the Vietnam War, in 1995 he published *In Retrospect: The Tragedy and Lessons of Vietnam* in which he admitted the war was a mistake and U.S. policies had been muddled and improvised from the beginning. He also maintained that the United States failed to recognize the power of Ho Chi Minh's appeal to Vietnamese nationalism, and he criticized his own and President Johnson's decision to send combat troops into a country whose internal political situation was highly unstable. Twenty years after the fall of South Vietnam his book generated considerable controversy and stirred passionate feelings among Americans from every part of the political spectrum.

Marshall, George C. (1880–1959)   Secretary of state, 1947–49; and secretary of defense, 1950–51. Born in Uniontown, Pennsylvania, in 1880, the son of a coal merchant, Marshall graduated from Virginia Military Institute in 1901. He joined the Army in 1902 and rose steadily through the ranks. During World War I he assumed high administrative and planning positions with U.S. forces fighting in Europe, and as chief of operations of the First Army he helped plan the 1918 Meuse-Argonne offensive. After the war Marshall served as General John Pershing's aide-de-camp, and between 1924 and 1927 he served in China. Prior to World War II he revamped the instructional program at the Infantry School at Fort Benning, organized Civilian Conservation Corps camps in several states and served as chief of the War Department's War Plans Division. In 1939 he became Army chief of staff. In that capacity Marshall oversaw the U.S. buildup for World War II, and his highly respected diplomatic skills helped resolve many disputes among the Allies. In 1944 he successfully opposed British Prime Minister Winston Churchill's Mediterranean strategy in favor of an invasion across the English Channel. However, because President Roosevelt considered him too valuable in Washington, D.C., Marshall was unable to lead the assault against Nazi-held Europe at Normandy Beach. That responsibility went instead to his protégé General Dwight D. Eisenhower. By the war's conclusion Marshall was a hero and one of the most highly regarded U.S. citizens. President Truman called him "the greatest living American." In November 1945, when Marshall retired from the military at the mandatory age of 65, he held the rank of five-star general and outranked all other U.S. military men except the Navy's Admiral William Leahy.

The week following Marshall's retirement Truman asked him to go to China to try to resolve the civil war between Mao Zedong's Communists and Chiang Kai-shek's Nationalists. As Truman's special emissary Marshall sought to form a coalition government in which all parties would be represented but the Nationalists would dominate. In addition to achieving a viable political settlement in China, Truman hoped that Marshall's stature would quiet domestic criticism by the right-wing China lobby that his administration was willing to sell out Chiang to the Communists. Despite deep, mutual mistrust between the Communists and Nationalists and seemingly irreconcilable demands by each side, Marshall succeeded in negotiating a truce and an agreement to create a national assembly to draft a national constitution. Moreover, both sides agreed to integrate their forces into a single, national Army. However in March 1946, while Marshall was in Washington to consult with Truman, the fragile truce fell apart. Conservative elements among the Nationalists refused to accept a coalition with Communists. Moreover, Nationalist forces attempted to stop Mao's armies from occupying areas abandoned when the Soviets vacated Manchuria. Unable to negotiate a new truce and fearful that Chiang had overextended his supply lines, Marshall declared an impasse and asked to be recalled. The mission officially ended in January 1947. In his reports Marshall cautioned that the United States would "virtually [have] to take over the Chinese government" in order to preserve Chiang's rule. "It would involve a continuing [U.S.] commitment from which it would practically be impossible to withdraw." Truman heeded the warning and gradually reduced aid to Chiang, leaving only token amounts to appease the China lobby and other right-wing critics.

While Marshall was still negotiating in China Truman asked him to succeed James Byrnes as secretary of state, a post that Marshall reluctantly assumed in January 1947 out of a sense of civic duty. In recognition of the high esteem in which the country held the retired war hero, the Senate took the unprecedented action of unanimously confirming his appointment without conducting a prior hearing. Marshall was the first military leader to become secretary of state. His appointment elevated Truman's sagging popularity and helped the president's attempt to forge a bipartisan foreign policy.

Nineteen forty-seven marked the beginning of the Cold War, when Communists took control in Bulgaria, Romania, and Poland and the East-West coalitions began to fall into place. The responsibility for formulating a foreign policy to react to these events fell to Marshall. The decisions he made and the policies he and Truman implemented ultimately created and defined the Cold War, at least from the U.S. side. His perception that the Soviets posed a genuine and significant threat to Western Europe became a fundamental axiom of the Cold War. Another was his belief that U.S. self-interest required the United States to meet the Soviet threat by strengthening the Western European democracies, which stood as the first line of defense against Communist expansion. Most centrist and right-wing politicians shared these assumptions, though in early 1947 not everyone concurred. Some liberals believed the United States and Soviet Union could reach a mutually acceptable political accommodation, and some conservatives feared the costs of internationalism and favored postwar isolationism instead. Historians continue to debate whether the Soviet threat to Western Europe was actually as serious as Marshall believed or whether Truman and Marshall's responses to the perceived danger in fact forced Stalin into an increasingly aggressive posture, thereby creating a type of self-fulfilling prophecy. In either case, by the time Marshall left office in January 1949 only those on the political extremes rejected Marshall's basic assumptions about sinister Soviet intentions and the need for a strong U.S. response against them.

Upon taking office Marshall reorganized the State Department, appointing Undersecretary Dean Acheson and later Undersecretary Robert Lovett to oversee the daily workings of the bureaucracy and to take care of the details of foreign policy planning. His own role was to determine general foreign policy goals and overall strategies. For long-term planning he created a Policy Planning Staff outside the State Department hierarchy, where it would be relatively free from internal department politics. In early 1947, after the British announced their withdrawal from Greece and Turkey, Marshall recommended that the United States send aid to those countries to prevent Communists from assuming power in the region. Acheson proposed sending $400 million to the two countries and, in order to win support from conservative congressmen, he suggested describing the aid package as part of a world crusade against Communism. Marshall objected to the ideological rhetoric and the open-ended U.S. commitment, but Truman endorsed Acheson's plan and submitted it to Congress with Marshall's support. Congress appropriated the money in May.

In March and April 1947 Marshall attended the Moscow Conference, where

Soviet intransigence strengthened his belief that the USSR sought to weaken Western Europe by creating economic and political chaos. Upon his return home Marshall announced that Europe would require immediate U.S. financial aid to avoid ruin: "The patient is sinking while the doctors deliberate." The next day he instructed George Kennan to formulate a proposal for European economic recovery. Kennan, Acheson, and William Clayton worked on the plan throughout the spring and Marshall announced the European Recovery Program (ERP) in June. He lobbied for its passage for almost a year in the face of opposition from Republicans who wanted to deny Truman an election-year foreign policy triumph and who resisted donating large sums of foreign aid. Marshall defended the program by pointing out that a revitalized Europe would strengthen the U.S. economy by stimulating production and trade. A Communist coup in Czechoslovakia in February 1948 helped convince reluctant senators that the ERP was necessary, and the program, popularly known as the Marshall Plan, passed in March.

Despite its substantial cost — $12 billion between 1948 and 1951— the Marshall Plan eventually became one of the great successes of the Cold War and one of the greatest testimonies to the vitality and creative energy of capitalism. By promoting Western European industrial production, bolstering Western European currencies, and promoting international trade, the Marshall Plan facilitated Western Europe's surprisingly rapid recovery from the devastation of World War II. And by ensuring the economic stability of non–Communist governments in France, Italy, and other countries where a Communist presence was strong, the Marshall Plan helped enable friendly, procapitalist governments to remain in power. It thereby fulfilled its Cold War objective of containing Communism. Though invited to participate in the ERP, the Soviets and their Eastern European allies rejected the offer and denounced the program, as Marshall had anticipated they would.

The Marshall Plan was the first in a series of policies that collectively became known as the Truman Doctrine. The other policies were the 1948 Four Point Program to provide technical aid to underdeveloped countries in Asia, Africa, and Latin America, and the creation of the North Atlantic Treaty Organization (NATO) in 1949. Though Marshall was no longer in office when NATO was ratified, he helped initiate the anti–Soviet military alliance among the United States and the Western European democracies.

When the Soviets blockaded the surface routes to Berlin in June 1948 Marshall argued against recommendations by General Lucius Clay and others that the United States send armed convoys to break the blockade. Instead, Truman adopted Marshall's proposal to airlift supplies to the cut-off city. Unable to achieve their political objectives, the Soviets lifted the blockade the following spring. Thus the United States realized its goals and avoided a military confrontation with the Soviets.

Parts of Marshall's proposal for an agency to coordinate military aid and foreign policy were enacted in the National Security Act of 1947, which created the National Security Council (NSC). The NSC was composed of the president and the secretaries of state, defense, Army, Navy and Air Force and was charged with advising on and coordinating defense and foreign policies. Marshall's proposal to achieve greater organizational efficiency by unifying the armed services was never realized, despite periodic attempts throughout the Cold War by various administrations. Marshall favored universal military training and the rearming of Western Europe to create stronger forces at home and abroad to counter Soviet aggression. Though he favored the Baruch Plan for UN control of atomic weaponry — which Acheson had originally formulated — Marshall quickly became disenchanted by the Soviets' failure to try seriously to establish viable atomic controls. Consequently, he raised no objections to U.S. atomic testing and opposed unilateral atomic disarmament. Marshall retained his desire to see a coalition government in China and remained firm in his belief that Chiang could not be saved by foreign aid. He told Chiang that "the fundamental and lasting solution to China's problems must come from the Chinese themselves" and declined to increase financial aid to the Nationalists or accede to right-wing demands that the United States intervene militarily. In December 1948 Marshall had a kidney operation and resigned the following month.

However, shortly after the outbreak of the Korean War in 1950 Truman asked Marshall to rejoin the administration as secretary of defense and again Marshall agreed out of sense of civic duty. He reorganized the Pentagon, eliminating political appointees and establishing stronger communication links between the State and Defense departments, especially at the lower organizational levels. Because he believed that ground troops would ultimately prove more decisive than atomic weapons, he worked to increase the number of active duty soldiers to 2.7 million and to increase the military budget to $6.5 billion. Over General Douglas MacArthur's objections Marshall supported Truman's policy of waging a limited war in Korea. In 1951 MacArthur publicly called for bombing Communist positions inside China and "unleashing" Chiang's Nationalist Army against the mainland Communists, policies that contradicted Truman's. Challenged by one of his subordinates on foreign policy, the president called for and received the general's resignation. Marshall concurred with Truman, and in his testimony before congressional hearings he successfully explained the administration's position, though the right wing attacked him severely for what they called a failure in Asian policy. Senator Joseph McCarthy, the most venomous and vocal of Marshall's critics, charged that Truman, Marshall, and Acheson had permitted the fall of China and had allowed known Communists to hold important posts in the State Department. He described Marshall as "an instrument of the Soviet conspiracy" with an "affinity for Chinese Reds." Because of the high regard that Marshall still enjoyed within the country, McCarthy's charges resulted in a Senate investigation into whether McCarthy should be expelled for his behavior. However, though the final report criticized McCarthy on several accounts, the Senate subcommittee recommended no action.

In 1951 Marshall retired and in 1953 he received the Nobel Peace Prize for the ERP. Though he withdrew from politics during the 1950s, he continued to receive impassioned criticism from the China lobby and right-wing Republicans until his death in 1959.

Nixon, Richard M. (1913–94)   Republican congressman and senator; vice president, 1953–61; and U.S. president, 1969–74. Born in Yorba Linda, California, to a middle-class Quaker family, Nixon received his B.A. from Whittier College in 1934 and a law degree from Duke University in 1937. After his application to become an FBI agent was turned down for budgetary reasons, Nixon returned to California where he began a private law practice. At the beginning of World War II he worked for eight months at the Office of Price Administration, an experience that forever disillusioned him about government bureaucracy. He served in the South Pacific as a noncombat naval officer from 1942 to 1945. In 1946 he won election to the U.S. House of Representatives where he served on the House Committee on Un-American Activities (HUAC) and earned a national reputation for his probes into alleged Communist infiltration of the federal government.

In 1948 Nixon persistently pursued accusations by Whittaker Chambers that Alger Hiss had been a Communist and had given classified information to the Soviets. A former ranking State Department official in the Roosevelt and Truman administrations and the first acting secretary-general of the United Nations, Hiss vehemently declared his innocence. When Chambers responded to a HUAC subpoena by submitting five roles of microfilm that he had concealed the day before inside a carved-out pumpkin at his farm in Maryland, Nixon arranged for extensive press coverage showing the theatrical retrieval of the microfilm, two roles of which contained classified State Department material bearing Hiss's initials. President Truman denounced the HUAC probe as a deliberate, political distortion and a Republican "red herring." In return Nixon criticized Truman for his flagrant "flouting of the national interests of the people."

A grand jury later indicted Hiss for perjury because the statute of limitations for espionage had expired, and after a mistrial Hiss was convicted. According to Nixon, "Hiss was clearly the symbol of a considerable number of perfectly loyal citizens whose theaters of operation are the nation's mass media and universities, its scholarly foundations, and its government bureaucracies. They are of a mind-set, as doctrinaire as those on the extreme right, which makes them singularly vulnerable to the Communist popular front appeal under the banner of social justice. In the time of the Hiss case they were 'patsies' for the Communist line."

Hiss steadfastly maintained his innocence and the case remains controversial. No records coming out of Russia since the collapse of the Soviet Union have indicated that he ever worked as a Soviet spy. Regardless of his innocence or guilt, his conviction provided the right-wing with credible evidence that its view of internal subversion was accurate and not paranoid, as its opponents charged. On the other hand, Hiss's defenders maintain that Chambers's accusations were fraudulent and that the right-wing prosecution and persecution of Hiss was part of a deliberately manipulated Republican attempt to discredit Roosevelt's liberal New Deal policies and undermine Truman's Democratic administration. And they point to the seemingly personal nature of Nixon's vendetta against the representative of the East Coast liberal establishment. The Hiss case played a major role in establishing Nixon's national reputation. He later wrote in *Six Crises*, "I received considerable credit for spearheading the investigation which led to Hiss's conviction. Two years later I was elected to the U.S. Senate and two years after that General Eisenhower introduced me as his running mate to the Republican national convention as 'a man who has a special talent and ability to ferret out any kind of subversive influence wherever it may be found, and the strength and persistence to get rid of it.'"

In 1950 Nixon defeated incumbent Senator Helen G. Douglas who, he claimed, "follows the Communist Party line" and was "pink right down to her underwear." Eisenhower selected him for his vice presidential running mate in 1952 in an effort to appeal to the Republican Party's right wing. Allegations of financial improprieties almost resulted in Eisenhower's dropping Nixon from the ticket, but Nixon generated strong public support when he defended himself on national television in his famous "Checkers" speech. Eisenhower and Nixon went on to defeat the Democrats by a landslide.

As vice president, Nixon contributed little to foreign policy, though he made several trips overseas and worked closely with the Republican Party. In May 1958 anti–American demonstrators in Peru and Venezuela attacked him while he was on a goodwill tour of Latin America. In response, Eisenhower placed soldiers in the Caribbean on a standby alert to protect the vice president. In July 1959, during a lull in the ongoing Berlin Crisis, Nixon opened the American National Exhibition in Moscow, where he engaged Soviet Premier Khrushchev in the so-called "Kitchen Debate." While touring an American-style ranch house Nixon and Khrushchev argued before a large following of reporters about the relative merits of each country's economic system. Khrushchev repeatedly predicted that the Soviets would supersede the United States in world influence, while Nixon pointed out the superiority in quality and variety of choice in such U.S. commodities as color televisions and washing machines.

Nixon received the 1960 Republican nomination but lost a close election to Democratic Senator John Kennedy. The Nixon-Kennedy debates were the first televised presidential debates and are often credited for giving Kennedy his small margin of victory. Kennedy's poise, charm, energy, and youthful good looks contrasted against Nixon's obvious discomfort with the television medium, his weariness after a recent hospitalization, and his more sinister appearance under the television lights. In 1962 he ran unsuccessfully for governor of California and after his defeat declared that the press would not "have Nixon to kick around anymore." However, he remained active in the Republican Party and helped persuade party congressmen to support Kennedy's 1963 nuclear test ban treaty and civil rights legislation in 1964 and 1965. After a weak bid to win the 1964 presidential nomination failed, Nixon campaigned hard for the Republican candidate, Senator Barry Goldwater, who was crushed by President Lyndon Johnson. Nixon reemerged from the power vacuum that followed Goldwater's stunning defeat and in 1968 beat out California's ultraconservative Governor Ronald Reagan for the Republican nomination. To win support from Senator Strom Thurmond, the Republican leader in the South, Nixon agreed to adopt a "Southern strategy" in which he promised not to name a liberal vice presidential candidate, to appoint conservatives to the Supreme Court, reduce the federal role in desegregation, and increase military spending. He also maintained that he possessed a secret plan to end the increasingly unpopular Vietnam War. Nixon narrowly defeated Vice President Hubert Humphrey and was inaugurated as president in January 1969. Congress, however, remained under Democratic control.

Upon taking office Nixon, national security adviser Henry Kissinger and Defense Secretary Melvin Laird began to implement the Vietnamization of the war, in which South Vietnam assumed increasingly greater responsibility for conducting the war and U.S. troops were gradually withdrawn. Thus between 1969 and 1972 Nixon withdrew 555,000 troops from Vietnam. At the same time he intensified the war in other ways. In early 1969 Nixon authorized secret bombings in Laos and Cambodia against North Vietnamese supply centers, and in March 1970 the administration supported a civilian-military coup that brought a pro–U.S. government to Cambodia. The regime quickly devolved into a corrupt military dictatorship and seriously destabilized the country. In April Nixon authorized a joint U.S.–South Vietnamese invasion into Cambodia to destroy North Vietnamese sanctuaries and disrupt the flow of soldiers and supplies from North Vietnam into South Vietnam along the Ho Chi Minh Trail that passed through Cambodia. He defended this expansion of the war into an officially neutral and sovereign nation by asserting that the limited action was not really an invasion of Cambodia because the areas under attack were under North Vietnamese control. The war expanded again in 1971 when, after Congress voted to forbid sending U.S. troops into Laos or Cambodia, the administration sponsored unsuccessful South Vietnamese incursions into Laos. In 1970 Nixon also permitted limited bombing of North Vietnam in "protective reaction" strikes that were made ostensibly to protect reconnaissance flights. However, he did not authorize renewed massive bombings of North Vietnam until the spring of 1972, following a major North Vietnamese offensive. The policy objective was to enable the United States to disengage from the conflict while still preserving the anti–Communist regime of South Vietnam's President

Nguyen Van Thieu. Kissinger maintained that U.S. credibility with other countries precluded a rapid withdrawal that might undermine Thieu.

Despite the troop withdrawals, Nixon's aggressive measures provoked widespread protests throughout the United States. The 1970 invasion of Cambodia closed college campuses across the country as students and faculty went on strike in protest. At demonstrations at Kent State University in Ohio and Jackson State College in Mississippi protesting students were shot and killed by the National Guard and state police, and the relationship between the Nixon and his antiwar opponents became increasingly hostile. Disposed to regard the protesters as potential revolutionaries and fearful that the antiwar coalitions might cripple his presidency, Nixon and his White House aides began formulating an "enemies list" and ordered the FBI, CIA, and other government agencies to maintain files on suspicious individuals and disrupt antiwar activities. Many of these government actions were illegal, and they were exposed during the Watergate scandal and the congressional investigations that followed.

Negotiations among the United States, North and South Vietnam, and the National Liberal Front (Vietcong) continued from 1968 to 1972 with little progress. Hoping to end the war prior to the 1972 elections, Nixon intensified the air war and ordered the mining of Haiphong Harbor after North Vietnam launched a major attack across the demilitarized zone that separated it from South Vietnam. These efforts prevented the collapse of the South Vietnamese Army in the northern region of South Vietnam, but they did not succeed in forcing the North Vietnamese to make major concessions at the bargaining table. However, in October — a month before the U.S. election — Kissinger announced a major breakthrough and declared, "We believe that peace is at hand." But Thieu refused to accept the new terms and demanded 69 amendments to the agreements. After new talks between Kissinger and North Vietnamese representative Le Duc Tho broke down in December, Nixon ordered massive Christmas bombings of Hanoi and Haiphong. Nixon told the joint chiefs of staff that he was lifting the restrictions on target selections to permit the bombing of railroads, power plants, radio transmitters, and other installations surrounding Hanoi, as well as docks and shipyards in Haiphong, adding "I don't want any more of this crap about the fact that we couldn't hit this target or that one. This is your chance to use military power to win this war, and if you don't, I'll hold you responsible." After 11 days of bombings the North Vietnamese returned to the bargaining table, and an agreement similar to the October accord was reached. Nixon then warned Thieu, "You must decide now whether you desire to continue our alliance or whether you want me to seek a settlement with the enemy which serves U.S. interests alone." On the other hand, the Christmas bombing had demonstrated U.S. willingness to bomb North Vietnam again should they violate the truce. In January 1973 all of the parties accepted a new peace agreement, and the last U.S. troops left Vietnam on March 29. However, unlike the 1954 peace accords, the 1973 agreement permitted the North Vietnamese armies to remain in southern regions they already controlled, and by the next year the war had begun anew. But Nixon left office in August 1974, and President Ford was unwilling to order a new U.S. intervention. On April 30, 1975, Saigon fell to the Communists. Cambodia also fell under Communist rule that month.

If his Vietnam policy was his most unpopular Cold War position, Nixon's decision to ease East-West tensions and promote a new era of détente earned him the most praise. By 1969 Mao Zedong had completed the first phase of his Cultural Revolution and consolidated power in China. Though a long-standing opponent of Chinese Communism, Nixon perceived that China was ready to assume an important leadership role in the world. Moreover, he realized that a U.S.-Chinese alignment would further pressure the Soviets. Nixon's strong reputation as a fierce anti–Communist protected him against accusations of being soft on Communism in attempting to normalize relations with the People's Republic of China (PRC). Thus in July 1971 he authorized Kissinger to fly secretly to Beijing to arrange a presidential visit that he made in February 1972.

That trip laid the groundwork for formal relationships between the two countries, something that President Carter accomplished on New Year's Day 1979. The rapprochement with China led to the replacement of Nationalist China by the People's Republic in the United Nations and otherwise destroyed the myth of a monolithic Communist movement controlled by the Soviet Union.

Largely under the influence of Kissinger, who became secretary of state in 1973, U.S.-Soviet relations also improved considerably during the Nixon era. Intended to reduce costly U.S. engagements overseas, the 1969 Nixon Doctrine ended the willingness of the United States to assume primary responsibility for the defense of nations besieged by Communism. Nixon thus backed away from the containment policies that had dominated U.S. Cold War behavior since the 1940s. He also pursued the Strategic Arms Limitation Talks (SALT) that had begun under Johnson as a means for slowing the arms race, and in May 1972, three months after going to China, Nixon traveled to Moscow where he signed a treaty to limit new armaments. He thereby became the first U.S. president to visit the USSR since Roosevelt went to Yalta in 1945. This trip led to further policies of détente between the superpowers, as Soviet Chairman Leonid Brezhnev aggressively sought American trade. In particular, he hoped to gain U.S. high technology and financial investment in return for access to Soviet markets and natural resources. In October 1972 Nixon and Brezhnev signed an Anti-Ballistic Missile (ABM) Treaty in hopes of reducing the arms race. And in 1973 Brezhnev visited the United States and signed a pact aimed at avoiding superpower confrontations that could lead to a nuclear war. Aided by the efforts of businessman Armand Hammer, the United States and Soviet Union also instituted a series of cultural exchanges, in addition to expanding business opportunities. A poor grain harvest in 1972 led the Soviets to purchase extensive U.S. grain reserves. Though the deal helped established commercial ties between the countries, it later fell under attack from Senator Henry Jackson, a foe of détente who argued that it benefited the Soviets at the expense of U.S. taxpayers. Jackson further undermined détente by amending the 1973 East-West Trade Relations Act to require the Soviets to permit the emigration of its persecuted Jewish population. The Soviets regarded the stipulation as interference in its internal affairs and canceled the agreement.

Détente also extended beyond the two superpowers to the Western allies during the Nixon era. With approval from the United States and Soviet Union, East and West Germany initiated diplomatic contacts in the late 1960s and signed a treaty granting mutual recognition in 1973. The United States acceded to East Germany's admission to the United Nations that year and officially recognized it in 1974. During the same period, West Germany signed nonaggression pacts with the USSR and Poland and improved relations with other Warsaw Pact countries. West German Chancellor Willy Brandt promoted the ultimate reunification of a single, independent Germany with ties to both superpowers.

On the other hand, Nixon retained a hard line against Communist expansion within the U.S. sphere of influence, and in 1973 secretly supported a military coup that overthrew Salvador Allende, the freely elected Marxist president of Chile. Allende had tried to turn Chile into a socialist state by nationalizing industries, promoting extensive land reform, and establishing closer ties with Communist countries. Allende was replaced by General Pinochet's military dictatorship, which later became notorious for its brutal and widespread human rights violations. In the Middle East Nixon supported Israel during the 1973 Yom Kippur War and briefly placed U.S. forces on a high state of alert in order to counter Soviet threats to intervene directly in the fighting. A crisis was averted when the United Nations worked out a cease-fire and established a peacekeeping force in the region. Two weeks later, in an effort to weaken Egyptian ties with the USSR, Nixon restored diplomatic relations with Egypt, ties that had been broken since the 1967 Arab-Israeli War. The renewed relations helped lay the foundation for the separate peace established between Israel and Egypt under the auspices of President Carter. On the other hand, the U.S. support for Israel angered the Arab nations and provoked an oil boycott against the United States and other Israeli allies. Lasting from December 1973 to March 1974, the boycott created an energy crisis in the United States that quadrupled oil prices, worsened the trade deficit, stimulated inflation, and created a worldwide recession later in the year.

Between 1972 and 1974 much of Nixon's efforts and attention became focused on the growing Watergate scandal that eventually forced him out of office. The affair began on June 22, 1972, when a security guard caught 5 men breaking into the Democratic Party National Committee offices in the Watergate complex in Washington, D.C. When Nixon learned that the burglars had been working for his reelection campaign committee, he ordered an illegal cover-up. Nixon was able to hide his involvement in this cover-up until after the election, which he won overwhelmingly against peace candidate George McGovern.

However, as more information continued to surface Congress ordered investigations that ultimately revealed a wide pattern of political dirty tricks and the surveillance and harassment of Nixon's political enemies. When in July 1974 the Supreme Court ordered the president to surrender 64 taped White House conversations, Nixon's involvement in the cover-up became established beyond doubt, and the House Judiciary Committee approved 3 articles of impeachment. When it became apparent that the House would vote to impeach him and the Senate would vote to convict him, Nixon decided to resign, which he did on August 9, 1974. He was replaced by Vice President Gerald Ford, who had come to office in 1973 after Vice President Spiro Agnew resigned after pleading no contest to charges of corruption. Ford then granted Nixon a blanket, unconditional pardon that forestalled any further criminal investigations against the former president. The only president to resign before completing his term, Nixon's reputation was redeemed somewhat in the 1980s and 1990s as he tried with a measure of success to assume the role of elder statesman.

Reagan, Ronald W. (1911–   )   Governor of California, 1967–75; and U.S. president, 1981–89. Born in Tampico, Illinois, to a working-class family, Reagan graduated from Eureka College in 1932. He worked as a radio sports announcer before beginning a career as a movie actor in 1937. As a liberal Democrat in the 1930s and 1940s he supported Franklin Roosevelt. He served as an officer during World War II, making Army training films and attaining the rank of captain. By the 1950s Reagan's political orientation had turned to the right, and he endorsed the Eisenhower-Nixon ticket in 1952. He served as president of the Screen Actors Guild from 1947 to 1951 and again in 1959. In that capacity he contributed to the conservative effort to eliminate Communists and Communist sympathizers from the Hollywood film industry. In 1962 he became a Republican and in 1964 campaigned for Barry Goldwater. In 1966 he was elected governor of California, promising to crack down on campus radicals protesting the Vietnam War, eliminate welfare fraud and reduce taxes. He easily won reelection in 1970. Reagan emerged as a national spokesman for the conservative cause and in 1976 narrowly failed to wrest the Republican presidential nomination from incumbent Gerald Ford.

In 1980 Reagan was elected president, despite concerns that at age 68 he was too old for the job. Two months after his inauguration he survived an assassination attempt in which he was shot in the chest. He recovered quickly and returned in time to defend his budget proposals before Congress. These introduced "supply-side economics," featuring lower taxes on businesses and individuals and reduced spending on social programs. "Reaganomics," as it was popularly known, was based on the "trickle-down theory" that held that tax cuts would stimulate business and thereby produce jobs and consequently reduce the need for welfare. Unemployment and inflation did drop during his tenure in office, and between 1983 and 1990 the United States experienced one of its longest periods of sustained economic growth. But Reagan also initiated a massive military buildup that he financed through deficit spending, and this undermined his goal of achieving a balanced budget. By the time he left office the national debt had more than doubled, exceeding $3 trillion in 1988.

By the time Reagan took office the Soviet invasion of Afghanistan in late 1979 had already ended détente and provoked President Carter to increase military spending and reintroduce draft registration. But Reagan took an even harder anti–Soviet line, calling the USSR an "Evil Empire" and denouncing Communist-supported popular movements in Central America and elsewhere. During his first term Reagan increased defense spending by 40 percent, providing for the MX missile, a 600-ship Navy with new aircraft carriers, new tanks, and other conventional weapons. He replenished ammunition stocks and reinstated the B-1 bomber that Carter had earlier canceled. He also achieved the deployment of intermediate-range, nuclear-armed Pershing and Cruise missiles in Western Europe, despite intense opposition by antinuclear activists in Great Britain and West Germany.

In early 1983 Reagan initiated the highly controversial Strategic Defense Initiative (SDI), more commonly known as "Star Wars," after a popular science fiction movie of the time. SDI proposed to provide a shield of laser-armed satellites in outer space capable of shooting down missiles targeted at U.S. cities and defense installations. Reagan viewed SDI as an alternative to the policies of mutually assured destruction (MAD), which had dominated the 1970s détente and which he believed to be highly dangerous, especially since he thought the Soviets were implementing policies to enable them to prevail in a nuclear war. Though SDI ostensibly violated the 1972 Anti-Ballistic Missile (ABM) Treaty, which had been a central element of the arms control process during the preceding decade, Reagan asserted that it was "consistent with our obligations under the ABM Treaty." Many scientists remained skeptical about SDI's feasibility, though the scientific community enjoyed the additional funding for basic research that accompanied it. Other critics attacked SDI for its enormous cost, which came at the expense of social programs and/or attempts to balance the budget. And, despite Reagan's claims that SDI was to be a purely defensive system that the United States would even be willing to share with the USSR, the Soviets greatly feared its offensive capabilities. Moreover, the European allies were concerned that a missile shield over the United States would increase U.S. isolationism and leave them vulnerable to a Soviet attack. When he later recognized that protecting every U.S. city was unrealistic, Reagan revised SDI's mission to protect American missile sites against a first strike. The redefined mission thus echoed the second-strike capability the United States developed during the Kennedy administration, guaranteeing that a Soviet first strike could not eliminate massive U.S. retaliation.

Some nuclear planners were also concerned that SDI might prompt the Soviet Union to launch a preemptive nuclear strike before the system could be deployed, since afterward the USSR would become vulnerable to a U.S. attack. Soviet fears were exacerbated by talk from ranking Reagan administration officials who began speaking publicly of winnable nuclear war. In 1981 Reagan approved a secret National Security Decision Document that outlined a plan for prevailing in a protracted nuclear war. The administration adopted the position that enhanced civil defense efforts would enable civilians to survive nuclear attacks. Deputy Undersecretary of Defense T. K. Jones also predicted that the United States would be able to return to prewar economic levels in as little as two to four years if it adopted Soviet civil defense practices.

Other administration officials expressed similar sentiments during the early 1980s, including Vice President George Bush and Reagan himself. Bush and Reagan maintained that since Soviet planning was based not on MAD but on winning a nuclear war, the United States needed a policy "of that kind." Thus, during Reagan's first term public fears of nuclear war rose to levels not experienced since the Berlin and Cuban Missile crises in the late 1950s and early 1960s. The administration's suggestion that nuclear war need not result in mutually assured destruction, its introduction of SDI, Reagan's verbal attacks on the Soviet Union, and his insistence that the Communist leaders were "godless" monsters who were not to be trusted because they had "less regard for humanity or human beings" further increased Cold War tensions.

These actions also led the Soviets to intensify their intelligence efforts for detecting early signs of an impending Western attack and to increase their own defense budget. Their downing of a Korean passenger plane (KAL-007) that had strayed into their air space on September 1, 1983, may have resulted from their state of heightened alert and fear of a U.S. first strike. Reagan condemned the attack as barbaric and offered it as new proof of Soviet disregard for human life. The incident further increased worldwide tensions. On September 8 Soviet Foreign Minister Gromyko cautioned, "The world situation is now slipping toward a very dangerous precipice. Problem number one for the world is to avoid nuclear war." Two months later the Soviets feared that a NATO exercise to coordinate nuclear command procedures, Able Archer 83, might actually be preparation for a real strike against the Warsaw Pact. A flurry of coded communications between the United States and Great Britain just prior to the early November exercise heightened their apprehensions, though these messages actually concerned the U.S. invasion of Grenada, which occurred on October 25. During the exercise the KGB mistakenly notified its intelligence stations that U.S. military bases had been put on alert. Thus Reagan's more aggressive posture increased the likelihood of a Soviet preemptive attack and/or Soviet overreaction to and misinterpretation of Western actions. On the other hand, apart from shooting down KAL-007 the Soviets did not initiate military action due to their heightened state of alert and Reagan's policy's did not result in nuclear warfare. Reagan's champions maintain that by compelling the Soviets to divert their resources to defense the president created the conditions that led to the economic collapse of the

USSR. They therefore argue that Reagan was largely responsible for ending the Cold War. His critics maintain that while Reagan's policies may have hastened the downfall of the USSR, internal Soviet corruption and economic failures would have created that result, regardless of the president's actions. They further argue that his policies needlessly endangered the world and that the budget deficit caused by Reagan's defense buildup crippled the U.S. economy.

Reagan initiated a number of policies that became collectively known as the Reagan Doctrine. Harking back to the 1950s policies of liberation advocated by John Foster Dulles, Reagan vowed to oppose Communist regimes and movements worldwide and to insist that any arms reduction agreement include reduction of Soviet conventional troops. U.S. support of rebels in Angola, Afghanistan, and Nicaragua and U.S. intervention in the Lebanese civil war resulted from the Reagan Doctrine. On October 23, 1983, a suicide bomber in Beirut penetrated U.S. Marine barracks and killed 241 American and 60 French soldiers who had been sent as peacekeepers to end a civil war between Christian and Druse militias in Lebanon. Two days later Reagan ordered full-scale invasion of the thinly defended Caribbean island of Grenada, which Marxist Maurice Bishop had taken over in a bloodless coup in 1979. Shortly before the U.S. invasion a pro–Soviet military coup overthrew and executed Bishop and allegedly endangered the lives of U.S. medical students studying on the island, though the actual danger to the students remains disputed. The threat to their safety emerged as the main pretext for the U.S. assault. The invasion was a success and a year later a democratic government was reestablished on the island. After a string of military failures ranging back to the Vietnam War, the failed attempt to rescue the Iranian hostages, and the deaths of the Marines in Lebanon, the success in Grenada helped reassert the military capability of the United States.

Even before taking office Reagan had denounced the pro–Communist Sandinistas who had deposed the Nicaraguan dictator Anastasio Somoza in 1979. Whereas Carter had tried to work with the Sandinistas to avoid driving them into the Soviet and Cuban camp, Reagan adopted an extremely hard line against them. He cut off U.S. and international aid and in 1981 directed the CIA to arm and organize Nicaraguan rebels trying to depose them. Reagan described these Contras as freedom fighters and likened them to the founding fathers of the American Revolution. However, Congress opposed his efforts and in 1982 passed the first Boland Amendment, forbidding the CIA to overthrow the Nicaraguan government. Nonetheless, the covert activities continued, largely directed from the National Security Council, and in 1984 the CIA secretly mined Nicaraguan harbors, which was technically an act of war. When these and other illegal covert activities became publicly known, Congress passed additional Boland amendments, denying government agencies funds to support "directly or indirectly military or paramilitary operations" in Nicaragua.

To bypass the Boland prohibitions on government involvement the Reagan administration, largely through high-ranking officers in the National Security

Council, sought ways to channel weapons and funds to the Contras through private individuals and agencies. This privatization of the country's handling of foreign affairs led directly to the Iran-Contra Affair of 1985 and 1986. An arms for hostages deal was originally suggested in the summer of 1985 by Israel, which acted as an intermediary in the trade in hopes of gaining improved relations with Iran, which was then fighting a war with Iraq. Despite Reagan's pledge never to swap arms for hostages, the Iran-Contra Affair involved the sale of U.S. weapons to Iran in return for the release of seven American hostages held by pro–Iranian terrorist groups in Lebanon. However, only three hostages were released, despite several transactions. The $48 million generated between September 1985 and October 1986 was diverted for various purposes, including arming the Contras ($16.5 million), running other covert operations ($1 million), establishing reserves for future operations ($4.2 million), bribing Iranian officials ($15.2 million), and paying commissions to middlemen who brokered the deals ($6.6 million). A 1987 congressional investigation revealed many top administration officials to be involved, including Reagan's national security advisers Robert McFarlane and John Poindexter and CIA Director William Casey. Secretary of State George Shultz opposed the scheme and was kept "out of the loop" of information. Marine Lieutenant Colonel Oliver North controlled the funds and used them "to run the covert operation to support the Contras." According to North, Casey saw the diversion of funds as part of a more grandiose plan to create a "stand-alone," "off-the-shelf" covert capability that would extend throughout the world while evading congressional review. Casey had a sudden stroke just as the scandal was unfolding and died without ever testifying about it. Reagan gave a series of conflicting accounts about his own role but claimed to be unaware of any illegal activities or any arms for hostages trades. However, he later admitted, "Mistakes were made."

Reagan's contradictions, his inability to recall important events, and his proclaimed ignorance of this major operation conducted by ranking members of his administration — in violation of his own publicly avowed principles — made the president appear either dishonest or incompetent or both, and the incident seriously undermined the administration's credibility and future effectiveness. During the 1988 presidential campaign Bush, the Republican candidate, claimed to be "out of the loop" when decisions were being made about the Iran-Contra deal. He thereby escaped serious political damage and easily won the election. However, new revelations by a special prosecutor a week prior to the 1992 elections hurt Bush's reelection bid, as documents showed him to be much more inside the loop than he had represented.

During Reagan's second administration the United States took actions against hostile Third World countries but adopted a less bellicose tone toward the Soviet Union. Reagan continued to oppose the Sandinistas and support the right-wing military regime that had seized power in El Salvador in 1979 and was fighting a civil war against Nicaraguan-backed populist rebels. In 1986 he ordered attacks against Libya, following alleged Libyan missile attacks on U.S. aircraft in the Gulf of Sidra (Sirte). These provoked Soviet warnings about the threat to world peace and sparked acts of terrorism throughout the world. In 1987 Reagan ordered naval escorts for Kuwaiti oil tankers passing through the Persian Gulf after Iran threatened shipping in the gulf, and in September U.S. helicopters fired on an Iranian ship laying mines in those waters. In April 1988 U.S. forces destroyed two Iranian oil platforms and sunk a patrol boat in retaliation for an attack on an American vessel. The Iran-Iraq war concluded in August and the situation in the gulf stabilized. Elsewhere, long-lasting regional conflicts began to conclude as Soviet Premier Gorbachev announced in early 1988 that the USSR would begin withdrawing troops from Afghanistan in May and conclude its withdrawal by February 1989. Also in early 1988 the United States participated in Angolan-Cuban talks that brought about a Cuban withdrawal from Angola and paved the way for Namibian independence.

Gorbachev became the Soviet premier in 1985 and soon introduced economic reforms and new principles of freedom (perestroika and glasnost). British Prime Minister Margaret Thatcher declared "I like Mr. Gorbachev. We can do business together," and Reagan's stance toward the Soviet Union became increasingly conciliatory. In November 1985 Gorbachev and Reagan issued a joint statement, declaring that nuclear war could never be won and must never be fought and that neither side would seek military superiority. They were unable to reach an arms agreement during an October 1986 mini-summit in Reykjavik, Iceland, because Reagan refused to comply with Soviet demands that the United States abandon SDI. Nonetheless, they surprised the world and their own staffs by reaching several startling agreements in principle: the elimination all intermediate-range missiles from Europe, the elimination of all ballistic missiles over a ten-year period, and the reduction of other nuclear delivery systems, including bombers and tactical weapons. Reagan later recalled, "For a day and a half, Gorbachev and I made progress on arms reduction that even now seems breathtaking." These agreements became the basis for the Strategic Arms Reduction Talks (START), which replaced SALT and eventually led to the 1991 START Treaty. Moreover, in February 1987 Gorbachev dropped his demand that the United States eliminate SDI, and in December he and Reagan signed the INF Treaty to eliminate all intermediate-range nuclear weapons in Europe. The INF Treaty was the first Cold War treaty to reduce the size of superpower nuclear arsenals, and it removed the Cruise and Pershing missiles that had provoked so much domestic opposition in Western Europe and Great Britain. In December 1988 Gorbachev further announced his intentions to unilaterally downsize the Soviet Army by 0.5 million soldiers and withdraw Soviet troops and tanks from Eastern Europe. His economic and military reforms opened the door for change not only within the Soviet Union but inside all Eastern Europe. Reagan's support of Gorbachev's reforms are additional reasons why his champions credit him for ending the Cold War.

Rosenberg, Ethel (1915–53), and Julius (1918–53)   Convicted atomic bomb spies. Born in New York City, both Ethel and Julius grew up on the Lower East Side, the children of workers in the garment industry. Ethel graduated from high school in 1931, attended a stenography course, and then secured a low-paying office job. After becoming active in her union she was fired for organizing a strike. Julius attended the City College of New York (CCNY) and received a degree in electrical engineering in 1939. As a teen he had become interested in radical politics and became a Communist while at CCNY. In 1939 he married Ethel, also a Communist, and took a job as civilian junior engineer in the Army Signal Corps. Ethel became a housewife and mother. Julius remained in the Signal Corps until 1945, when he was fired for being a Communist. Afterward he went to work at the Emerson Radio Corporation before forming his own hardware business with Ethel's brother, Bernard Greenglass. When that venture failed he operated a small machine shop with David Greenglass, Ethel's other brother.

On June 16, 1950, nine days before the outbreak of the Korean War, FBI agents arrested the Rosenbergs and charged them with passing atomic secrets to the Soviets during World War II. Specifically, they were charged with participating in a Soviet spy ring involving the British physicist Klaus Fuchs, Harry Gold, Morton Sobell, and Ethel's brother, David Greenglass. Their greatest alleged crime was the theft between 1944 and 1945 of a limited amount of technical information about the atomic bomb, which was then under development in Los Alamos, New Mexico. Upon their arrest Fuchs, Gold, and Greenglass confessed their involvement in the spy ring, but Sobell and the Rosenbergs steadfastly proclaimed their innocence.

Their 1950–51 trial took place during one of the most intense periods of the Cold War, and fears of domestic subversion were rampant. The Korean War was in full force; the Soviets had tested their first atomic bomb a year before; Alger Hiss had been recently convicted of perjury; and Senator Joseph McCarthy had recently initiated his accusations that the State Department had knowingly allowed Communists to occupy top positions. Despite the Rosenbergs' invocation of the Fifth Amendment when asked about their Communist ties, the prosecution succeeded in establishing their Communist background and beliefs, and former ranking Communist Elizabeth Bentley testified about how the Soviets controlled the American Communist Party. The prosecution's chief witness was David Greenglass, who declared that Julius had recruited him into the ring and received from him sketches and diagrams of the lens that detonated the bomb. Max Elitcher, a college classmate of Julius, also testified that Julius had tried to recruit him for espionage during World War II. Other witnesses corroborated parts of Greenglass's story.

The defense tried to undermine Greenglass's testimony, suggesting that he was turning on his sister as part of a family feud, and his wife Ruth had developed the plan to blame Julius and Ethel in order to have their own sentences reduced. Harry Gold admitted receiving documents from Greenglass but denied ever meeting the Rosenbergs. The Rosenbergs testified that they were innocent. On March 29, 1951, a federal jury convicted them. Judge Irving Kaufman sentenced Sobell to 30 years in prison and Greenglass to 15. Believing the Rosenbergs to have headed the spy ring, he sentenced both to death declaring, "I believe your conduct in putting into the hands of the Russians the A-bomb years before our best scientists predicted Russia would perfect the bomb has already caused, in my opinion, the Communist aggression in Korea, with the resultant casualties exceeding 50,000 and who knows but that millions more of innocent people may pay the price of your treason."

The Rosenbergs appealed the conviction, arguing that the espionage statute was vague and that Kaufman had been prejudiced in favor of the prosecution. In particular, they objected to his admitting evidence of their Communist beliefs, since this prejudiced the jury against them. In 1952 the Federal Court of Appeals rejected the Rosenbergs' appeal, stating that their Communist background was relevant because it helped establish a motive for the crime and that Kaufman had repeatedly warned jurors not to come to a verdict on the basis of their Communism. Later that year the Supreme Court unanimously turned down a further appeal. After the Supreme Court overturned a last-minute stay of execution that Justice William O. Douglas had granted, the Rosenbergs were executed in New York's Sing Sing Prison on June 19, 1953.

The Rosenberg case was highly controversial and provoked strong passions while it was in progress. It remained controversial throughout the Cold War. On the one hand, there were those who, like Kaufman, believed in the Rosenbergs' guilt and believed their acts of espionage had seriously harmed and endangered the United States. For these people the death sentence was well merited. On the other hand, many believed that the Rosenbergs were innocent, their trial had been severely biased against them, and/or the death penalty was excessively severe and unwarranted. The Rosenbergs' defenders maintained they were victims of the ferocious anti–Communist Red Scare of the early 1950s, that their conviction and sentencing were tainted by anti–Semitism, and/or that their execution stemmed from a national desire to punish a scapegoat for recent Communist military and political successes. Other defenders have argued that the stolen information was not crucial to the Soviets' development of the atomic bomb and that Kaufman was inaccurate when he stated that the Russians had developed the bomb years before our best scientists had predicted they would. Thus, guilty or innocent, the Rosenbergs were not responsible for the Russian A-bomb. Among those who pleaded for a more lenient sentence were physicist Albert Einstein and Pope Pius XII. Neither President Truman nor President Eisenhower responded to pleas on the Rosenbergs' behalf, despite mass rallies and petitions shortly before the couple's execution. No consensus has yet been reached on their guilt, the fairness of the trial, the appropriateness of their sentence, the motivations of the judge and prosecutors, or the importance of the stolen information to the Soviet atomic research program. To date no documents released from Russia after the breakup of the Soviet Union, including those from the Communist Party's archives, have shown that the Rosenbergs participated in a spy ring. On the other hand, in July 1995 the CIA released documents from the Venona Project that decoded cables to the Soviet Union from suspected spies in the 1940s. These documents do indicate the Rosenbergs' complicity.

Rusk, Dean (1909–94)   Secretary of state, 1961–69. Born in Cherokee County, Georgia, Rusk was the son of an ordained Presbyterian minister who worked as a farmer. His mother was a mail carrier. He worked his way through Davidson College and graduated in 1931. Afterward he attended Oxford University on a Rhodes scholarship. In 1934 Rusk became a professor of political science at Mills College in California and dean of the faculty in 1938. During World War II he served in the China-Burma-India theater and became deputy chief of staff to General Joseph Stilwell. He also gained the attention of Army chief of staff General George Marshall, who encouraged Rusk to join the State Department after the war as assistant chief of international security affairs. During the Truman years Rusk worked as special assistant to the secretary of war and as an aide to Robert Lovett and Dean Acheson. In 1950 Acheson appointed Rusk assistant secretary of state for Far Eastern affairs. Subsequently, Rusk helped formulate the Korean War policy of fighting a limited action in Korea and not expanding the war into China, as General MacArthur and other conservatives advocated. In 1952 Rusk left the State Department to assume the presidency of the Rockefeller Foundation. In that capacity he promoted programs designed to improve agriculture and public health in underdeveloped African, Asian, and Latin American countries.

When Kennedy was elected in 1960 he believed foreign policy was the paramount issue and wanted to assume primary responsibility for it. Thus he sought a secretary of state who would be willing to allow the president to dominate foreign policy. Rusk, who believed the secretary should function primarily as a presidential adviser and had attractive connections to the New York Eastern establishment, made a congenial choice. Having largely removed himself from policymaking, Rusk personally directed the State Department's daily operations during times of crisis.

Rusk declined to contribute to the April 1961 discussion over whether Kennedy should authorize the Bay of Pigs invasion of Cuba by anti–Castro exiles, other than to warn against excesses and point out that a failure could undermine domestic and international confidence in the new president. Therefore, he recommended that the invasion be authorized by someone else who could be used as a scapegoat in the event of defeat. Otherwise Rusk did not offer a recommendation as to whether to proceed with the attack. Kennedy declined Rusk's suggestion and indeed suffered extreme embarrassment after the invasion failed. Rusk later wrote that he had "served Kennedy badly…. Having been in the China-Burma theater in World War II, I knew that this thin brigade of

Cuban exiles did not stand a snowball's chance in hell of success. I didn't relay this military judgment to President Kennedy because I was no longer in the military." Rusk also played only a secondary role during the 1962 Cuban Missile Crisis. Nonetheless, his remark just after the crisis peaked is one of the most widely quoted, "We are eyeball to eyeball, and the other fellow just blinked." Likewise, Rusk largely acceded to Kennedy's preference for having Robert McNamara's Defense Department formulate policy pertaining to Vietnam, though during the Johnson administration he became one of the more eloquent defenders of the war. Rusk left office after Nixon's inauguration and later joined the faculty at the University of Georgia. His eight years in office was the second longest tenure of any secretary of state during the twentieth century.

Shultz, George P. (1920–) Secretary of labor, 1969–70; head of the Office of Management and Budget, 1970–72; secretary of the treasury, 1972–74; and secretary of state, 1982–89. Born in New York City, Shultz received his Bachelor's degree from Princeton in 1942 before serving in the Pacific as a Marine artillery officer during World War II. He received his doctorate from the Massachusetts Institute of Technology (MIT), where he taught until 1955. In 1957 Shultz joined the faculty of the University of Chicago's School of Business and from 1962 to 1969 served as dean of the university's Graduate School of Business. During this time he gained a reputation for his skills in arbitrating labor disputes. A conservative Republican, Shultz served as an economic and labor consultant to the Eisenhower, Kennedy, and Johnson administrations. President Nixon appointed him secretary of labor in 1969, head of the newly created Office of Management and Budget in 1970, and secretary of the treasury in 1972. He resigned in 1974 because of recurring disagreements with the president.

Shultz subsequently joined the Bechtel Corporation and became president of the Bechtel Group, a large engineering and construction firm. In 1976 he became part of the newly revived Committee on the Present Danger, which reformed two days after the election of Jimmy Carter. The fiercely anti–Communist committee opposed the SALT II Treaty and argued for increased defense spending. Other members included Ronald Reagan and several of his future appointees, among them William Casey, Richard Allen, Jeane Kirkpatrick, Paul Nitze, and Richard Perle.

After Al Haig abruptly resigned as secretary of state in June 1982, President Reagan named Shultz to replace him and Shultz held that position until 1989. Never one of Reagan's inner circle of advisers, he threatened to resign several times after being omitted from important decisions, including the 1983 invasion of the Caribbean island Grenada. In cabinet meetings he opposed the illegal Iran-Contra exchange of weapons for hostages and was left "out of the loop" of decisionmaking when plans were formulated to proceed. In 1984 Shultz helped convince the president to meet with Soviet Foreign Minister Andrei Gromyko and discuss the possibility of resuming arms control talks. Afterward

Shultz and Gromyko met and agreed to resume arms negotiations with the Strategic Defense Initiative (SDI) on the agenda. These meetings with Gromyko represented the first major thaw in U.S.-Soviet relations since Reagan assumed office. During the 1986 breakthrough summit in Reykjavik, Iceland, when Reagan and Gorbachev surprised the world and their own staffs by reaching several startling agreements in principle (the elimination of all intermediate-range missiles from Europe, the elimination of all ballistic missiles over a ten-year period, and the reduction of other nuclear delivery systems), Shultz withheld his reservations. "I really felt he's the President. He got elected twice. He has made no secret of his view on nuclear weapons. So who am I to stop him from saying what he believes and what he campaigned on." In 1988 he helped negotiate further arms agreements with the Soviets and helped arrange the withdrawal of Soviet troops from Afghanistan.

Though a member of administrations tainted by major scandals — including Watergate and Iran-Contra — Shultz retained his reputation for honesty. When asked how, Shultz replied, "The way to maintain your integrity is to act with integrity. I think it's very simple." In 1989 Shultz joined the Graduate School of Business at Stanford University.

Truman, Harry S. (1884–1972)   Democratic senator, 1935–45; vice president, 1945; and U.S. president, 1945–53. Born in Lamar, Missouri, the son of an agricultural businessman, Truman grew up in Independence, Missouri. His mother was a devout Baptist who valued education, and both parents were committed Democrats. After graduating from high school Truman wanted to pursue a military career, but West Point rejected him because of his poor vision. He held a number of jobs prior to World War I. He served as an artillery officer during the war, and afterward he and a friend opened a haberdashery store in Kansas City. However, the joint venture failed during the economic slump in 1921–22 and subsequently Truman turned to politics. Supported by Missouri's powerful Democratic Party, he was elected county judge in 1922. His position was administrative, and from 1926 to 1934 he served as president of the court, in which capacity he supervised public building projects and administered a substantial road extension program. Again supported by the Democratic political machine, Truman won election to the U.S. Senate in 1934. Though more moderate than Franklin Roosevelt, Truman consistently supported the president and generally voted along Democratic Party lines. His major legislative achievements were his contributions to the Civil Aeronautics Act of 1938 and the Railroad Transportation Act of 1940. During World War II he rose to national prominence when a committee he chaired revealed corruption and inefficiency within the defense program.

In 1944 Roosevelt selected Truman as a compromise vice presidential candidate over incumbent Vice President Henry Wallace, whom the party's left wing favored, and the director of war mobilization James F. Byrnes, who had the support of the party's more conservative element. Cognizant of Woodrow Wilson's difficulties after World War I, Roosevelt hoped that Truman's popularity in Congress could help the administration win ratification of the forthcoming World War II peace treaties and the charter for the United Nations. In his three months as vice president Truman was, in his own words, "a political eunuch" who was not greatly involved in policy planning or decisionmaking. However, after Roosevelt died suddenly on April 12, 1945, he assumed the presidency.

Truman was initially awed by the new responsibilities that had befallen him. Upon taking office he told reporters, "Boys if you ever pray, pray for me now.... When they told me yesterday what had happened, I felt like the moon, the stars and all the planets had fallen on me." Many politicians and political observers doubted whether Truman was up to the job. For instance, David Lilienthal, who chaired the Tennessee Valley Authority, wrote in his diary, "Consternation at the thought of that Throttlebottom Truman. The country and the world doesn't [sic] deserve to be left this way." On the other hand, many of those who knew him in Congress had a higher assessment of Truman's potential. Speaker of the House Sam Rayburn declared that although he would not be flashy like Roosevelt, "By God, he'll make a good President, a sound President. He's got the stuff in him."

Truman assumed office at a dynamic moment in world history. Within two weeks of his inauguration he signed the UN Charter; within a month Germany surrendered and World War II concluded in Europe; and within two months the terms of the Cold War were already beginning to emerge as the Allies partitioned Germany into four sectors to be controlled individually by the United States, Great Britain, France, and the Soviet Union. During his first months in office Truman was advised by Averell Harriman, Admiral William Leahy, and former Vice President Wallace. Wallace counseled Truman to continue Roosevelt's policies of cooperating with the Soviets, while Harriman and Leahy took a harder line, urging Truman to force concessions on Soviet domination of Eastern Europe. Prior to the German surrender Truman turned down Winston Churchill's suggestion that the U.S. Army should move deeper into Eastern Europe in order to give the United States a stronger bargaining position, and he reaffirmed Roosevelt's decision to acquire Soviet entry into the Japanese War in return for political concessions to the Soviets in Asia.

In July Edward Stettinius stepped down as secretary of state and Truman appointed Byrnes to replace him. The two men did not work easily together, but they initially shared the same basic foreign policy objectives: to sustain the wartime alliance and inhibit the Soviets' attempts to take full control of Eastern Europe. Neither man viewed the Soviets as ideologues bent on world conquest. Instead, they regarded Stalin as a fellow politician willing to negotiate a political arrangement. Disregarding the Soviet insistence on secure borders with Eastern Europe, Truman and Byrnes promoted the revitalization of Germany, the founding of democratic governments in Germany and Eastern Europe, and the eventual evacuation of Soviet troops from occupied European territories. Prior to the Potsdam Conference, which convened in July 1945, Truman insisted that the Soviets reaffirm their support for the provisions of the Yalta Declaration calling for representative governments and free elections in Eastern Europe, and he reduced U.S. aid to the USSR to pressure Stalin on the issue. He also sent one of Roosevelt's favorite advisers, Harry Hopkins, to Moscow to resolve outstanding disagreements. Hopkins obtained an agreement for a compromise government in Poland and for the Soviet entry into the war against Japan.

At Potsdam the so-called big three — the United States, Great Britain, and the Soviet Union — set policies for controlling Germany during the occupation. They agreed to foster democratic ideals and introduce representative and elective principles of government in Germany. The Soviets reluctantly acceded to the economic redevelopment of the Germany, which Truman believed was crucial to the revitalization and security of Europe. Stalin also agreed to restrict Soviet reparation claims on West German goods. Left unrestricted, reparation claims could have seriously impeded Germany's economic recovery. In return for Stalin's concessions Truman consented to the transfer of part of eastern Germany to Poland where it fell under Soviet control pending a final peace treaty (which was not signed until 1990). The big three also warned Japan to surrender unconditionally or risk total destruction.

While attending the Potsdam Conference, Truman, who had not even known about the atomic bomb project before he became president three months earlier, learned that the bomb had been successfully tested. He declined to inform Stalin. In early August, four days after the conference concluded, Truman authorized the atomic bombing of Hiroshima and Nagasaki; shortly thereafter Japan surrendered.

Truman's decision to drop the atomic bomb on military/civilian targets — the only time nuclear weapons have ever been employed in warfare — remains highly controversial. Prior to the bombings Truman had already decided to mount a massive invasion of the Japanese islands. Thus in August 1945 most Americans hailed the atomic attacks as a pragmatic way to end the war quickly and avert an invasion that would have taken far more lives — American and Japanese — than were lost in Hiroshima and Nagasaki. Total casualties from an invasion were anticipated to number in the millions, and many U.S. soldiers who expected to participate in the Japanese invasion credit the atomic bomb for saving their lives. On the other hand, recent scholarship suggests that the bombings may not have been necessary, that the Japanese might soon have been willing to negotiate a surrender, and that the U.S. military might have been at least as motivated by a desire to observe how the bombs would perform in wartime conditions as by a desire to end the war quickly. (Hiroshima was chosen as the bomb site because it was a "virgin target," untouched by conventional air raids. It thus permitted a controlled experiment: the U.S. scientists who were sent there immediately after the war to investigate the bomb's effects could attribute all of the devastation to the atomic explosion.) A letter to Truman written by head atomic scientist Robert Oppenheimer and signed by 67 other prominent scientists urged him not to use the bomb, but Oppenheimer's superior, General Leslie Groves, routed the letter so it would not reach Washington, D.C., until after Truman had left for Potsdam, and Truman never received it. Despite the controversy in later years over the decision to use the bomb, Truman never expressed any regret; nor did he waver from his claim that using the bomb had forestalled an otherwise inevitable invasion.

For Byrnes the atomic bomb also promised to "make Russia more manageable in Europe," but in the September 1945 London Conference of Foreign Ministers he found that the Soviets seemed unimpressed by America's atomic monopoly. The Soviets demanded U.S. recognition of the governments they had imposed in Romania and Bulgaria. In return Byrnes acknowledged that the United States would tolerate governments friendly to the Soviet Union but insisted that they be democratically elected. The two sides reached an impasse, and Byrnes became discouraged about Soviet willingness to reach political compromises. He told administration officials, "We are facing a new Russia, totally different than the Russia we dealt with a year ago.... Now that the war was [*sic*] over they [are] taking an aggressive attitude and stand on political and territorial questions that [is] indefensible." In November Byrnes went to Moscow, where he agreed to recognize the Soviet-controlled regimes in Bulgaria and Romania in return for broader representation within those governments. Angered by Byrnes's refusal to keep him informed during the conference and by the secretary's announcement of the agreement before reporting to him, Truman disassociated himself from Byrnes who, he claimed, had "lost his nerve at Moscow." Republican Senator Arthur Vandenberg, a vocal critic of the administration's foreign policy, termed the agreement "one more typical American give away."

Truman had also fallen out with Byrnes over the question of atomic energy. Truman favored international control and had stated his position publicly in October 1945, while Byrnes still viewed the U.S. atomic monopoly as a useful political weapon. Despite Byrnes's misgivings, in 1946 Undersecretary of State Dean Acheson convened a committee to prepare a U.S. plan for international control. To make the plan more appealing to Congress Truman asked Bernard Baruch to present it to the United Nations. However, Baruch insisted on amendments that virtually assured Soviet refusal. Baruch threatened to resign if his changes were not accepted and Truman acquiesced, despite Acheson's prediction that the Soviets would certainly veto the amended plan. As Acheson forecast, the Soviets indeed vetoed the proposal in the Security Council in December 1946. The subsequent intensification of the Cold War rendered any further top-level efforts for international control politically impossible.

As the USSR continued to make gains in postwar Eastern Europe, as Mao

Zedong's Communists won victories in China, and after the Canadians uncovered a Soviet spy ring, Soviet intentions became increasingly suspect. Public and congressional pressure compelled Truman to gradually assume a harder line against the Communists. In February 1946 George Kennan wrote his detailed "Long Telegram" analyzing U.S. policy toward the USSR, and Truman made it the intellectual basis for subsequent Soviet policy. Departing from Byrnes's earlier view that the Soviets were pragmatic politicians who sought to achieve their goals primarily through diplomacy, the Long Telegram maintained that Soviet foreign policy was predicated on the Communist ideological belief that conflict between Communism and capitalism was historically inevitable. Consequently, Kennan argued that Stalin would consolidate his power at home and insulate the Soviet Union by surrounding it with allied client states. Being too weak to attack the West militarily, the Soviets would attempt to isolate the United States through the political subversion of capitalist countries.

Truman thus adopted a policy of "patience with firmness," in which the United States would negotiate with the USSR but expect any further concessions to come from the Soviets. When Soviet troops occupied part of Iran in early 1946 in a dispute over oil rights, the administration exerted diplomatic pressure until the two countries reached a formal agreement and the Soviets withdrew their soldiers. That summer at the Paris Peace Conference Byrnes became convinced that the Soviet Union would not honor its Potsdam commitment to create an independent and democratic Germany. Consequently, the administration moved toward establishing a separate, democratic West German government rather than allow a single Soviet-dominated German state. Truman also began to move toward a policy of containment that Kennan more fully developed in 1947. During this period Truman and Kennan believed containment should be achieved through economic rather than military measures.

In January 1947 George Marshall replaced Byrnes as secretary of state, an appointment that signaled a harder, less conciliatory position toward the Soviet Union. Truman greatly admired Marshall who, as Army chief of staff, had emerged from World War II a five-star general and a highly decorated hero. As secretary of state, the decisions Marshall made and the policies he and Truman implemented ultimately created and defined the Cold War, at least from the American side. Despite remaining claims that the two superpowers could still reach a viable political settlement through good-faith diplomacy, Marshall believed the Soviets posed a genuine and significant threat to Western Europe. Truman concurred and the existence of a severe Soviet threat to Western Europe emerged as a fundamental axiom of the Cold War.

Truman and Marshall also agreed that U.S. self-interest required the United States to meet the Soviet threat and strengthen the Western European democracies that stood as the first line of defense against Communist expansion. In 1946 Truman authorized economic aid to the governments in Greece and Turkey, which were resisting Communist takeovers. In March 1947, two months after taking office, Marshall attended the Moscow Conference, where he became further convinced of the Soviets' lack of good faith. Concluding that European economic recovery was essential for preserving Western Europe, he had his advisers, including Kennan and Acheson, develop the European Recovery Plan (ERP). More popularly known as the Marshall Plan, the ERP passed through the Congress in 1948. Despite its substantial cost — $12 billion between 1948 and 1951 — the Marshall Plan eventually became one of the great successes of the Cold War and one of the greatest testimonies to the vitality and creative energy of capitalism. By promoting Western European industrial production, bolstering Western European currencies, and promoting international trade, the Marshall Plan facilitated Western Europe's surprisingly rapid recovery from the devastation of World War II. And by ensuring the economic stability of non–Communist governments in France, Italy, and other countries where a Communist presence was strong, the Marshall Plan helped enable friendly, procapitalist governments to remain in power. It thereby fulfilled its Cold War objective of containing Communism. Though invited to participate in the ERP, the Soviets and their Eastern European allies rejected the offer and denounced the program, as Marshall had anticipated they would.

Collectively known as the Truman Doctrine, the Marshall Plan, the 1948 Four Point Program to provide technical aid to underdeveloped countries in Asia, Africa, and Latin America, and the 1949 formation of the North Atlantic Treaty Organization (NATO) became the basis of U.S. policy for containing Soviet expansion. Truman favored an economic approach over military-based policies. He declined to intervene in the Communist takeover of Czechoslovakia in February 1948, and when the Soviets blockaded the surface access routes to West Berlin he rejected a plan by General Lucius Clay to force entry into the city using armed convoys. Instead, he adopted Marshall's proposal for airlifting supplies. The Berlin Airlift, which lasted from June 1948 to May 1949, ultimately achieved its objectives: the Soviet Union finally lifted the blockade and abandoned its demand that West Berlin accept a single, Soviet-controlled currency to be used in all four sectors of Berlin. The Truman administration regarded the single-currency plan as a Soviet attempt to derail the creation of a separate West German government.

The success of the Berlin Airlift also enabled Truman to avert an unpopular, election-year military expedition. Efforts by Florida's Senator Claude Pepper and other prominent Democrats notwithstanding, Truman won his party's nomination in 1948. Despite possible defections to Wallace — who was running as the Progressive Party candidate — Truman sought to retain Roosevelt's New Deal coalition of poor, urban, and agricultural voters. Moreover, Truman's decision in May to recognize the newly formed state of Israel helped attract Jewish voters. On whistle-stop train trips across the country he attacked the conservative Congress for refusing to pass his social programs. When Truman called a special session of Congress that summer to work on social legislation,

Republican intransigence helped validate the president's charges that the eightieth Congress was a "do nothing Congress." When he proclaimed, "If you send another Republican Congress to Washington, you're a bigger bunch of suckers than I think you are," crowds shouted back, "Give 'em hell, Harry": words that became Truman's slogan. With support from blacks and the emerging class of blue-collar, middle-class industrial workers, Truman achieved one of the greatest political upsets in U.S. history. He defeated highly favored Republican Thomas E. Dewey by 2 million popular votes and 114 electoral votes. Wallace, whom the American Communist Party had endorsed, received slightly more than 1 million popular votes and no electoral votes.

Elected in his own right, Truman felt freer to pursue his own policies. Maintaining that "every segment of our population and every individual has a right to expect from his government a fair deal," he submitted to Congress extensive social legislation. The comprehensive housing bill for aiding veterans and people from low-income groups became the basis for most government housing programs during the 1950s. Truman also led the effort to extend social security benefits, increase the minimum wage, expand rural electrification and flood control programs, and tighten farm price supports. He tried unsuccessfully to enact universal health insurance. Truman also advanced civil rights legislation and used his executive power to achieve rights for blacks when Congress resisted. He ordered the desegregation of the armed services and appointed a black judge to the federal judiciary. His administration also supported efforts to end segregation in the public schools.

Even before his election Truman had to respond to right-wing demands for tighter security against internal subversion by domestic Communists. In 1947 he ordered an investigation of Communist activities and subsequently issued Executive Order 9835 that required everyone holding a civilian post within the government to pass a loyalty check. Anyone accused of disloyalty could demand a hearing with a lawyer present, but could not confront his or her accusers. The attorney general's list of subversive organizations also expanded during the Truman years and figured more prominently in congressional and executive branch investigations. Despite these measures, however, Truman was far more moderate in his pursuit of Communist subversion than his right-wing critics believed he should be. In 1948 he attacked the House Committee on Un-American Activities' investigation of Alger Hiss, calling it a "red herring," and in 1951 he refused at some political cost, to produce loyalty files on China specialist Professor Owen Lattimore, citing executive privilege. Republican Senator Joseph McCarthy had accused Lattimore of being a top Soviet spy. A committee investigating McCarthy's charges dismissed them but later conservative Democratic Senator Patrick McCarran reopened the case, and his committee recommended that Lattimore be indicted for perjury. However, subsequent grand jury indictments were eventually either dropped or dismissed.

In 1948 Truman successfully opposed the Mundt-Nixon bill's "police state tactics," which would have required all Communists to register with the government. However, under McCarran's leadership Congress passed the 1950 Internal Security Act that not only incorporated the requirements of the Mundt-Nixon bill but provided for the internment of Communists and other suspected subversives in concentration camps in the event of a national emergency. Truman vetoed the legislation but Congress overrode the veto.

In February 1950, less than a month after a federal jury convicted Alger Hiss for lying when he denied he had acted as a Soviet agent while serving in the Roosevelt administration, McCarthy dramatically declared that he had a list of 205 known Communists within the State Department. With time the size of the list fluctuated between 57 and 207, but the Truman administration was never able to dispel McCarthy's charges of espionage and internal subversion, despite the senator's inability ever to produce the name of a single Communist serving in the State Department. In the spring of 1950 Truman established a special task force to counter each of McCarthy's charges and he attacked McCarthy in his own press conferences and speeches. But he never confronted McCarthy directly or compelled McCarthy to substantiate his charges. Several anti–Truman candidates whom McCarthy had endorsed won during the 1950 midterm elections and McCarthy's power grew even stronger.

Truman thus had to forge his Cold War policy while under constant attack from the right, which was claiming that he was soft on Communism, especially in Asia, and that his State Department was riddled with subversive, pro–Soviet agents. As early as November 1945 Truman had asked Marshall to go to China to resolve the civil war between Mao's Communists and Chiang Kai-shek's Nationalists. In addition to achieving a viable political settlement in China, Truman hoped that Marshall's stature would quiet domestic criticism by the right-wing China lobby that his administration was willing to sell out Chiang to the Communists. Marshall succeeded in negotiating a truce and an agreement to create a national assembly to draft a national constitution. However, in March 1946 the truce fell apart. In his final report Marshall cautioned that the United States would "virtually [have] to take over the Chinese government" in order to preserve Chiang's rule. "It would involve a continuing [U.S.] commitment from which it would practically be impossible to withdraw." Truman heeded the warning and gradually reduced aid to Chiang, leaving only token amounts to appease the China lobby and other right-wing critics.

Marshall retired due to ill health in January 1949, and Acheson replaced him as secretary of state. Acheson pictured the superpower confrontation as a matter of power politics and did not believe in formulating policies according to abstract principles of morality or internationalism. He thought that such idealistic motivations would compel the United States to avoid its responsibilities as a superpower to exercise power in order to create and sustain world order. He also believed that negotiation with the Soviet Union was futile since that nation was unwilling to bargain in good faith. Acheson's view of a world polarized into distinct Eastern and Western spheres of influence came to dominate Truman's Cold War foreign policy.

Unlike Marshall and Kennan, who viewed containment as fundamentally a matter of foreign aid and economic stimulation, Acheson increasingly understood it in military terms. He advocated a massive U.S. military buildup to counter the Communists, and he asserted that the United States must be willing to assume unilateral responsibility for the defense of the non–Communist world. Though Truman initially resisted Acheson's call to increase the annual military budget to $35 billion — 20 percent of the gross national product — the president supported the request after the outbreak of the Korean War in 1950. Acheson also worked to establish the German Federal Republic (West Germany), which he helped bring into the Western, anti–Communist alliance and whose eventual rearmament he promoted. He continued Marshall's China policy of reducing aid to the ineffectual Chiang. Acheson publicly declared that Chiang lacked the support of the Chinese people and that the United States would be unwise to waste its resources propping him up or to intervene militarily on his behalf. A month later the Communists assumed complete control of the Chinese mainland. Chiang's defeat allowed Acheson's right-wing critics to charge him and his State Department with betraying Chiang's anti–Communist cause. This fierce right-wing attack compelled Acheson and Truman to reject their original plan to recognize Mao's Communist government. Instead, the administration agreed to provide economic aid to Chiang's government-in-exile on Taiwan (then called Formosa) but refused to commit the United States to its military defense, especially since the island held no strategic value.

In June 1950 Communist North Korea launched a surprise attack against South Korea. Believing the USSR was behind the North Korean action, probing for weaknesses in the Western alliance, Truman committed U.S. troops to the UN "police action" that became the Korean War. Commanded by General Douglas MacArthur, who engineered a brilliant surprise attack behind enemy lines at Inchon, the mostly American UN forces soon took the offensive and appeared headed for a quick victory. Acheson and MacArthur advocated liberating North Korea after the military situation in South Korea stabilized. However, both men seriously underestimated the Chinese resolve to attack if the UN forces crossed the thirty-eighth parallel into North Korea, and they were caught off guard when the Chinese Communists entered the war in November 1950. Unable to negotiate a suitable peace treaty, Truman resisted calls from leading Republicans to extend the war to China.

Arguing that "there is no substitute for victory," MacArthur wanted to expand the war by bombing Chinese supply depots in Manchuria and destroying bridges over the Yalu River that separates China from North Korea. Truman and Marshall, who rejoined the administration as secretary of defense after the war began, preferred to fight a limited police action rather than provoke an all-out war that might eventually involve the Soviets, who had developed their own atomic bomb a year earlier. MacArthur's public criticisms of administration policy angered Truman. On April 5, 1951, Representative Joseph Martin read on the floor of Congress a letter from MacArthur objecting to the administration's pursuit of a limited war. Truman regarded the letter as an act of insubordination and fired MacArthur on April 11. Truman's highly controversial action provoked a congressional inquiry. McCarthy declared "the son of a bitch [Truman] should be impeached." Nonetheless, Truman weathered the storm. But opposition from a conservative Congress continued to undermine his social agenda and push him to take strong anti–Communist measures both at home and in foreign policy.

Truman declined to run for reelection in 1952. He supported the Democratic Party nominee, Adlai Stevenson, but felt rebuffed when Stevenson distanced himself from him. Stevenson's Republican opponent, Dwight Eisenhower, declared that he would "go to Korea" to resolve the ongoing war, and Eisenhower won decisively. In his final State of the Union Message in January 1953 Truman warned Stalin against provoking a war with the United States and urged the West to continue resisting worldwide Communist expansion, but avoid a nuclear war at the same time. He also attacked the Red Scare and warned against legislation directed against domestic Communists that would promote "enforced conformity."

Vance, Cyrus R. (1917–) Secretary of the Army, 1962–64; undersecretary of defense, 1964–67; and secretary of state, 1977–80. Born in Clarksburg, West Virginia, Vance graduated from Yale in 1939 and received his law degree there in 1942. He served in the Navy in the Pacific theater during World War II and entered private legal practice in 1947. A Democrat, Vance was special counsel for Senate investigating committees from 1957 to 1960 and general counsel for the Defense Department from 1961 to 1962. In July 1962 he became secretary of the Army and advised President Kennedy to send troops to the South, following riots over racial integration in 1962 and 1963. Vance became undersecretary of defense shortly after Kennedy's assassination. He served as President Johnson's special envoy to Panama, the Dominican Republic, and Korea, and helped negotiate a cessation of the 1967 fighting between Greece and Turkey over Cyprus. As undersecretary he helped plan the growing U.S. military buildup during the Vietnam War, which he supported through 1968. In that year, however, the deteriorating military situation in Vietnam and the domestic protest in the United States led him to advocate halting the bombing of North Vietnam and initiating peace negotiations. He subsequently represented the United States in the first Paris peace talks. When Richard Nixon became president in January 1969, Vance returned to his private legal practice and remained out of government until 1977, when President Carter appointed him secretary of state.

As a member of the Carter administration Vance worked to continue the U.S.-Soviet détente initiated by Henry Kissinger during the Nixon and Ford administrations. He advocated nuclear arms limitation, sought to improve relations with China, and promoted negotiations between Israel and its Arab enemies. He frequently clashed with national security adviser Zbigniew Brzezinski, who advocated a harder line against the Soviets, even at the expense of détente and arms reduction. When in 1977 Colonel Mariam Mengistu led a pro–Soviet coup in Ethiopia, Brzezinski perceived a serious Soviet attempt to gain power in Africa. Vance, on the other hand, offered a more tolerant view: "We in the State Department saw the Horn [of Africa] as a textbook case of Soviet exploitation of a local conflict. In the long run, however, we believed the Ethiopians would oust the Soviets from their country as had happened in Egypt and the Sudan. Meanwhile we should continue to work with our European allies and the African nations to bring about a negotiated solution of the broader regional issues. We believed that in the long run, Soviet-Ethiopian relations undoubtedly would sour and Ethiopia would turn again to the West." In the long run Vance proved accurate, but the Mengistu regime lasted until 1991. Likewise, Vance and Brzezinski clashed over the U.S. response to the December 1979 Soviet invasion of Afghanistan. Vance hoped to continue the process of détente while Brzezinski again took a more forceful position. Sensitive to election-year pressures not to appear tolerant of Soviet aggression, Carter sided with Brzezinski, withdrawing the SALT II Treaty from Senate consideration, canceling a grain sale to the USSR, boycotting the 1980 Moscow Olympic games, and otherwise ending détente.

The national security adviser and secretary of state also differed in their response to the 1979 crisis in Iran. Brzezinski wanted to inform the shah that the United States would tolerate military suppression of rebellious dissidents while Vance disagreed. Consequently, the shah received ambiguous messages about U.S. intentions. After the shah was overthrown and Islamic fundamentalists seized the U.S. embassy and took 66 hostages, Brzezinski and Vance again disagreed on how the United States should respond. Brzezinski favored a military rescue while Vance advocated diplomatic measures. Carter initially followed Vance's advice, but after five months he authorized a rescue attempt. However, a sandstorm debilitated the U.S. helicopters and the mission failed. Eight soldiers died in the attempt and Vance resigned in protest. The hostages were finally released on the day Carter left office. Vance later participated in several international diplomatic efforts, and in 1991 and 1992 he headed an unsuccessful UN effort to negotiate an end to the warfare that followed the dissolution of Yugoslavia.

Weinberger, Caspar (1917–   )   Secretary of health, education, and welfare, 1972–75; and secretary of defense, 1981–87. Born in San Francisco, Weinberger graduated from Harvard in 1938 and from Harvard Law School in 1941. As an Army captain during World War II he served on General MacArthur's intelligence staff. After the war he practiced law in California and in 1952 ran successfully as a Republican candidate for the state legislature. He won reelection in 1954 and 1956. Weinberger chaired California's Republican Central Committee during the early 1960s and in 1968 Governor Ronald Reagan appointed him finance director. In that post he acquired a reputation for cost-cutting, which led to subsequent appointments within the Nixon administration. He served on the Federal Trade Commission in 1969, and in 1970 joined the Office of Management and Budget (OMB), becoming its director in 1972 and acquiring extensive experience in working with Pentagon budgets. In November 1972 Nixon appointed Weinberger secretary of health, education and welfare, where he oversaw budget cuts. He resigned in 1975 and managed San Francisco construction and engineering firms until President-elect Reagan appointed him secretary of defense in 1980.

Weinberger shared with Reagan, Vice President Bush, and other ranking members of the administration the assumption that the Soviets were attempting to gain nuclear superiority over the United States and preparing to prevail in a nuclear war. He thus adopted a policy of strengthening the U.S. military so that the United States would prevail in any nuclear war scenario. In 1981 he told Congress that the administration would increase U.S. capacity "for deterring or prosecuting a global war with the Soviet Union," and that year he presented a defense spending plan intended to give the United States nuclear superiority before the end of the decade. During Reagan's first term defense spending increased by 40 percent, providing for the MX missile, a 600-ship Navy with new aircraft carriers, new tanks, and other conventional weapons, replenished ammunition stocks, and the reinstated the B-1 bomber that Carter had earlier canceled. The United States further achieved the deployment of intermediate-range, nuclear-armed Pershing and Cruise missiles in Europe despite intense opposition by antinuclear activists in Great Britain and West Germany. Weinberger also supported Reagan's Strategic Defense Initiative (SDI), which proposed to create a shield of orbiting, laser-armed satellites able to shoot down incoming missiles targeted for U.S. cities and military installations. Weinberger resigned in November 1987 to care for his sick wife.

Biographies of Superpower
and Allied Leaders

Adenauer, Konrad (1876–1967)   Chancellor of West Germany, 1949–63. Born in Cologne, Adenauer studied law before entering politics in 1904. He was elected mayor of Cologne in 1917. An early opponent of Hitler, he had to flee from the city after refusing to fly swastika flags or meet with Hitler in 1933, and he spent most of the next 12 years secluded in a monastery. He reassumed his position as mayor when Cologne was liberated by the U.S. armies in 1945, but after the peace was concluded the city became part of the British sector and Adenauer was soon replaced. This experience soured his feelings for Great Britain throughout the rest of his political career. It also induced him to run for national office, and in 1946 he became chairman of the newly created conservative Christian Democratic Union (CDU).

Coinciding with the end of the 1948–49 Berlin Airlift, Germany became two states, the Federal Republic of Germany (West Germany) and the German Democratic Republic (East Germany). West Germany's constitution, the Basic Law, declared that this partition was to be temporary, until the nation could be united, and in August 1949 the West Germans elected Adenauer their first chancellor. From the beginning he took a strong anti–Communist stand. He perceived the Soviet Union as a hostile nation and sought protection by aligning West Germany with the United States and the NATO allies. In 1950 Adenauer proposed a rapprochement with France and, despite an initial rejection, his initiative was enacted in the Schuman Plan that allowed France and Germany to pool their coal and steel resources. This was the first step toward greater European integration, and it represented West Germany's acceptance into "the community of free European nations."

That year Adenauer also agreed to West German participation in a proposed European Defense Community (EDC), but France refused to approve the treaty when it came up for ratification shortly after the Korean War ended, for Stalin had died and the need for German remilitarization no longer seemed so great. Adenauer threatened that without a defense agreement West Germany would be compelled to reach an accommodation with the USSR. In response West Germany was invited to join NATO and the Western European Union. However, to allay French fears of renewed German militarism Adenauer agreed to limit the size of the German military and allow some 50,000 British soldiers to be stationed in West Germany through the end of the century. In 1955 Adenauer rejected a Soviet offer to reunify Germany, which he felt was an insincere attempt to delay West Germany's complete entrance into the Western alliance. Shortly afterward West Germany achieved full membership in NATO. Adenauer subsequently visited Moscow and agreed to open diplomatic relations in return for the return of German prisoners of war from World War II. The USSR had officially recognized East Germany as a sovereign state in 1954, and thus prior to the late 1960s it was the only major power to maintain relations with both Germanys. The United States did not recognize East Germany until 1974.

In 1957 Adenauer helped form the European Economic Community, (Common Market) which further integrated West Germany within the Western alliance. In 1958, after Charles De Gaulle came to power in France, Adenauer intensified his efforts to seek greater German-French cooperation. The two leaders met in September 1958 and discovered that they shared similar aspirations for Europe. In 1963 they signed the Franco-German Friendship Treaty, which called for regular meetings between the heads of state and foreign ministers, consultation on major foreign policy decisions, greater military cooperation, and cultural exchanges between France and West Germany.

Adenauer received criticism for not responding more vigorously to the erection of the Berlin Wall in 1961 and for sacrificing German reunification for alignment with the West. In 1961 the CDU lost its absolute majority and formed a coalition government with the Free Democratic Party (FDP). Adenauer, then 85 years old, declined to step down despite pressure to allow Economics Minister Ludwig Erhard to replace him. He finally resigned in October 1963 in favor of Erhard, whom he considered a political lightweight. But Adenauer remained chairman of the CDU through 1966, and he died on April 19, 1967.

Andropov, Yuri (1914–84) Soviet general secretary, 1982–84. The son of a railway worker, Andropov was born in the northern Caucasus region. He worked as a telegraph operator and film projectionist and attended a local university but did not graduate. During World War II he led guerrilla activities behind the German lines and afterward was named party leader in Petrozavodsk, the capital city of the Karelo-Finnish Republic. He joined the Communist Central Party in Moscow in 1951 and completed his university education at the Higher Party School, where he received military and political instruction. After serving with the ministry of foreign affairs in Czechoslovakia and Poland he transferred to Hungary in 1953 and became ambassador in 1954. His duplicitous but effective handling of events during the 1956 Hungarian Revolution won him respect from the Soviet leadership, and he subsequently helped rebuild the

Hungarian Communist Party and introduced economic reforms that made Hungary the most liberal Communist country in Eastern Europe during the 1970s and 1980s. These successes in Hungary influenced his policies when he later headed the Soviet Union. In 1957 Andropov assumed responsibility for party relations with the Communist parties of other countries throughout the world, and in 1962 he joined the Central Committee. In 1967 he was made a nonvoting member of the Politburo and became a voting member in 1973.

In 1967 Andropov also assumed the leadership of the KGB, the Soviet secret police and international intelligence organization. Brezhnev appointed him because he believed Andropov was the candidate least likely to use the post for a personal political power base. Under Andropov the KGB discarded its Stalin-era terror tactics and altered its international focus from political espionage to industrial spying in order to assist Soviet industry's effort to catch up to the West. Though domestic political dissidents were usually not murdered or tortured they were nonetheless suppressed, often by being consigned to psychiatric hospitals where they were given psychoactive and/or debilitating drugs. In 1979 Andropov was rewarded for his work when the Politburo published a collection of his speeches. The volume's positive reception in official reviews signaled Andropov's emergence as a major leader.

Following Brezhnev's death on November 10, 1982, Andropov became the party's general secretary. He entered as a reformer who had attacked the corruption of Brezhnev's family and friends. Thus Andropov also implicitly attacked his political rival and Brezhnev's personal choice for successor, Konstantin Chernenko. Five days after taking office Andropov gave a major speech identifying economic failures from the previous two years. He proposed to stimulate the economy through industrial decentralization and by offering incentives to workers. He also endorsed linking wages to productivity, advocated greater independence for agricultural and industrial enterprises and encouraged new technologies. Believing that the economy could no longer absorb the drain from Brezhnev's military buildup, Andropov advocated freezing nuclear strategic arsenals as the initial step for achieving arms reduction with the West. He also signaled his willingness to return to the East-West détente that had ended in 1979. However, Andropov died from kidney failure on February 9, 1984, before he could complete his reforms. In many respects he anticipated the changes Mikhail Gorbachev instituted a few years later, though his program suffered an immediate, short-term setback when Chernenko, a hard-line conservative, assumed power following Andropov's death.

Attlee, Clement (1883–1967)   British prime minister, 1945–51. Born to a British middle-class family, Attlee attended Oxford before entering a law practice. Interested in social reform he joined the Labour Party in 1908 and was elected to Parliament in 1922. In 1924 he served in Britain's first Labour government as undersecretary of state for war and later assumed other administrative posts. In 1935 he was elected head of the Labour Party over pacifist George Lansbury. However, after Germany invaded Poland his refusal to join a nationalist government headed by Neville Chamberlain enabled Conservative Winston Churchill to become prime minister in 1940. Attlee became Churchill's deputy prime minister and worked closely with Churchill throughout the war.

As the war concluded in May 1945, however, Attlee forced an election and defeated Churchill. Since the result of the election was still undetermined at the beginning of the Potsdam Conference, both men attended, and Attlee assumed responsibility for the negotiations after his victory was announced. Attlee sustained Churchill's demand for Polish independence and addressed the central questions about the postwar administration of Germany and Soviet demands for extensive reparations. At the conference Attlee became convinced that the Soviets were intent on expanding their domination throughout Europe.

Attlee appointed Ernest Bevin as foreign minister, and the two men formulated most of Britain's foreign policy in the formative days of the Cold War. Central to their policy was a close alliance with the United States, since Attlee recognized that Britain and the rest of Europe would have to depend on US military and economic aid in the near future. In July 1946 he obtained a $937 million loan from the United States. Though he disagreed with President Truman's view that all national Communist parties were controlled by the Soviet Union, and he correctly anticipated a split between the People's Republic of China (PRC) and the USSR, Attlee supported the Korean War and sent British troops to be part of the UN forces fighting there. Under the Bizonal Agreement of 1946 Attlee agreed to merge the U.S. and British zones in West Germany into a single administrative unit, and in 1948 he ordered the Royal Air Force to join in the Berlin Airlift when the Soviets blocked Western access to West Berlin. During the airlift Truman and Attlee agreed to base U.S. nuclear-armed bombers in Great Britain, and in 1949 they formed the NATO alliance with other Western powers to protect against possible Soviet aggression. Attlee also authorized development of Britain's own atomic weapons program, something he believed was necessary for Great Britain to remain a world power. His only major policy conflict with the United States came when he recognized the PRC in October 1949, arguing that political control and not ideology should determine recognition. The United States did not fully recognize the PRC until 1979.

World War II drained the British economy and made it impossible for the country to sustain its overseas empire. Thus during his administration Attlee oversaw the British withdrawal from Egypt and the end of its rule in India, Burma, Sri Lanka (then Ceylon), and Palestine. Unable to commit sufficient funds to protect Greece from a Communist takeover immediately following the war, Attlee and Bevin helped convince Truman to expend U.S. aid.

Churchill defeated Attlee in the general elections of 1951 and returned the Conservative Party to power. Attlee stepped down from the leadership of the Labour Party in 1955 and died on October 8, 1967.

Brandt, Willy (1913–92)   Chancellor of West Germany, 1969–74. Born as Herbert Ernst Karl Frahm, Brandt was an early participant in the Social Democratic Party (SPD). However, when the SPD failed to effectively oppose Hitler in 1932, he joined the more extreme Socialist Workers Party for whom he wrote newspaper articles under the pseudonym "Willy Brandt." Fearing arrest by the Nazis, he fled from Germany in 1933 and remained in exile throughout World War II, living in Scandinavia and working for the exile office of the German Socialist Workers Party. He acquired Norwegian citizenship during the war but renounced it in 1947 after returning to Germany, first as a journalist and then as a member of the press assigned to the Norwegian Military Mission at the Allied Control Council. He soon rejoined the SPD and became director of the party's Berlin liaison office. In that capacity he helped the Western allies remain in contact with East Germany during the Berlin Airlift of 1948–49. He was elected to the West German legislature in 1949 and to the Berlin House of Representatives in 1950.

From 1957 to 1961 Brandt served as mayor of West Berlin. His tenure in office coincided with the Second Berlin Crisis, which culminated in the late summer and fall of 1961 when East Germany erected the Berlin Wall to stem emigration to West Germany, and Soviet and U.S. tanks faced each other at the wall. Brandt insisted that West Berlin should be included in the Western alliance and that it be allowed to make decisions independent from those of the Western military commanders. At the same time he rejected a 1958 Soviet demand that West Berlin become "an independent political entity," since he believed such a move would result in Soviet domination. When the Soviets built the Berlin Wall Brandt vigorously protested U.S. failure to take immediate steps against it. Subsequently, President Kennedy strengthened the U.S. commitment to West Berlin, sending an additional 1,500 troops from West Germany. During the crisis, which finally defused in late fall, Brandt lobbied actively to win international support for West Berlin and emerged as a leading West German political figure.

During the Berlin Crisis Brandt brought the SPD closer to the political center, and in 1959 the party adopted a platform that renounced doctrinaire Marxism and advocated private property, freedom of religion, and free enterprise. In 1961 and 1965 he ran unsuccessfully against Konrad Adenauer as the SPD's candidate for West German chancellor. But in 1966, following the split between Adenauer's Christian Democratic Union (CDU) and the Federal Democrat Party (FDP), Brandt became foreign minister and vice chancellor in a coalition government led by Kurt Kiesinger. He subsequently devised a new *Ostpolitik*, or Eastern policy, designed to defuse East-West tensions by improving West German relations with Eastern Europe. The establishment of diplomatic relations with Romania and Yugoslavia culminated Brandt's efforts as foreign minister, though efforts by the CDU kept him from developing his Ostpolitik as fully as he desired.

However, in September 1969 the SPD won the largest number of seats in the general election, and Brandt became chancellor in a coalition government with the Federal Democrats. He quickly renewed his efforts for Ostpolitik, meeting in March 1970 with East German President Willi Stoph to discuss the normalization of diplomatic relations. However, the two sides were unable to reconcile what Brandt termed as their "contradictory social orders" and their "utterly different basic interests." Nonetheless, Brandt succeeded in negotiating 1970 nonaggression pacts with the Soviet Union and Poland, in which West Germany recognized its borders with East Germany and East Germany's borders with Poland. This provided a first step in Western recognition of the Soviet Union's de facto territorial gains following World War II and thereby helped bring about the East-West détente of the 1970s. Brandt's initiatives were well received by France, and Great Britain was enticed to acquiesce by Brandt's support of British membership in the European Economic Community. After an initially cool response the United States also supported Brandt, and in August 1971, Great Britain, France, the Soviet Union and the United States signed the Quadripartite Agreement that allowed West Berliners to travel to East Berlin, provided for uninhibited travel from West Germany to West Berlin, and normalized the status of West Berlin with West Germany.

In 1971 Brandt also received the Nobel Peace Prize for his efforts to alleviate Cold War antagonisms. The following year he signed a treaty with East Germany that normalized diplomatic relations, reunified families, and released prisoners. Campaigning on these successes, Brandt's SPD-FDP coalition easily won reelection. In his second term Brandt continued to establish closer ties with the East, signing economic agreements with the USSR and Romania and a treaty with Czechoslovakia. However, he was forced to resign in April 1974 after a close aide, Günter Guillaume, was arrested as an East German spy. Brandt, who acknowledged that he had been negligent, was replaced by Helmut Schmidt.

Nonetheless, Brandt remained chairman of the SPD and thus retained considerable influence in West Germany's foreign affairs. In 1976 he won election as president of the Socialist International, and in 1980 his Brandt Commission, which studied the relationship between developed and underdeveloped countries, recommended that the rich, industrialized nations donate some $8 billion annually in food aid and $60 billion in developmental aid and loans over the next five years. It advocated a universal tax to cover the costs.

During the 1980s Brandt opposed the hard turn to the right taken by President Reagan and unsuccessfully opposed the U.S. efforts to place Cruise and Pershing II missiles in Germany. In the process he emerged as a major proponent of Europe's antinuclear movement, a position consistent with his concern throughout the Cold War that Germany would be the likely battleground in the event of an East-West nuclear exchange. In 1984 Brandt unsuccessfully tried to mediate an end to the civil war in Nicaragua. Disappointing results in the 1987 general election and a sex scandal reduced Brandt's influence within the SPD, and he was forced to resign after chairing the party for 23 years.

Brezhnev, Leonid (1906–82)   Soviet general secretary, 1964–82. The longest-serving Soviet leader during the Cold War era, Brezhnev was born in the Ukraine to a working-class family. He began working in the steel industry at age 15 while he attended night school studying metallurgy. He joined the Communist Party in 1923 and strongly backed Joseph Stalin, who was then in the process of consolidating power. In the 1930s he assisted in Stalin's purges in the Ukraine, which wiped out the Kulaks and forced farmers to join government-owned collective farms. In 1938 Brezhnev became secretary of the Ukrainian Communist Party and served under Nikita Khrushchev with whom he established a long working relationship. During World War II he initially served as a political commissar attached to the Red Army with the rank of lieutenant colonel, but he was promoted to major general in 1943. Following the war he assumed responsibility for imposing Soviet rule on portions of Romania, Czechoslovakia, the Ukraine, and Moldavia. His severe methods met with Stalin's approval, and in 1952 he came to Moscow as a member of the party's Central Committee and a nonvoting member of the Politburo. However, during the power struggle following Stalin's death Brezhnev was removed from the Politburo. Between 1953 and 1956 he distanced himself from Stalin and aligned with Khrushchev. In 1956 he assisted in Khrushchev's program of deStalinization, rejoined the Politburo as a nonvoting member, and helped develop the Soviet Union's rocket and guided missile program. In 1957, as Khrushchev consolidated power, he became a voting member of the Politburo.

In the early 1960s Brezhnev rose dramatically within the party becoming chairman of the Presidium of the Supreme Soviet in 1960 and the Central Committee's secretary for personnel selection in 1963. In the latter post he strengthened his power base by promoting supporters to important positions and became the second most powerful person in the party after Khrushchev. He did not play a major role in the October 1964 coup that removed Khrushchev but emerged as the most powerful leader afterward. Initially, he ruled as part of a *troika* with Prime Minister Alexei Kosygin and Andrei Kirilenko. Brezhnev became the party's general secretary, and his ties with the military gave him greater power than the other two members of the triumvirate. By 1970 Brezhnev had established nearly complete control, though Kosygin remained prime minister. In 1976 Brezhnev promoted himself to field marshal, the Red Army's highest rank, and in 1977 he also assumed the presidency of the USSR, becoming the first Soviet leader to hold both the top party and top government positions. The next year he received the Soviet Union's highest military honor, the Order of Victory. During this period he began developing a personality cult akin to Stalin's as posters with his portrait adorned city walls and streets and towns were named after him.

Brezhnev was a Communist hard-liner who reversed some of Khrushchev's social and economic reforms and sought to return the party to the traditional values of Marxist-Leninism. He avoided the purges and other excesses of the

Stalin years but strengthened the secret police (KGB) and curtailed political dissent. While he was in power, dissenters were sent to labor camps or psychiatric hospitals. He forbade Jewish emigration except for a brief period during the 1970s détente. Threatened by the liberal policies of Czechoslovakia's Alexander Dubček, Brezhnev ordered the Warsaw Pact invasion of that country on August 20, 1968. Within a week some 650,000 foreign soldiers were stationed on Czech soil and the liberal reformers were removed from power. On November 12 he issued the Brezhnev Doctrine justifying the invasion. The doctrine acknowledged respect for the sovereignty of Communist-ruled countries but added that "when internal and external forces that are hostile to socialism try to turn the development of some socialist country toward the restoration of a capitalist regime ... [it becomes] a common problem of all socialist countries."

Brezhnev geared the Soviet economy toward heavy industry and defense at the cost of providing consumer goods and ample food supplies. He built up the Soviet nuclear arsenal to levels roughly comparable to those of the United States. Having attained military parity with the West in the early 1970s and feeling concern about the newly established U.S. ties to China, Brezhnev began to promote a limited détente. In May 1972, three months after Nixon's historic trip to China, Brezhnev hosted the president in Moscow where they signed the Strategic Arms Limitation Treaty (SALT I). They also agreed to cultural exchanges and improved trade relations, and in October they signed an agreement for both sides to forego antiballistic missile (ABM) systems. In 1975 Brezhnev, President Ford, and the leaders of Eastern and Western Europe signed the Helsinki Accords that, for the first time during the Cold War, granted de facto Western recognition of the Soviet territorial gains following World War II. This had been a major Soviet objective throughout the Cold War. In return Brezhnev acceded to Western demands for increased trade and cultural exchange and greater commitment to human rights and political expression.

Even as détente continued, however, Brezhnev insisted that the ideological competition between capitalism and Communism must continue, and in the mid–1970s the CIA, under the leadership of future President George Bush, came to the controversial conclusion that Brezhnev was preparing for Soviet victory in any all-out nuclear war. This contradicted the assumption of mutually assured destruction (MAD) that underlay détente. Disagreements over the emigration rights of Soviet Jews led to the eventual cancellation of the 1974 East-West Trade Relations agreement. Soviet support of Communist insurgency in Ethiopia, South Yemen, Mozambique, Angola, and elsewhere in the underdeveloped regions of the world also weakened the East-West détente. Moreover, Brezhnev's decision to deploy SS-20 intermediate-range nuclear missiles in Europe provoked NATO's controversial decision in December 1979 to deploy Cruise and Pershing II nuclear missiles. Détente was finally destroyed on Christmas Day 1979, when the Soviet Union invaded Afghanistan. In response President Carter withdrew the SALT II Treaty from Senate consideration, canceled a large grain sale, and boycotted the 1980 Moscow Olympic games. Relations with Carter's successor, Ronald Reagan, were even colder as Reagan dubbed Brezhnev the leader of an "Evil Empire."

The Afghanistan invasion also alienated elements in Western Europe that had promoted détente. Those ties were further weakened in 1980 when Brezhnev imposed an antireform government in Poland that outlawed the Solidarity trade union and introduced martial law. Prior to that he had established good working relationships with France's presidents De Gaulle, Pompidou, and Giscard d'Estaing, though relations deteriorated with Socialist President Mitterrand. He also worked well with West Germany's Social Democratic chancellors Willy Brandt and Helmut Schmidt. However, he established no rapport with British Prime Minister Thatcher, whom he called "The Iron Lady." Brezhnev distrusted China's Mao Zedong, and in the early 1970s he proposed a joint U.S.-Soviet nuclear strike against China, with whom the Soviet Union had clashed in 1969. The plan was rejected, and just prior to his death on November 10, 1982, Brezhnev called for an end to Chinese-Soviet hostility.

Callaghan, James (1912–   )   British foreign secretary, 1974–76; and prime minister, 1976–79. Educated in the British state school system, Callaghan joined the civil service and soon became involved with the unions. He joined the Labour Party at age 19 and became a full-time union official in his early twenties. He served in the British Naval Intelligence during World War II and entered Parliament in the 1945 elections that overthrew Winston Churchill's government. In 1956, after Churchill and the Conservatives returned to power, Callaghan became the Labour Party's spokesman for colonial affairs. When the Labour Party regained power in 1964 he was named chancellor of the exchequer, though he resigned in 1967 after Prime Minister Harold Wilson compelled him to devalue the pound. He returned to Wilson's government as home secretary and then became Labour's spokesman for foreign affairs after the Conservatives took office again in 1971. When Wilson became prime minister again in 1974 he named Callaghan as foreign secretary.

As foreign secretary, Callaghan continued Great Britain's close relationship with the United States. Along with U.S. Secretary of State Kissinger he helped negotiate a settlement to the 1974 Greek-Turkish conflict in Cyprus that threatened to weaken NATO's southern flank. Labour's $11 billion defense cut in late 1974 resulted in troop reductions in Hong Kong and Cyprus and withdrawals from Singapore and Mauritius. Callaghan was not a strong supporter of the East-West détente, though in 1975 he helped negotiate an agreement offering $2.4 billion in low-interest credits to the Soviet Union. He called the deal a "new phase in Anglo-Soviet relations," but the USSR used only a small fraction of the credit. Following the collapse of Portuguese power in Angola and Mozambique, Callaghan helped dissuade Kissinger and President Ford from sending troops to Angola or supporting a South African invasion, arguing that a country that supported a South African military action would "find itself pilloried all over Africa." At the same time he opposed the Soviet Union's efforts to expand its influence in those countries, and he objected to the introduction of Cuban troops into Angola. He also tried unsuccessfully to deal with the ongoing crisis in Rhodesia that had begun in 1965, when a white supremacist government under Ian Smith declared independence from Great Britain and sparked a civil war with black nationalists.

Wilson stepped down as prime minister in April 1976 and the Labour Party elected Callaghan to replace him. He soon formed a close relationship with President Carter, who took office in January 1977. Despite fierce opposition within his own party, Callaghan accepted a U.S. offer to replace Great Britain's small fleet of aging nuclear-armed Polaris submarines with newer Trident submarines and missiles. Carter and Callaghan also coordinated their policies in southern Africa and attempted unsuccessfully to pressure Smith into allying with a moderate black leader. The Rhodesian situation was not finally resolved until six months after Callaghan left office, when Conservative Prime Minister Margaret Thatcher oversaw the creation of the new state of Zimbabwe.

Callaghan's ruling coalition fell apart in 1979 and Thatcher replaced him in May. Callaghan remained leader of the opposition for a short time before resigning in October 1980, after the Labour Party adopted several left-wing positions and committed itself to unilateral nuclear disarmament. Unlike other more conservative members of the party who left to form the new Social Democratic Party, Callaghan stayed in the Labour Party but became one of the strongest inside critics of its antinuclear platform.

Chernenko, Konstantin (1911–85)   Soviet general secretary, 1984–85. Born to a Siberian peasant family, Chernenko joined the Communist Youth Movement in the 1920s and became regional party secretary of Krasnoyarsk in 1941. In 1948 he was placed in charge of propaganda in Moldavia, where he later met Leonid Brezhnev who had been appointed Moldavian party leader. The two formed a close working relationship that eventually brought Chernenko to the seat of Soviet power. He accompanied Brezhnev to Moscow in 1956 when the latter became a nonvoting member of the Politburo, and when Brezhnev became chairman of the Presidium in 1960 he named Chernenko chief of staff. Chernenko retained that position until Brezhnev's death. Chernenko joined the party's Central Committee in 1971 and became a full member of the Politburo in 1978. He was a member of the delegation that met with President Carter in Vienna to sign the 1979 Strategic Arms Limitation Treaty (SALT II), and during Brezhnev's final years he controlled access to the infirm leader. Though he was Brezhnev's personal choice to succeed him, Chernenko lacked the political base to become general secretary. After Brezhnev died on November 10, 1982, Chernenko's rival, the more liberal Yuri Andropov, became the Soviet leader. Despite their differences, Chernenko nominated Andropov in a public display of party unity. When Andropov died on February 9, 1984, after a little more than a year in office, Chernenko replaced him.

Chernenko sought to return the party to Brezhnev's conservative policies and orientation. He sentenced several prominent dissidents to internal exile, strengthened relations with Eastern Europe, and took a hard line in nuclear arms negotiations with the West. He demanded the removal of U.S. intermediate-range, nuclear-armed Cruise and Pershing II missiles from Western Europe and the elimination of President Reagan's Strategic Defense Initiative (SDI) as preconditions for further talks. And he increased the budget for military spending by 12 percent in November 1984. He died on March 10, 1985, following a combination of illnesses including emphysema, hepatitis, and cirrhosis of the liver. Reformer Mikhail Gorbachev succeeded him.

Chiang Kai-shek (1887–1975)   Leader of Nationalist China, 1949–75. Born to a merchant family in Chekiang province Chiang grew up in poverty but managed to attend the Paoting Military Academy in 1906. He then received advanced instruction in Japan, where he met Dr. Sun Yat-sen. Sun became Chiang's mentor and the founder of modern China. In 1911 Chiang became one of Sun's military leaders in his revolution, and by 1921 Chiang emerged as chief of staff for Sun's Nationalist government based in Canton. Sun's Kuomintang Party allied with the Chinese Communists in the early 1920s and received assistance from the newly formed Soviet Union. Chiang went to the USSR in 1923 to learn about Soviet institutions and military structure. Afterward he became commandant of the Whampoa Military Academy that was organized along Soviet lines.

Following Sun's death in 1925 Chiang assumed control of the Kuomintang. In 1927, when he realized that the Communists threatened his power base, he eliminated most of them in a bloody purge that killed thousands. The survivors fled with Mao Zedong first to Kiangsi province in the south. Then in 1934, after Chiang's Army nearly destroyed them, they made the Long March to Shenshi province 6,000 miles to the north.

In the meantime the Japanese had begun their invasion of China, and the Soviet Union supported the United Front — Communists and Kuomintang — to fight them. Chiang refused until he was kidnapped by Communists and northern warlords in the December 1936 Sian Incident and forced to join the anti–Japanese alliance. Negotiations conducted by Zhou En-lai spared his life. The United Front collapsed in 1941, shortly before the United States entered World War II and gave full financial and military support to Chiang's Nationalist government. During this time Chiang and his wife cultivated the friendship of Henry Luce, the influential publisher of *Time* and *Life* magazines. President Roosevelt projected Chiang as the future leader of a democratic China that would create stability in Asia after the war. Over the objections of Stalin and Churchill, Roosevelt insisted on including Chiang as one of the big four leaders during the war and admitting China to the United Nations Security Council afterward. However, General Joseph Stilwell, who commanded U.S. forces in the region, and John Davies and John Service, senior members of the State Department, objected to Chiang's corruption, inefficiency, and greater attentiveness to defeating his political enemies than to fighting the Japanese. Chiang managed to have Stilwell replaced but the Roosevelt administration changed its policy to support a coalition government that would be dominated by Chiang but include the Communists.

After the war President Truman sent retired General George Marshall to negotiate such an arrangement. Marshall achieved a truce between the Nationalists and Communists, who initially agreed to create a National Assembly that would represent both parties. Both sides further agreed to integrate their forces into a single, national Army. However, in March 1946, while Marshall was in Washington, D.C., to consult with Truman, the fragile truce fell apart. Conservative elements among the Nationalists refused to accept a coalition with Communists. Moreover, Nationalist forces attempted to stop Mao's armies from occupying areas abandoned when the Soviets vacated Manchuria. Following the collapse of the negotiations, the Chinese Civil War broke out between the two factions. In his reports Marshall cautioned that the United States would "virtually [have] to take over the Chinese government" in order to preserve Chiang's rule. "It would involve a continuing [U.S.] commitment from which it would practically be impossible to withdraw." Truman heeded the warning and gradually reduced aid to Chiang, leaving only token amounts to appease Luce's China lobby and Chiang's other right-wing supporters.

Chiang's armies (3 million strong) outnumbered Mao's of 1 million, and with the assistance of limited U.S. aid Chiang won initial victories. But by 1947 the tide had turned, and Beijing fell in October 1949. Shortly thereafter Mao declared China to be the People's Republic of China (PRC) and Chiang fled with his Army and gold and silver reserves across the Taiwan Straits to the offshore island of Taiwan (then Formosa), where he established the Republic of China. The United States recognized Chiang's government as the official Chinese government, and Chiang's Nationalists held the UN Chinese seat until 1971. Upon declaring the existence of the republic in October 1949, Chiang imposed martial law due to possibility of a Communist attack. The state of emergency, which lasted through the late 1980s, also allowed Chiang to control the 15 million Taiwanese with whom his 2 million exiles shared the island.

During the Korean War Chiang presented himself as a strong U.S. ally and hoped to use the war to reconquer the mainland. As UN forces approached the Chinese border in 1950 he proposed attacking the Chinese Communists from the south, thereby diverting their troops from the Korean border. Soon after General MacArthur flew to Taiwan to discuss the plan with Chiang, the Communist Chinese leadership decided to enter the war since the threat of a U.S.-led invasion appeared increasingly genuine. However, Truman rejected Chiang's proposal since he thought it would provoke Soviet intervention and further escalate the war. At the same time he feared a Communist invasion of Taiwan; so he stationed the Seventh Fleet in the Taiwan Straits to preclude an attack by either side.

In December 1954, Chiang signed a mutual defense treaty with the United States following Communist attacks on the nearby islands of Quemoy and Matsu. At that time President Eisenhower threatened to use atomic weapons if necessary to defend Chiang. The crisis died down but flared up again in 1958 when Eisenhower again threatened to use nuclear force. At the same time Secretary of State Dulles flew to Taiwan to inform Chiang that the United States would not support an attack on the mainland and insist that Chiang renounce the use of force against the PRC, which Chiang reluctantly did. Willingness to defend Quemoy and Matsu was later a major topic in the 1960 Nixon-Kennedy presidential debates.

Unable to pursue reconquest of the mainland, Chiang consolidated control of Taiwan. He created a near dictatorial political structure and formed a secret police force headed by his son Chiang Ching-kuo, who assumed most of the administrative responsibility for running the country and gained a reputation for ruthlessness and authoritarianism. In the 1970s the United States began separating itself from Chiang, first when the PRC replaced Nationalist China in the United Nations in 1971 and then when President Nixon visited the PRC in 1972. Finally, on January 1, 1979, almost four years after Chiang's death, President Carter severed relations with the Republic of China and recognized the PRC. For all practical purposes Taiwan was then removed from Cold War politics.

Churchill, Sir Winston (1874–1965)   Prime minister of Great Britain, 1940–45, and 1951–55. Born into one of England's most prestigious families, Churchill was a dominant figure in twentieth-century politics. Originally a member of the Liberal Party, he developed a lifelong hatred for Communism when he served as home secretary in 1911. Later, as first lord of the admiralty he helped strengthen the British Royal Navy prior to World War I. He switched to the Conservative Party in the early 1920s and stridently warned against the threat posed by Hitler in the 1930s. His efforts resulted in the upgrading of the British military. Neville Chamberlain's efforts to appease Hitler failed in 1939, and Churchill became prime minister in 1940, following the start of World War II. He led the British war effort and worked with Roosevelt and Stalin to coordinate Allied efforts.

In October 1944 Churchill and Foreign Secretary Anthony Eden met in Moscow with Stalin. In respect to existing "spheres of influence," they agreed to give the Soviets 90 percent predominance in Romania and the British 90 percent in Greece, where their respective armies were already stationed. They would share dominance in Yugoslavia. The Soviets later pointed to this agreement as a tacit understanding that the Allies would respect each other's spheres of influence following the war, though Churchill insisted that the arrangement was understood to be only temporary. At the same Moscow Conference Churchill and Stalin had their first major disagreements over postwar plans for Poland, and these differences soon extended to plans for Germany and the structure of the United Nations. At the Yalta Conference Churchill and Roosevelt, faced with the existing presence of the Soviet Red Army in Poland, agreed to significant changes in the Polish border in return for Soviet promises of free elections in Poland. However, the free elections never materialized. Churchill represented Great Britain at the beginning of the Potsdam Conference, but was replaced by his successor Clement Attlee after his defeat in the general elections in July 1945.

After losing the election Churchill became leader of the opposition and a vocal critic of Stalin. In a speech in Fulton, Missouri, on March 5, 1946, he warned, "From Stettin in the Baltic to Trieste in the Adriatic an iron curtain has descended across the continent of Europe. The Communist parties ... have been raised to preeminence and power far beyond their numbers and are seeking everywhere to obtain totalitarian control.... Whatever conclusions may be drawn from these facts — and facts they are — this is certainly not the liberated Europe we fought to build up. Nor is it one that contains the essentials of permanent peace." The iron curtain offered a powerful image of Communist oppression that dominated the Cold War. Its concrete manifestation came 15 years later in the cement and barbed wire of the Berlin Wall. While out of power Churchill supported Attlee's foreign policy, including the Berlin Airlift, the merging of the British and U.S. zones in Germany, negotiations with the USSR for a German peace treaty, and the formation of NATO.

Churchill was elected prime minister once again in October 1951. Placing U.S. relations at the center of his foreign policy, he flew to Washington, D.C., in early 1952 to reassure President Truman of Great Britain's continued support of the Korean War. He tried to secure U.S. cooperation in nuclear weapons research, but the McMahon Act (1946) forbade sharing nuclear secrets with foreign powers. Believing that possession of nuclear weapons was essential for Great Britain to regain its status as a world power, Churchill pursued an independent atomic research program, and in October 1952 Britain exploded its first atomic bomb. Shortly before retiring in 1955 he also authorized production of a British hydrogen bomb. He promoted an independent land-based missile system for delivering British nuclear weapons, though the so-called Blue Streak program was canceled in 1960 due to its great cost.

Following Stalin's death in March 1953, Churchill proposed trying to improve relations with the Soviet Union. He helped organize an East-West summit in December, but it did not achieve the mutual agreements Churchill had hoped for. In 1954 he resisted U.S. efforts to win British support for the French cause in Vietnam. However, he failed to convince Secretary of State Dulles to accept the Geneva Accords which his foreign secretary, Anthony Eden, helped negotiate after the French defeat at Dien Bien Phu. In 1954 Churchill also agreed to permanently base 50,000 British troops in West Germany in order to allay French fears that German rearmament might permit renewed German militarism.

Churchill retired as prime minister and leader of the Conservative Party on April 5, 1955. He remained a representative in the House of Commons and won reelection in 1959 but no longer played a significant role in shaping world affairs.

De Gaulle, Charles (1890–1970)   President of France, 1945–46, 1958–69. Born into the lesser French nobility, De Gaulle attended the French military academy at Saint-Cyr where he graduated in 1912. He won the Legion of Honor in World War I and led the Free French movement in World War II. His relations with Roosevelt and Churchill were stormy although he got along more smoothly with Stalin. He led the Allied liberation of Paris in August 1944 and was unanimously elected provisional president of France in November 1945. However, De Gaulle resigned in 1946 because he felt constrained by party politics. The Fourth Republic was formed shortly thereafter. In 1947 he organized his own Rally of the People Party, which became better known as the Gaullist Party. It centered around De Gaulle personally and fully endorsed his vision of France as a major world power with himself at its head.

In July 1947 De Gaulle reversed his earlier policy of cooperating with the Communists. He charged that the Soviet Union threatened "the same rights and liberties" as the Nazis had and declared that European governments needed to attract citizens who were drawn to Communism in order to avert "an immense and unpardonable war." He also called for U.S. economic assistance in resisting Communism. In return the Soviet foreign minister attacked De Gaulle as an "admirer and imitator" of Hitler. However, De Gaulle could not gain the support of big business or the Truman and Eisenhower administrations, which instead backed governments headed by Jules Moch and Robert Schuman. Unable to achieve his objectives, De Gaulle retired in July 1955 announcing, "We shall not meet again until the tempest again looses itself on France."

Turmoil surrounding France's Algerian War led to the collapse of the Fourth Republic, and on June 1, 1958, the National Assembly elected De Gaulle premier and gave him near-dictatorial powers. The constitution for the Fifth Republic, which De Gaulle formulated, created a strong presidency, and De Gaulle was elected the first president of the Fifth Republic in December 1958. He met with West Germany's Chancellor Adenauer in September 1958 and discovered they shared similar aspirations for Europe. In 1963 they signed the Franco-German Friendship Treaty that called for regular meetings between the heads of state and foreign ministers, consultation on major foreign policy decisions, greater military cooperation, and cultural exchanges between France and West Germany.

De Gaulle pursued a policy of greater French independence and military strength. He made France a nuclear power in 1960 declaring, "Hurrah for France! Since this morning she is stronger and prouder," and his administration oversaw the production of France's first hydrogen bomb in 1968. In addition to giving France greater influence and prestige De Gaulle's nuclear policy served as a hedge against possible U.S. refusal to defend France against a limited Soviet attack. De Gaulle opposed the 1962 Nassau Pact in which Great Britain agreed to buy missiles from the United States because it undermined his attempt to reduce U.S. influence in Europe. In early 1966 De Gaulle called for the dissolution of NATO whose domination by the United States he resented and distrusted. Shortly thereafter he announced France's intention to withdraw its forces from the integrated NATO military command and ordered all U.S. and NATO troops from French soil. On July 1 France withdrew all of its troops from NATO, and NATO headquarters moved to Brussels. Nonetheless, De Gaulle proclaimed his willingness to adhere to the NATO mutual defense pact in the event of an unprovoked attack against alliance members.

De Gaulle was reelected in 1966 but a massive student-worker uprising in 1968 undermined his ability to rule, and he resigned in 1969 after losing a national referendum. Georges Pompidou succeeded him. De Gaulle died the following year, on November 9, 1970.

Deng Xiaoping (1904–) Leader of the People's Republic of China since 1977. Born to a wealthy landowner in Szechwan province, Deng studied in Paris where he met Zhou En-lai and joined Zhou's Chinese Communist Party. After completing his studies in France, Deng attended Oriental University in Moscow before returning to China. He taught at the Chungshan Military Academy in 1926 and 1927 but fled after Chiang Kai-shek conducted a bloody purge of Communists from the Kuomintang Party alliance. He eventually joined Mao Zedong in the southern province of Kiangsi and headed the Red Army's Propaganda Bureau. He served as deputy commander of the 12th Division during the Communists' 6,000 mile Long March to northwestern China following their defeat by Chiang's Army and as a political commissar to the Red Army during its fight against Japan in World War II and then afterward in its battles against Chiang during the Chinese Civil War. After the Communists prevailed and Mao declared the People's Republic of China (PRC) in October 1949, Deng was appointed party leader of southwest China.

Throughout the early and mid–1950s Deng assumed a number of increasingly important posts. He allied with the moderate Liu Shaoqi in the political center between pro–Soviet Kao Kang and radical Mao. Their power increased in 1955 when Kao was purged, Liu was promoted to a leadership position second only to Mao, and Deng was appointed to the Politburo. As part of his effort to lessen Soviet influence in China, Deng reduced Soviet control of Chinese industry and railways. He contributed to the split between the PRC and the

USSR when he criticized Khrushchev's anti–Stalinism in 1957 and again in 1960 when he attacked Khrushchev's policy of peaceful coexistence with the West. As leader of a 1963 delegation charged with settling differences with the Soviets, Deng resisted efforts at conciliation and the negotiations failed.

After the failure of Mao's 1958 peasant-based economic Great Leap Forward, Liu and Deng became even more powerful. In November Mao stepped down as chairman of the Republic and Liu replaced him. But Mao remained party chairman. In 1965 Mao reasserted himself by launching his Cultural Revolution aimed at driving Liu and Deng from power and restoring his agrarian-based policies. In 1967 Mao succeeded in having Deng labeled a "capitalist roader" and removed him from all of his party and government positions. Deng remained inconspicuous until April 1973 when he reemerged in Chinese politics at a state dinner for Cambodia's Prince Sihanouk. A few months later he rejoined the party's Central Committee and in 1974 was renamed to the Politburo. In the final two years of Zhou En-lai's life Deng assumed many of the premier's duties, though he never held Zhou's title. Deng participated in most of Mao's meetings with foreign leaders and in 1975 traveled to France, where he became the highest-ranking Chinese official to visit a NATO country. After Zhou died in January 1976 Mao fell under the influence of his own wife, Jiang Qing, and the other members of the radical Gang of Four, and he purged Deng from power in April. The Gang briefly assumed power after Mao died in September. But in 1977 Hua Guofeng, Mao's chosen successor, was able to displace them and rehabilitate Deng.

Deng soon emerged as the dominant Chinese leader, even though Hua retained the title of prime minister. In January 1979, shortly after the United States officially recognized the PRC and severed diplomatic ties with Nationalist China, Deng visited President Carter in Washington, D.C. While there he forewarned U.S. officials of Chinese plans to attack Vietnam in reprisal for Vietnamese raids over the previous six months.

Deng preferred to exert power indirectly, and in 1980 he consolidated his leadership when Hua resigned in favor of Deng's protégé, Zhao Ziyang. In 1981 Hua surrendered the party chairmanship to another protégé, Hu Yaobang. As chairman of the party's Central Military Commission, Deng retained direct control of the armed forces; he also held the title of deputy prime minister. In September 1982 Deng further consolidated power when the Chinese Communist Party restructured the constitution and elected him chairman of its new Central Advisory Commission. Though he retained actual power, Deng retired from the party's Central Committee in 1987 and thereby forced other elderly leaders to do likewise. In this way he eliminated conservative opponents to his economic reforms. He also forced Hu to resign as general secretary after Hu accepted responsibility for policy errors in responding to massive student protests calling for greater democracy. The more conservative Zhao replaced him.

Deng used his power to introduce many reforms. He decentralized aspects of the economy, gave farmers greater individual control over their production and profits, and encouraged individual responsibility for decisionmaking. These changes led to greater agricultural output in the early 1980s. Deng also sanctioned material incentives for industrial achievement and formed cadres of well-trained technicians and managers to lead China's industrial development. He was in power in 1979 when the United States officially recognized the PRC and severed ties with Nationalist China, and he moved to further strengthen China's trade and cultural relations with the West and open Chinese enterprises to foreign investment. However, Deng did not match his economic liberalization with democratic reforms, and he retained a tight control on power via the Army.

The Tiananmen Square demonstrations occurred while Gorbachev was visiting Beijing in the spring of 1989. Inspired by the Soviet reformer, 3,000 students began a hunger strike on May 13 and demanded Deng's resignation. On May 20 the government imposed martial law. The internationally televised protest gained world attention and the support of some Army units, but on June 4 the Army crushed it. Public executions of protest leaders began the next week. Deng blamed Zhao and replaced him with a more conservative protégé, Jiang Zemin. Jiang later replaced Deng as chairman of the Central Military Commission, but Deng remained the most influential figure in the PRC. Though the Tiananmen Square massacre drew international protest, it did not create any long-term impairment of China's relations with the West. Despite stiff opposition in Congress, China retained most favored nation trade status with the United States during the early 1990s, and trade continued to expand between the countries.

Eden, Anthony (1897–1977)   British prime minister, 1955–57. The son of a baronet, Eden was schooled at Eton and Oxford University. During World War I he became the youngest brigade major in the British Army, and he first won election to the House of Commons in 1923. After joining the Foreign Office in 1931 he became the first British minister to meet Hitler in 1931 and in 1935 the first to meet Stalin. In December 1935 he was appointed foreign secretary. During World War II he served on Churchill's cabinet and played a large role in negotiating such wartime agreements as the Atlantic Charter, the Lend-Lease Program, and the formal alliances with the United States and Soviet Union. In 1941 he negotiated an agreement granting Soviet sovereignty over the Baltic States following the war. He also attended the Teheran, Cairo, Yalta and, Potsdam conferences, which helped shape the postwar political environment, and he represented Great Britain at the founding meeting of the United Nations in 1945.

Churchill and Eden left office in July 1945 after the Labour Party won the general election, and Eden became spokesman on foreign affairs for the opposition Conservative Party. Unlike Churchill, Eden believed relatively harmonious East-West relations could be achieved. However, after a 1947 coup placed

Communists in control of Hungary, Eden became more antagonistic toward the Soviets. He concurred with Labour's foreign policy of developing close relations with the United States and participated in Great Britain's bipartisan support for the Truman Doctrine, the Marshall Plan, the Berlin Airlift, NATO, and the Korean War.

When the Conservatives regained power in October 1951, Eden was named foreign secretary and deputy prime minister. As Churchill's heir apparent he tried to maintain Great Britain's status as one of the world's dominant superpowers and the leader of an extensive empire. This orientation created conflicts with U.S. Secretary of State Dulles, who disliked European colonialism and regarded the United States as the world's preeminent power. Nonetheless, when Iran's Prime Minister Mohammad Mossadegh nationalized the Anglo-Iranian Oil Company in 1951, Eden worked with U.S. representatives to arrange for his overthrow.

At the Berlin Conference of Soviet, British, French, and U.S. foreign ministers in early 1954 he presented the Eden Plan for German Reunification, which proposed free, democratic elections throughout all of Germany, after which a united national government would be formed. However, Soviet Foreign Minister Molotov rejected the proposal, reiterating Soviet calls for a unified provisional government prior to the elections, the exclusion of political parties "hostile to democracy and peace," and assurances that the reunified Germany would remain free from military alliances. The Eden Plan was the last significant attempt to reunite Germany prior to the end of the Cold War. On March 26 the Soviets recognized East Germany as a separate, sovereign state, and in 1955 they and the Western powers recognized West Germany.

Like Churchill, Eden supported European unity but wished to avoid formal British participation. Consequently, after France rejected the proposal for a European Defense Community (EDC) in 1954, Eden successfully proposed extending the 1948 Brussels Treaty to West Germany and Italy and — to allay French fears about German remilitarization — he agreed to permanently station 50,000 British troops in West Germany.

In July 1954 Eden helped negotiate the French withdrawal from Vietnam following their defeat by the Communist-led Vietminh at Dien Bien Phu. Prior to that battle the Eisenhower administration had sought to send British and U.S. troops to support the French and thereby prevent a Communist victory. However, Eden refused to participate because he believed military support would only complicate and prolong a messy, hopeless political situation. Subsequently, Eisenhower likewise declined to offer substantial military assistance, though the Americans refused to endorse the peace treaty Eden helped to negotiate between the French and the Vietminh. The U.S. and South Vietnamese refusal to agree to the treaty — which called for national elections in 1956 to unify the country — later became the basis for the U.S. involvement in the Vietnam War. The United States did agree to two other proposals by Eden. The first guaranteed the neutrality of Laos, Cambodia, and Vietnam and was signed by China, the USSR, and the Western allies. The second was to form a military alliance among the non–Communist nations in Southeast Asia. It resulted in the 1954 Treaty on Indochina and the formation of the Southeast Asia Treaty Organization (SEATO).

Eden became prime minister in April 1955 after Churchill retired. Feeling the need for a national mandate, he called for general elections the following month and the Conservatives won an even larger majority. In hopes of easing East–West tensions he hosted a visit by Soviet President Nikolai Bulganin and First Secretary Nikita Khrushchev in 1956. In November 1956 Eden supported a British-French-Israeli invasion of Egypt following Egypt's seizure of the Western-owned Suez Canal. However, Eisenhower opposed the venture and threatened to withdraw U.S. support for the British economy. Eden capitulated and the British and French withdrew their troops. A UN agreement called for Egypt to repay the investors who owned the canal, though it deprived Israel access to it. The Suez Crisis formed a serious breach in British-U.S. relations. Eden retired on January 9, 1957. He had been quite ill during the crisis and cited ill health as his reason, but the Suez fiasco doubtlessly contributed to his decision to step down. Harold Macmillan succeeded him.

Erhard, Ludwig (1897–1977)   Chancellor of West Germany, 1963–66. Born in Bavaria, Erhard was wounded while fighting for Germany during World War I. He studied economics at Frankfurt University and in 1928 joined the faculty of the Industrial Research Institute of Nuremberg. However, he lost his post when he refused to join the Nazi Party, and during World War II he worked outside of the government as a freelance economics consultant. He developed a plan for the postwar reconstruction of the country, and when officials in the U.S. occupying force read his proposal they made him an economic adviser. He then became director of economics and assumed responsibility for the currency reforms that established the economic foundation of West Germany. In 1949 Chancellor Konrad Adenauer appointed him the first economics minister in the newly formed Federal Republic of Germany (West Germany).

Erhard earned much of the credit for Germany's postwar economic revival. He rejected the welfare-state policies of Great Britain's Labour government, arguing that Germany's future lay "not in the leveling of scarcities but in the just sharing of a growing prosperity." He thus endorsed free trade and a market-driven economy, and in 1948 eliminated food rationing. Though prices initially rose sharply, soon production was able to fulfill the demand and the economy flourished.

In 1961 Erhard's conservative Christian Democratic Union (CDU) lost its absolute majority and formed a coalition government with the Free Democratic Party (FDP). Adenauer, then 85 years old, declined to step down, despite pressure to allow Erhard to replace him. Adenauer finally resigned as chancellor in

October 1963 in favor of Erhard, whom he considered a political lightweight. But Adenauer remained chairman of the CDU through 1966.

Adenauer, like French President Charles De Gaulle, had begun to doubt U.S. commitment to fighting off a Soviet nuclear attack against Western Europe and had moved to create a West German defense independent of the United States. As part of this strategy he signed a friendship treaty with De Gaulle shortly before resigning. Erhard, on the other hand, favored stronger relations with the United States and deeper reliance on U.S. forces based in Europe. This weakened West Germany's bond with France and led De Gaulle to establish a rapprochement with the USSR. Erhard's position was unpopular with members of his government, but he was able to assert the chancellor's constitutionally given responsibility for setting foreign policy. Success in the 1965 elections strengthened his position. Erhard continued to forge close ties with the United States, backing the Vietnam War and U.S. policy on China and forming a close working relationship with President Johnson. However, they clashed over proposals for NATO's Multinational Nuclear Force and payments to defray the expense of stationing U.S. troops to protect West Germany. Erhard also established full diplomatic relations with Israel. He resigned on November 30, 1966, after his coalition splintered following calls for tax increases to offset an anticipated 1967 budget deficit. He was succeeded by Social Democrat Willy Brandt. Erhard died on May 5, 1977, of heart failure.

Giscard d'Estaing, Valéry (1926–   )   French president, 1974–81. Born into a wealthy family of minor nobility, Giscard attended the prestigious École Nationale d'Administration and joined the ministry of finance after World War II. He won election to the National Assembly in 1956 as a member of the conservative National Center of Independents and Peasants and soon gained a reputation for being among the most intellectual members of the assembly. When De Gaulle became president of the newly formed Fifth Republic in 1959, he appointed Giscard secretary of state for finance. Giscard assumed responsibility for drawing up and implementing the national budget. In January 1962 he became finance minister and soon after formed his own pro–Gaullist Independent Republican Party. Giscard cut government spending, imposed wage and price controls, and increased taxes. He succeeded in balancing the budget for the first time in 36 years and lowering inflation to 2.5 percent. However, his austere measures were unpopular and De Gaulle dropped him from his cabinet in 1966. After De Gaulle resigned in 1969 Giscard returned as finance minister in Georges Pompidou's government, and in the following three years France's economy enjoyed an annual growth rate of 6 percent. However, the 1973 oil crisis and subsequent inflation ended the French "economic miracle."

After Pompidou's death in April 1974 Giscard narrowly defeated the Socialist candidate François Mitterrand. A few weeks later he met with West German Chancellor Helmut Schmidt and reaffirmed the French-German alliance and the European Community. Giscard also improved France's relations with the United States, Great Britain, and NATO. He met with President Ford in December 1974 and agreed to compensate the United States $100,000 for financial losses stemming from De Gaulle's unilateral decision to remove NATO military bases and troops from French soil. In return Ford agreed to coordinate more closely with the Western allies on economic and energy-related issues. Giscard got along well with Secretary of State Kissinger, whose pragmatic sense of realpolitik he admired. He had more difficulty with the Carter administration's emphasis on human rights that Giscard believed could undermine détente. In 1979 he hosted the Guadeloupe Summit where he and the heads of West Germany, Great Britain, and the United States endorsed the anticipated second round of Strategic Arms Limitation Talks (SALT II), and discussed how to address Soviet fears that closer Western ties with China would diminish the West's commitment to détente. Giscard's own relations with China included hosting visits by Foreign Minister Deng Xiaoping in 1975 and Prime Minister Hua Guofeng in 1979 and visiting China in October 1980.

He also sought closer ties to the Soviet Union and Eastern Europe, something that De Gaulle had earlier initiated. He met with Brezhnev in December 1974, after which the Soviet leader declared the meeting was the "perfect convergence of our points of view down to the last details." In June 1975 he went to Poland and signed agreements improving economic, cultural and political relations. He and Brezhnev met again in October 1975 but disagreed over the meaning of détente. Giscard wanted it to extend to ideological as well military rivalries but Brezhnev maintained that "International détente in no way puts an end to the struggle of ideas." Nonetheless, the two leaders met regularly and signed a ten-year economic agreement in 1979. However, they were unable to reach agreements for proceeding with arms reduction, as Giscard refused to join SALT III nuclear talks and Brezhnev refused to approve a general European conference to reduce conventional weapons. Giscard angered U.S., British, and West German leaders when he met with Brezhnev in May 1979, after giving the Western leaders only two-day's notice. Giscard warned Brezhnev that if the Soviets deployed their intermediate-range nuclear SS-20 missiles NATO would probably deploy U.S. missiles. However, Brezhnev ignored the warning and in December NATO agreed to deploy the Cruise and Pershing II missiles. Following the Soviet invasion of Afghanistan that December, Giscard issued a joint statement with Schmidt declaring that the act was "unacceptable and create[d] grave dangers for the stability of the region and for peace." They warned that the invasion made détente "more difficult and uncertain."

Nonetheless, Giscard tried to preserve détente, and in 1981 he won *Pravda's* endorsement as a "prudent and careful politician." Mitterrand, whom *Pravda* had criticized as vague and inconsistent, used the endorsement against Giscard in the 1981 election and defeated Giscard by a comfortable margin. In 1984 and 1988 Giscard won election to the National Assembly and in 1989 visited Moscow for talks with Gorbachev as a member of the Trilateral Commission. His Gaullist-UDF coalition won the largest number of seats in the 1989 election.

Gorbachev, Mikhail (1931–   )   Soviet general secretary, 1985–91. Born to a peasant family, Gorbachev studied law at Moscow State University. While in school he became an official in the Communist Youth League in Stavropol, and in April 1970 became the first secretary of the Stavropol Territory Party Committee. His powers were equivalent to those of a governor and he won recognition for increasing agricultural productivity in the region. This earned him the favor of the head of the secret police (KGB), Yuri Andropov, and Mikhail Suslov, a prominent member of Brezhnev's administration. They arranged for Gorbachev's election to the Supreme Soviet in 1970 and the Central Committee in 1971. Gorbachev joined the secretariat of the Central Committee in 1978 and assumed responsibility for Soviet agriculture. He tried to introduce limited reforms but poor weather and the party's strict adherence to collective farming led to a series of poor crops. Nonetheless, Gorbachev continued to ascend the power structure, becoming a nonvoting member of the Politburo in 1979 and a full member in 1980. When Andropov succeeded Brezhnev in November 1982, Gorbachev played a major role in implementing his political and economic reforms and his program to eliminate corruption. In May 1983 Gorbachev led a Soviet delegation to Canada. Though he appeared likely to succeed Andropov when Andropov died in February 1984, party conservatives selected Brezhnev's protégé Konstantin Chernenko instead. In turn Gorbachev received the prestigious and powerful post of party ideologue. As the elderly and infirm Chernenko sought to reverse Andropov's reforms, Gorbachev consolidated his power base. In December 1984 he met with British Prime Minister Thatcher, who declared of Chernenko's heir apparent, "I like Mr. Gorbachev. We can do business together." Chernenko died on March 10, 1985, and Gorbachev assumed power the next day. Thatcher's endorsement helped considerably to allay President Reagan's skepticism about the new Soviet leader.

Like his mentor Andropov, Gorbachev directed his greatest efforts toward restoring the economy. He introduced perestroika, a policy of reforms that pushed the economy in the direction of capitalism. These called for eliminating price controls on nonessential goods and services, establishing a currency convertible in the world market and selling off state properties and state-owned enterprises.

In his acceptance speech on May 11, 1985, Gorbachev offered to freeze nuclear weapons and stop deploying missiles. He reduced the military drain on the economy by withdrawing Soviet troops from East Germany, Hungary, Mongolia, and the Chinese border area. In December 1988 Gorbachev further announced his intentions to unilaterally downsize the Soviet Army by 500,000 soldiers and withdraw Soviet troops and tanks from Eastern Europe. And in 1989 he completed the Soviet troop withdrawal from Afghanistan.

Gorbachev also introduced a policy of political openness and reform known as glasnost, which provided greater personal liberties, religious freedom, and freedom of the press. He freed dissident Anatoly Shcharansky and pardoned Andrei Sakharov in 1986. He also permitted increased Jewish emigration in 1987 and eased emigration laws for all Soviets in 1991. In January 1988 he passed legislation restricting the practice of consigning political dissidents to psychiatric hospitals.

Gorbachev consolidated his power in September 1988 when opponents of his reforms were voted out of office and he was appointed president of the Soviet Union. In March 1989 he authorized elections to select representatives to the new Congress of People's Deputies. These were the first nationwide elections since 1917. The new Congress then reconfirmed him when it elected Gorbachev president in May. On September 24, 1990, the Soviet Parliament gave him near dictatorial powers so he could handle every aspect of reform. The economic reforms were not successful though, and they caused discontent among party hard-liners. Moreover, the political reforms were leading to independence movements within the Baltic States. In November and December 1990 Gorbachev tried to appease internal opposition by elevating hard-liners to important posts and giving greater authority to state security forces. In response, Gorbachev's long-time adviser Foreign Minister Eduard Shevardnadze resigned after warning of an impending dictatorship.

In March 1991 separatist leaders spearheaded a successful boycott of national unity elections in six regions, while the Ukraine voted for independence. On April 4 the Soviet Parliament learned that the nation faced imminent economic collapse because 15 Soviet republics had not made their payments to the central budget, and on April 9 Georgia proclaimed its independence from the Soviet Union. In June Gorbachev and regional leaders renamed the USSR the Union of Soviet Sovereign Republics, but this was not sufficient to appease the aspirations for independence.

Between 1985 and 1988 Gorbachev and Reagan met four times. The first was in Geneva in November 1985. They agreed in principle to a 50 percent reduction in nuclear weapons and suggested an interim agreement on intermediate-range nuclear forces (INF). They also issued a joint statement declaring that nuclear war could not be won and must never be fought, and vowed that neither side would try to achieve nuclear superiority. They disagreed over Reagan's Strategic Defense Initiative (SDI), which Gorbachev strongly opposed, but Reagan left the summit declaring that the meeting represented a fresh start in superpower relations. The leaders were unable to reach an arms agreement during an October 1986 mini-summit in Reykjavik, Iceland, because Reagan refused to abandon SDI. Nonetheless, they surprised the world and their own staffs by reaching several startling agreements in principle: the elimination of all intermediate-range missiles from Europe, the elimination of all ballistic missiles over a ten-year period, and the reduction of other nuclear delivery systems, including bombers and tactical weapons. Reagan later recalled, "For a day and a half, Gorbachev and I made progress on arms reduction that even now seems breathtaking." These agreements became the basis for the Strategic Arms Reduction Talks (START) that replaced SALT and eventually led to the 1991 START Treaty. Moreover, in February 1987 Gorbachev dropped his demand that the U.S. eliminate SDI, and in December he and Reagan signed the INF Treaty to eliminate all intermediate-range nuclear weapons in Europe. The INF Treaty was the first Cold War treaty to reduce the size of superpower nuclear arsenals. In May 1988 Reagan visited Moscow and endorsed Gorbachev's reforms.

Nonetheless, in 1988 Vice President Bush campaigned by taking a hard line against Gorbachev, declaring that "Gorbachev is not a freedom-loving friend of democracy, but an orthodox, committed Marxist," and later claiming, "the jury is still out on the Soviet experiment [with reforms]." Shortly after Bush's inauguration national security adviser Brent Scowcroft publicly accused Gorbachev's reforms of being "a peace offensive" designed to make "trouble within the Western alliance." Despite this initial skepticism, the quickly spreading collapse of Communism in Eastern Europe and the Soviet Union forced Bush to reevaluate and offer greater support to Gorbachev. During the summer of 1989 Gorbachev and Bush engaged in secret dialogues to arrange a summit meeting, and the Soviets assured the Americans that they would not intervene militarily to inhibit the political reforms taking place in Eastern Europe.

Soon after Gorbachev made this position public the rapid fall of Communism ensued. In June 1989 the Solidarity trade union won general elections in Poland, and its nominee, Tadeusz Mazowiecki, became the first non–Communist prime minister in the Eastern bloc. In September Hungary opened its borders with Austria, affording 60,000 East Germans access to the West, and in October the Hungarian Communist Party dissolved and renounced Marxist-Leninism in favor of a social democracy. On November 10 East Germany dismantled the Berlin Wall and opened access to West Germany. By the end of the year a new liberal cabinet was in place in East Germany, led by reformer Hans Modrow. Also in 1989 Bulgaria's Communist government was replaced; the Czechoslovakian Communist politburo resigned and was replaced by a non–Communist government; and Romanian Communist President Nicolae Ceauşescu was overthrown by the Army and executed on Christmas Day. The United States was on the verge of achieving one of its most central Cold War objectives: Germany whole and free in a Europe whole and free.

By 1990 Bush and Gorbachev had come to some basic agreements. Both wanted to preserve political stability during these times of immense change. Both accepted the internal changes within the Warsaw Pact countries but recognized the Soviets' need for security. They agreed that for the sake of stability the Warsaw Pact and NATO should be continued, if only temporarily, and both recognized the need for each side to retain its armies in Europe during the period of transition. In September 1990 Great Britain, France, the United States, and the Soviet Union signed a peace treaty with East and West Germany, officially concluding World War II and establishing the withdrawal of the Soviet Army from Eastern Europe. They thus realized the objectives of Eisenhower's Secretary of State John Foster Dulles, who had advocated a "liberation policy" some 35 years earlier. On October 3 East and West Germany united into a single Germany with its capital in Bonn, the capital site of the former West Germany. This fulfilled another major, long-standing U.S. Cold War objective. And on November 17–19 leaders of all the European states, the United States, Soviet Union, and Canada met in Paris where they signed a new charter regulating relations among all the participants and a nonaggression agreement between members of NATO and the Warsaw Pact. Bush then announced, "The Cold War is over."

In the aftermath of the Cold War Bush and Gorbachev worked together to promote world stability and begin to establish "a new world order." In July 1991 the Warsaw Pact dissolved, and shortly thereafter Bush traveled to Moscow where he and Gorbachev signed the Strategic Arms Reduction Treaty (START). This was the first Cold War treaty actually to reduce long-range nuclear stockpiles instead of merely limiting their growth. Afterward Bush flew to Kiev in support of Gorbachev's efforts to hold the Union together. He warned the citizens of the Ukraine that "Freedom is not the same as independence" and "Americans will not support those who seek independence to replace a far-off tyranny with a local despotism." However, Bush declined to grant Gorbachev the massive amounts of economic aid the Soviet leader insisted he needed to maintain stability and which he had counted on in return for concessions on arms control and for withdrawing Soviet troops from Afghanistan.

Politically weakened at home, Gorbachev was placed under house arrest during a coup by Communist hard-liners on August 19, 1991. Boris Yeltsin, the president of the Republic of Russia, led the populist opposition that toppled the coup on August 21 and restored Gorbachev to power. Thereafter, however, Yeltsin's power increased as Gorbachev's waned. On August 23 Yeltsin banned the Communist Party and seized its assets, and on August 24 he recognized the independence of the Baltic States. The Ukraine declared its independence on August 24 as well, and on August 25 Gorbachev resigned as head of the Soviet Communist Party. He resigned as Soviet president on Christmas Day, and on December 31, 1991, the Union of Soviet Socialist Republics was officially dissolved. Gorbachev, who won the 1990 Nobel Peace Prize, became more revered abroad than at home. In 1996 he ran for president of Russia but Yeltsin won the election.

Heath, Edward (1917–96)   British prime minister, 1970–74. Heath attended Oxford where he joined the Conservative Party and strongly opposed Neville Chamberlain's policy of appeasing Hitler. He served as an officer during World War II and was elected to Parliament in 1950. He was minister of labour under Harold Macmillan from October 1959 to July 1960. He then became lord privy seal and assumed responsibility for handling the negotiations leading to Britain's planned entry into the European Economic Community (EEC), more popularly known as the Common Market. However, France's President De Gaulle vetoed the agreement. In October Heath became president of the Board of Trade. He was elected leader of the opposition Conservative Party in July 1965 and became prime minister when the Conservatives regained power in June 1970.

To secure British acceptance into the EEC Heath sought a closer relationship with De Gaulle's successor, French President Georges Pompidou, and distanced himself from President Nixon. Subsequently, U.S.-British relations cooled but Great Britain gained admission to the Common Market in January 1972. Heath continued the Labour policy of withdrawing British troops from east of the Suez. He supported the Vietnam War and encouraged closer Western ties to the People's Republic of China (PRC). He was suspicious of the Soviet Union, and relations with that country chilled considerably after Great Britain expelled 105 Soviet citizens accused of spying.

Heath fell from power following the energy shortages in 1973, when his government instituted fuel rationing and a three-day work week. He failed to put together a governing coalition following elections in February 1974, and Labour's Harold Wilson succeeded him as prime minister after assembling a minority government. In 1975 the right-wing element of the Conservative Party removed Heath as party leader and replaced him with Margaret Thatcher. She excluded him from cabinet roles within her government when she became prime minister in 1979, and Heath became one of her major critics within the party.

Khrushchev, Nikita (1894–1971)   Soviet general secretary, 1953–64. Born into a working-class Russian family, Khrushchev received a rudimentary education before taking a job as a pipe fitter at age 15. His factory work kept him from military service during World War I and introduced him to labor organizations. He joined the Communist Party in 1918 and became a political commissar attached to the Red Army, which was then fighting the Polish and White Russian armies in Lithuania. He completed his education in 1922 and attended the 1925 Party Congress in which Joseph Stalin defeated his rival Leon Trotsky. Afterward, Khrushchev worked to become closer to the Stalin faction. In 1934 he was elected to the Communist Party's Central Committee, and the following year he became general secretary of the Moscow Communist Party. In that position he was the city's de facto mayor. Khrushchev fully supported Stalin and was one of only three provincial party secretaries to survive the purges and executions of the 1930s. Following the Soviet-German agreement to divide and absorb Poland in 1939, Khrushchev assumed responsibility for integrating the Soviet portion into the Union.

When Germany broke the pact and invaded the USSR in 1941, Khrushchev was appointed lieutenant general and made responsible for organizing the resistance in the Ukraine and moving heavy machinery to safe havens in the east. After the Red Army liberated the Ukraine in 1944 Khrushchev was charged with reestablishing the political and economic institutions in the region. He had his first major disagreement with Stalin in the famine year of 1946, when Khrushchev made restoring food supplies his first priority. Stalin cared more about revitalizing industrial production and Khrushchev was demoted in 1947. However, by 1949 he had regained Stalin's good graces and resumed his post as Moscow's general secretary.

A power struggle ensued following Stalin's death in March 1953. Initially, Georgi Malenkov appeared to dominate the field that included Lavrenty Beria, Vyacheslav Molotov, Nikolai Bulganin, Lazar Kaganovich, and Khrushchev. However, after Malenkov suddenly resigned as secretary of the Central Committee and Beria was liquidated, Khrushchev emerged as the general secretary, though Malenkov remained party chairman. At Khrushchev's recommendation Bulganin succeeded Malenkov as premier in 1955, and he remained loyal to Khrushchev until 1957.

In February 1956 Khrushchev gave an important speech at the Twentieth Party Congress in which he denounced Stalin's "personality cult." He accused Stalin of distorting political and economic objectives and murdering many innocent people. Though the speech was intended solely for party insiders, its content was leaked. The sentiments sparked waves of protest throughout Eastern Europe. In June riots erupted in Poland and Khrushchev was compelled to accept the return of reformer Władysław Gomułka in order to hold the Polish Communist government together and keep it within the Soviet camp. In October Hungarians briefly overthrew their Communist government, installed a neutral one instead, and appealed to the West for assistance. The assistance did not come, and on November 4 Khrushchev ordered Soviet tanks into Budapest to crush the Hungarian Revolution. Khrushchev and Malenkov struggled for power through 1957, when an attempt by Malenkov, Molotov, and Kaganovich to topple Khrushchev failed and the challengers fell from power. Bulganin also fell about that time.

Ironically, Khrushchev went on to adopt many of Malenkov's economic and foreign policies. He promoted greater production of consumer goods and became less confrontational in the Cold War. He also initiated the Soviet space program and a program to build intercontinental ballistic missiles (ICBMs). Both reached fruition in 1957 when the ICBMs were successfully tested and Sputnik I became the first human-made satellite to orbit the earth in outer space. Some analysts now believe that Khrushchev pursued a nuclear weapons program for the same reason as his U.S. counterpart, President Eisenhower: nuclear weapons were more cost effective. In the mid–1950s Khrushchev called for peaceful coexistence between the Communist and capitalist states, even while they continued to compete in the economic field. He met with Eisenhower in 1955 and in 1959 became the first Soviet leader to visit the United States.

However, that trip came as a break in the tensions stemming from the Second Berlin Crisis, which Khrushchev initiated in November 1958 when he demanded that the Western allies evacuate Berlin. Khrushchev's visits with Eisenhower failed to resolve their fundamental differences over Germany, and threats of war rose to new levels after the Soviets shot down an American U-2 spy plane over Soviet air space in May 1960. As a result Khrushchev scuttled a Paris summit conference scheduled for the following week. Some historians believe he used the incident to appease hard-line opponents who disapproved of additional accommodations with the West. That fall Khrushchev addressed the United Nations and vehemently opposed UN actions in the Congo. When he became enraged and pounded his shoe on the table to emphasize a point, he provided a strong visceral image of an out of control fury that seemed to underlie the Communist approach to the Cold War. Likewise his 1956 pledge that "We will bury you" was taken at face value as a clear expression of Soviet Cold War goals. Though Khrushchev later claimed he meant the pronouncement metaphorically, most Americans took him literally.

In June 1961 Khrushchev personally delivered an ultimatum to President Kennedy that the West must remove its troops from Berlin within six months or risk nuclear war. In response each side initiated military moves to intimidate the other. The crisis intensified throughout the summer and early fall. In early August Khrushchev ordered the construction of the Berlin Wall to stem the tide of East Berliners fleeing to West Berlin, and later that month the Soviets canceled a voluntary moratorium on nuclear testing and exploded a 60 megaton hydrogen bomb. The crisis came to a head in the fall when U.S. and Soviet tanks faced each other at Checkpoint Charlie, a Berlin Wall crossing point, but then Khrushchev allowed it to defuse. On October 17 Khrushchev declared that "the Western powers were showing some understanding of the situation and were inclined to seek a solution to the German problem and West Berlin." He subsequently eased off from his ultimatum for the Western evacuation of Berlin by December 31 without actually renouncing his demands (see chapter 11).

The Berlin Crisis humiliated Khrushchev, who received criticism from hardliners at home and abroad. That may have induced him to place offensive nuclear weapons in Cuba in 1962, only 150 miles from the U.S. mainland. However, U-2 reconnaissance flights detected the missiles in September, before most were fully operational. In the resulting Cuban Missile Crisis Khrushchev was again forced to back down after Kennedy instituted a naval blockade and demanded the missiles' removal. Khrushchev gained a U.S. pledge not to invade Cuba and an unwritten agreement to remove nuclear-armed missiles based in Turkey, but his failure to stand up to the Americans made him further vulnerable at home and contributed to his fall from power the following year. However, the flirtation with nuclear war invigorated negotiations for the Nuclear Test Ban Treaty that Khrushchev signed with Kennedy in 1963.

In addition to Cuba, Khrushchev spread Soviet influence to other under-developed nations throughout the world. He provided military, financial, and technical assistance to Egypt, Ghana, India, North Korea, Mongolia, and Afghanistan, and supported Communist liberation movements in the Congo, Vietnam, Laos, Malaysia, and the Philippines, amongst others. He initially pursued close ties with China, but Mao criticized him for revisionism when he proposed peaceful coexistence with the West and attacked him for backing down in Berlin and Cuba. In 1960 Khrushchev withdrew some 1,300 Soviet technicians from China.

A bloodless coup by his hard-line opponents toppled Khrushchev on October 15, 1964. He then retired quietly to his country house outside Moscow. In 1970 he published his memoirs, *Khrushchev Remembers*. He died of a heart attack on September 11, 1971.

Kiesinger, Kurt (1904–88)   Chancellor of West Germany, 1966–69. Kiesinger studied law at Berlin and Tübingen universities before entering private practice. He joined the Nazi Party in 1933 but in 1938 refused to join the newly formed National Socialist Lawyers' Guild and considered leaving the country. Instead, he monitored radio broadcasts for the foreign ministry. After the war his opponents pointed to his Nazi ties, but he had used his post to curtail anti–Semitic propaganda, and the Allies' de–Nazification program cleared him. Kiesinger helped found the conservative Christian Democratic Union (CDU) and established himself as an expert on foreign affairs. However, Chancellor Adenauer served as his own foreign minister, and Kiesinger was relegated to chairman of the Bundestag's foreign policy committee. When Adenauer appointed Heinrich von Brentano foreign minister in 1957 Kiesinger resigned in protest and returned to his native province of Baden-Württemberg where he served as prime minister. He did not participate significantly in the CDU-led coalition government headed by Ludwig Erhard from 1963 to 1966, but on November 26, 1966, he emerged as chancellor of a new coalition between the CDU and the Social Democratic Party (SPD) led by Willy Brandt.

Kiesinger took the first steps toward normalizing relations with Eastern Europe. Brandt later realized these more fully in his *Ostpolitik* (Eastern policy). In January 1967 West Germany established diplomatic relations with Romania; in August it concluded a trade agreement with Czechoslovakia; and in January 1968 it established formal ties with Yugoslavia. Kiesinger also sought closer relations with East Germany, including youth exchanges, free interchange of newspapers and literature, increased trade and technical cooperation, and other proposals that would improve life for East Germans without undermining West German sovereignty. However, East Germany rejected his proposals, demanding that West Germany first recognize it, establish full diplomatic ties, and allow West Berlin to be incorporated into East Germany. Despite his inability to improve relations with East Germany, Kiesinger declared in May 1968, "We have begun to build our bridges in the East. The opening of relations with Romania and Yugoslavia is a beginning. We are prepared to create a friendlier political climate in the whole of Europe."

However, the Warsaw Pact's invasion of Czechoslovakia in August 1968 abruptly thwarted Kiesinger's efforts to achieve an East-West détente. He attacked the military action as a gross violation of human rights and especially denounced East Germany for its role in the invasion. In September 1969 a new coalition led by Brandt but excluding the CDU removed the CDU from power for the first time since West Germany was founded in 1949. Out of power, Kiesinger opposed Brandt's more aggressive Ostpolitik, which he felt offered the Soviets too much too soon. He particularly attacked Brandt's confusing notion of forming two states within a unified German nation. Kiesinger stepped down as leader of the CDU in October 1971. He died on March 9, 1988.

Kohl, Helmut (1930–   )   Chancellor of West Germany, 1982–90; and the first chancellor of reunited Germany, 1990–   . As a teenager Kohl joined the conservative Christian Democratic Union (CDU) and remained active within the party throughout the 1950s and 1960s. In 1973 he became chairman of the CDU's national executive, a post that placed him in line for chancellor when the party regained power in 1982.

Like his predecessors from both parties, Kohl pursued close relations with France. He increased French-German defensive cooperation in order to alleviate West Germany's heavy reliance on the United States, and in 1988 Kohl and France's President Mitterrand established a joint defense council that placed a joint defense brigade in West Germany. He also supported U.S. efforts to deploy intermediate-range, nuclear-armed Cruise and Pershing II missiles in West Germany despite the strong protests of antinuclear critics who feared that Germany would become the battleground in any NATO–Warsaw Pact nuclear exchange. Kohl supported President Reagan's hard line against the Soviet Union and his plans for a Strategic Defensive Initiative (SDI), though in deference to opposition within his coalition Kohl rejected formal German participation or funding of the effort. When Reagan and Soviet Premier Gorbachev proposed eliminating intermediary nuclear weapons in Europe, Kohl became concerned and supported the 1987 INF treaty only reluctantly.

On the other hand, Kohl opposed later efforts by President Bush and British Prime Minister Thatcher to upgrade NATO's German-based short-range nuclear weapons. He argued that these weapons would increase the probability of a nuclear war being fought on German soil, while simultaneously decreasing the likelihood that the Western allies would come to West Germany's aid. He further feared that the upgrades would harm his party's chances in the coming elections. Bush resolved the issue with a compromise linking the weapons modernization to reductions in conventional weapons.

Kohl followed up slowly on his Social Democrat predecessors' initiatives to normalize relations with East Germany and the Soviet Union. He remained suspicious of Gorbachev, comparing him in a *Newsweek* interview to the Nazi chief of propaganda Joseph Goebbels. However, after the fall of East Germany's Communist government in 1989, Kohl helped bring about the reunification of Germany. In September 1990 he signed the peace treaty with Great Britain, France, the United States, and the USSR officially concluding World War II and establishing the withdrawal of the Soviet Army from Eastern Europe. After obtaining Gorbachev's agreement to allow a unified Germany to remain in NATO, Kohl first unified East and West Germany economically, and then followed with political unification in October 1990. In November he participated in the official end of the Cold War when Germany signed the Treaty on Conventional Armed Forces in Europe. The people of reunited Germany then elected him their first chancellor on December 2, 1990. He was reelected in 1994.

Liu Shaoqi (1892–1969)   Chairman of the People's Republic of China, 1959–68. Born in Hunan province to a wealthy peasant family, Liu joined the Socialist Youth League in 1920. He then studied in Moscow where he joined the fledgling Chinese Communist Party. Liu returned to China to work with Mao Zedong organizing unions in Hunan and eventually followed Mao to Kiangsi province after Chiang Kai-shek purged the Communists from the Kuomintang alliance in 1927. When Mao and his troops made the Long March to Shenshi in 1934 Liu went to Beijing to organize antigovernment activity and played a major role in the outbreak of student violence in December 1935. He rejoined Mao in 1939 and was named to the important post of party ideologue. In 1943 he became secretary of the Central Secretariat, and by the end of World War II he was the ranking party leader behind Mao. When Mao declared the People's Republic of China (PRC) in 1949 Liu was named vice chairman.

Liu's economic philosophy lay between Mao's peasant-based agrarian beliefs and Kao Kang's pro–Soviet, industrial-based orientation. He reduced Soviet control over Chinese industry and railways but the Soviets retained domination over the military and foreign policy, while Mao controlled agriculture. Liu's position strengthened in 1955 when Deng Xiaoping joined the Politburo, Kao was purged, and Liu was promoted to the number two position in government. Liu oversaw most of the government administration, but Mao remained in charge of party doctrine and policy.

In 1958 Mao launched his program of economic reforms called the Great Leap Forward, but these failed and he stepped down at the end of the year as chairman of the PRC, though he retained his chairmanship of the party. Liu replaced him as head of state and instituted a number of economic reforms, deviating from Mao's hard ideological line and introducing more consumer goods into the economy. He also became more actively involved in foreign policy and forged closer links to Ghana, North Vietnam, Cambodia, Pakistan, North Korea, Cuba, and Indonesia. Deng took a more active role in engineering the Chinese split with the Soviet Union in the late 1950s, but it is unlikely he would have done so without Liu's support. In the early 1960s Mao regained power by forging an alliance with Defense Minister Lin Biao, and in 1965 he inaugurated his Cultural Revolution, which was aimed at displacing Liu and Deng. By December 1966 Liu ceased to appear in public. He was purged from the party in October 1968 and Lin succeeded him as Mao's designated heir in April 1969. Liu died on November 12, 1969, though his death was not reported in the West until 1974.

Macmillan, Harold (1894–1986)   British prime minister, 1957–63. The son of an American woman and the head of the Macmillan Publishing Company, Macmillan was educated at Eton and Oxford and was badly wounded in World War I. He first entered the House of Commons in 1924 as a Conservative. His strong opposition to Hitler kept him out of the government until Winston Churchill became prime minister in 1940. As British minister in Algiers he developed good working relationships with Dwight Eisenhower and Charles De Gaulle, both of whom he later worked with as prime minister. In 1951 he became minister of housing and in October 1954 Churchill appointed him secretary of defense. After Churchill retired in April 1955 Macmillan became foreign secretary in the government of Anthony Eden. However, because Eden, a former foreign minister, insisted on overseeing foreign affairs himself, Macmillan soon transferred to the post of chancellor of the exchequer. In that capacity he informed the government during the 1956 Suez Crisis that Great Britain could not afford to wage war with Egypt if the United States followed through on its threat to withdraw economic support. When Eden retired due to ill health immediately following the crisis, Macmillan became prime minister.

One of his first tasks was to repair relations with the United States that the Suez Crisis had weakened. He met with Eisenhower in March 1957 and established a precedent by agreeing to purchase U.S. missile systems. In October they met again to discuss sharing scientific resources following the Soviet launching of Sputnik. They also met to discuss a nuclear test ban treaty in 1958 and 1960 and to discuss the Berlin situation in December 1959. Though strongly anti–Communist, Macmillan resisted the inflexible, ideological approach of Eisenhower's Secretary of State Dulles and sought instead to establish a working relationship with the Soviets. His negotiations with Khrushchev helped arrange the May 1960 Paris summit, where leaders of the four major powers were to try and resolve the growing Berlin crisis. However, Khrushchev scuttled the conference following the downing of a U.S. spy plane in Soviet air space a few days earlier.

After John Kennedy became president in 1961, he and Macmillan formed a close relationship. According to Arthur Schlesinger, Kennedy liked Macmillan's relaxed, "patrician approach to politics" and Macmillan admired Kennedy's "courage, his ability to see events unfolding against the vast canvas of history ... his unfailing sense of the ridiculous." However, Kennedy's initial failure to advise Macmillan of his decision to blockade Cuba during the 1962 Missile

Crisis undermined Macmillan's power at home. To reassert Macmillan's prestige Kennedy allowed British sources to release the first public photographs of the Soviet missile sites. Kennedy also embarrassed Macmillan when the United States unilaterally abandoned the Skybolt missile project, since Great Britain had planned to use the Skybolt to replace its own unsatisfactory Blue Streak program. In December 1962, however, Kennedy and Macmillan signed the Nassau Agreement in which the United States agreed to sell Polaris missiles to Great Britain. The agreement both increased British reliance on U.S. nuclear technology and angered French President De Gaulle, who was then trying to limit U.S. influence in Europe. In 1963 Macmillan signed the Nuclear Test Ban Treaty forbidding above-ground testing of nuclear weapons.

In addition to his interactions with the other major powers, Macmillan also oversaw Great Britain's relatively smooth process of decolonization. He recognized that many of the independence movements were becoming attracted to the ideas and support offered by Communists. Therefore, he asserted in his "winds of change" speech of February 1960 that in order not to "imperil the precarious balance of East and West" Britain must support the progressive, nationalist forces in Africa. He was reelected in 1960 but resigned in October 1963 — ostensibly for health reasons — following a sex/spy scandal within his cabinet. Toward the end of his life he denounced Prime Minister Thatcher's economic policies.

Mao Zedong (also spelled Mao Tse-tung; 1893–1976)   Chairman of the Communist Party of the People's Republic of China, 1949–76. Born to a wealthy peasant family in Hunan province, Mao participated in the revolution against the Manchu Dynasty when he was 18 years old. He helped found the Chinese Communist Party in 1922 and in 1925 developed his theory of Communist revolution based on the peasantry instead of industrial laborers, as Marx and Lenin had envisioned. In 1923 the Communists allied with Dr. Sun Yat-sen to form the Kuomintang alliance, but the partnership fell apart when Sun died in 1925 and Chiang Kai-shek succeeded him. After Chiang's 1927 bloody purge of the Communist Party, Mao and the few remaining Communists fled to the southern province of Kiangsi and began to implement his revolutionary theories. Mao and his chief military assistant, Chu Teh, developed a form of guerrilla warfare that they conducted from bases in the countryside. After a series of successes Mao declared a Chinese Soviet Republic in Kiangsi in 1931, with himself as first chairman. However, Chiang's Army eventually surrounded the Communists and almost eradicated them. Mao's troops broke through the enemy lines on October 16, 1943, and began their famous Long March, a 6,000-mile trek to the northwestern province of Shenshi. The march took a full year to complete, but at its end Mao united with a substantial peasant Army.

In 1936 he and friendly northern warlords kidnapped Chiang and compelled him to join the United Front — Communists and Kuomintang — against

Japan, a country that was then invading China. The struggle against Japan enabled Mao to strengthen and build his own Army, and by the end of World War II his Army of 700,000 soldiers controlled an area inhabited by almost 85 million people. Mao introduced agrarian reform into the regions he controlled, and U.S. observers during the war compared his administration favorably to Chiang's more corrupt and inefficient government.

Following the war the Chinese Civil War broke out as Chiang and Mao turned on each other. In late 1945 George Marshall came as President Truman's emissary to try to end the fighting. Marshall sought to form a coalition government in which all parties would be represented but the Nationalists would dominate. Despite deep, mutual mistrust between the Communists and Nationalists and seemingly irreconcilable demands by each side, they agreed to a truce and the creation of a National Assembly to draft a unifying national constitution. Both sides further agreed to integrate their forces into a single national Army. However, in March 1946, while Marshall was in Washington, D.C., to consult with Truman, the fragile truce fell apart. Conservative elements among the Nationalists refused to accept a coalition with Communists. Moreover, Nationalist forces attempted to stop Mao's armies from occupying areas abandoned when the Soviets vacated Manchuria. Unable to negotiate a new truce and fearful that Chiang had overextended his supply lines, Marshall declared an impasse and asked to be recalled. The mission officially ended in January 1947. In his reports Marshall cautioned that the United States would "virtually [have] to take over the Chinese government" in order to preserve Chiang's rule. "It would involve a continuing [U.S.] commitment from which it would practically be impossible to withdraw." Truman heeded the warning and gradually reduced aid to Chiang, leaving only token amounts to appease the China lobby and other right-wing critics.

By 1947 Mao was able to seize the offensive, despite Chiang's larger armies, and by 1949 he maintained full control of the Chinese mainland. On October 1, 1949, he proclaimed the People's Republic of China. Meanwhile, Chiang fled to the offshore island of Taiwan (then Formosa) where he established the Republic of China. The United States recognized Chiang's government and continued to provide at least minimal forms of military assistance. Fearful of U.S. intervention, Mao signed a mutual defense pact with Stalin in 1949 that granted the Chinese financial and military aid as well. Nonetheless, Mao's concern over a possible U.S.-led invasion greatly influenced his decision to enter the Korean War when UN forces closed in on the Chinese border. China remained active in the war until the fighting ceased in 1953. Following China's entry into the war, the United States increased its aid to Chiang. On December 1, 1954, the United States and Nationalist Chinese signed a mutual security pact, and throughout the 1950s President Eisenhower threatened retaliation if Mao's armies attacked Chiang's Nationalists on Taiwan or the nearby islands of Quemoy and Matsu. However, the most intense period of confrontation with the United States occurred between 1958 and 1962, when Mao was largely out of power.

After forging the alliance with the Soviet Union, Mao stepped down from the daily administration of the republic, though he retained the role of chairman. However, as Soviet technical and military advisers soon became more influential, Mao's program for a peasant-based revolution became subordinated. In 1955 he tried to reassert his authority, but on December 17, 1958, Mao was forced to step down as head of the government after his economic policies in The Great Leap Forward failed. Liu Shaoqi replaced him as chairman of the People's Republic, though Mao remained party chairman. During the late 1950s and early 1960s Mao was unable to successfully challenge the reforms sponsored by Liu and Deng Xiaoping. But in the early 1960s an alliance with Defense Minister Lin Biao enabled Mao to reassert himself as head of the Socialist Campaign Movement to lead the country back to what Mao considered the true path of Communism. Between 1962 and 1964 a major rift between China and USSR developed as Mao attacked Khrushchev's reforms and accused him of "revisionism." Mao also chided the Soviet leader for backing down in Berlin and Cuba. During this period Mao's stance toward the West was bellicose. Thus as U.S.-Soviet tensions eased somewhat following the 1962 Cuban Missile Crisis, China emerged as the most hostile Communist power in the 1960s. The potential of China's threat increased in 1964 when it exploded its first atomic bomb.

By 1964 Mao was able to purge the Army of some of Liu and Deng's supporters, and on September 2, 1965, Mao declared his Cultural Revolution to return Chinese Communism back to its peasant foundations. Universities were closed and students were organized into units of Red Guards, each given copies of *The Quotations of Chairman Mao*, also known as the Little Red Book. They were then sent into the countryside to work or organize peasant rebellions against the reformers. Many of the intelligentsia, teachers, and skilled laborers were purged or killed and a near civil war ensued. Industrial production also suffered, dropping by 12 percent between 1966 and 1968. But by 1969 Mao had consolidated his power and established a personality cult in the process. In 1970 he became supreme commander of the Army and Navy and assumed full control by 1971.

During the Cultural Revolution the split between China and the Soviet Union widened, and Mao began to solicit closer ties with the United States. His efforts culminated in February 1972 when he and Prime Minister Zhou En-lai hosted President Nixon in Beijing. The visit brought improved political and trade relations, and eventual U.S. recognition of China in 1979. Mao was 78 when he met Nixon and his health was beginning to fail. Thereafter, he was primarily influenced by Zhou, a moderate, and his own radical wife, Jiang Qing. After Zhou died in January 1976 Jiang and her cohorts known as the Gang of Four dominated Mao's thinking and induced him to continue aspects of the Cultural Revolution. In April Mao purged Deng at their behest. When Mao died on September 9, 1979, the Gang of Four briefly took control, but shortly afterward Deng reemerged as China's most powerful leader. The Gang of Four was tried and convicted of treason in 1980, and Mao was officially discredited for mistakes in leadership in 1981.

Mendès-France, Pierre (1907–82)   Premier of France, 1954–55. Born in Paris, he studied law and became a barrister. He joined the Radical-Socialist Party in the 1930s and served in the Air Force during World War II. The Vichy government imprisoned him, but Mendès-France escaped in 1941 and joined the London-based Free French Air Force in 1942. From 1943 he served in General Charles De Gaulle's Free French government as commissioner for finance and minister of national economy, but he resigned in 1945 when his austere policies were not adopted. During the 1940s and early 1950s Mendès-France sharply criticized the successive French governments of the Fourth Republic for their economic policies, their handling of the situation in Algeria, and their conduct of the war in Indochina (Vietnam, Laos, and Cambodia). Following the French defeat at Dien Bien Phu in 1954, Mendès-France was made prime minister. He oversaw the French withdrawal from Southeast Asia and approved the Geneva accords that ended the fighting and partitioned Vietnam. However, opposition to his drastic economic policies and his handling of the situation in North Africa caused his government to fall in 1955. Mendès-France became deputy premier in Guy Mollet's government for four months in early 1956, but resigned when Mollet refused to adopt a more liberal policy toward Algeria. He failed to be reelected to the National Assembly in 1958. In 1959 he left the Radical Party to join the Unified Socialist Party and supported Socialist candidate Pierre Mitterrand in his failed 1965 election bid against De Gaulle. Mendès-France was reelected to the Assembly in 1967 but then voted out of office in De Gaulle's 1968 victory.

Mitterrand, François (1916–96)   President of France, 1981–95. After Mitterrand received an advanced law degree from the University of Paris he enlisted in the Army and was wounded and captured by the Germans in 1940. He escaped in 1941 and returned to France, where he worked for the Vichy government. At the same time he was secretly a member of the French Resistance. He was elected to the National Assembly in 1946 and held a number of cabinet posts during the Fourth Republic, which dissolved in 1958. Among his positions were minister for overseas territories, minister for state justice, and minister of the interior. He opposed De Gaulle's new constitution for the Fifth Republic and was voted from the Assembly in 1958. He returned in 1962 as a strong voice for the left. In 1965 he embarrassed De Gaulle by forcing a runoff election, though De Gaulle won handily. Mitterrand joined the French Socialist Party in 1971 and negotiated with the Communist Party to form the Common Program in 1972. The Common Program committed both parties to improving social welfare, reducing presidential powers, nationalizing certain industries, maintaining membership in NATO and the European Economic Community (EEC) and seeking higher wages and pensions. The French voters received it warmly, electing more Socialists to the Assembly in March 1973 and then giving Mitterrand a plurality lead in the first round of presidential elections that May. However, Valéry Giscard d'Estaing narrowly defeated him in the runoff. During Giscard's term Mitterrand continued to lead the French left wing.

In May 1981 he defeated Giscard and became France's first Socialist president since De Gaulle came to power in 1958. Moreover, Communists were included in the French government for the first time since World War II. However, they received only minor appointments and were not involved in defense, security, or foreign policy. Feeling isolated and ineffectual, the Communists left Mitterrand's coalition in July 1984.

It was ironic that the right-wing Giscard won praise from the Soviet Union, where *Pravda* called him a "prudent and careful politician," while the Socialist Mitterrand, whom *Pravda* had criticized as vague and inconsistent, supported NATO and the U.S. military buildup during Reagan's first term. Mitterrand first revealed his sympathies at the European summit in July 1981 when he surprised the other heads of government by warning against "the dangers of galloping neutralism" in Western Europe. He also supported NATO's decision to deploy nuclear-armed U.S. Cruise and Pershing II missiles in Europe to offset the Soviet SS-20 intermediate-range nuclear missiles. He declined to give an official response to Reagan's 1983 proposal for a Strategic Defense Initiative (SDI) but allowed French companies to participate in and profit from the research and development efforts. He thus supported French industry, while retaining some political distance from the controversial proposal. At the same time Mitterrand departed from the traditional Socialist position by promoting the further development of France's own nuclear arsenal. He believed that a nuclear deterrent was less expensive than conventional means, and, like the Gaullists, retained serious doubts about the depth of the U.S. commitment to aid Europe in an actual nuclear war. Therefore, Mitterrand maintained that France needed its own nuclear force since it could not depend on the United States to risk an all-out nuclear war on its behalf. For the same reason he sought to strengthen defensive alliances within Western Europe that excluded the United States. In 1984 he thus revived the Western European Union among Great Britain, France, Italy, West Germany, Belgium, Holland, and Luxembourg, and in 1985 he inaugurated the European Research Agency to coordinate Western Europe's development of high technology.

In October Mitterrand met with Reagan to celebrate the bicentennial anniversary of the end of the Revolutionary War. They found considerable common ground and formed a strong working relationship; however, they disagreed over relations toward Central America and other underdeveloped regions of the world. Mitterrand argued that Reagan's policy of supporting a right-wing dictatorship against populist, left-wing guerrillas in El Salvador and right-wing guerrillas against a populist, leftist government in Nicaragua ultimately served

Soviet interests. "The reality is that El Salvador lives under an unbearable, dictatorial oligarchy.... We believe that the prolongation of those outdated systems in Latin America is a danger for the whole world. Now we speak of Communism? This is how it is introduced!" He believed it was important to develop closer ties with the leftist Nicaraguan Sandinista government, and in May 1985 he hosted Sandinista leader Daniel Ortega, promising to expand the Nicarguan trading relationship with France.

Like his Gaullist predecessors, Mitterrand promoted a strong French-German alliance. Meetings held with West German Chancellor Helmut Schmidt led to a 1986 treaty with Schmidt's successor, Helmut Kohl, to increase military cooperation between the countries. Shortly thereafter Mitterrand promised to consult West Germany before employing prestrategic weapons on its territory. In January 1988 Mitterrand and Kohl celebrated the twenty-fifth anniversary of the Franco-German Friendship Treaty by establishing a defense council to better coordinate military strategy, troop deployment, and weapons acquisition. They also established a joint military brigade to be stationed in West Germany and formed a joint economic council to strengthen economic ties and coordinate financial policies. However, fearful of the military, economic, and political developments that might come from a unified Germany, Mitterrand did not warmly receive the German reunification of 1990.

Mitterrand also established a good relationship with British Prime Minister Thatcher, though he criticized her tepid support of the European Economic Community (EEC). The two governments agreed to establish joint research and production programs for both nuclear and conventional arms. During the U.S.-Soviet negotiations for the Intermediate-Range Nuclear Forces Treaty (INF), Mitterrand and Thatcher both strongly rejected Soviet attempts to include their missiles. The Soviets argued that their intermediate-range missiles were necessary to counter those held by France and Great Britain and that a reduction in Soviet missiles would have to be matched by reductions in the French and British nuclear arsenals. But Mitterrand and Thatcher would not accept this argument.

Mitterrand took a hard line against the Soviet Union. He denounced its imposition of martial law in Poland in December 1981 and canceled Foreign Minister Gromyko's visit to Paris following the Soviet downing of a Korean passenger plane in September, 1983. Mitterrand also cracked down on Soviet spying in France, something that De Gaulle and his successors had tolerated in order to maintain a special relationship with the Soviet Union. Despite the less cordial political atmosphere, Mitterrand sought to retain French-Soviet trade relations. In early 1982 he signed a contract to purchase natural gas for 25 years, beginning in 1984. Then Mitterrand convinced the EEC to condemn a U.S. trade ban on companies involved with the gas pipeline to the Soviet Union. The Reagan administration dropped the ban a year later. Also in 1984 France agreed to a 5-year economic cooperation pact with the USSR. After Gorbachev came to power in 1985 Mitterrand became the first Western leader to host him. They met again in 1989 when they signed 21 agreements on issues ranging from military exchanges, to French training programs for Soviet managers, to a cease-fire in Lebanon. Mitterrand also established closer ties with Poland. In December 1985 he became the first Western leader to host General Jaruzelski following the imposition of martial law. And in June 1989 Mitterrand traveled to Poland, where he agreed to restructure the Polish debt and provide an additional $100 million in bank loans. He also helped create the European Recovery Bank. Mitterrand declined to run for a third seven-year term in 1995 due to his declining health.

Pompidou, Georges (1911–74)   Premier of the Fifth French Republic, 1962–68; and president, 1969–74. The son of a teacher, Pompidou taught school in Marseilles and Paris before serving as a lieutenant in the French Army during World War II. He met General Charles De Gaulle in 1944 when De Gaulle was leading the Free French government in exile, and Pompidou proved adept at presenting the general's policies. He served on De Gaulle's personal staff from 1944 to 1946 and remained a part of his shadow cabinet after De Gaulle abruptly resigned in January 1946. In 1955 he left government for a position in the Rothschild Bank in Paris and in 1959 became the bank's director general. When De Gaulle returned to power during the Algerian crisis in 1958, Pompidou became his chief personal assistant, playing a large role in drafting the constitution for the Fifth Republic and planning for France's economic recovery. After De Gaulle was elected president of the Fifth Republic Pompidou returned to the private sector, though in 1961 he conducted secret negotiations with the Algerian Liberation Front. These talks eventually led to a cease-fire.

De Gaulle then appointed Pompidou premier in April 1962. He remained in office through July 1968. In May 1968 he negotiated with striking students and workers and concluded the Grenelle Agreement that ended the strikes, which had threatened to topple De Gaulle's government. In June he campaigned on a law and order platform and led the Gaullists to their strongest majority ever in the National Assembly, but in July De Gaulle dismissed him. His six years as premier was the longest term in office of any French premier in four generations. Pompidou remained active within the Gaullist Party, and when De Gaulle resigned in 1969 Pompidou was elected to replace him as president.

Pompidou continued De Gaulle's basic foreign policy. He retained economic ties with the Arab countries. However, he was less successful in forging a closer defensive alliance with West Germany. Like De Gaulle, he did little to build closer relations with the United States. Pompidou supported Great Britain's entry into the European Economic Community and gave France a stable government for five years and strengthened its economy. He died in office on April 2, 1974, and was succeeded by Valéry Giscard d'Estaing of the pro–Gaullist Independent Republican Party.

Schmidt, Helmut (1918–   )   Chancellor of West Germany, 1974–82. As a child growing up in Nazi Germany, Schmidt joined the Hitler Youth, and he served in the German Army before being captured during the Battle of the Bulge. While a prisoner of war he became converted to the cause of socialism and joined the Social Democratic Party (SPD) in 1946. He won election to the West German legislature in 1953 and initially opposed the placement of U.S. nuclear weapons in West Germany. Schmidt resigned his seat in 1961 because he felt he was unable to advance within the SPD. He returned to Hamburg where he became the city's minister for internal affairs. He sprang to national prominence in February 1962 when he coordinated relief efforts that saved thousands of lives following sudden floods. He returned to the legislature in 1964 and became the SPD's deputy chairman in 1966. When a coalition between the SPD and the Federal Democratic Party (FDP) replaced the Christian Democratic Union (CDU) — which had ruled West Germany since its inception — Willy Brandt became chancellor and Schmidt was named minister of defense. In that capacity he became Brandt's heir apparent.

As defense minister Schmidt reversed his earlier anti–American position and advocated full military cooperation with the United States. He also abandoned his earlier endorsement of a nuclear-free zone. In his 1967 book *The Balance of Power* he supported Brandt's détente with the East but added, "It would be foolish to strive for détente while neglecting to provide for the military protection of one's own existence." These positions pushed Schmidt from the SPD's left wing to its right. Schmidt served as minister of economics and finance between 1972 and 1974 and became chancellor in 1974 after Brandt resigned following a spy scandal.

As chancellor Schmidt strived to retain good relations with the United States. Though he got along well with President Ford and Henry Kissinger, his relationship with President Carter was strained. He disagreed with Carter's cancellation of the neutron bomb, a step that Schmidt felt showed Western weakness. He also argued that Carter's tougher stand on human rights would lead to greater Soviet intransigence. At the same time Schmidt encouraged closer ties with the USSR, and a West German–made pipeline connecting to Soviet natural gas was eventually constructed, despite U.S. opposition. Schmidt also supported the 1978 SALT II Treaty to limit the nuclear arms race. He continued Brandt's *Ostpolitik*, or Eastern Policy, which sought to normalize relations between West Germany and Eastern Europe. In 1975 he agreed to pay Poland 2.3 billion deutsche marks as World War II reparations, in return for permission for ethnic Germans residing in Poland to return to West Germany. Schmidt also promoted improved relations with East Germany, and in 1975 he and Erich Honecker became the first leaders of East and West Germany to meet. In the middle and late 1970s Schmidt oversaw transit agreements and continued a policy of compensating East Germany for the lost services of workers who emigrated to the West. In this way he enabled some 1,000 workers to emigrate in 1978 at a cost of about $50 million.

The Soviet invasion of Afghanistan in late 1979 and its 1980 crackdown on the Solidarity movement in Poland put the brakes on West Germany's détente with the USSR. Despite a strong nuclear freeze movement in Germany — where any tactical nuclear exchange between NATO and the Warsaw Pact was likely to occur — Schmidt supported the U.S. deployment in Germany of Cruise and Pershing II missiles. Between 1980 and 1982 Schmidt struggled to maintain support for this policy and it passed only narrowly. In response, the left wing of the SPD formed a new party, the Democratic Socialists, and in October 1982 the weakened Schmidt lost the chancellorship to a coalition led by Helmut Kohl. Out of power and alienated from his own party, Schmidt resigned from politics in 1986.

Stalin, Joseph (1879–1953)   Soviet general secretary, 1922–53. If any individual can be said to have started the Cold War it was Stalin, at least in the eyes of Americans. Born as Vissarionovich Dzhugashvili in Georgia to an impoverished peasant woman, Stalin participated in revolutionary activities prior to the 1917 Russian Revolution. He was in exile in Siberia when the czar was overthrown, but returned shortly afterward to become a member of the Communist Party's Central Committee and Politburo. After initially advocating cooperation between Bolsheviks and Mensheviks, he joined Lenin and Trotsky in the November 7 revolution. During the ensuing civil war he developed an antipathy for Great Britain, France, Japan, and the United States because those countries sent troops and supplies to aid the non–Communist White Russians. Stalin later maintained that this experience convinced him of the West's innate hostility toward the Soviet Union and greatly influenced his foreign policies throughout his life. During the civil war Stalin revealed his willingness to employ torture and brutal killings as methods for implementing policy. The war ended in 1921 and in 1922 Stalin became the party's general secretary. The post was not then a seat of power, but Stalin used the administrative position to seize control of the party and the nation. He opposed Lenin's new economic policies as too capitalistic and attacked Lenin's plan to create a confederacy of highly autonomous Soviet republics instead of a more centrally controlled union. Lenin's final political testament in 1924 called for Stalin's removal, but Stalin suppressed it. In the following five years all of Stalin's political enemies were either killed or exiled. After his greatest opponent, Leon Trotsky, fled to Mexico in 1929, Stalin assumed near dictatorial powers. Trotsky was assassinated in 1940.

In 1928 Stalin imposed a massive program of agricultural collectivization, forcing some 25 million farmers onto vast state-run farms. Those who refused were shot. Widespread terror and famine followed and some 10 million people are estimated to have died as a result. But Stalin succeeded in establishing a Communist plan for Soviet agriculture. He also increased industrial production, making the USSR the second most productive nation in the world by 1937. In 1934 Stalin began a massive purge of all his real and imagined political enemies.

Some 3 million people are estimated to have died during this period of political terror, which featured show trials, false confessions, and executions of ranking party leaders, local party committees, university professors, artists, writers, and doctors. Revelations of the 1930 purges and show trials led many U.S. Communists to leave the party.

During the 1930s Stalin opposed Hitler and tried unsuccessfully to ally with Great Britain and France against Nazi Germany. After their refusal he signed the 1939 nonaggression pact with Hitler that called for the division of Poland. This gave Hitler tacit approval to invade Poland, the act that began World War II. Stalin is believed to have agreed to the pact in order to buy time to build up Soviet defenses and consolidate his own domestic power base. After Germany launched a surprise invasion of the USSR in June 1941, British Prime Minister Winston Churchill immediately offered to ally with Stalin, but differences in positions about the postwar world delayed the formal treaty for another year. In December 1941 Stalin met with British Foreign Minister Eden to discuss plans for postwar Europe. Stalin demanded moving the Soviet-Polish border to the Curzon Line and realigning the Soviet borders with Romania and Finland. He then proposed compensating Poland and Romania with land seized from the defeated Germany and Hungary. He insisted that Poland and Romania should be recognized as existing within the Soviet sphere of influence, that the USSR should be allowed to station troops in Romania and Finland, and that Lithuania, Estonia, and Latvia should remain within the Soviet Union. Stalin had forcibly annexed the three Baltic States in 1940. In return Stalin offered to allow Great Britain to establish military bases in France, Norway, and Denmark after the war. Stalin's proposals contradicted the Atlantic Charter that Churchill and Roosevelt had already signed and that called for national self-determination through free elections in the postwar era. Furthermore, these proposals promised to cast Great Britain and the Soviet Union as land-grabbing expansionist powers who were using the war to expand their own territory and influence: not much different from Germany. The vague 20-year Treaty of Mutual Assistance that Churchill and Stalin signed in 1942 remained noncommittal on these issues, and Stalin later pointed to his 1941 meeting with Eden to justify his postwar actions.

During the war Stalin demanded that the United States and Great Britain should open a second front in Europe to alleviate the intense German effort against the Soviet Union. He feared that his Western allies were stalling until Germany and the USSR each became so weakened that neither could challenge Western supremacy. He later claimed that the especially heavy Soviet losses during the war entitled the USSR to a greater share of the spoils of war, but Churchill rebutted him by blaming his nonaggression pact for starting the war and for not entering the war prior to 1941 when Great Britain alone stood against Hitler. Roosevelt, Churchill, and Stalin first discussed the postwar world at the 1943 Teheran Conference, where Roosevelt's objections to Soviet plans for Poland were not as strong as Stalin had anticipated. Poland remained a central issue during the 1945 Yalta and Potsdam conferences as well. Churchill insisted that restoring Polish sovereignty had been the initial cause of the war and objected to Soviet desires to treat Poland as a satellite country. Stalin, on the other hand, maintained that Poland had been the traditional avenue for attacks on the Soviet Union from Western Europe and demanded control over it for security reasons. However, at Yalta he agreed to permit free elections in order to avoid a confrontation on the issue. The failure of those elections to take place created a major rift at the Potsdam Conference. But the Red Army occupied all of Eastern Europe and half of Germany, so Great Britain and the United States had little leverage. At Yalta Stalin also won Asian territories occupied by Japan as a concession for entering the war against Japan following the defeat of Germany. The USSR thus emerged from World War II as the dominant land power in Europe and Asia and one of the world's superpowers.

During the 1930s the Soviet Union harbored European Communists who had fled from Fascist domination in their own countries. Many of these were trained to seize political control when they returned to their homelands after the war. Poland's Bolesław Bierut was one such exile. In 1943 Stalin had recognized Bierut's Moscow-based Polish government in exile and rejected the London-based exile government recognized by the Western allies. When the Red Army conquered Poland, Stalin placed Bierut in power. Stalin likewise imposed other sympathetic governments in Romania, Hungary, Czechoslovakia, Albania, Bulgaria, East Germany, and North Korea.

The suppression of free elections and the forceful imposition of Communist rule in these nations convinced the Western allies that Stalin was bent on Soviet domination of Europe. This belief led directly to the Cold War. In the immediate aftermath of World War II much of the conflict centered on Germany. Stalin sought massive wartime reparations from Germany and desired to see it destroyed as an independent economic and political power. Having experienced Germany's resurrection into a dominant military power after its defeat in World War I, Stalin did not want to risk further attacks from a remilitarized Germany after World War II. He believed that Germany should either fall under Soviet domination or remain weakened and neutral. Great Britain and the United States, on the other hand, believed that Germany's revitalization was crucial to the economic recovery of postwar Europe, which in turn was necessary to keep Western Europe from falling under Soviet domination. By 1946 Communist parties were already exerting their strength in France, Italy, and Greece. Furthermore, the Western allies insisted on leaving West Berlin free of Soviet domination while Stalin wanted to have the British and U.S. sectors fall under Soviet control. On June 24, 1948, Stalin ordered a Soviet blockade of West Berlin, and the United States responded with the Berlin Airlift. By the spring of 1949 the round-the-clock flights were averaging 8,000 tons of fuel and food supplies daily. Unable to achieve his objective of gaining control over the city, Stalin lifted the blockade on May 12, 1949. Later that year Germany divided into two separate republics, East and West Germany, but the division was to be temporary until the superpowers could agree on the terms for German unification. However, they were unable to reach agreement and in 1954, the year after Stalin's death, the USSR recognized East Germany as a sovereign nation.

In September 1947 Stalin formed the Communist Information Bureau (Cominform), an alliance of the Communist parties in Eastern Europe. Cominform's publicly stated goal was to direct the activities of Communist parties throughout the world, and this contributed to the common impression in the West that the Communist threat took the form of a monolithic, united front personally directed by Stalin. In 1948, however, Stalin expelled Yugoslavia's Marshal Tito, who had removed Stalinists from the Yugoslavian Communist Party and purged them from the Army. In late 1949, following the Communist takeover of China, Stalin hosted Mao Zedong in Moscow and signed a mutual defense pact that gave Soviet military and financial assistance to the newly formed People's Republic of China (PRC).

In September 1949, a week before the final Communist victory in China, the Soviet Union exploded its first atomic bomb. These events and the start of the Korean War in June 1950 prompted fears in the West that Stalin was trying to siphon off Western forces to Asia in order to use the atomic bomb and the Red Army to conquer Western Europe. In response the West made a strong show of unity, forming the NATO alliance in 1949 and taking other steps to contain Communism. Subsequently, Stalin became fearful of both an attack by the West and an internal coup. According to his successor, Nikita Khrushchev, and his daughter Svetlana, from 1949 onward Stalin became increasingly paranoid and out of touch with reality. In January 1953 he arrested several doctors in the Kremlin whom he accused of having murdered several important Communist leaders. Stalin was apparently planning to use the "Doctors' Plot" to justify another massive purge when he died suddenly on March 5, 1953. The armistice ending the Korean War was signed the following month, and recently released documents from the former Soviet Union suggest that his death, more than Eisenhower's threat to use atomic weapons, made the truce possible.

Thatcher, Margaret (1925–   )   British prime minister, 1979–90. The daughter of working-class parents, Thatcher graduated from Oxford in 1947 with a major in chemistry. Running as a Conservative, she won election to the House of Commons in 1959. Prime Minister Heath appointed her secretary of state for education in 1970, and in Heath's Conservative government she gained a reputation for her strong opposition to socialism and détente and her support of a military buildup. After the Conservative Party was voted out of power in 1974 Thatcher led a right-wing challenge to the more moderate Heath, and in 1975 she was elected the party's leader. As opposition leader she attacked the Soviets in early 1976 for insincerity in their pursuit of détente, and she declared that Soviet intervention in Angola demonstrated that the USSR was "bent on world domination." She further warned against weakening NATO's defenses. Her attack drew an official protest from the Soviet ambassador, who complained of "extreme hostility and even open hostility." A Soviet newspaper called her "The Iron Lady," but the intended slur became a popular symbol for Thatcher's resolution to stand firm against Communism. Her party won the election in 1979, and she became prime minister.

For her first three years in office Thatcher largely entrusted foreign policy to Peter Carrington, who succeeded in resolving the long-standing Rhodesian crisis in 1979. However, after the Foreign Office failed to foresee the invasion of the Falkland Islands by Argentina, Carrington departed from the government and Thatcher took control of the 1982 Falklands War, which she prosecuted aggressively. Thatcher supported the 1979 NATO decision to place intermediate-range U.S. Cruise and Pershing II missiles in Europe and took a strong stand against antinuclear demonstrators who protested the deployment of 166 of those missiles in 1983. She also adopted a hard line in negotiations with the Soviets over an Intermediate-Range Nuclear Forces (INF) Treaty. The Soviets argued that their intermediate-range missiles were necessary to counter those held by France and Great Britain and that a reduction in Soviet missiles would have to be matched by reductions in the French and British nuclear arsenals, as well as in the arsenals supplied by the United States. But Thatcher and France's President Mitterrand rejected this argument. Despite stiff opposition from the Labour Party and the revived Campaign for Nuclear Disarmament, Thatcher also succeeded in replacing the Royal Navy's obsolete Polaris submarine fleet with Trident II submarines and nuclear missiles.

After Reagan was elected president in 1980 he and Thatcher developed a close working relationship. She was the first foreign leader he hosted after taking office and the last before he left. Thatcher supported Reagan's tough stand against the Soviet Union, his military buildup, and his aggressive policies in Nicaragua, Libya, and Chile. However, Reagan's invasion of Grenada in 1983 embarrassed Thatcher since the Caribbean island is part of the British Commonwealth. And she opposed U.S. economic sanctions against South Africa, though these were imposed by Congress over Reagan's objections.

Thatcher never established any rapport or trust with Brezhnev or his two immediate successors, Andropov and Chernenko. However, after she first met Gorbachev in December 1984, a few months before he became general secretary, she announced, "I like Mr. Gorbachev. We can do business together." Her endorsement played a significant role in winning Reagan's willingness to deal with Gorbachev in 1986. Nonetheless, Thatcher also urged caution in arms negotiations since she believed Gorbachev was vulnerable to being overthrown by Communist hard-liners who would be less accommodating. Thatcher, whose tough economic policies were blamed for high unemployment and class conflict, lost leadership of the Conservative Party in 1990 and consequently stepped down in November, after serving the longest term in office of any British prime minister during the Cold War.

Wilson, Harold (1916–95)   British prime minister, 1964–70, and 1974–76. The son of an industrial chemist, Wilson studied economics at Oxford and taught there following his graduation. While at Oxford he and Sir William Beveridge wrote the report that established the foundation for Great Britain's postwar welfare state. During World War II he served as director of economics and statistics at the ministry of fuel and power and wrote a book that became the intellectual basis for the Labour Party's nationalization of the coal industry after the war. Wilson won election to the House of Commons in 1945 as a Labour candidate and in 1947 was named president of the Board of Trade, a cabinet post. However, he resigned in protest in April 1951, when the government imposed a surcharge on national health services to finance the Korean War.

With the support of the Campaign for Nuclear Disarmament (CND), which advocated Great Britain's unilateral nuclear disarmament, Wilson became prime minister in October 1964. Prior to his election he informed President Kennedy that if he was elected he would "de-negotiate" the Nassau Pact in which Great Britain had agreed to purchase missile systems from the United States. At that time he declared that "if being a first-rate military power means being a nuclear power" he would not oppose Britain's being a second-rate power. However, once he took office Wilson's position softened. He agreed to retain Britain's U.S.-supplied Polaris missiles and its nuclear-armed Vulcan bombers, though he proposed integrating them into an Atlantic Nuclear Force (ANF) in which the NATO allies would exercise a greater voice than the United States in determining how the nuclear weapons would be deployed and used. Though the ANF proposal was unsuccessful, Wilson allowed the Polaris missiles to become operational, thereby alienating him from the Labour Party's left wing and the country's antinuclear forces. Afterward, the antinuclear movement lost strength until 1980 when Margaret Thatcher agreed to deploy U.S. intermediate-range Cruise and Pershing II missiles.

Wilson wavered in his support of the Vietnam War. In February 1967 he attempted unsuccessfully to negotiate a settlement in conjunction with the Soviets. President Johnson objected to Wilson's decision to withdraw British troops east of the Suez Canal in 1967, since he believed this would create a power vacuum that would invite Communist activity. But Wilson felt that the British economy required the move. He tried to placate Johnson by allowing the United States to establish a military base on the strategic, British-held island of Diego Garcia in the Indian Ocean.

Wilson also tried to develop a special relationship with the Soviets. In February 1966 he made his first of several visits to Moscow, and he was host to Alexei Kosygin in February 1967. These moves anticipated the U.S.-Soviet détente of the early 1970s by promoting trade between East and West. British-Soviet trade nearly doubled between 1964 and 1968, and in August 1968 the USSR held the largest trade exhibition in London that it had ever staged overseas. However, the Warsaw Pact's invasion of Czechoslovakia in 1968 considerably cooled Wilson's efforts for détente. He labeled the action a "flagrant violation of the United Nations Charter and of all accepted standards of international behavior," but urged the West not to return to "the frozen immobilism of the Cold War."

In 1970 the Conservative Party led by Edward Heath deposed Wilson and the Labour Party. However, Wilson returned as prime minister in February 1974 after Labour won a narrow victory. During a five-day visit to Moscow in 1975, he signed a series of political and economic agreements. The weak British economy forced Wilson to cut the defense budget by $11 billion and seek payments to defray the costs of maintaining 50,000 soldiers in West Germany, as called for by a 1955 agreement negotiated by Anthony Eden. Even after the United States and West Germany assumed nearly 90 percent of the costs, however, Wilson still removed some British forces stationed in Germany from the Army of the Rhine and the Royal Air Force.

Wilson promoted the formation of an independent, multiracial government in the British colony of Rhodesia, but white supremacists under the leadership of Ian Smith refused to comply. After Smith's government declared independence in 1965, a civil war broke out. Wilson embargoed Rhodesia but was criticized for not sending in troops to squelch what he described as a "treasonable" rebellion. However, Wilson did not believe military action was feasible. Throughout his tenure in office he tried to resolve the situation, which was not finally settled until 1979. Wilson resigned unexpectedly in March 1976.

Zhou En-lai (also spelled Chou En-lai; 1898–1976)   Premier of the People's Republic of China, 1949–76. Born into a wealthy middle-class family, Zhou attended schools in Japan and France and formed a Chinese Communist Party in Europe while studying in Paris. He joined Dr. Sun Yat-sen's Kuomintang alliance in 1924 but fled after Sun's successor, Chiang Kai-shek, purged Kuomintang of Communists in 1927. He joined Mao Zedong in Nankow and was elected to the party's Politburo in April 1927. Zhou assumed political responsibility for the Army but had to relinquish that duty after a series of military losses in 1934. Thereafter, he joined Mao on the famous 6,000 mile Long March to the northwest region of China. In 1936 he worked out an agreement to save Chiang's life after Communists kidnapped Chiang and forced him to commit to a United Front against Japan, which was then invading the country. During World War II Zhou represented Communist interests in Chiang's headquarters in Chungking and afterward represented the Communists in negotiations to create a National Assembly that would unify a China divided by Chiang's Nationalists and Mao's Communists. However, those negotiations failed in 1946 and the Chinese Civil War followed.

Mao eventually prevailed, and when the People's Republic of China (PRC) was declared on October 1, 1949, Mao was its first chairman and Zhou the first premier and foreign minister. As premier he oversaw the administration of the entire government and issued an annual state of the nation report for more than 25 years. He surrendered the post of foreign minister in 1958, the same year Mao stepped down as chairman of the Republic following the failure of the Great Leap Forward. But Zhou retained most of his duties and responsibilities. He traveled extensively among the world's underdeveloped countries and worked to form ties with them. He also participated in the 1950 defense alliance between China and the Soviet Union and coordinated their relations during the Korean War. He refrained from entering the war until he became convinced that UN forces under General MacArthur genuinely threatened to invade China. He then prosecuted the war vigorously. Zhou also formed China's policy later during the 1950s when the PRC threatened Chiang's armies on the islands of Quemoy and Matsu. Twice Zhou ordered heavy artillery bombardments, but each time President Eisenhower intervened to protect the islands from a Communist invasion and simultaneously prevent Chiang from counterattacking.

In 1954 Zhou participated in the Geneva Conference following the French defeat at Dien Bien Phu. He pressured the Communist Vietminh to end the fighting before reaching a political settlement and to accept a less favorable settlement than they had won on the battlefield. The agreement required the Vietminh to remove its armies from the south, permit temporarily partitioning Vietnam at the seventeenth parallel, and postpone national elections for two years, though the elections subsequently never took place. Contrary to the Vietminh's primary objective of unifying Vietnam under a single Communist government, Zhou indicated his willingness to accept the partition of Vietnam into two separate nations with which China would maintain relations. He toured Eastern Europe in 1957 and, while not directly undermining Soviet authority, tried to establish relations with the Communist bloc independent of Moscow. This, and his advice that the Soviet Union abandon "great power chauvinism," contributed to the rift between China and the USSR that continued to widen throughout the 1960s. In 1969, however, he negotiated an agreement that ended their intensifying border clashes.

Seeking additional support against the Soviet Union, Zhou employed an informal channel between the U.S. and Chinese embassies in Poland in order to enter into talks with U.S. national security adviser Henry Kissinger who visited China in July 1971. President Nixon's visit in February 1972, the first by any U.S. president to the PRC, culminated Zhou's efforts and created closer political and trading ties between the United States and China. Though Nixon also met with Mao, Zhou conducted all of their negotiations. The two countries eventually established formal relations in 1979, at which time the United States ceased to recognize Nationalist China.

During the Cultural Revolution of the 1960s Zhou served as a mild restraint on Mao, though he never directly opposed the chairman. In this way he retained power while acting as a moderating force, and he managed to protect several ministers who had been threatened by the revolution. After Zhou died on January 8, 1976, Mao's radical wife, Jiang Qing, and her cohorts in the Gang of Four exerted the greatest influence on the aging Mao. In April they purged Zhou's protégé, Deng Xiaoping, and briefly seized power after Mao's death in September. However, Deng reclaimed power shortly afterward and remained the most powerful leader in the PRC through the mid–1990s.

Selected Bibliography

General Studies of the Cold War

Bradley, J. F.N. *War and Peace since 1945: A History of Soviet-Western Relations*. New York: Columbia University Press, 1989.

Crockatt, Richard. *The Fifty Years War: The United States and the Soviet Union in World Politics, 1941–1991*. London: Routledge, 1995.

Hill, Kenneth L. *Cold War Chronology: Soviet-American Relations, 1945–1991*. Washington, DC: Congressional Quarterly, 1993.

Hyland, William G. *The Cold War*. New York: Random House, 1991.

Judge, Edward H. and John W. Langdon. *A Hard and Bitter Peace: A Global History of the Cold War*. Upper Saddle Incorporated, NJ.: Prentice Hall, 1996.

Kugler, Richard L. *Commitment to Purpose: How Alliance Partnership Won the Cold War*. Santa Monica, CA: Rand Corporation, 1993.

La Feber, Walter. *America, Russia, and the Cold War, 1945–1992*. New York: McGraw-Hill, 1993.

Maier, Charles S. *The Cold War in Europe*. New York: M. Wiener, 1991.

Paterson, Thomas G. *The Making and Unmaking of the Cold War*. New York: W. W. Norton, 1992.

Pessen, Edward. *Losing Our Souls: The American Experience in the Cold War*. Chicago: I. R. Dee, 1993.

Walker, Martin. *The Cold War: A History*. New York: Henry Holt, 1993.

Young, John W. *Cold War Europe, 1945–89: A Political History*. New York: Routledge, Chapman and Hall, 1991.

Origins of the Cold War

Gormly, James L. *From Potsdam to the Cold War: Big Three Diplomacy, 1945–1947*. Wilmington, DE: SR Books, 1990.

Jensen, Kenneth M., ed. *Origins of the Cold War: The Novikov, Kennan, and Roberts "Long Telegrams" of 1946*. Washington, DC: Institute of Peace, 1991.

Kennan, George F. *Measures Short of War: The George F. Kennan Lectures at the National War College, 1946–47*, ed. Giles D. Harlow. Washington, DC: National Defense University Press, 1991.

_____. "The Sources of Soviet Conduct." *Foreign Affairs* (July 1947). (Kennan published this article anonymously as "Mr. X." It introduced and provided the rationale for U.S. containment policy.)

Parrish, Scott D. *New Evidence on the Soviet Rejection of the Marshall Plan, 1947: Two Reports*. Washington, DC: Woodrow Wilson International Center for Scholars, 1994.

Reynolds, David. *The Origins of the Cold War in Europe: International Perspectives*. New Haven, CT: Yale University Press, 1994.

Woods, Randall Bennett. *Dawning of the Cold War: The United States' Quest for Order*. Athens: University of Georgia Press, 1991.

The Bomb

Bundy, McGeorge. *Danger and Survival: Choices about the Bomb in the First Fifty Years*. New York: Random House, 1988.

_____. *Reducing Nuclear Danger: The Road Away from the Brink*. New York: Council on Foreign Relations Press, 1993.

Calder, Nigel. *Nuclear Nightmares*. New York: Viking, 1980.

Cohn, Carol. "Slick'ems, Glick'ems, Christmas Trees, and Cookie Cutters: Nuclear Language and How We Learned to Pat the Bomb." *Bulletin of the Atomic Scientists* 43, no. 5 (June 1987): 17–24.

Kahn, Herman. *On Thermonuclear War: Thinking about the Unthinkable*. Princeton, NJ: Princeton University Press, 1960.

Kissinger, Henry. *Nuclear Weapons and Foreign Policy*. New York: Harper, for the Council on Foreign Relations, 1957.

McNamara, Robert. *Blundering into Disaster: Surviving the First Century of the Nuclear Age*. New York: Pantheon, 1986.

Pauling, Linus. *No More War!* New York: Dodd, Mead, 1958.

Rhodes, Richard. *The Making of the Atomic Bomb*. Simon and Schuster, 1986.

Sagan, Scott. *The Limits of Safety: Organizations, Accidents, and Nuclear Weapons*. Princeton, NJ: Princeton University Press, 1993.

Scheer, Robert. *With Enough Shovels: Reagan, Bush and Nuclear War*. New York: Random House, 1982.

Schell, Jonathan. *The Fate of the Earth*. New York: Alfred A. Knopf, 1982.

Teller, Edward, and Albert Latter. *Our Nuclear Future: Facts, Dangers and Possibilities*. New York: Criterion, 1958.

McCarthyism and the Red Scare

Alsop, Joseph and Stewart. *We Accuse! The Story of the Miscarriage of American Justice in the Case of J. Robert Oppenheimer*. New York: Simon and Schuster, 1953.

American Business Consultants. *Red Channels*. New York: Counterattack, 950.

Bentley, Eric, ed. *Thirty Years of Treason: Excerpts from Hearings before the House Committee on Un-American Activities, 1938–1968*. New York: Viking, 1971.

Buckley, William F. *The Committee and Its Critics: A Calm Review of the House Committee on Un-American Activities*. New York: Putnam, 1962.

Buckley, William F., and L. Brent Bozell. *McCarthy and His Enemies: The Record and Its Meaning*. New York: McDowell Oblensky, 1954.

Carr, Robert K. *The House Committee on Un-American Activities*. Ithaca, NY: Cornell University Press, 1952.

Chambers, Whittaker. *Odyssey of a Friend: Whittaker Chambers' Letters to William F. Buckley, Jr.* New York: Putnam, 1970.

_____. *Witness.* New York: Random House, 1952.

Cogley, John. *Report on Blacklisting,* 2 vols. 1956. Reprint, New York: Arno, 1971.

Fried, Richard. *Nightmare in Red: The McCarthy Era in Perspective.* New York: Oxford University Press, 1990.

Goodman, Walter. *The Committee: The Extraordinary Career of the House Committee on Un-American Activities.* New York: Farrar, Strauss and Giroux, 1968.

Hellman, Lillian. *Scoundrel Time.* Boston: Little, Brown, 1976.

Hiss, Alger. *In the Court of Public Opinion.* New York: Alfred A. Knopf, 1957.

Hoover, J. Edgar. *From the Secret Files of J. Edgar Hoover,* ed. Athan Theoharis. Chicago: I. R. Dee, 1991.

_____. *Masters of Deceit: The Story of Communism in America and How to Fight It.* New York: Holt, 1958.

Jones, Dorothy. "Communism and the Movies: A Study of Film Content." In John Cogley, ed., *Report on Blacklisting,* vol. 1, *The Movies.* 1956. Reprint, New York: Arno, 1971.

Keller, William W. *The Liberals and J. Edgar Hoover: Rise and Fall of a Domestic Intelligence State.* Princeton, NJ: Princeton University Press, 1989.

Lattimore, Owen. *Ordeal by Slander.* Boston: Little, Brown, 1950. Reprint, Westport, CT: Greenwood, 1971.

Leffler, Melvyn P. *A Preponderance of Power: National Security, the Truman Administration, and the Cold War.* Stanford, CA: Stanford University Press, 1992.

_____. *The Specter of Communism: The United States and the Origins of the Cold War, 1917–1953.* New York: Hill and Wang, 1994.

Lewis, Lionel S. *Cold War on Campus: A Study of the Politics of Organizational Control.* New Brunswick, NJ: Transaction Books, 1988.

Miller, Merle. *The Judges and the Judged.* Garden City, NY: Doubleday, 1952. Reprint, New York: Arno, 1971.

Navasky, Victor. *Naming Names.* New York: Viking, 1980.

Nizer, Louis. *The Implosion Conspiracy.* Garden City, NY: Doubleday, 1973. (About the Rosenbergs' conviction as atomic spies.)

Philbrick, Herbert A. *I Led 3 Lives: Citizen, "Communist," Counterspy.* 1952. Reprint, Washington, DC: Capitol Hill, 1972.

Reeves, Thomas C. *The Life and Times of Joe McCarthy: A Biography.* New York: Stein and Day, 1982.

Rogin, Michael. *The Intellectuals and McCarthy: The Radical Specter.* Cambridge, MA: MIT Press, 1967.

Rosteck, Thomas. *"See It Now" Confronts McCarthyism: Television Documentary and the Politics of Representation.* Tuscaloosa: University of Alabama Press, 1994.

Schneir, Walter and Miriam. *Invitation to an Inquest: Reopening the Rosenberg "Atom Spy" Case.* Baltimore: Penguin, 1973.

Schrecker, Ellen. *The Age of McCarthyism: A Brief History with Documents.* Boston: Bedford, 1994.

_____. *No Ivory Tower: McCarthyism and the Universities.* New York: Oxford University Press, 1986.

Vaughn, Robert. *Only Victims.* New York: G. P. Putnam's Sons, 1972.

Weinstein, Allen. *Perjury: The Hiss-Chambers Case.* New York: Knopf, 1978.

The Korean War

Blair, Clay. *The Forgotten War: America in Korea, 1950–1953*. New York: Random House, 1988.
Cummings, Bruce. *The Origins of the Korean War*. 2 vols. Princeton, NJ: Princeton University Press, 1981.
Isserman, Maurice. *The Korean War*. New York: Facts on File, 1993.
Lowitt, Richard. *The Truman-MacArthur Controversy*. Chicago: Rand McNally, 1967.
Marshall, S. L. A. *The Military History of the Korean War*. New York: F. Watts, 1963.
Summers, Harry G. *Korean War Almanac*. New York: Facts on File, 1990.
Weathersby, Kathryn. *Soviet Aims in Korea and the Origins of the Korean War, 1945–1950*. Washington, DC: Cold War International History Project, Woodrow Wilson International Center for Scholars, 1993.

The Second Berlin Crisis

Beschloss, Michael R. *The Crisis Years: Kennedy and Khrushchev, 1960–1963*. New York: Edward Burlingame, 1991.
Schlesinger, Arthur. *A Thousand Days: John F. Kennedy in the White House*. Boston: Houghton Mifflin, 1965.
Slusser, Robert M. *The Berlin Crisis of 1961: Soviet-American Relations and the Struggle for Power in the Kremlin, June–November, 1961*. Baltimore: Johns Hopkins University Press, 1973.
Zubok, V. M. *Khrushchev and the Berlin Crisis (1958–1962)*. Washington, DC: Cold War International History Project, Woodrow Wilson International Center for Scholars, 1993.

The Cuban Missile Crisis

Beschloss, Michael R. *The Crisis Years: Kennedy and Khrushchev, 1960–1963*. New York: Edward Burlingame, 1991.
Blight, James, and David Welch. *On the Brink: Americans and Soviets Examine the Cuban Missile Crisis*. New York: Hill and Wang, 1989. (An oral history of the Cuban Missile Crisis.)
Brugioni, Dino. *Eyeball to Eyeball: The Inside Story of the Cuban Missile Crisis*, ed. Robert F. McCort. New York: Random House, 1991.
Central Intelligence Agency. *CIA Documents on the Cuban Missile Crisis, 1962*. Washington, DC: History Staff, Central Intelligence Agency, 1992.
Cuban Missile Crisis, 1962: A National Security Archive Documents Reader. New York: New Press, 1992.
Kennedy, Robert. *Thirteen Days: A Memoir of the Cuban Missile Crisis*. New York: W. W. Norton, 1969.
Rhodes, Richard. "The General and World War III." *The New Yorker* (June 19, 1995), 47–59. (Discusses General Curtis LeMay.)
Schlesinger, Arthur. *A Thousand Days: John F. Kennedy in the White House*. Boston: Houghton Mifflin, 1965.
Thompson, Robert Smith. *The Missiles of October: The Declassified Story of John F. Kennedy and the Cuban Missile Crisis*. New York: Simon and Schuster, 1992.

The Vietnam War

Halberstam, David. *The Best and the Brightest.* New York: Random House, 1972.

_____. *Ho.* New York: Random House, 1971.

_____. *The Making of a Quagmire.* New York: Random House, 1965.

_____. *One Very Hot Day.* Boston: Houghton Mifflin, 1967. (A Novel.)

Isserman, Maurice. *The Vietnam War.* New York: Facts on File, 1992.

Karnow, Stanley. *Vietnam: A History.* New York: Viking, 1983. (This was the basis for the PBS television documentary "Vietnam: A Television History," 1983.)

McNamara, Robert. *In Retrospect: The Tragedy and Lessons of Vietnam.* New York: Times Books, 1995.

Santoli, Al. *Everything We Had: An Oral History of the Vietnam War by Thirty-Three American Soldiers Who Fought It.* New York: Ballantine, 1981.

Sheehan, Neil. *A Bright Shining Lie: John Paul Vann and America in Vietnam.* New York: Random House, 1988.

Summers, Harry G. *Vietnam War Almanac.* New York: Facts on File, 1985.

Intelligence Agencies and Covert Operations

Adams, James. *Sellout: Aldrich Ames and the Corruption of the CIA.* New York: Viking, 1995.

Agee, Philip. *Dirty Work: The CIA in Western Europe.* Secaucus, NJ: L. Stuart, 1978. (Agee was a former CIA agent.)

_____. *Inside the Company: CIA Diary.* 1975. Reprint, New York: Bantam, 1976.

Donovan, James B. *Strangers on a Bridge: The Case of Colonel Abel.* New York: Atheneum, 1964. (The FBI caught Abel spying for the Soviets in the 1950s.)

Grose, Peter. *Gentleman Spy: The Life of Allen Dulles.* Boston: Houghton Mifflin, 1994.

Hunt, E. Howard. *Undercover: Memoirs of an American Secret Agent.* New York: Berkley, 1974. (Hunt was a former CIA agent who was operations officer on the Bay of Pigs invasion. He was also one of the convicted Watergate burglars.)

Kessler, Ronald. *Spy vs. Spy: Stalking Soviet Spies in America.* New York: Charles Scribner's Sons, 1988.

Kornbluh, Peter and Malcolm Byrne, eds. *The Iran-Contra Scandal: The Declassified History.* New York: New Press, 1993.

Loftus, John, and Mark Aarons. *The Secret War against the Jews.* New York: St. Martin's, 1994. (Documents information about U.S. espionage activities during the Cold War and the origins of the Iran-Contra Affair.)

Mills, Ami Chen. *CIA off Campus: Building the Movement against Agency Recruitment and Research,* 2d ed. Boston: South End, 1991.

O'Toole, G. J. A. *The Encyclopedia of American Intelligence and Espionage: From the Revolutionary War to the Present.* New York: Facts on File, 1988.

Philby, Kim. *My Silent War.* New York: Grove, 1968. (Philby was a top British agent who defected to the Soviets.)

Richelson, Jeffrey. *American Espionage and the Soviet Target.* New York: William Morrow, 1987.

Rockefeller, Nelson A. *Report to the President by the Commission on CIA Activities within the United States.* Washington, DC: U.S. Government Printing Office, 1975.

Smith, Russell Jack. *The Unknown CIA: My Three Decades with the Agency.* Washington, DC: Pergamon-Brassey's, 1989.

United States House of Representatives Permanent Select Committee on Intelligence.

Report of Investigation: Aldridge Ames Espionage Case. Washington, DC: U.S. Government Printing Office, 1994.

United States House of Representatives Select Committee to Investigate Covert Arms Transactions with Iran and U.S. Select Committee on Secret Military Assistance to Iran and the Nicaraguan Opposition. *Iran-Contra Affair.* Washington, DC: U.S. Government Printing Office, 1987.

United States Senate Select Committee on Intelligence. *An Assessment of the Aldrich H. Ames Espionage Case and Its Implications for U.S. Intelligence.* Washington, DC: U.S. Government Printing Office, 1994.

United States Senate Select Committee to Study Governmental Operations with Respect to Intelligence Activities. *Alleged Assassination Plots Involving Foreign Leaders.* New York: W. W. Norton, 1976.

_____. *Covert Action in Chile, 1963–1973.* Washington, DC: U.S. Government Printing Office, 1975.

_____. *Final Report of the Senate Select Committee to Study Government Operations with Respect to Intelligence Activities.* Washington, DC: U.S. Government Printing Office, 1976. (This is also known as the *Church Committee Report.*)

Williams, Robert C. *Klaus Fuchs, Atom Spy.* Cambridge, MA: Harvard University Press, 1987.

Woodward, Bob. *Veil: The Secret Wars of the CIA, 1981–1987.* New York: Simon and Schuster, 1987.

Zubok, V. M. *Soviet Intelligence and the Cold War: The Small Committee of Information, 1952–53.* Washington, DC: Cold War International History Project, Woodrow Wilson International Center of Scholars, 1992.

Memoirs and Personal Histories of Major American Leaders

Acheson, Dean. *Present at the Creation: My Years in the State Department.* New York: W. W. Norton, 1969.

Baruch, Bernard M. *The Public Years.* New York: Holt, Rinehart and Winston, 1960.

Byrnes, James F. *All in One Lifetime.* New York: Harper, 1958.

Carter, Jimmy. *Keeping Faith: Memoirs of a President.* New York: Bantam, 1982.

Eisenhower, Dwight D. *The Churchill-Eisenhower Correspondence, 1953–1955,* ed. Peter G. Boyle. Chapel Hill: University of North Carolina Press, 1990.

_____. *The White House Years.* Garden City, NY: Doubleday, 1963.

Ford, Gerald R. *A Time to Heal.* New York: Harper and Row, 1979.

Hammer, Armand, and Neil Lyndon. *Hammer.* New York: Putnam, 1987.

Johnson, Lyndon B. *Vantage Point: Perspectives of the Presidency.* New York: Holt, Rinehart and Winston, 1971.

Kennan, George F. *Memoirs.* Boston: Little, Brown, 1967.

Kissinger, Henry. *White House Years.* Boston: Little, Brown, 1979.

_____. *Years of Upheaval.* Boston: Little, Brown, 1979.

LeMay, Curtis E., and Mackinlay Kantor. *Mission with LeMay; My Story.* Garden City, NY: Doubleday, 1965.

MacArthur, Douglas. *Reminiscences.* New York: McGraw-Hill, 1964.

Marshall, George C. *George C. Marshall: Interviews and Reminiscences for Forrest C. Pogue.* Lexington, VA: G. C. Marshall Research Foundation, 1991.

Nixon, Richard M. *In the Arena: A Memoir of Victory, Defeat, and Renewal.* New York: Simon and Schuster, 1990.

_____. *RN: The Memoirs of Richard Nixon.* New York: Simon and Schuster, 1978: Reprint, with new introduction, 1990.

_____. *Six Crises.* Garden City, NY: Doubleday, 1962.

Rusk, Dean. *As I Saw It,* ed. Daniel S. Papp. New York: W. W. Norton, 1990.

Truman, Harry S. *The Autobiography of Harry S. Truman,* ed. Robert H. Ferrell. Boulder: Colorado Associated University Press, 1980.

_____. *Letters Home,* ed. Monte M. Poen. New York: Putnam, 1984.

_____. *Memoirs.* Garden City, NY: Doubleday, 1955.

_____. *Off the Record: The Private Papers of Harry S. Truman,* ed. Robert H. Ferrell. New York: Harper and Row, 1980.

Udall, Stewart L. *A Personal Exploration of Our Tragic Cold War Affair with the Atom.* New York: Pantheon, 1994.

Weinberger, Caspar. *Fighting for Peace: Seven Critical Years in the Pentagon.* New York: Warner, 1990.

Memoirs and Writings by Foreign Leaders

Adenauer, Konrad. *Memoirs.* Chicago: H. Regnery, 1966.

Andropov, Yuri. *Speeches and Writings.* Oxford, England: Pergamon, 1982.

Attlee, Clement C. *As It Happened.* New York: Viking, 1954.

Brandt, Willy. *People and Politics: The Years 1960–1975.* Boston: Little, Brown, 1978.

Brezhnev, Leonid. *Memoirs.* Oxford, England: Pergamon, 1982.

Callaghan, James. *Time and Chance.* London: Collins, 1987.

Churchill, Sir Winston. *The Churchill-Eisenhower Correspondence, 1953–1955,* ed. Peter G. Boyle. Chapel Hill: University of North Carolina Press, 1990.

De Gaulle, Charles. *Implacable Ally.* New York: Harper and Row, 1966.

_____. *Memoirs of Hope, Renewal and Endeavor.* New York: Simon and Schuster, 1971.

De Gaulle, Charles, and Andre Malraux. *Fell Oaks; Conversation with De Gaulle.* New York: Holt, Rinehart and Winston, 1971.

Dubček, Alexander. *Dubček Speaks.* New York: I. B. Tauris, distributed by St. Martin's, 1990.

_____. *Hope Dies Last: The Autobiography of Alexander Dubček,* ed. and trans. Jiri Hochman. New York: Kodansha International, 1993.

Eden, Anthony. *The Reckoning: The Memoirs of Anthony Eden, Earl of Avon.* Boston: Houghton Mifflin, 1965.

Gorbachev, Mikhail. *The August Coup: The Truth and the Lessons.* New York: HarperCollins, 1991.

Havel, Václav. *Open Letters: Selected Writings 1965–1990,* ed. Paul Wilson. New York: Alfred A. Knopf, 1991.

_____. *Summer Meditations,* trans. Paul Wilson. New York: Alfred A. Knopf, 1992.

Khrushchev, Nikita. *Khrushchev Remembers.* Boston: Little, Brown, 1970.

Macmillan, Harold. *At the End of the Day, 1961–1963.* New York: Harper and Row, 1973.

Mao Zedong. *The Writings of Mao Zedong, 1949–1976,* ed. Michael Y. M. Kau and John K. Leung. Armonk, NY: M. E. Sharpe, 1986.

Schmidt, Helmut. *Men and Power: A Political Retrospective.* New York: Random House, 1989.

Thatcher, Margaret. *Downing Street Years.* New York: HarperCollins, 1993.

Tito, Josip Broz. *The Essential Tito,* ed. Henry M. Christman. New York: St. Martin's, 1970.

Wałęsa, Lech. *Struggle and the Triumph: An Autobiography,* ed. Franklin Philip. New York: Arcade, 1992.

Zhou En-lai. *Selected Works of Zhou En-lai.* Beijing: Foreign Language Press (distributed in the United States by Pergamon, Elmsford, NY), 1981.

Collected Biographical Sketches of Political Leaders

Arms, Thomas S. *Encyclopedia of the Cold War.* New York: Facts on File, 1994.

Frankel, Benjamin, ed. *The Cold War, 1945–1991.* Detroit: Gale Research, 1992.

Lichtenstein, Nelson, ed. *Political Profiles.* 5 vols. New York: Facts on File, 1976. (Provides in-depth profiles of major and minor political figures from the Truman, Eisenhower, Kennedy, Johnson, and Nixon/Ford presidencies.)

The Influence of the Cold War on American Culture

Anisfield, Nancy, ed. *The Nightmare Considered: Critical Essays on Nuclear War Literature.* Bowling Green, OH: Bowling Green State University Popular Press, 1991.

_____. *Vietnam Anthology: American War Literature.* Bowling Green, OH: Bowling Green State University Popular Press, 1987.

Biskind, Peter. *Seeing Is Believing: How Hollywood Taught Us to Stop Worrying and Love the Fifties.* New York: Pantheon, 1983.

Dowling, David. *Fictions of Nuclear Disaster.* Iowa City: University of Iowa Press, 1987.

Enloe, Cynthia H. *The Morning After: Sexual Politics at the End of the Cold War.* Berkeley: University of California Press, 1993.

Halberstam, David. *The Fifties.* New York: Random House, 1993.

Hinds, Lynn Boyd. *The Cold War as Rhetoric: The Beginnings, 1945–1950.* New York: Praeger, 1991.

Hirshberg, Matthew S. *Perpetuating Patriotic Perceptions: The Cognitive Function of the Cold War.* Westport, CT: Praeger, 1993.

Inglis, Fred. *The Cruel Peace: Everyday Life in the Cold War.* New York: Basic Books, 1991.

Lindey, Christine. *Art in the Cold War: From Vladivostok to Kalamazoo, 1945–1962.* London: Herbert, 1990.

May, Lary, ed. *Recasting America: Culture and Politics in the Age of Cold War.* Chicago: University of Chicago Press, 1989.

Medhurst, Martin J. *Cold War Rhetoric: Strategy, Metaphor, and Ideology.* New York: Greenwood, 1990.

Rosteck, Thomas. *"See It Now" Confronts McCarthyism: Television Documentary and the Politics of Representation.* Tuscaloosa: University of Alabama Press, 1994.

Sayre, Nora. *Running Time: Films of the Cold War.* New York: Dial, 1982.

Schaub, Thomas Hill. *American Fiction in the Cold War.* Madison: University of Wisconsin Press, 1991.

Schwartz, Richard A. *Cold War Culture.* New York: Facts on File, 1997. (Encyclopedia describing the influence of the Cold War on American fine arts, performing arts, literature, film, television, and popular culture.)

Shaheen, Jack G. *Nuclear War Films.* Carbondale, IL: Southern Illinois University Press, 1978.

Siebers, Tobin. *Cold War Criticism and the Politics of Skepticism.* New York: Oxford University Press, 1993.

Steel, Ronald. *Walter Lippmann and the American Century.* New York: Random House, 1980.

Whitfield, Stephen. *The Culture of the Cold War.* Baltimore: Johns Hopkins University Press, 1991.

Yoder, Edwin. *Joe Alsop's Cold War: A Study of Journalistic Influence and Intrigue.* Chapel Hill: University of North Carolina Press, 1995.

Other Cold War–Related Books

Beschloss, Michael R. *At the Highest Levels: The Inside Story of the End of the Cold War.* Boston: Little, Brown, 1993.

Borstelmann, Thomas. *Apartheid's Reluctant Uncle: The United States and Southern Africa in the Early Cold War.* New York: Oxford University Press, 1993.

Brands, H. W. *The Devil We Knew: Americans and the Cold War.* New York: Oxford University Press, 1993.

Freedman, Lawrence, ed. *Europe Transformed: Documents on the End of the Cold War.* London: Tri-Service, 1990.

Gleason, Abbott. *Totalitarianism: The Inner History of the Cold War.* New York: Oxford University Press, 1995.

Kanet, Roger E., and Edward A. Kolodziej, eds. *The Cold War as Cooperation.* Baltimore: Johns Hopkins University Press, 1991.

Lebow, Richard Ned, and Janice Gross Stein. *We All Lost the Cold War.* Princeton, NJ: Princeton University Press, 1994.

Levine, Alan J. *The Missile and Space Race.* Westport, CT: Praeger, 1994.

McMahon, Robert J. *The Cold War on the Periphery: The United States, India, and Pakistan.* New York: Columbia University Press, 1994.

Partos, Gabriel. *The World that Came in from the Cold: Perspectives from East and West on the Cold War.* London: Royal Institute of International Affairs, BBC World Service, 1993. (Based on the BBC World Service Series, The World That Came in From the Cold.)

Simmons, P. J. *Archival Research on the Cold War Era: A Report from Budapest, Prague and Warsaw.* Washington, DC: Woodrow Wilson International Center for Scholars, 1992.

Young, John W. *France, the Cold War and the Western Alliance, 1944–49.* Leicester, England: Leicester University Press, 1990.

Index